CHICAGO'S
WHITE CITY
OF 1893

CHICAGO'S
WHITE CITY
OF 1893

DAVID F. BURG

The University Press of Kentucky

ISBN: 0-8131-1331-8

Library of Congress Catalog Card Number: 75-3542

Copyright © 1976 by The University Press of Kentucky

A statewide cooperative scholarly publishing agency
serving Berea College, Centre College of Kentucky,
Eastern Kentucky University, Georgetown College,
Kentucky Historical Society, Kentucky State University,
Morehead State University, Murray State University,
Northern Kentucky State College, Transylvania University,
University of Kentucky, University of Louisville, and
Western Kentucky University.

Editorial and Sales Offices: Lexington, Kentucky 40506

*This book is dedicated to Helen
for whom I would gladly
launch a thousand ships*

CONTENTS

ILLUSTRATIONS

PREFACE

THE WHITE CITY was the most popular title of that most remarkable event, the World's Columbian Exposition, otherwise known as the Chicago World's Fair of 1893. The White City's life was brief but legendary. It inspired hundreds of publications—catalogs, photographic albums, speeches, essays, novels. It was the subject of four full-length histories and a fifth unfinished one which alone consist of thousands of pages. A merely cursory investigation reveals that the World's Columbian Exposition evoked far more commentary than any exposition in history. Obviously this study cannot do justice to all that commentary. But from the written records it gleans the important outlines of the story and the meaning of the exposition. In addition to the plethora of commentary published in its own time, the exposition has been referred to since by numerous social, architectural, and intellectual historians. It has been sometimes extravagantly praised; more often, resoundingly damned. Whether laudatory or damnatory, however, historians have generally conceded that the exposition was an event of genuine cultural import. Even so, retrospectively, no attempt has been made to evaluate that import in a study of sufficient length to do justice to the subject. This study makes the attempt.

It is not enough to assume merely on the basis of voluminous accumulated commentaries that the White City deserves the attempt. Consequently, one purpose of this study is to argue the exposition's historic merit. There are several reasons why such a study rewards interest. One is the nature of the event itself. International expositions are of recent origin. The first was the Great Exhibition held in London in 1851 which was the scene of

Joseph Paxton's Crystal Palace—the first large-scale, prefabricated iron and glass building—which alone attested that fair's significance. From then until 1893 there were several European expositions, probably the most famous being that held in Paris in 1889, celebrated for its Eiffel Tower. The United States had hosted several trade fairs but only one full-scale international exposition, that held in Philadelphia in 1876, the celebration of the centennial of American independence. The World's Columbian Exposition would be the fifteenth world's fair and the second American one. But it was of vastly greater scope than any of its predecessors. Early expositions had consisted simply of one large exhibition hall, as at the Great Exhibition, or of such a hall augmented with attached or nearby sheds. The main hall might be artfully designed, but little attempt was made to lay out the surrounding grounds or to embellish the buildings with sculpture and paintings. The Paris Exhibition of 1867 originated both the idea of gridlike layouts for buildings and a park site plan. By the time of the 1889 Paris Exhibition many buildings, such as the Trocadero, were permanent, as successive expositions there were always held at the Champs de Mars. It was the 1889 exhibition that inspired the World's Columbian Exposition. But the progeny far surpassed its forebears. Paris, London, Vienna temporarily transformed their appearances to host their expositions. Chicago created a veritable new city. That city was not only larger than any previous exposition but also more elaborately designed, more precisely laid out, more fully realized, more prophetic. First of all, this was to be a celebration of the four hundredth anniversary of Columbus's discovery of the New World, of which the United States was only a part, though, as the Americans assumed, the greatest part. Given the historic setting, it would have been inconceivable that a Latin American country would have hosted the event. It was intended from the start, however, to be a genuinely international exposition. That is, it was the first exposition truly to solicit the participation of the entire world. Hence in an era of intense nationalistic rivalries and imperialistic ambitions, the World's Columbian Exposition reflected a unique spirit of internationalism.

Another and more important reason for studying the exposition is the fact that the White City was intended to inform all visitors of the momentous achievements in such areas as fine arts, industry, technology, and agriculture of the United States, "the first new nation," in Seymour Martin Lipset's phrase, whose political, cultural, and economic endeavors had prepared her to join the ranks of the world's great nations. In short, the exposition was a celebration of America's coming of age—a grand rite of passage. It was also the primary representative event of an era that Henry Steele Commager has aptly designated as the watershed of American history. "On the one side lies an America predominantly agricultural; concerned with domestic problems; conforming, intellectually at least, to the political, economic, and moral principles inherited from the seventeenth and eighteenth centuries. . . . On the other side lies the modern America, predominantly urban and industrial; inextricably involved in world economy and politics . . .; experiencing profound changes in population, social institutions, economy, and technology; and trying to accommodate its traditional institutions and habits of thought to conditions new and in part alien."[1] Thus Commager referred to the entire decade of the 1890s as the historic divide between past and present America. Though an early event of the nineties, the exposition embodied and portended that truth. The World's Columbian Exposition was both hail and farewell.

It is therefore instructive of how Americans saw themselves in a period of profound and complex change. The extraordinary responsiveness of visitors, both informed critics and lay public, to the wonders of the White City is highly revealing of American values, anticipations, and aspirations. The making of the exposition, as an achievement of cooperative endeavor and technical expertise and as a singular agglomeration of inventive and exotic amusements, is a story of high culture and popular culture combined.[2] It is a story of masterful artistic and engineering achievement. The creation of the White City provided a giant index of an urban-industrial environment that might have been, had the public's enthusiastic regard been honored; had the vicissitudes of rapid change, commercial enterprise, and political priorities developed differently. As such the fair is an incomparable event in American history. It demonstrated at a timely juncture that the artistic capacity and technical knowledge were available to transform new industrial cities into well-designed centers of business, culture, and humane community in agreeable combination. For the White City was in itself such a well-designed center.

Furthermore, as Howard Mumford Jones has commented, "Tempting as it is to chronicle the swift and efficient solution of a series of technological problems, one must agree that the national significance of the World's Columbian Exposition lay in three great achievements: the working together of painters, architects, decorators, landscape designers, engineers, and lay laborers in realizing an ideal that kindled their enthusiasm and redoubled their energies; the beauty of the Exposition as a whole; and the range and variety of intellectual congresses held at the Fair or called by it in 1893."[3] These three achievements highlighted the fair's effectiveness as a shared and inspiring experience for Americans representing every segment of the populace. It was a cooperative fulfillment of various arts—architecture, painting, sculpture, music, theatre, poetry, fiction—and the source of ideas and creations in those arts. In this respect alone it far surpasses the role of historic curiosity.

But even as curiosity it has merit. Not the least of considerations is the lingering memory of past events. There are still alive people who experienced the White City either firsthand or vicariously through the accounts of friends and relatives, and for them the legacy of the fair is personal and therefore more vivid and perhaps more vital than it is for the historian. For that reason alone the White City remains worthy.

Anyone who writes a book owes innumerable debts of gratitude, some of them to sources long since forgotten, as insights and ideas are gleaned over the course of many years. As F. O. Matthiessen wrote in *American Renaissance:* "During the course of this long volume I have undoubtedly plagiarized from many sources.... I doubt whether any criticism or cultural history has ever been written without such plagiary, which inevitably results from assimilating the contributions of your countless fellow-workers, past and present. The true function of scholarship as of society is not to stake out claims on which others must not trespass, but to provide a community of knowledge in which others may share." That has always seemed to me a most sensible statement and I hope that, with apologies to Matthiessen for the borrowing, I may offer it as a comprehensive thank you to all of those whose thoughts may somehow have contributed to this volume.

Some institutions and persons deserve specific mention. I wish to thank the University of Pennsylvania, the Philadelphia Free Library, and especially the Franklin Institute for the use of their excellent library facilities. Mrs. Diane Barelli and Mr. Fred Westing, formerly of the staff of the Franklin Institute, showed me many kindnesses and earned my sincere gratitude. I would like also to thank the University of Kentucky for the use of its libraries, with special thanks to Hunter Adams, director of the architecture library, and her former assistant Kit Duke; Stuart Forth, former director of libraries; and Dr. Jacqueline Bull, head of special collections. In addition, I wish to thank the Art Institute of Chicago and the Chicago Historical Society for the use of their facilities, with special thanks to Mrs. Mary Frances Rhymer, Curator of Prints at the Historical Society. The University of Kentucky Research Foundation awarded me two grants—for typing and for photographs—for which I am most thankful.

My special thanks also go to Neil Leonard, whose counsel and guidance were most helpful to me when I first began writing of the Columbian Exposition, and to his colleagues Anthony N. B. Garvan and Charles Rosenberg, all of the University of Pennsylvania. Naturally none of them is responsible for whatever failings this book contains.

Lastly, I would like to thank Rollin Henry Rendlesham, without whose support this book could never have reached fruition, and Floris Johnson Burg, whose generous efforts and clerical skills facilitated its completion. Most of all, heartfelt thanks to my wife Helen for her editing, encouragement, counsel, and understanding.

1

AMERICA ON THE
EVE OF CELEBRATION

The city is the nerve center of our
civilization. It is also the storm center. The
fact, therefore, that it is growing much more
rapidly than the whole population is
full of significance.

Josiah Strong

ATTEMPTING TO summarize any age in the brevity of a few
pages may seem foolhardy. The attempt is plagued by problems of
selection, generality, interpretation. Yet summarizing may not be
entirely sinful. The essence of an era might, after all, be evoked in
a single phrase. Certainly historians of the American 1890s, and
the decades immediately preceding and following, have an addic-
tion to epithets—the Mauve Decade, the Age of Enterprise, the
Great Barbecue, the Age of Excess—that are meant to convey an
image of the dominant milieu of an exceptional and preoccupying
era; and to varying degrees they do accomplish just that. Nevertheless, neither evocative epithets nor extensive histories have served
to explain late nineteenth-century America. Perhaps such explanation is impossible. But the attempt to summarize remains somehow necessary and irresistible. It becomes doubly necessary in a
study that purports to discuss the World's Columbian Exposition
as a quintessential event of the times.

What, then, was the essential nature of the dominant American
culture in the immediate years leading up to the World's Colum-

bian Exposition? As Thomas Beer had it, the color of the age was hardly an imperial purple. Nevertheless, his evocation of its colorfulness reveals something more akin to kaleidoscopic hues and electrical energy than was the case perhaps with his own 1920s, to which he compared "The Mauve Decade." Perhaps the 1890s primary color was mauve; certainly the era's primary motive was enterprise. Still, because of its embracing ambiguity, what seems a most appropriate epithet is that of Howard Mumford Jones. His *Age of Energy* considers the entire period from 1865 to 1915; but one can well argue that the early nineties, as the midway mark in that fifty-year period, constituted both apex and watershed. For these years witnessed par excellence in the World's Columbian Exposition, and in manifold other events, "the discovery, use, exploitation, and expression of energy, whether it be that of personality or of prime movers or of words" which caused Jones to see energy as the overriding principle of the age.[1] Jones regards the age as one in which "everything was flexible, everything was possible" and in which one of the chief elements was its being "in search of a style."[2] It may be this flexibility and this search which led near the turn of the century to the adoption of middle-class values as the norm for Americans; to the consolidation of the drive toward urbanizing and industrializing the nation; and, as Jones concludes, to the conviction, expressed through the various arts of the time, "that the world is as we see it and that the business of style is to be a mode of representing things as they are . . . as physical fidelity. . . . This was the great transformation in style these fruitful years accomplished."[3] That transformation in style most certainly reflected a transformation in substance. Both transformations would be strikingly represented at the World's Columbian Exposition.

In discussions of national character, in political, social, and economic histories, and in statistical profiles are revealed the general truth that modern America was largely prophesied in the 1880s and 1890s. There have since been changes in amenities, in material goods, in fashions, and so on; but the nineties foretold, in essential outline, what twentieth-century America would be. Probably above all other developments in importance, America would be urban. "Underlying all the varied developments that made up American life," wrote Arthur Schlesinger, "was the momentous shift of the center of national equilibrium from the countryside to the city."[4] The modern city was the primary product of the consummation of industrialism in the late nineteenth century. The only sections of the nation to which such statements might not have applied in 1893 were the vast open areas of the West and the agriculture-oriented South, where industry was still aborning, where rural culture remained ascendant, but where nonetheless the rudimentary introduction of industrialism foreshadowed the future.

The East was already urban. The heartland of America was nearly so. "In the Middle West and the North Atlantic states rural America, like a stag at bay, was making its last stand. The clash between the two cultures—one static, individualistic, agricultural, the other dynamic, collectivist, urban—was most clearly exhibited in the former section," wrote Arthur Schlesinger with a succinctly descriptive phraseology that evinces the vast social, political, and economic significances of this shift.[5] And there was no question about the ultimate triumph of urbanization. "The extraordinary growth of its bigger cities was one of the marvels of Middle Western life in the eighties. Chicago, which best represented the will power and titanic energy of the section, leaped from a half million in 1880 to more than a million ten years later. . . . The Twin Cities trebled in size; places like Detroit, Milwaukee, Columbus and Cleveland increased from sixty to eighty percent."[6] This extraordinary growth resulted not merely from a growing shift of population from rural to urban centers but also from the enormous influx of immigrants that occurred in the eighties and nineties. "The population of the country was 47 million in 1877; 67 million in 1893. The rate of growth was just over a million per year in the late 1870's; thereafter until 1893 it was about 1.3 million per year. In most years from a third to a half of the

3

population increase was due to immigration, and much of the growth of the American economy can be attributed to this flow of immigrants."[7] Quite naturally these developments had their attendant problems. American society had experienced in the nineteenth century periods of intense hostility toward immigrants, periods of rabid nativism. This nativism reached a peak in the 1890s because after 1880 the largest proportion of the immigrants came from Italy and the Eastern European countries; they had two suspicious aspects—they were neither Anglo-Saxon nor Protestant.

These later immigrants probably bore the brunt of a hostility engendered in part by workingmen's fears of unemployment and by the participation of some earlier immigrants, prominently Germans, in agitation for political and economic reform or revolution. Unions and employers that had advocated immigration began to insist upon its termination. "Where one saw the foreigner as a tool of oppression, the other discerned an agent of unrest. The two lines of attack had little in common except their origin in a common situation: both reacted to the immigrants as a disruptive wedge in a dividing society."[8] The crisis came in the mid-eighties. The focal event precipitating a nativist hysteria was the notorious Haymarket Riot which occurred on May 4, 1886, in Chicago.[9] To this day the facts of that event have not been entirely clarified. But as a symbol of a presumed workingmen's threat to capitalism the riot and the heinous trial that followed it, together with a resultant era of labor turmoil punctuated by the Homestead Strike of 1892—all combined with recessions, the most severe beginning in 1893—led to the Quarantine Act of 1893 and the organization in 1894 of an Immigration Restriction League. The mid-nineties recession itself, however, apparently solved the problem.[10] And it may fairly be said that, although the immigrant-nativist tension had deepened divisions in American society, the expansive immigration of the eighties had effected two salient changes in the life of American cities by 1890: it made them simultaneously more pluralistic and more cosmopolitan.

It was industrialization that created America's giant cities. And that creation in turn has had pervasive results. "It is impossible to exaggerate the role of business in developing great cities in America, and it is impossible to exaggerate the role of the cities in creating our business culture. . . . Creating a national market for standardized goods, they also created a national model of the successful man: the thrifty, shrewd, and practical clerk or mechanic who rose from the ranks to leadership."[11] Probably the single industry most responsible for the evolution of the cities and the model successful man was transportation, namely, the railroads. "If the late nineteenth century [in America] is to be named for any aspect of its technology, there is not a doubt in the world that it should be called the railroad age."[12] The period was the great age of "railroad imperialism." The rate of growth of the nation's railroads after the Civil War was nothing short of spectacular, in spite of recessions, and "by 1893 . . . 150,000 miles [of track] had been laid since the war. Capital invested in American railroads jumped . . . from two to nearly ten billion dollars. Though most of this mileage and most of this capital went to complete old trunk lines and their links to new centers in the valleys of the Ohio, Mississippi, and Missouri, the most spectacular of all the roads and perhaps the most important were the transcontinentals." The growth of these roads gave the nation its heroes, and its villains as well.[13] It was the railroads that secured the commercial future of such cities as Chicago, Saint Louis, Omaha, and Kansas City by making them into gathering places and distribution centers for the nation's wealth of lumber, iron, wheat, cattle. For close upon the heels of railroad development followed the burgeoning of other gigantic industries in steel, oil, sugar, meat-packing. This was the age of giant trusts which created the fortunes of such incomparable entrepreneurs as steel magnate Andrew Carnegie and oil magnate John D. Rockefeller, prime examples of the rags-to-riches gospel of hard work, thrift, and determination that was preached in the best-selling novels of Horatio Alger. And it was the age of holding companies which were based upon the expertise, machinations, and fortunes of men like the banker John Pierpont Morgan. In short, it was an age in which the industrialist and the banker were the monarchs. "Outside steel and oil, similar combinations were being pushed to completion by Armour and Swift in meat packing, Pillsbury in flour milling, Havemeyer in sugar, Weyerhauser in lumber. By 1893 all had become leaders of great corporations composed in part of shoestring competitors that had fallen in every financial storm."[14] During the thirty years leading up to the World's Columbian Exposition the number of millionaires in the United States had increased from a mere handful to over 4,000.

Not only was the late nineteenth century the age of consolidation, monopoly, multimillionaires; it was also the age of America's rise to industrial supremacy among the nations of the world. By 1893 that supremacy had been achieved. "In the manufacture of timber and steel, the refinement of crude oil, the packing of meat, the extraction of gold, silver, coal, and iron the United States surpassed all competitors. America had more telephones, more incandescent lighting and electric traction, more miles of telegraph wires than any other nation. In specialties like hardware, machine tools, arms and ammunition, she retained the leadership assumed before the Civil War, while her pianos as well as her locomotives had become the best in the world."[15] It would be a few years yet before this rapid and exultant ascent to the pinnacle of industrial might was translated into imperial muscle-flexing; but its internal effects, its influences upon American culture, were pervasive. Most notably, industrial supremacy made secure the power and position of the entrepreneur not only in commerce and finance but also in politics and society, and even in the fine arts. The entrepreneur's public image, his extreme wealth and his conspicuous taste, made him a genuine American hero. The self-made multimillionaire was the man to emulate. He had power, status, mobility; he built mansions and collected artworks; he dominated industries and politicians—and all by means of money. "Thus the ideals of our business leaders became the ideals of the great majority of the people, though only a few were themselves endowed with talent for leadership."[16] Thus also by 1893 America, now primarily a business culture, had attained that orientation which allowed Calvin Coolidge years later to assert, "The business of America is business." The "money ethic" had become a respectable value. "The American people subordinated religion, education, and politics to the process of creating wealth. Increasing production, employment, and income became the measures of community success, and personal riches the mark of individual achievement."[17] The acquisitive society—given to conspicuous consumption and devoted to the Gospel of Success—had taken form, already augmented by a superabundance of goods and by that transformed and growing institution of affluence, advertising. "The Tenth United States Census gives the value of advertisements in the American press in 1880 at $39,136,306, and the next census shows that these figures had increased in 1890 to $71,243,361—a gain of eighty-two per cent in ten years."[18] Moreover, the nature and quality of advertising had changed. It now appeared in streetcars and large billboards; it contained illustrations; the use of color printing was appearing. While modern advertising is quite different, an industry of astronomically greater wealth, than that of the 1890s, its future was already clear.

As the hero of the era, the entrepreneur set the standard of munificence in residential architecture, cultural aspiration, and social pretension. His wealth conferred responsibility. Andrew Carnegie, more enlightened than many of his compeers, had in 1889 already begun to preach what William T. Stead, editor of the *Pall Mall Gazette*, labeled "The Gospel of Wealth"—Carnegie's belief that the rich should live simply and frugally, regarding themselves as caretakers of personal fortunes which they should use for the commonweal.[19] And some titans of wealth were, like Carnegie, often philanthropic, endowing libraries, universities, observatories, museums; but many were given to ostentatious self-aggrandizement. They hired the most prestigious architects to design for them the most renowned residences of the era—indeed, of any era in American history, for the 1880s and 1890s witnessed a style of residential grandeur that remains unsurpassed. As the palace of a prince made his power readily evident to his subjects, so the mansion of the entrepreneur, the prince of late-Victorian America, revealed his stature. Nor was opulence confined to the houses of the wealthy—on their own scale the middle class displayed their more modest wealth in their residences.

The two sites for the most conspicuous and most profuse display of palatial residences were New York City and Newport, Rhode Island. At both sites the architect nonpareil was the grand old man of American architecture, Richard Morris Hunt. He was the first American architect to be trained in Europe, at the École des Beaux-Arts. And it was in his office that the American Institute of Architects was founded in 1857. He was at the height of his fame in the 1880s and early 1890s. He designed more of the great mansions of his time than any architect. His forte was the style of the French Renaissance. Deviating from this style was one of Hunt's most renowned houses, the Breakers, designed in the Italian Renaissance style and constructed in the years 1892-1895 at Newport for railroad tycoon Cornelius Vanderbilt. But nearly as famed were several mansions in his favorite style, such as Belcourt, built in 1892 for Oliver H. P. Belmont, son of banking magnate August Belmont, who was one of the few Jews to win acceptance in American society. Also at Newport was Marble House, the Roman-style mansion Hunt designed for William K. Vanderbilt. The same patrons and others besides had hired Hunt to design their New York houses. But Hunt's most imposing and notable work was Biltmore, begun in 1890 and finished in 1895, the Asheville, North Carolina, palace of George Vanderbilt. Designed in the French (François I) chateau style, measuring 500 feet in length, containing 250 rooms, and located on a 120,000 acre tract of land that was laid out by Frederick Law Olmsted, America's greatest landscape architect, Biltmore was a triumph of size and sumptuousness. It was Hunt's masterpiece. Hunt's residential work was confined to the East, but architects and entrepreneurs in other areas of the nation contracted to erect original mansions or imitative versions of Hunt's Newport "cottages." Among them were such nationally known residences as the Charles Crocker house in San Francisco and the Potter Palmer house in Chicago. These great mansions of the age of energy, especially those designed by Hunt, laid claim to international repute and respect.

Montgomery Schuyler, respected architectural critic of the time, remarked, "The Bourgeois mansion of the 1850's has expanded to a palace." And the expansion of that house, especially as witnessed at Newport from 1855 to 1895, "affords an epitome of the history of the United States for the interval and furnishes matter for the discourse of the social philosopher as well as of the architectural critic."[20] Schuyler's point was well taken. Not only was the millionaire's mansion a symbolic declaration of equality with European royalty and an object for public admiration but also, and most importantly, it signified a revolution in American life. As the exhibition site for the entrepreneur's wealth and tastes the mansion evidenced the complete triumph of industrialism and therefore of the social revolution industrialism had created. Symptomatic of that revolution, on a most mundane but quite telling level, was the observation of a French visitor: "Before assigning a man his standing, people ask him in England, 'Who is your father?' in France, 'Who are you?' in America, 'How much have you?' "[21] The mansion was visible proof of how much. It obviated the same French visitor's view that in America there were three aristocracies: Society, plutocracy, and talent.[22] At the time talent had no hope of entering the top two aristocracies, but the aristocracy of money was able to buy its way into Society. After all, membership in Society derived mostly from inherited wealth. "But all of the old fortunes were being dwarfed, in fact and in publicity, by the new riches which accrued between the Civil War and the Great War—the longest crescendo in the history of American wealth."[23]

The life-style elaborated by the scions of Society was perhaps nowhere better exemplified than in the adventures of Alva Smith,

who came to New York from Mobile, wed William Kissam Vanderbilt, persuaded him to hire Hunt to design their famous $3 million
house at Fifty-second Street and Fifth Avenue, and then managed
the grandest social bash of her time in a house-warming fancy-
dress ball held on March 26, 1883, with 1,200 invited guests. It
was a smash hit. Thereafter Alva Smith Vanderbilt maneuvered her
husband into erecting and furnishing Marble House at a total cost
of $9 million. Apparently not satisfied with these achievements,
she finally divorced Vanderbilt in 1895 and in the next year
married Oliver H. P. Belmont.[24] Not least of her many triumphs,
as an index of Society's values, was Alva Smith's splendid waste,
the conspicuous consumption of her lavish parties and ornate
mansions. "In summary it may be said that the quarter century
before 1914 was the great age of the social leader in America, of
the dominant personality who—by a mixture of wealth, family,
aggressiveness, social skill, originality, and a measure of publicity—
was able to shape into a more or less compact group the casual,
shattered materials cast up by successive tides of new riches and
luxurious living."[25] The milieu of such elegant flotsam may seem
remote from events which move and shake the world; but Society
set a standard of behavior that lesser mortals might choose to
imitate or to admire. That behavior may, in retrospect, seem more
akin to Phinias T. Barnum's *Struggles and Triumphs* than to
taste-maker and dictator of etiquette Ward McAllister and his dicta
on social graces for nabobs. But suspect though it was, the world
of wealth also would eventuate in such literary achievements as
Edith Wharton's, in the creation of some of the foremost collections of art in the world, and in the finest flowering of American
architecture.

When not given over to the frivolities of Society, the wealthy
walked the very substantial ground of commerce. And in this
realm their feet were not always so clayish. The greatest witness to
that fact was the emergence in the 1880s and 1890s of an
architecture which was summarily referred to under the rubric
"commercial style." And rightly so, for it was the lords of com-

merce who, in near perfect partnership with a new and experimental generation of architects, were responsible for the giant structures that came to dominate the business centers of every major city in the nation. These structures, skyscrapers as they came to be called, represented a revolution in architectural design and vertical construction. Thus commerce created the most important buildings to be erected in America in the late nineteenth century, whether viewed structurally or culturally. "The development of the high office building has been so rapid in this country within the last few years and it has reached so high a degree of evolution at the hands of American architects that it must now be considered the representative and characteristic type of American architecture," editorialized one of the architectural journals.[26] Astute observers, foreign and domestic, had to agree. The beauty and utility of the skyscrapers represented the combined genius of American architects and engineers. But the skyscrapers' origin and existence evidenced the triumph of industry and commerce. Industry provided the necessary building materials and devices—cheaper steel of greater tensile strength for skeleton construction, the high-speed hydraulic elevator—and commerce provided the capital and the incentive. Thus the skyscraper was both index and artifact of an ascendant urban-industrial culture. Aesthetic or otherwise, the skyscraper was entirely a capitalistic creation, the result of investments generated by the profit motive.

The "commercial style" was attaining full blossom in the city of Chicago. Its stylistic inspiration there derived from Boston architect Henry Hobson Richardson's Marshall Field Wholesale Store (1885), but its increasing utilitarian simplification and height derived from the design adaptations of glass and improved steel by William LeBaron Jenney, architect of the Leiter Building I (1879), the Manhattan Building (1890), and the Leiter Building II (1891). The mantle of leadership fell to the leading firms of Adler and Sullivan and Burnham and Root. The memorable maxim "form follows function" was Louis Sullivan's; but it was John Wellborn Root who assumed the major responsibility of architectural advo-

11

cate of the commercial style through both his words and his designs. No one better understood the significance of the tall commercial building as a primordial representation of a new social order, as a symbol of a commercially oriented and dominated society, than Root. He said of such structures, "In them there should be carried out the ideas of modern business life, simplicity, breadth, dignity. To lavish upon them profusion of delicate ornament is worse than useless. . . . Rather should they by their mass and proportion convey in some elemental sense an idea of the great stable, conserving forces of modern civilization."[27] The Chicago architects were the champions of such theory as the most experimental group of architects in the nation, and their achievement has never been surpassed. In the latter part of the nineteenth century architects had been searching for a genuinely American style and in the "commercial style" they had found it. It would gradually invade every city in the nation. At the time, however, other styles held their own—the neoclassical and renaissance styles in the East through such outstanding firms as Hunt's and that of McKim, Mead, and White; the same styles in parts of the Middle West, through the efforts of such architects as former Bostonian Henry Van Brunt; the perpetuation in many areas of the nation of the Romanesque style of Richardson, who had died in 1886, through the efforts of his successors Shepley, Rutan, and Coolidge and other imitators. Thus the 1880s and 1890s were a period of enormous architectural vitality.

Much the same might be said of the associated arts of painting and sculpture, where the scions of industry and Society also had their influence, though their interest here was less pronounced. In fact, for the most part the wealthy families had their agents build collections of foreign art, chiefly French, and they rather ignored domestic painters and sculptors. Nevertheless, the eighties and nineties marked an age of impressive achievement in these fields. And some support was forthcoming, especially for artists whose fame derived from what was acknowledged to be that most characteristic field of American painting inherited from the Hudson

River school of painters—that is, the landscape. In 1888 George W. Sheldon reported that in New York alone there were some twenty collectors who bought American works exclusively, especially those of the renowned landscapists George Inness, Alexander Wyant, and Dwight W. Tryon.[28] By this time, too, some of the younger generation of painters—Will H. Low, William Merritt Chase, Wyatt Eaton, George de Forest Brush, Frank Millet, Frank Duveneck, and others—had established reputations through exhibitions in the late seventies of the National Academy of Design and thereafter of the Society of American Artists. But they never attained popular acceptance. For one thing, most American artists were trained abroad, primarily at the École des Beaux-Arts, and it was there that they both learned their techniques and adopted their subject-matter. Though capable, they certainly could not surpass their mentors in technical achievement nor in their feel for the indigenous sites and peoples of Europe. Why should American collectors buy American painters' imitations of European work when they could buy the originals? The attraction of native American art would have to lie in native forms and subjects.

Thus it is not surprising that the most touted painters of the time were landscape artists. Though the gigantic renderings of Albert Bierstadt of the spatial and natural wonders of the West had waned in popularity, those of Thomas Moran elicited warm praise. The legacy of the Hudson River school had gone West, as witnessed in the giant works of the Rocky Mountain school of painters. And that legacy still obtained in the East through the works of Frederick Church, Dwight W. Tryon, and George Inness. Inness was doubtless the master. It was he who best captured in his panoramic landscapes the essential quality of nature so admired by Thomas Cole, but he did so with individual talent and interpretation. His talent seemed both native and distinctive. Inness was "from the first a vigorous, individual portrayer of our home landscape in a style of great massiveness and sincerity."[29] Inness's work influenced the art of Winslow Homer, who established his reputation as a magazine illustrator and a genre painter but whose major achievement was landscapes and seascapes which represent the consummation of America's nineteenth-century native school of landscape art. The realism and candor of his works marked a high attainment, as critic Russell Sturgis would conclude: "Truly there is hope for a country that has produced a painter of such uncompromising honesty. Such art is a good foundation for the future—all the better that it is sometimes a little rude. But Mr. Homer has other claims upon our admiration than his independence: his Americanism, so pronounced that one might call him the Walt Whitman of our painters."[30]

Walt Whitman calls to mind the other giant painter of the times, the friend and portraitist of the poet, Thomas Eakins. Eakins had studied at the École and yet he would supersede that training to become distinctively American. Mrs. Schuyler Van Rensselaer, prominent critic of art and architecture, had judged his achievement generously after a visit to the 1881 exhibition of the Society of American Artists. "Of all American artists," she wrote, "he is the most typically national, the most devoted to the actual life about him, the most given to recording it without gloss or alteration." American life was often ugly, she continued, but ugliness did not deter Eakins, whose skill could create good results from dubious subjects. She foresaw his final reputation as superior to his contemporaries.[31] Though Van Rensselaer was a discerning critic, Eakins was not to attain popularity or esteem in his own time. He achieved for America in genre and portrait work what Homer achieved in landscape painting, but the laurels in these popular fields went to others.

Those others had also trained abroad and their works would remain derivative. Nevertheless, it was such men as J. Gari Melchers, J. Carroll Beckwith, Frank Millet, Edwin Blashfield, Elihu Vedder, and Frank Duveneck who attained greater repute than Eakins. Some of these artists and others of larger ability, most notably the versatile John LaFarge, would see to fruition the prophecy of Frederic Crowninshield: "Architecture may yet beget a race of painters through the medium of mural decoration."[32]

For America's golden age of architecture did bring about a furious endeavor in mural work. The giant of this field was LaFarge who, by enlisting his assistance in many projects, furthered the career of the outstanding sculptor of the era, Augustus Saint-Gaudens. There were a number of sculptors of national reputation—Karl Bitter, Lorado Taft, Daniel Chester French, William Rimmer—but none attained the stature of Saint-Gaudens, who already had created the *Shaw Memorial*, the *Farragut*, the *Puritan*, the *Adams Memorial*, and the *Diana*, the famous statue that was created to rise atop the Madison Square Garden designed by Stanford White. And, under the aegis of LaFarge, he had also created bas-reliefs, frescoes, and medallions for such capitalists as Cornelius Vanderbilt II and Jacob Schiff.

Such art and architecture belonged to the domain of high culture. Middle-class culture, circumscribed by limited capital and perhaps by taste, would content itself with lesser art. The middle-class family might conceive of its home as a modest version of the rich man's mansion, but they were not likely to afford a first-ranking architect nor to decorate with the works of an Inness or a Saint-Gaudens. Instead they were likely to have lithographs by Currier & Ives and the sentimental family groups of the popular sculptor John Rogers, and "The 'chromo' or chromolithograph was the most popular single item of late Victorian interior decoration."[33] Some writers, notably Mark Twain, even began to refer to their society as the "chromo civilization." The subjects of many of these chromos were curious and noteworthy—fire engines, trains, earthquakes, train wrecks. Photographs were also popular. But even on this level the prevalence of the nature school of art pertained through representations of the Rocky Mountains, the Grand Canyon, and the Yosemite Valley. A French observer, remarking that our nation was given to enterprise and the pursuit of material advantages, explained that such an atmosphere might reduce art to the level of advertisement; that is, artistic value might be measured in dollars. And overall, he concluded, "the taste for painting . . . tends to assume the character of a costly

15

luxury. There is nothing in this surprising to anyone acquanted [*sic*] with the Yankee's life of overstrain. Absorbed by constant preoccupations of a material nature, he cannot have that free and untroubled mind which is needed by a seeker after the beautiful. Leisure is wanting, nor has his early education prepared him to appreciate the delicate refinements of art."[34] Though his comment sounds condescending, there is truth in the Frenchman's conclusion. Nevertheless, he acknowledged that there were some fine private collections in the United States, some of which already augmented the works exhibited in museums. And certainly it is notable that the 1870s and 1880s were the great age of the establishment of academies and museums, among them the Metropolitan Museum of Art in New York in 1870, the Boston Museum of Fine Arts begun in 1870, the Pennsylvania Academy in Philadelphia (1871-1876), the Chicago Art Institute (1879), the San Francisco Institute of Art (1871), the Cincinnati Art Museum (1880), and the Cleveland Institute of Art (1882). Such museums would make available to the American people exhibits of fine works of art and sculpture.

Two other art forms were readily available to the public: music and literature. In the early 1890s music was on the verge of what might be called an America-consciousness, a reaction against the still prevailing dominance of German and Austrian influences. One of the spearheads of that consciousness was Antonin Dvořák, whose *New World Symphony,* finished in the year of the exposition, incorporated native folk songs. Dvořák would openly argue in 1895 for the use of Negro melodies and other folk songs as the basis for a native music.[35] But the Teutonic influence was still dominant. William Dean Howells remarked upon the fact that in the 1870s and 1880s German opera was predominant. But in New York at least Italian and French opera began to displace the vogue of Wagner. Though opera companies traveled throughout the United States, there could be no doubt that New York City's Metropolitan Opera, designed by J. Cleveland Cady and built in 1883, was the national center of opera. The only house to rival it was Louis Sullivan's Auditorium in Chicago, where opera was inaugurated in 1889 by a company under the management of Henry Abbey and Maurice Gran.[36] The "undisputed queen of the opera" at the time was Adelina Patti, though she had a worthy competitor in the American soprano Lillian Nordica.[37] Other American singers, such as Clara Louise Kellogg and Annie Louise Cary, were rising to prominence, but the stalwarts of the opera remained foreign-born.

Certainly of greater import at the time and since for the musical experience of a large segment of the American public was the development of symphony orchestras. And in this sphere one man stands supreme. "Theodore Thomas is an epic figure in American history—one of our great heroes. . . . It is through his efforts that this country is the home of the best in orchestral music, that almost all of our major cities have symphony orchestras of the first rank, and, what is more important, that in each of these cities there is a public that will listen to the finest symphonic works."[38] Thomas had been brought from Germany to the United States by his parents in 1845 when he was ten. He began his musical career as a youthful concert violinist. On December 7, 1860, he became a conductor, as a substitute for the regular conductor in an opera program at New York's Academy of Music. Soon thereafter Thomas was launched upon a perilous, sometimes successful but frequently disastrous, career of trying to educate the American public in the appreciation of instrumental music. He formed the Theodore Thomas Orchestra and began years of touring the nation. In 1873 he began the Cincinnati May Festivals that continued into the twentieth century. In 1877 he became conductor of New York's Philharmonic Society, a position he held for fourteen years. Then in 1891 the scions of Chicago offered him the opportunity to fulfill his lifelong desire to establish the first permanent symphony orchestra in America. He made the best of the opportunity, even managing to secure the Chicago Symphony Orchestra a permanent home in Orchestra Hall shortly before his death in 1905.[39] "The modern symphonic ideal, according to which dozens of players submit through careful rehearsal to the rigorous, not to say autocratic, direction of a conductor in the interests of polished perfection, was Thomas's ideal."[40] That ideal he achieved in the Chicago Orchestra. With that orchestra and through his forty years of tireless effort in the service of his ideal, Thomas immeasurably influenced orchestral music across America. Along with his efforts came the establishment of several conservatories. The Peabody Institute reached a delayed fruition in Baltimore in 1868; 1867 saw the founding of the New England Conservatory in Boston, the Cincinnati Conservatory, and the Chicago Musical College. Furthermore, professorships in music were set up in the 1870s at such universities as Harvard, Pennsylvania, and Yale.[41]

That the music of the great European composers dominated concerts and instruction at the time might suggest there were no serious American composers, or at least none who were taken seriously. And the truth is that few of the names of the period's leading composers remain familiar to today's patrons of serious music. What one musicologist has called the Second New England School of Composers included Arthur Foote, George Chadwick, Arthur Whiting, Horatio Parker, Mrs. H. H. A. Beach, Daniel Gregory Mason, and John Knowles Paine, oldest and perhaps most prominent of the group, who was the erstwhile teacher of some of the others at Harvard.[42] Most gifted and enduring of this generation of composers was Edward MacDowell. But it is doubtful that even MacDowell, trained in France and Germany, was a distinctly American composer, although he sometimes employed native subjects and idioms.[43] And the question of a national music did loom large at the time, along with the concern for national styles in painting and architecture; but its strongest advocacy and fruition in serious music belonged to the future.

Where the nation's musical taste most obviously appeared was where it always appears: in popular music. Certainly among the most popular was band music. It was a golden age of bands. "Before 1890, it was estimated that there were more than ten thousand amateur military-type bands in the United States, and there were probably twice that many by the end of the century."[44] Most famous of all such bands was the United States Marine Band directed by John Philip Sousa from 1880 until 1892, when Sousa organized his own concert band. Sousa's popular success was enormous, and before the opening of the World's Columbian Exposition he had established his reputation as a composer with such enduring march favorites as *Semper Fidelis, The Thunderer,* and *The Washington Post.*[45] The other great band of the era, the Twenty-second Regiment Band of New York, passed from the direction of its famous leader Patrick S. Gilmore, who died in 1892, to the direction of Victor Herbert in that same year.[46]

Certainly an important reflection of the Age of Energy was the nature of its popular songs. "Moralizing songs, quoting well known mottoes, maxims, and proverbs, were exceedingly popular in the '70's, and remained so right through the '80's and '90's."[47] In the eighties appeared those song-writers whose products would command the popular taste of the century's last decade: Paul Dresser, Charles Graham, Monroe H. Rosenfeld, Reginald DeKoven. The titles alone of their songs are revealing and also evocative of memories that still linger. There was, for example, Rosenfeld's *Johnny Get Your Gun* (1886), *With All Her Faults I Love Her Still* (1889). The still durable Paul Dresser had his first hit in 1886 with *The Letter That Never Came.* Thereafter the popular and profligate Dresser, generous and high-spirited man about town in New York, produced nearly annual favorites, such as *The Convict and the Bird* (1888), *The Pardon Came Too Late,* and *Her Tears Drifted Out with the Tide* (1891). Dresser is best remembered to this day for his immortal *On the Banks of the Wabash* (1899), in which his younger brother Theodore Dreiser professed to have had a hand. Reginald DeKoven's fame also rests upon a single piece—*Oh! Promise Me* (1889) which attained tremendous success through the vehicle of his light opera *Robin Hood,* first produced in Chicago in 1890. Charles Graham's great hit of these years was

The Picture That Is Turned toward the Wall (1891). It was also in that year that *Ta-ra-ra-boom-der-e*, by Henry J. Sayers, first appeared and became one of America's enduring nonsense songs. The smash hit of 1892 was Charles K. Harris's doggeral verse waltz tune, *After the Ball*. "The year 1893 presented another strange mixture of comedy, sentiment and religion," witnessing such songs as *Mamie, Come Kiss Your Honey Boy* by May Irwin; Charles Graham's *Two Little Girls in Blue;* and James M. Black's *When the Roll Is Called up Yonder.*[48] Though such titles suggest ephemera that might evince a smile, it must be assumed that such music, popular as it was, bespeaks the sentiments of the time. Nor should one forget that this was an age of enthusiasm for the imported musical comedies of Gilbert and Sullivan. Perhaps a counterpart of such stage productions—and a counterpart that led to distinctly American operettas—was the legacy of Harrigan and Hart, whose careers began in 1871. By 1885 Tony Hart had left the partnership; but Ned Harrigan's success still continued through his association with the English-born David Braham. Their 1890 production of *Reilly and the Four Hundred* contained one of their most popular songs, *Maggie Murphy's Home*. Harrigan recalls also the legacy of the minstrel show cum vaudeville. The minstrel shows, still dominated by whites and songs composed by whites about Negroes, had a large audience; but a Negro porter, Gussie L. Davis, beginning his career as a composer in the mid-eighties, would become prominent in the nineties.[49] It was the nineties, too, that made a craze of ragtime music through player pianos, pianists, dance bands, and thus forecast the coming prominence of jazz.[50] But except for such a propitious beginning, the judgment of the critical chronicler of our popular music Sigmund Spaeth might serve to highlight the meaning of the era's popular music: "The songs of the Nineties were perhaps more cruelly characteristic of their time than ever before, inexorable in their revelation of limited human understanding, commonplace emotions and the platitudes of social intercourse."[51]

A similar comment might apply to some of the popular literature of the period, but it has to be conceded, nonetheless, that this was a time of monumental and serious literary production in the United States. And literature may have been the most public and most revealing art form. Certainly it was the most accessible, prolific, and useful of all our arts. "Indeed it was an age of books, of print, of oratory, an age of words. . . . From 1875 until 1891, when the International Copyright Law was passed, paperback books were manufactured and distributed at extremely low prices. Literature was meant for the masses. . . . By 1891 books crowded household and library shelves throughout the nation. . . . [and] they were read, not merely displayed."[52] The new copyright law would shortly lead to a plethora of indigenous novels which in numbers at least would for the first time in 1894 outpace foreign-produced novels. In that year *Harper's Monthly* listed 617 publishers—187 in New York, 60 in Philadelphia, 52 in Boston, 51 in Chicago, 12 in San Francisco.[53] Certainly there was no dearth of American publishers, nor was there any lack of native talents. "But in 1893 . . . a canvass of leading libraries showed that Dickens was the most widely read novelist, with Scott, Cooper, Eliot, Alcott, Hawthorne, O. W. Holmes, Bulwer-Lytton, and Thackeray as his rivals. Twain held thirteenth and Howells twenty-sixth place."[54] It must be said retrospectively that such a list does not reflect serious discredit upon the American reading public, though that public had its curious literary passions certainly. Frank Luther Mott has evoked the general atmosphere: "The intellectual and spiritual climate of the early nineties was well adapted to literary fevers. Enthusiasms for certain books and authors gathered force suddenly and spread widely through the country, with all the exaggerations and the delirium of eulogy that follow upon such epidemics."[55]

Nevertheless, compared to some more recent periods, even the best-sellers of the eighties and early nineties suggest respectable taste in literature. For among them are Joel Chandler Harris's *Uncle Remus*, Lew Wallace's *Ben-Hur*, Gustave Flaubert's *Madame Bovary*, James Whitcomb Riley's poems, Mark Twain's *Life on the*

Mississippi and *The Adventures of Huckleberry Finn*, Leo Tolstoi's *War and Peace*, Guy de Maupassant's *Stories;* Arthur Conan Doyle's early Sherlock Holmes tales, and works by Rudyard Kipling and Robert Louis Stevenson.[56] Of course, the curiosities on the best-seller list might be of more interest as indexes of the period's values, for they divulge fascination with adventures, juvenile literature, romances, and utopian literature. *Ben-Hur* would qualify among the first, as would the works of Stevenson and Doyle; but even more so in this vein were H. Rider Haggard's *King Solomon's Mines* and *She.* Juvenile literature was represented by such renowned works as Margaret Sidney's *Five Little Peppers and How They Grew*, Johanna Spyri's *Heidi*, Frances Hodgson Burnett's *Little Lord Fauntleroy*, and Stevenson's *A Child's Garden of Verses.* As for romances, there was Marie Corelli's *Thelma*, Mrs. Humphrey Ward's *Robert Elsmere*, and Archibald Clavering Gunter's extraordinary tale of *Mr. Barnes of New York*, which combined romance and high adventure. Utopian literature was splendidly represented by Edward Bellamy's landmark *Looking Backward*, originator of an enormous spate of such works, none of which attained the great popularity of Bellamy's seminal novel.[57]

The influence of European literature still loomed very large, as was the case in architecture, painting, and music. But again American writers were intent upon creating a literature that would be distinctly native and thus freed to the largest possible extent from Europe's legacy. The impetus of this intention was the quest for the Great American Novel. Creation of this mythical monster was first intoned by novelist John W. DeForest in an essay published in 1868. The Great American Novel, as one observer saw it, would require an American Balzac, whose "breadth, depth, strength, and fearlessness . . . would be at once a joy and a terror; for he would run the gamut of our social, religious, commercial, and political sins and virtues, with a voice whose volume would be overwhelming, and whose compass would not be strained by the furthest extremities of exertion."[58] The Great American Novel would have to possess qualities which the literary arbiter of the age, William

Dean Howells, defined as "breadth," "spaciousness," and "amplitude."[59] In short, the Great American Novel should be an American equivalent of the *comedie humaine* within the covers of a single volume. Howells conceded implicitly and rather unhappily that no such leviathan was likely to be born. Nevertheless there were any number of works that might have been knights errant in the quest, among them Howells's own *Rise of Silas Lapham* and *A Hazard of New Fortunes*. With the works of Howells, Mark Twain, Henry James, George Washington Cable, Henry Blake Fuller, Harold Frederic, and Stephen Crane, the era was a most productive and important one in our history and it may fairly be said that it did evince a literature that is distinctly American. The novel was its mode of expression. Though there were manifold poets, it was clearly an age of prose. "This is preeminently the age of the novel," wrote Charles Dudley Warner. "So we have novels for children; novels religious, scientific, historical, archaeological, psychological, pathological, total-abstinence; novels of travel, of adventure and exploration; novels domestic, and the perpetual spawn of books called novels of society."[60]

It was also an age of the theatre. So popular and appealing was the drama that many of the novelists—including Mark Twain, Howells, James, Thomas Bailey Aldrich, and Hamlin Garland—succumbed to the ambition to be playwrights. Their works fared poorly on the stage. For the theatre was dominated by a taste that had emerged during and after the Civil War, inspired in great part by the extravagant and wildly popular *The Black Crook*, which was first performed in 1866 and produced almost annually thereafter for nearly thirty years. Charles M. Barras's play was perhaps an unequaled stage spectacle. "Almost every scene gives ample scope for theatre magic: displays of fire, water, transformations of all sorts, phantasmagorias of horror, caverns, grottos, necromancy and conjury, and most important of all, the ballet extravaganzas."[61] What the American playgoing public most admired was not drama but spectacle. As the well-known drama critic Brander Matthews attested, "there has been no falling off in the splendor of theatrical spectacle; indeed, it is often a reproach to the modern stage that it is prone to sacrifice acting, which is the vital essence of theatric art, to adornment, which is but external, superficial, and accidental."[62] Although there were both serious actors and playwrights, such as Bronson Howard and James A. Herne, they received only niggardly public support. And in critical circles the age was largely summarized in a commonly employed phrase, "the decline of the drama." The famous playwright Dion Boucicault complained near the end of his life that we had produced no essentially American dramatist, that in fact the American drama of the time was growing only "the most worthless and gaudy weeds. The prominent features of the theatre are burlesque and operetta; and the kind of farce we used to call extravaganza."[63] His characterization was obviously very close to the mark. It was not an age of dramatic achievement, but rather one of extravagant theatre.

The truth of that judgment was revealed even in the careers of the three great stage managers of the time: John Augustin Daly, James Steele MacKaye, and David Belasco. Daly dominated the milieu of theatrical production. He was influenced by the popularity of *The Black Crook*, which led him to emphasize careful and elaborate staging. Daly's first success was *Under the Gaslight*, which appeared in 1867 and was produced regularly thereafter for about twenty years. Its most famous and sensational scene portrayed the heroine effecting a last-minute rescue of a male character who lay trussed upon railroad tracks with a train bearing down upon him; that in itself suggests the tenor of the era's theatrics. But Daly could be serious as well as spectacular. He was an exacting director and his company of actors included the so-called Big Four—Ada Rehan, John Drew, Mrs. G. H. Gilbert, and James Lewis. His company became most famous, among both the playgoing public and the critics, for presentations of Shakespeare, especially in the decade following 1886. His productions of Shakespeare were memorable. They "were to be lavishly, magnificently staged; an attempt was made to suit the decor to the poetry. . . . Of course, there were also specially chosen musical pieces, choruses and crowds; authentically designed costumes, and some of the most elaborate sets ever mounted on an American stage."[64] Thus even the work of Shakespeare took on the aura of the Greatest Show on Earth.

It is noteworthy that the era's great erratic genius of American theatre, Steele MacKaye, began his career as a Shakespearean actor. He was incomparably successful playing Hamlet in England in 1873. In later years MacKaye wrote, produced, and acted in a number of plays, two of which—*Hazel Kirke* (1880) and *Paul Kauvar* (1887)—were quite successful and of some enduring interest. But, like Daly, his chief rendering of theatre came in the form of spectacle. *Paul Kauvar*, for example, was famous for one scene of indescribable carnage. And as the reviewer for the *New York World* saw it, "The performance, of unusual magnitude, held the large assemblage till nearly one o'clock. The dramatic intensity, the constant succession of incidents, the splendour of ensemble, the notable brilliancy of the cast and staging made a genuinely profound impression."[65] Obviously MacKaye was not to be outdone as a creator of spectacle. His great contributions to the theatre, however, were numerous patented and ingenious staging devices, such as the double stage, a flood-lighting contrivance called the Luxauleator, a mechanism to create clouds or cloud shadows called the Nebulator, and a machine to create scenic effects of sunlight, darkness, sunrise called the Illumiscope, all of which he planned to employ in a magnificent production for the World's Columbian Exposition.

MacKaye influenced the third member of this triumvirate of managers, David Belasco, who admired his effects, especially in *Paul Kauvar*. Belasco was the only Westerner among the three, having made his beginning as an actor in San Francisco. He traveled east in 1882 via Chicago and McVicker's Theater, where he teamed with another famous manager, Charles Frohman. In New York Belasco assumed control of MacKaye's old post at the Madison Square Theater, and when it finally failed he moved to the Lyceum to work with MacKaye. In 1886 Belasco assumed managership of the Lyceum, a position he held until 1890. In the nineties he emerged to prominence. His great success of the exposition year was *The Girl I Left behind Me*. Belasco's intent was to create total realism through introducing such effects as mounted cavalry, real trains and tracks, and actual fires. "And so," wrote Montrose J. Moses in his compendious study of the American theatre, "the art of the drama is the art of all arts, where proportion, perspective and color accumulate for a given effect. No one has studied this fact to greater purpose than David Belasco. . . . When the story of scenic realism is told, he will occupy a distinctive position."[66] Moses was right. Belasco would carry such heady realism into the 1920s, when as "the Bishop of Broadway" he shined as one of the New York theatre's stellar lights; but by that time theatre had given way to cinema as the art medium of spectacle.

The coming dominance of the cinema had long since been forecast in the nineteenth century by that adjunct of the theatre, scene painting, which often took the extraordinary and highly popular form of the panorama. These were enormous canvases depicting such events as the destruction of Pompeii, the great fire of London, the conflagration of Moscow. These immense panoramas—some of them were four hundred feet wide and over sixty feet high—were unrolled before outdoor audiences with the breathtaking accompaniment of floodlighting, fireworks, and flames.[67] A well-known English scene-painter of the period who worked with Daly, among others, reported, "Panoramas at that time were all the rage in America, and some fine spectacular shows were presented."[68] Theatrics and panoramas both would be in evidence at the World's Columbian Exposition.

Such amusements as the spectacle theatre and panorama might be included among the ephemeral enthrallments of devotees of both high culture and popular culture. In other areas Americans gave themselves up to pursuits that were novel at the time but are with us still. With the rise of the city came a burgeoning of social and sometimes secret societies, which had existed in small numbers up to 1880, "but between that year and the turn of the century close to 500 new orders were founded."[69] These included such stalwarts as the International Order of Odd Fellows, the largest of the groups, and university fraternities and sororities. Americans became joiners. Some of the societies they joined were of quite serious intent. Prominent among these were such social purity movements as the Woman's Christian Temperance Union, founded in 1874 but grown forceful after 1879 under the redoubtable Frances E. Willard, who led it until her death in 1898.[70] There was a very strong linkage between the waxing woman's movement and the crusades to prohibit alcohol and to eliminate prostitution. After all, alcohol was a serious threat to family life and prostitution was the most degrading vestige of the double standard. Women joined in both social battles; in fact, they led many of the skirmishes.

With regard to joining, this also was the age of the country club. It is therefore not surprising that Americans abandoned themselves to playing or watching sports. Bicycling and croquet were "the two great crazes of the era"; but tennis and golf became increasingly popular and basketball made its appearance in 1891.[71] Boxing was dominated by the attractions of John L. Sullivan and "Gentleman Jim" Corbett and baseball secured its ascendancy as the all-American game. There were other amusements, some of them, though regarded by their devotees as manifestations of the sporting life, perhaps not quite so wholesome as athletics. Although under attack and in some states prohibited, the saloon was holding its own. And the conviviality that made the saloon appealing could be enhanced. Commercialism enhanced immorality. The police inspector of New York, for example, estimated in 1893 that there were 40,000 prostitutes in his city.[72] That meant roughly one prostitute for every fifty residents, a far higher ratio than that of doctors to patients. Of course, there are varied means of ministering to the needs of the body. And the means most prominently augmented by the expanding cities was not the respectable institution of marriage, but the blatant assignation of prostitution. The 1890s marked the golden age of the American brothel.

It is not surprising that American religious leaders found themselves put to the test. The emergence of the city pinpointed the problems of the church. America had always been a largely Protestant community and it was the Protestant denominations which saw the city as the primary challenge of the new era. The time of evangelizing of frontier populations was past; the time for salvation of city-dwellers had come. The age marked the early growth of the Social Gospel. The Presbyterian minister Josiah Strong, representative in Ohio of the American Home Missionary Society, pinpointed the crisis forcefully when he wrote in the 1891 edition of his gospelizing tract *Our Country*, "The city has become a serious menace to our civilization, because in it, excepting Mormonism, each of the dangers we have discussed is enhanced, and all are focalized."[73] Those dangers were immigration, Romanism, public educational policies, intemperance, socialism, and Mammonism. The city, itself an extraordinary problem, magnified these real dangers tenfold. Thus for the Protestant denominations, "the great task during the decades that followed the war was to win and to hold the vast tide of people flowing into the cities."[74] The means to these ends were city mission societies, chief among them the Young Men's Christian Association. The most influential of all YMCA leaders was the gargantuan 280-pound Chicago-based revivalist Dwight L. Moody, who in tandem with his organist and hymnist Ira S. Sankey formed a remarkable team that through rhetoric and music brought theatrics to the church and disseminated evangelism worldwide through the tracts of the Chicago Bible Institute founded in 1889. These two had counterparts in other cities. Philadelphia, for example, boasted Russell H. Conwell whose famous lecture *Acres of Diamonds*, first delivered in 1888 and thereafter to earn millions of dollars through more than 6,000 deliveries, exhorted Americans to make money as a Christian obligation. His great religious edifice, the Temple Baptist Church, opened its doors in 1891 and along with his Temple University, chartered in 1888 to serve the offspring of the poor, benefited from his lecture income.[75]

Such men, gospelizing giants of their time, were exemplary of a legion of famous Protestant clergy—Phillips Brooks, Washington Gladden, Lyman Abbott, T. DeWitt Talmadge, and Charles M. Sheldon, who would publish in 1896 one of the all-time best-selling books *In His Steps*. These years were also the great age of the American pulpit. "Sermons were often front-page news in the daily press, and those of some of the more prominent clergy were regularly syndicated nationally in their entirety."[76] Such dynamic clergymen held sway over the imagination of part of the American public with an authority never since equaled. As that most astute foreign observer Lord Bryce saw it, "In the great cities the leading ministers of the chief denominations, including the Roman Catholic and Protestant Episcopal bishops, whether they be eminent as preachers or as active philanthropists, or in respect of their learning, are among the first citizens, and exercise an influence often wider and more powerful than that of any layman."[77] It is notable, however, that the speeches of the popular Robert Ingersoll, the Great Infidel and the scourge of religion, were front-page news and his works were widely read. The leading denominations in America according to the 1890 census and in order of number of congregants were Roman Catholics, Methodists, Baptists, Presbyterians, Lutherans, Disciples of Christ, Episcopalians, Congregationalists, with the Protestant churches holding a ratio of two to one over the Catholics.[78] The cities were, by virtue of immigration, the seats of Roman Catholicism in America. "These were the years—roughly from 1870 to 1900—which fixed the American Catholic pattern as predominantly an urban one with the immigrants settling for the most part in the large industrial centers."[79] Most prominent of the leaders was James Cardinal Gibbons of Baltimore—"probably the greatest single figure the Church in the United States has produced."[80] His efforts on behalf of American workers and his sympathy toward Terrence V. Powderly's Knights of Labor found support in Pope Leo XIII's famous 1891 encyclical *Rerum novarum*. One of Gibbons's supporters was John Lancaster Spalding, bishop of Peoria, whose efforts in Catholic education led to the establishment in 1889 of the Catholic University of America in Washington, D.C. The third major religion in America, Judaism, also found its center in the cities largely because of the great streams of immigrants in the period. Perhaps most notable among its leaders was Isaac Mayer Wise, leader of the Reform movement and founder in 1875 of Hebrew Union College in Cincinnati. Reform Judaism received its major impetus in the 1880s when upper-class Jews began to experience exclusion from Society at the same time that many of them, especially the German Jews, were experiencing increasing prosperity.[81] Reform Judaism promised to obscure the distinctions between Jewish experience and American experience. That impetus led, through the efforts of Felix Adler, to the prominence of the virtually nonreligious Ethical Culture Society, which Adler founded in 1876. It also led to a counterreaction by the Conservatives to hold fast to the traditions of Judaism. This struggle within Judaism is indicative of the terrible strains to which urban life subjected religion, as well as every other aspect of American society.

Indeed, prominent though religious leaders were, their actual importance resulted from their being combatants against a rising tide of Secularism. Some of them, in fact, were fellow travelers, consciously or otherwise—as *Acres of Diamonds* would suggest. And, his evangelical zeal notwithstanding, it is clear that in *Our Country* Josiah Strong was aiding and abetting not so much Christian missionary work as American imperialism and nationalism, the very offshoots of the Satanic enemy materialism. That intense nationalism, known rhetorically as spread-eagleism, would eventuate in the imperialism of the Spanish-American War and like events. Thus unwittingly or otherwise, many religious leaders, like Conwell and Strong, were making their peace with secularism. They had become spokesmen of the New Theology, which identified Jesus Christ with cultural ideals and institutions, assumed that the dominant cultural and social processes were redeeming, obscured the distinction between church and society. Responding to the vicissitudes of urban life, many ministers, prominently Washington Gladden, joined the incipient Social Gospel movement—at this point struggling for a philosophy, but soon to become a practical attempt "to establish the Kingdom of God" on earth.[82] They intended the Christianization of society, but they sealed the fate of the socialization of Christianity. Perhaps exemplary of the weakness inherent in the clergy's compromise with secularism was the statement of Charles F. Thwing, Congregational minister and president of Western Reserve University, who wrote, in admonishing preachers to minister to businessmen, "The church should not denounce money or money-making. The church should rejoice in all the money which its members either have or gain. The church wants money, must have it."[83] He was right; the church must have money. But in an age of rampant commercialism, how far must the church go toward accommodating itself to Mammon? Another prominent academician, Richard T. Ely, professor of economics at Johns Hopkins University and the University of Wisconsin in these years and himself a godly man, perceived the danger. The church, he wrote, was guilty of "the sin of concession to the powers of this world, so that they might hear nothing to terrify or alarm them, or even to make them uncomfortable; and the result has been sin, sin, sin, until in the markets of the world you cannot distinguish a Christian from one who professes to live for this world only."[84] The church, Ely conceded, was this-worldly; but its mission should not therefore be to make peace with prevailing social, economic, and cultural circumstances—rather, its mission should be to reform them. As an advocate of what he termed ethical political economy, Ely exhorted the church to push forward reforms in such areas as child labor, working conditions for women, the abolition of Sunday labor, recreational facilities, public guardianship of deprived children, public and political corruption, Saturday half-holidays, a redistribution of wealth, and a war on the false optimism and nationalism of society.[85]

Ely was one of those social reformers of the period who refused to see the evils of society sanctified by religion, philosophy, or stasis. In spite of his nationalism, Josiah Strong was equally forceful in his indictment of society's shortcomings and his advocacy of reform. "Our wonderful material prosperity," he intoned, ". . . may hide a decaying core."[86] That decaying core, as he saw it, could largely be attributed to Mammonism, which constituted not only a vile materialism and a corruption of morals but also an impediment to reform and an undermining of the political process, resulting largely from the concentration of too much wealth and power in too few hands.[87] Lyman Abbott agreed. "In the evolution of the race, as of the individual," he wrote, "the body precedes the soul. The eagerness of America is not for character but for possession. The American people . . . are covetous; partly because they wish to possess, partly because possession is the symbol of success, and they wish to succeed. Get rich, honestly if you can, but at all events get rich" was the watchword of all too many Americans.[88] If American society could not reform itself, then its evolution might result in disaster, its great experiment in democracy might become a colossal failure. But Strong and Abbott were confident that the society could reform itself.

Others were not so certain. In his great work on the evils of the tenements of New York and the hopeless lives of the city's poor masses, *How the Other Half Lives* (1890), Jacob Riis defied optimism in his declaration, "We know now that there is no way out; that the 'system' that was the evil offspring of public neglect and private greed has come to stay, a storm center forever of our civilization. Nothing is left but to make the best of a bad bargain."[89] He was no more hopeful two years later in his study of *The Children of the Poor*. The children of the toiling masses would determine the destiny of the nation, Riis believed, especially because "the cities long since held the balance of power," and cities were home to the oppressed, impoverished slum-dwellers. "Clearly, there is reason for the sharp attention given at last to the life and the doings of the other half, too long unconsidered.

Philanthropy we call it sometimes with patronizing airs. Better call it self-defense."[90] In Riis's view the society was embattled and endangered. But philanthropy and reform were raising their heads. Largely at the behest of the church, settlement houses were springing up in New York, Boston, and Chicago. The most famous of them was Jane Addams's Hull House in Chicago, founded in 1887. The decay at the core was larger than such humanitarian institutions could manage, but they were a beginning. They at least helped to make known the existence and the plight of the cities' slums. And that knowledge, in turn, helped spur movements for political reform, which resulted in 1894 in formation of the National Municipal League.

Information and opinion are necessary adjuncts to change and it was in this realm that newspapers and magazines contributed to the reform movement. Newspapers and periodicals proliferated. Newspaper dailies increased from 500 at the close of the Civil War to 2,000 by 1900.[91] The American public had become avid newspaper readers and their opinions were greatly influenced by what they read. "The American press may not be above the moral level of the average good citizen,—in no country does one either expect or find it to be so,—but it is above the level of the Machine politicians in the cities. In the war waged against these worthies, the newspapers of New York, Boston, Philadelphia, and Chicago have been one of the most effective battalions."[92] Though given largely to sensationalism, such newspapers as Joseph Pulitzer's *New York World* actively crusaded against vice and scandal, against municipal corruption and political chicanery. One of their most effective weapons was the editorial cartoon, which such artists as Thomas Nast of *Harper's* had raised to the level of extraordinary influence. Magazines like *Harper's* joined in the crusading effort, but foremost among the reform periodicals were *Arena* and *Forum*. Other journals like *Century Magazine, McClure's,* and *Nation* were outlets for the reform-minded writings of Ely, Benjamin O. Flower, E. L. Godkin, George Washington Cable, and others.

Cable was one of the few reformers interested in improving the living conditions, opportunities, political influence, and education of the nation's Negroes. He eloquently underscored the plight of blacks in such statements as, "over a million American citizens, with their wives and children, suffer a suspension of their full citizenship, and are virtually subjects, not citizens, peasants instead of free men."[93] If immigrants who were not even citizens, who did not share the native heritage, could be assimilated into American society, Cable argued, then why not the Negroes? His protests fell upon either hostile ears in the South or indifferent ears in the North. Only blacks were listening, among them educator Booker T. Washington. Washington shared that idea, common to many reformers, that education might solve the problems not only of individuals but also of an entire society.

It was, on the university level especially, an age that emphasized education. School enrollments were comparatively high. "According to the most recent statistics—those for 1890—the total number attending public and private schools of the three orders, primary, secondary, and higher, was 14,512,778. . . . It amounts to over 23 percent of the entire population of the country, and makes a good showing for us, inasmuch as 19 or 20 percent is to be regarded as first-class school enrollment."[94] The figure was four to seven percentage points higher than that of the leading nations of Europe. Attendance did not quite match enrollment figures, but those figures testify to the American public's general regard for the desirability of schooling. That regard was especially evident in the Middle West. The stalwarts of the schooling process were the old standbys, reading, writing, and arithmetic. The 1880s and 1890s, however, saw the beginning of a progressive and experimental approach to education; a movement away from the stress on rote memory, which presaged the later pioneering educational work of John Dewey, already the author of *Psychology* (1886) and *Outline of a Critical Theory of Ethics* (1891).

The reasons why there should be such an emphasis upon education may be arguable; but some were suggested by the popular literature of the time and at least one observer placed the emphasis within some dominant aspects of the society. Our devotion to reading, wrote W. T. Harris, first United States commissioner of education, resulted from the social evolution of the age. "For the age is intent on individual self-help, and the greatest means of all self-help is the printed page of book or newspaper." Reading books frees one from dependence and personal control and makes one more critical. "In short, the American characteristic of text-book instruction is the preparation of a people for a newspaper civilization—an age wherein public opinion rules."[95] Harris's contention about the rule of public opinion may seem dubious, but he was surely right in thinking that in an age of newspapers the public should be literate. In addition, Harris was of the opinion that the schools, especially the kindergartens, held the key to the civilizing of slum-dwellers. A later historian of American education, Edwin Grant Dexter, agreed with Harris on the influence of newspapers and also, like Harris, pointed out the significance to education of America's expanding public libraries. There was a most impressive increase in the number of libraries and in the volumes of books they housed. Traveling libraries were begun in 1893 and the size of bequests to libraries throughout the nineties was huge—this followed Andrew Carnegie's initial philanthropy in 1881.[96] With respect to higher education, the most significant development was the growth of state universities sponsored by the Merrill Land Grant Act of 1862, which had resulted by the time of the World's Columbian Exposition in public-supported universities throughout the nation. Increases in enrollment, faculty, and facilities at these institutions were prodigious.

It was perhaps this proliferation of institutes of higher learning combined with the experiences of American professors abroad, primarily in the graduate schools of Germany, that led to a new emphasis upon graduate schools. "The most important development of our higher institutions of learning during the last fifty years," wrote Dexter in 1904, ". . . has been in . . . graduate work."[97] There had been graduate work to the extent of the master's degree in this nation for some years, but it was not until this period, with the importation of German methods at universities like Johns Hopkins, Clark, and Chicago, that modern graduate education was established. And it was established in an era of imposing presidents: Daniel Coit Gilman at Johns Hopkins, Charles W. Eliot at Harvard, William Rainey Harper at Chicago. Such men were able to attract and to encourage scholar-educators of singular stature. There were Brander Matthews and George Edward Woodberry in literature at Columbia; Moses Coit Tyler in history and literature at Cornell; Richard T. Ely in economics at Johns Hopkins; the philosopher and historian John Fiske at Harvard; William Graham Sumner in political and social sciences at Yale; William James in psychology at Harvard; Frederick Jackson Turner in history at Wisconsin; Josiah Willard Gibbs in mathematical physics at Yale; Henry A. Rowland in physics at Johns Hopkins; Albert A. Michelson in physics at Chicago. There were others outside the universities: the historian Henry Adams, the sociologist Lester Ward, the former law teacher turned judge Oliver Wendell Holmes, Jr. Some of these men made enduring contributions to the literature of the humanities and the sciences. Moreover, in colleges and universities curricula had begun to stress science as well as the humane disciplines, reflecting on this highest educational level the realities of an industrial age that had called forth on a lower level schools of technical, industrial, and engineering instruction. The consolidating of higher education, like the incorporation of American industry, is indicated by formation in the decade prior to the exposition of the Modern Language Association, the American Historical Association, the American Economic Association, the American Mathematical Society, and the National Statistical Association. However, with respect to America's contribution to science Daniel Coit Gilman made this rather lamenting assessment: "We may with propriety speak of the scientific men of America, or of American institutions for the advancement of science, or of the progress of science in the United States; but to speak of American science is to speak of that which does not exist."[98] Gilman may have been right. Nevertheless, merely to toll off the names of the men of science in the period, adding to them imposing figures in other fields, is to reveal that it was a time of enormous intellectual endeavor.

That endeavor spilled over into many areas. Given the industrial nature of the age, it is not surprising that a huge amount of ideational energy, exemplified most notably through Thomas Edison, went into the inventing of mechanical devices and processes: incandescent electric lighting; perfected electrical transformers and generators; the telephone; the typewriter; the linotype—all of which represented revolutions in energy and communications. The full significance of such developments far exceeded their technical import. "The typewriter, the telephone and the telegraph were important for more than technological reasons; they played a unique part in the liberation of the American woman."[99] That is to say, they had been largely responsible by 1890 for the creation of the office girl. "The number of women wage earners increased from over two and one-half million in 1880 to four million in 1890."[100] In addition, since women could become useful adjuncts to the labor force, they found increasing acceptance into American colleges and universities; new residential living arrangements—the boardinghouses—mushroomed in cities, the meccas for both male and female wage earners; and a great impetus was given to the still young feminist movement, as is evidenced in the formation of the General Federation of Women's Clubs in 1889.

Women were active in cultural endeavors, in social purity movements, in philanthropic enterprises, and in the woman's rights movement. By the 1890s "the new woman" had emerged. Her emergence evidenced the rapid growth of feminism as a national social and political force. Under the leadership of Elizabeth Cady Stanton, Julia Ward Howe, Lucy Stone, Susan B. Anthony—and abetted by the support of enlightened men like Thomas Wentworth Higginson, Wendell Phillips, and Henry Ward Beecher—feminism had attained national status and organization in the National Women's Suffrage Association. But feminists aroused some horrified opposition by advocating divorce and sympathy for prostitutes as Stanton did, or free love, as Victoria Woodhull did.[101] Such advocacy was too much for a society bred on the sentimental adoration of the noble flower of American womanhood—innocent, motherly, tender, passive. The cynic might argue that liberation could produce more women like Lizzie Borden, presumed guilty of the bizarre murder of her parents in 1892. But at least the American woman had come alive. And one astute foreign visitor, the learned Matthew Arnold, found that fact appealing. "But almost everyone acknowledges," he wrote, "that there is a charm in American women. . . . It is the charm of a natural manner, a manner not self-conscious, artificial and constrained."[102]

Growing independence of women, coupled with public emphasis on education, also explains in part the era's plethora of periodicals and books and that singular outgrowth of self-help and instruction, the Chautauqua movement. Begun in 1874 as a school and summer camp for teachers, the Chautauqua Assembly soon had offshoots throughout the nation; after 1880 and until 1914 it had its own monthly magazine, the *Chautauquan;* and its improvement courses in literature, science, theology, and other subjects drew avid followers from all elements of the populace. At one time or another the original Chautauqua Assembly boasted such lecturers as Washington Gladden, Phillips Brooks, Richard T. Ely, Bliss Perry, Jacob Riis, and William James.[103] The popularity of the Chautauqua movement generated the revival of the Lyceum lecture circuit under the leadership of James Redpath. The Lyceum circuit became a platform for exponents of social reform and exposers of political corruption.

In American politics there was ample corruption to be exposed. On every level of government the political system was saturated with mediocre or corrupted office holders. American cities had virtual international notoriety as seats of venal politics. "The government of cities," said Lord Bryce, "is the one conspicuous failure of the United States."[104] Considering the staggering rapidity of their growth, and recalling that that growth was swollen by immigrants, such a circumstance is not surprising. It might have been simply inevitable. But, whatever the case, the political chicaneries of city politicians exacerbated some of the other problems of rapid growth—sanitation, health, transportation— while they simultaneously helped immigrants to survive in a strange environment in exchange for their votes. But the reform movement was gaining steam and in the later nineties some outstanding mayors would come to the fore, in fulfillment of the promise suggested by the election in 1889 of the honest Hazen S. Pingree in Detroit. And on the state level reformers could take hope from the 1892 gubernatorial election in Illinois which sent to the governor's mansion the seemingly anomalous but certainly admirable John Peter Altgeld—so fiercely honest that he could not be corrupted even by that champion predator, Charles T. Yerkes. On the national level politicians behaved gingerly or scandalously. "Congress in this era was powerful; but not particularly distinguished, either in the opinion of contemporaries or in the perspective of history."[105] Such men as Congressman Henry Cabot Lodge, Senators Roscoe Conkling, George F. Hoar, and James G. Blaine do not call forth visions of political grandeur or imperial rhetoric. And although by 1890 Thomas Reed had managed to make the Speakership of the House a position of such dominance as to control committees and legislation, the Congress fluctuated every other year between Democratic and Republican control. Congress managed to pass landmark though ambiguous laws like the act establishing the Interstate Commerce Commission and the Sherman Anti-trust Act, and to indulge in standard arguments over the tariff and free silver, the prevalent issues of the time. But it was a period of neither forthcoming legislation nor forceful leadership.

"The parties, closely balanced, hesitated to take clear positions on controversial questions lest by so doing they destroy the precarious balance of power. . . . Control of Congress and the White House shifted back and forth, not because of drastic alterations in voter opinion, but because the balance between the parties was so delicate that minor changes and chance events easily tipped it one way or the other."[106] Partly for this reason, partly out of deference to Congress, partly due to the prevailing philosophy that presidents should merely execute laws, the presidency in these years fell to two men who, though capable, were in no way remarkable chief executives—the Democratic Grover Cleveland and the Republican Benjamin Harrison, two men who hardly stood comparison with their contemporaries in England, Benjamin Disraeli and William Gladstone. When the World's Columbian Exposition was first envisioned those who wished to host it had to deal with the Republicans, since Benjamin Harrison had been elected president in 1888 in what is still regarded as the most corrupt election in American history. Many knew that the election had been paid for. In Indiana, for example, though votes in 1884 "had cost $2 to $5; the price in 1888 was $15 to $20. Those corporate contributions came in handy."[107] The politicians merely reflected the realities of the time—after all, commerce was king. Or as the perceptive Frenchman Paul de Rousiers saw it, "The most remarkable fact about present-day politics in America is that honest men seem to have abandoned them to professional politicians, and to interest themselves only in private enterprises. . . . There are some men entitled to the highest consideration, who occupy seats in the Supreme Court and in the Senate; but very few of them are to be found in the House of Representatives, and still fewer among the magistrates or civil servants."[108] And why not? For it was proper to assume that free enterprise was the worthiest enterprise of Americans. Ultimately politics and all other matters would evolve as they should; Herbert Spencer, the dominant philosophic presence of the time, proved as much.

Reflective of that prevalence of Spencer's popularized views of Darwin's ideas of evolution and natural selection, of the inevitability of progress and improvement, Andrew Carnegie began his munificent view of the republic, *Triumphant Democracy* (1886), with these words: "The old nations of the earth creep on at a snail's pace; the Republic thunders past with the rush of the express. The United States, the growth of a single century, has already reached the foremost rank among nations, and is destined soon to out-distance all others in the race. In population, in wealth, in annual savings, and in public credit; in freedom from debt, in agriculture, and in manufactures, America already leads the civilized world."[109] It was quite apt that Carnegie chose the hurtling express train as the image of an America of towering and accelerated growth. Whether democracy was triumphant might be debatable, but no one could deny the supremacy of industry and commerce symbolized by the railroad. Carnegie's view that the Republic represented the future of the world was agreeable to the American majority.

America might be in a state of enormous turmoil, of flux and adaptation. Certainly it was, as editor of the exposition-year Baedeker guide to the United States James F. Muirhead titled it, *The Land of Contrasts*. The contrasts were extravagant. "Society, always fluid in America, seemed in process of disintegration; the reintegration, though persistent and effective, was less obvious. The rapid growth of big cities, the torrential increase in immigration ..., the decline of the planter class in the South and the assault upon the social citadels of the North by the new rich, the emancipation of women and the decline in the birth rate, all contributed to the dislocation. The rise of the city was not merely a social or an economic phenomenon; it was psychological as well."[110] Nevertheless, the city itself was physical evidence of the democracy's astounding energy, of the supremacy of commercial endeavor, of the possibility that any man, given the rapidity of change and the fluidity of society, might ascend the ladder to success. Though the certitude of the cosmos was dissipated, most Americans, like Carnegie, remained confident of the democracy's future. The recent past proved that anything might be possible. The assurances of historians, philosophers, businessmen, clergy, foretold that the American era had come. And just as the manifold tendencies of American life conjoined in our cities, so they would

41

inevitably reveal themselves in the World's Columbian Exposition. Four hundred years after the arrival of Columbus America stood upon the threshold of her final destiny. The past as preparation was already history. The future had arrived. The American eagle, wings wide spread, had left its perch and was about to soar heavenward. Enter the White City.

Appropriately, the entrance to the White City was opened through money and through Chicago. Various cities vied for the honor of hosting the exposition; but the competition was essentially a two-way struggle between the titans, New York and Chicago. It was a struggle between East and West. New Yorkers promulgated a deprecating verbal battle with their rival, whereas Chicago went to work with political maneuvering and money. Chicago's maneuvering began in July of 1889 when her mayor, DeWitt C. Cregier, appointed a committee of one hundred citizens, later expanded to two hundred, to secure the fair. They raised $5 million for that purpose and began a campaign, urging Congress to select their city for the exposition because it was centrally located with excellent transportation access, because its locale would allow foreign and other visitors to see how the nation had developed west of the Allegheny Mountains, and because, "The marvelous growth of Chicago from a frontier camp to the active city of more than a million souls, with a corresponding advance in commercial, industrial, and intellectual activities, can best typify the giant young nation whose discovery the projected fair is to commemorate."[111] Adding impetus to this movement were tracts propagandizing the citizens of Chicago. One urged that the Lake Front be chosen as the site of the celebration because it was "emphatically the people's site for the Fair" and because such a locale would best help secure for Chicago the honor of being host city.[112] The argument and the lobbying campaign in Washington, headed by George R. Davis, succeeded. Chicago was chosen ahead of New York, Saint Louis, and Washington to be the site of the fair. And on April 25, 1890, Benjamin Harrison signed into law a bill authorizing the exposition to be held there in 1892. A corporation was established to organize, plan, and direct all the aspects of the exposition, its board members consisting of such Chicago scions as John V. Farwell, Jr., Lyman J. Gage, Harlow N. Higinbotham, Cyrus H. McCormick, Joseph Medill, Potter Palmer, Charles H. Schwab, and Charles T. Yerkes.[113] Thus it was assumed by such diverse types as the reformer Lyman Gage and the robber baron Charles T. Yerkes that Chicago's aspirations transcended their differences.

Chicago accepted the prize of the exposition as her rightful and inevitable due. What could be more appropriate than that the greatest of national endeavors, the celebration to eclipse all celebrations, should be held in the new metropolis of the West whose destiny, her citizens believed, was to become the greatest city of the world? What other city could have been so deserving of honor as the giant whose bulk sprawled along the southern shore of Lake Michigan, the mightiest inland lake in the world? It was most fitting that the colossus of the West should win. For Columbus had discovered the future when he discovered the New World, and Chicago was the future of America. As one historian of the exposition said of the city, "Here, for the present epoch at least, is the seat of empire, and here was properly placed the great Exposition that fitly marked the closing years of our century."[114] Now the star of the nation's destiny hovered not over the Atlantic seaboard but over the Great Lakes-Mississippi Valley urban-industrial empire. The West was the new and vital America and Chicago was its heart. For the moment at least Chicago would be the capital city of the New World.

2

CHICAGO

The growth of Chicago is one of the marvels
of the world. . . . There is in history no
parallel to this product of a freely acting
democracy: not St. Petersburg rising out of
the marshes at an imperial edict; nor Berlin,
the magic creation of a consolidated empire
and a Caesar's power.

Charles Dudley Warner

LONG BEFORE Carl Sandburg sang Chicago's praises, its citizens believed their city deserving of such euphoric epithets as "City of the Big Shoulders," for the development of the great city of America's inland empire was truly epoch-making. Chicago lived up to her motto, "I will." No visitor overlooked the significance of Chicago's growth; some exaggerated it. Clarence Clough Buel's view seems one of the latter: "Homer's deities might well have shrunk from the building in sixty years of the seventh city of the modern world; but here it has been done by the ordinary earthworm actuated only by the spirit of barter and gain."[1] Nevertheless, Chicago's history fairly validated his statement. In fact, so rapid was the growth of "The Garden City"—the motto on its official seal is *Urbs in Hortus*—that it seemed inexorably destined to become the chief metropolis of the nation. Natives and visitors alike sensed the thrilling rawness and verve of Chicago's giant industrial power, its robust and unrestrained cultural strivings. There was about Chicago, in its raucous and endless activity, its traffic-cluttered streets, its money-getting, and its crudeness, an electrical sensation of colossal energy, of dreams to be achieved, of impossible aspirations. Even its smoke-filled air, blown by gusty winds through cavernous streets, amid its mammoth buildings, seemed the essence of elemental power. Chicago was a microcosm of America. It was both the spirit and embodiment of the Age of Energy.

Indeed, Chicago was the epitome of energy. It was a thoroughly vivacious city, booming, optimistic, boastful. "It was so strong, so rough, so shabby, and yet so vital and determined. It seemed more like a young giant afraid of nothing, and that it was that appealed to me."[2] So wrote the novelist Theodore Dreiser in recalling the city where he went to seek his fortune in 1887. Dreiser was caught up by the spirit of Chicago, moved by the faith of its residents that one day their city would surpass in size and culture all other American cities and perhaps even become the first city of the world. Chicago's spirit was well described in Henry Blake Fuller's *The Cliff-Dwellers*, published at the time of the World's Columbian Exposition, in which a skeptical Bostonian visitor to "The Garden City" is regaled by some Chicagoans who expect their city to become America's greatest metropolis. Can this expectation be true, asks the Bostonian in dismay. And a mature, gray-haired Chicagoan responds, " 'Chicago is Chicago. . . . It is the belief of all of us. It is inevitable; nothing can stop us now.' "[3] For Chicagoans of all ages nothing seemed impossible. Hyperbole was their native idiom. And there was just cause for the Chicagoans' boastful pride.

After all, Chicago was now on the threshold of hosting America's greatest celebration a mere twenty years after the catastrophic devastation of the Great Fire of October 1871. Even her detractors lauded Chicago for having risen phoenixlike from her own ashes—the phrase that invariably flowed from the commentator's pen. The Great Fire's destruction seemed bewilderingly extensive. "Approximately two thousand acres lay waste; about eighteen thousand people left homeless,"[4] that is, nearly 6 percent of Chicago's population at the time. Nearly the entire commercial area of the city was destroyed; the total loss of property was estimated at $196 million; and at least 250 people had been killed. The fire was a monstrous tragedy. But the spirit of Chicago would prevail. As a native account invoked, "From the wreck and ruin of this great calamity, there is no one who questions the restoration and continued growth of Chicago. The first issue of her papers proclaimed, as its motto, *Resurgam.* . . . nor [is] any one weak enough to doubt the reconstruction, and on a grander scale, of this great marvel of the world."[5] Some observers had thought the city was doomed to oblivion, but Chicagoans implicitly and determinedly believed in the confident assertion of Joseph Medill's *Tribune:* "In the midst of a calamity without parallel in the world's history, looking upon the ashes of thirty years' accumulations, the people of this once beautiful city have resolved that *Chicago Shall Rise Again.*"[6] Their resolution was justified. "By October, 1872, only a year after the Great Fire, a new city had risen. An official estimate showed new buildings valued at $34,292,100 on the South Side, at $3,848,500 on the North Side, and at $1,893,000 on the West Side. . . . Trade was satisfyingly greater than in the year of destruction, real estate sold at advanced prices, and bank clearings attested the confidence generally held."[7] Despite the advent of a severe depression, such progress and confidence prevailed, so that Chicago was both rebuilt and greatly expanded; her trade mushroomed and her population exploded to estimates of 1.5 million by the time of the exposition. Thus the city's spirit was made tangible. Chicago's growth was exceptional, even astounding. And if such growth were possible under adverse conditions, then perhaps all things were possible.

Little wonder that architect Louis Sullivan, who came to Chicago in 1873, found the city incomparably vital. As he recalled years later: "Louis thought it all magnificent and wild: A crude extravaganza; An intoxicating rawness; A sense of big things to be done. For 'Big' was the word. 'Biggest' was preferred, and the 'biggest in the world' was the braggart phrase on every tongue. . . . [Chicago] shouted itself hoarse in réclame."[8] Apparently such réclame was a durably immodest expression of the city's spirit. Certainly at least it prevailed from 1873 to 1893, when even an outsider, the author Julian Ralph from archrival New York, became so enthralled with the Garden City's aura that he extolled it unequivocally: "America is Great and Chicago is her Prophet."[9]

Though extravagant, Ralph's words were in keeping with the elaborate rhetoric of his time. And his faith in Chicago as spokesman for America was also in keeping with the views of contemporary foreign observers. London's *Saturday Review*, for example, referred to Chicago as the "concentrated essence of Americanism."[10] European travelers in the United States almost invariably regarded Chicago as singularly American. A typical statement is that of the French traveler Paul de Rousiers: "Chicago . . . is . . . the most active, the boldest, the most American, of the cities of the Union."[11] One English traveler even shared the Chicagoans' faith in their city's future. "In speaking of the general impression left upon me by American cities," he wrote, "I trust I shall not be accused of Philistinism if I give, unhesitatingly, my preference to the brand new city of Chicago. . . . with all its defects . . . this city seems to me destined by its unrivalled position, and by the energy and public spirit of its citizens, to be the future metropolis of America."[12] Not all foreign visitors were so awe-struck by Chicago; some even thought the city hateful. Rudyard Kipling, for example, who professed deep love for the Americans, found Chicago merely a rather splendid chaos. "I have struck a city,—a real city,—and they call it Chicago," he wrote. "The other places do not count. . . . This place is the first American city I have encountered. . . . Having seen it, I urgently desire never to see it again. It is inhabited by savages. Its water is the water of the Hugli, and its air is dirt." He described spending ten hours in Chicago's business section, a "huge wilderness," wandering through its "terrible streets" and jostling "terrible people who talked money through their noses."[13] Fortunately he managed to escape. Chicago always inspired visitors to grandiloquent rhetoric, and more often than not the rhetoric was laudatory. As an epitome of the new urban age, Chicago, whether promising or portentous, had to be taken seriously. "For . . . she is at least the typical American city, the point of fusion of American ideas, the radical center of American tendencies."[14] That Chicago aroused such extreme feelings among both visitors and residents is not surprising. Barely extant as a fur-trapper's village in 1830, it had by 1890 developed, despite holocaust and depression, into one of the commercial centers of the world. And raw though it seemed, Chicago was so vital that it had generated a revolution in world architecture and a significant modern literary movement, which together with its Art Institute, symphony orchestra, and university, made even this rude city into a cultural, as well as a commercial, center.

As a major crossroad for America's railroads, Chicago was in a promising position. Even before the Great Fire Chicago had attained primacy as the commercial center of the West. And she would maintain that primacy. In the grain trade, for example, Chicago was unequaled. "As a primary transfer market no city was the peer of Chicago. In 1880 she received more than two and a half times as much grain and flour as did her closest competitor, St. Louis. In 1890 about 41 per cent of all taken in by the ten chief markets came to Chicago."[15] Thus Chicago's boosters justifiably boasted that their city was the greatest grain market in the world. Another factor in Chicago's commercial dominance was the lumber trade. Until the late 1880s Chicago had a virtual monopoly as locus of accumulation and distribution throughout the United States. Even after the eighties Chicago remained the greatest single lumber center of the United States because of large local consumption. "With population nearly quadrupling from 1870 to 1890, demands for timber mounted. Between 1871 and 1893 the city put up 98,838 buildings of all types" which were worth nearly $450 million.[16] The Columbian Exposition itself was the incentive for a building boom of such proportions that "local consumption alone amounted to the entire trade of New York, the second largest market of the country."[17] Even so, the lumber trade in Chicago never attained the volume and wealth of the grain trade, nor of that third lynchpin of the city's commerce which was burgeoning by the 1890s—the meat packing industry. From being a center for the transfer of live cattle, Chicago switched in the seventies and eighties to slaughtering and packing. By the time of the exposition these endeavors had attained staggering growth. "The measure of growth evidenced in the dollar value of the packers' products was . . . impressive and prophetic. The $19,153,851 of 1870 appeared insignificant indeed in light of . . . the $194,337,838 of 1890—an expansion of over 900 per cent in twenty years! At the same time capital mounted 511 per cent."[18] Much of this trade had become international, with Chicago shipping large quantities of packed meats to France, Germany, and Great Britain. Focal point for this trade was the place of disembarkation for unfortunate cattle, the monstrous Union Stock Yard, a city in itself. "In the Union Stock Yard, with its pens of wood and ugly, somber buildings of board and brick, resided the authority and action of the greatest enterprise of its kind in the world; a place of mud and smells, of overhead runways, and of shabbily clothed men seated on horses, cracking their whips over the incoming herds to hurry them on their way."[19] This huge enterprise sprawled over 400 acres of land which were visited annually by hundreds of domestic and foreign travelers. The Frenchman Paul Bourget was intrigued with his visit: "This walk through that house of blood," he wrote, "will always remain to me one of the most singular memories of my journey."[20] Surely the most curious tourist attraction in the nation, the Union Stock Yard was described by the *Chicago Tribune* as "the eighth wonder of the world."[21]

These three giant industries alone accounted for the creation of an imposing number of Chicago multimillionaires, including Jesse Spalding, Martin Ryerson, Turlington W. Harvey, Philip D. Armour, Gustavus Swift, and Nelson Morris. But there were still other enterprises which created fortunes for some Chicagoans. Again because of its railroad tie-ins and its strategic position, Chicago was an obvious locus for the iron and steel industry.

Chicago was near both to the sources of ore and to the coalfields of the Middle West. The giant Illinois Steel Company, formed through the combination of three already large manufacturers in 1889, pushed Chicago production of iron and steel into rivalry with Pittsburgh.[22] Along with growth in the steel industry came the manufacture of railway equipment and the fortunes of George M. Pullman. Similarly, the production of agricultural equipment became one of Chicago's chief enterprises. "By 1890 the city's six factories produced about one-seventh of all the machines made in this country."[23] King of this hill was Cyrus H. McCormick. Chicago also became an important center for the manufacture of wood products, among them organs and pianos—the W. W. Kimball Company was the leader here—and for ready-to-wear garments. No suggestion of Chicago's commercial activity could overlook the importance of the wholesale and retail dry goods concerns, which included the nationally famous enterprises of John V. Farwell & Co., Carson Pirie Scott & Company, Schlesinger and Mayer, and Marshall Field & Company. These famous stores were complemented by Chicago's dominance of mail-order merchandising, first begun by its native Aaron Montgomery Ward—sometime employee of the former firm of Field, Palmer, & Leiter—who set up his business in 1873. He was followed in 1886 by Sears, Roebuck & Company, founded by Richard Sears and Alvah Roebuck. The career of the best known of the dry goods dealers, Marshall Field, was representative of the Horatio Alger myth, of the wondrous climb to success of so many of the entrepreneurs of Chicago. "As with many other Chicago business giants, Marshall Field had risen from lowly beginnings—a clerkship paying $400 a year in 1856—to the headship of a mercantile establishment with the largest dry goods business in the United States, if not in the world, and possessing in 1890 a fortune estimated at $25,000,000. Like others, he prospered by investment in banking, real estate, railroads, iron mines, and city traction."[24] Among those others were the men already mentioned and such Chicago luminaries as banker Lyman Gage, hostelier Potter Palmer, traction magnate

Charles T. Yerkes, wire maker John W. "Bet-a-Million" Gates, and brewer Conrad Seipp—all self-made men, men of new riches. Indeed, Dixon Wecter described Chicago as "the paradise of parvenus."[25] As Chicago rose out of her own ashes, so it seems her most famous citizens rose from humble circumstances to wealth and power with a rapidity and energy commensurate to the atmosphere of their chosen city. These men were largely responsible for Chicago's cultural growth. Their fortunes stimulated developments in architecture, art, and music.

Chicago's major cultural achievement before the exposition was the development of the "commercial style," or Chicago style, of architecture. That development was the happiest and most immediately impressive outgrowth of the Great Fire calamity. The fire demanded in effect that Chicago be built entirely new. That fact alone attracted many young architects to the burned-out metropolis, among them two of the period's greatest architects, French-trained Louis Henry Sullivan and American-trained John Wellborn Root. It was Chicago architect W. L. B. Jenney who in the 1880s began steel-frame construction, and it was Henry Hobson Richardson whose Marshall Field Wholesale Store (1885) inspired the uniquely American unadorned skyscraper style. But it was Sullivan and Root who brought both the mode and the style to perfection. The firm of Burnham and Root was foremost in designing Chicago's renowned office buildings.

Of these buildings, Boston architect C. H. Blackall opined in 1887, Chicago could be justifiably proud, since they were all products of local genius and mostly of local money.[26] Their development he credited both to the need for rebuilding after the fire and to the artistic influence of the Centennial Exhibition of 1876, an interesting and perhaps prophetic observation. Chicago's buildings were not necessarily more original than those in other cities, Blackall argued, "but certainly the changes have been at least towards new methods and better and larger arrangements."[27] He credited Chicago architects with having tried every conceivable scheme for the designing of tall buildings. Without doubt Chicago

Marshall Field Wholesale Store

Courtesy of Chicago Architectural Photographing Company

was the city where the commercial style was most available for and most worthy of study. A striking feature of the commercial style in Chicago was its use of enormous size. Chicago had dared to create something new on a massive scale. Thus the great buildings of Chicago's commercial district deserved Blackall's enthusiasm: "It goes without saying that the buildings are grand and imposing. No structure can be erected covering the area that these do, and carried up into the air ten or twelve stories, without being majestic and awe-inspiring. . . . Such structures seemed more than human. One such building is imposing, but a whole street of such huge structures seems like the work of giants."[28] Buildings of superhuman character built by giants—it is an awe-impregnated opinion that evinces Chicago's atmosphere of superlative energy.

Chicago was obviously a very imposing physical presence. In its architecture, above all things, Chicago expressed its vibrant energy, its self-pride, and its soaring ambitions. Its unique skyscrapers attested the immensity of the city's development. They transformed Chicago into a city of giants. Few people realized how big those giants were. A common response from visitors was to count stories in order somehow to grasp the height of the skyscrapers. Such a response augmented Chicagoans' national reputation of wanting the biggest and best architecture in the world—a desire that sometimes led to actual or proposed absurdities, such as, Frederick Baumann's plan to erect a fifty-story skyscraper mausoleum and crematory.[29] Nevertheless, brash though Chicago was, her citizens had just cause to take pride in their massive buildings.

For by the time of the World's Columbian Exposition Chicago's reconstruction efforts had resulted in an amalgam of remarkable structures, many of them regarded since either as masterpieces of modern architecture or as significant influences upon the development of that architecture. Any list of such structures is imposing. On the eve of the exposition Chicago boasted W. L. B. Jenney's Manhattan Building (1890), Fair Store (1890-1891), and Leiter Building II (1891); Burnham and Root's Rookery Building (1886), Monadnock Building (1891), Ashland Block (1891-1892), Woman's Temple (1891-1892), and Masonic Temple (1891-1892); Adler and Sullivan's Auditorium Building (1887-1889), Schiller Building (1891-1892); Holabird and Roche's Tacoma Building (1887-1889) and Pontiac Building (1891); plus scores of other huge structures erected in earlier years. Any city that contained buildings designed by Sullivan and Root alone deserved to boast. Chicago's architecture was structurally innovative and artistically impressive. It constituted America's distinctive contribution to world architecture. Enlightened critics quickly perceived as much. What Chicago's architecture meant was succinctly expressed by John Wellborn Root when he argued the need for unity: "But the unity must spring from within the structure, not without it. The great styles of architecture are of infinite value but they are to be vitally imitated, not servilely copied. Continually return to nature and to nature's ways."[30] After all, there had never before in history been a society quite like this one. And since this society and this age were commercially oriented and urban centered, they needed an architecture of commensurate design. Chicago provided that architecture. "Chicago is not a city of big office buildings alone . . . ; but the office building has undergone so marked an evolution in the last few years at the hands of Chicago architects, the city is so full of them, that they may unquestionably be taken as the typical buildings of Chicago."[31] In this respect especially Chicago thoroughly justified the foreign travelers' view that it was the truly American city.

It would have been a most happy circumstance had Chicago's achievement in other arts reflected the vitality and genius that infused her architecture. But such was not the case. Though as in her architecture so in her art Chicago aspired to be the biggest and best, her artistic ambitions were not fulfilled. Chicago produced few noteworthy painters in the late nineteenth century. Perhaps the atmosphere that helped create the skyscraper was withering to the more delicate flora of painting. When Frank Duveneck had returned to the United States from Munich in 1873 he had discovered to his dismay that no art materials were available in

Rookery Building

Courtesy of Chicago Architectural Photographing Company

Monadnock Building

Courtesy of Chicago Architectural Photographing Company

Chicago. He had to send away for them. Fortunately, by the time of the exposition art in Chicago was in better straits.

By that time the dean of American portrait painters, George Peter Alexander Healy, had made Chicago his home. But he would survive there for only two years, dying in 1894, his powers long since spent. Nevertheless, he had made a sound choice of locales. For the early beginnings of art interest in Chicago, cut short by the Great Fire, were since resumed with the founding in 1878 of the Academy of Fine Arts and subsequently with the more important creation in May 1879 of the Art Institute of Chicago, with which the Academy promptly merged. Chicago's enthusiastic response to the Institute enabled the erection of its own building within four years of its founding. Thereafter it began to acquire large numbers of works. The importance of the Academy was permanently acknowledged in 1892 when, in conjunction with preparations for the exposition, a grand new building was erected to house the Institute's collections, classrooms, and studios. On the Lake Shore rose a splendid structure designed by Shepley, Rutan, and Coolidge, the successors to Henry Hobson Richardson.[32] Its facilities were used during the exposition for the World's Congress Auxiliary meetings. It was permanently opened as an art center in December 1893. In spite of such auspicious developments, however, Chicago was never to secure primacy in the effort to produce great artists and art. For already in the 1880s her archrival New York had become America's artistic mecca. Thus the good, bad, and mediocre artists of Chicago mostly abandoned their city and went east.

Nevertheless, the Institute achieved significance and impact as a museum and as a host for exhibitions, for by means of these two functions it fired the art aspirations of the city and the acquisitive instincts of its wealthy residents. Rich patrons began to collect paintings of excellent quality. For example, Mrs. Potter Palmer, the nabobish matron of Chicago society and an organizer of the exposition, acquired a huge collection of late nineteenth-century French paintings. She also had a fair representation of the works

Auditorium Building

Courtesy of Chicago Architectural Photographing Company

of American painters: Gari Melchers, Mary Cassatt, George deForest Brush, Eastman Johnson, and others.[33] The Palmer collection was open to the public, which it presumably helped to educate in the art of the Barbizon and Impressionist schools. Other scions of wealth who accumulated important collections which, like Palmer's, were later willed to the Institute included Henry Field, Elizabeth Hammond Stickney, and A. A. Munger.

The person who perhaps most thoroughly caught the art fever of Chicago was the writer Hamlin Garland, who moved to the city in the year of the exposition. There he became the most outspoken of propagandists for the Impressionists and for new developments in art. Among those he touted was Chicago's most noted sculptor, his brother-in-law Lorado Taft. And it must be said that Chicago is fortunate in sculpture with the works of Taft and others, most notably Augustus Saint-Gaudens, whose *Seated Lincoln*, done several years after the turn of the century following many difficulties, remains a tribute to Chicago's good taste.

In her music the city was more fortunate than in her art: Chicago had Theodore Thomas. Thomas came to the city from New York in 1891 to be director of the Chicago Symphony Orchestra, which was founded especially for him and with which he remained until his death in 1905. There were ironies and triumphs both in this capstone to his career. Probably the greatest of the ironies was that the earlier Thomas Orchestra had been booked for a two-week engagement in Chicago which was to have begun the day after the Great Fire broke out in Mrs. O'Leary's barn. The Crosby Opera House, where the orchestra was to perform, went up in the flames that destroyed the downtown. The result for Thomas was financial disaster.[34] But twenty years later he had returned, the most famous musical personage in America, to become the driving force behind Chicago's spirited devotion to music. Thomas had always been highly respected in Chicago, where he had conducted periodically for many years and whose German and Scandinavian residents avidly supported serious music. "It has always been reasonably musical, Chicago; it had

Schiller Building

Courtesy of Chicago Architectural Photographing Company

been one of the first cities in America to guess what Thomas was aiming at and to give him effective support."[35] In succeeding to the task of bringing serious music to Chicago, which Hans Balatka had pursued unsuccessfully years earlier, Thomas would receive effective support. His board of directors, unlike his ambivalent New York City backers, absorbed years of deficits without criticism and thus insured the ultimate success of his efforts. It remains a tribute to this day to the boosterism of Chicago businessmen that they gave unstinting financial support to their orchestra. Their confidence was justified. In Thomas they had chosen the right man. He was orchestral music in America; not merely because of his indefatigable energy and imposing expertise in the service of such music but also because of the educative effects of his programs. "For the last half of the nineteenth century he was the acknowledged master of the symphony orchestra, the first American virtuoso conductor."[36] That extraordinary virtuosity, together with a stubborn pursuit of his ideals, Thomas brought to Chicago. By the time of his death these qualities had secured the permanence of the Chicago Orchestra and a new home for it, Orchestra Hall, designed by Daniel H. Burnham and completed in 1905. Thomas was the logical choice as musical director for the World's Columbian Exposition. It is a pity that the city had no composer of commensurate skills, though she could boast the songwriter George Frederick Root and the composer Rossetter Gleason Cole. Root was famous for his Civil War songs, such as *Tramp, Tramp, Tramp* and *Just before the Battle, Mother* and for his hymn, *The Shining Shore*—all suitably sentimental works. Cole, on the other hand, composed symphonic works, choral works, and sonatas. Neither man was outstanding. But it was enough for Chicago to have Thomas. New York wished she had never given him up and Boston tried to lure him away. It was Chicago's good fortune that he honored his commitment to her.

The home of Thomas's Chicago Orchestra was the Auditorium Building. Thomas was never happy with that circumstance—hence his final great effort to secure Orchestra Hall—because he considered the acoustics of the Auditorium unsuitable for symphonic music. But for opera the acoustics were excellent. "Musicians shortly pronounced the Auditorium an acoustical dream. . . . [Mary Garden] says she once asked Jean de Reszke, the famous tenor, what he considered the finest theater in the world for acoustics. Without hesitation he answered, 'The Auditorium in Chicago.' "[37] Frank Lloyd Wright would later express the same opinion; but he had worked on the building's designs as a drafts- man for Louis Sullivan. Music lovers, in any event, could certainly be proud of such a fine home for opera in Chicago, especially as there had been none since the Crosby Opera House had suc- cumbed to flames. Consequently the excitement over the dedica- tion ceremonies was understandable. On December 9, 1889, a large audience, including President Benjamin Harrison and Vice President Levi P. Morton, had assembled for the ceremonies. They were treated to "the undisputed queen of opera," Adelina Patti, singing *Home Sweet Home*. On the following night Patti had the soprano role in the first opera to be performed in the Auditorium, Gounod's *Romeo and Juliet*.[38] In the next few years Chicagoans would have the opportunity to hear such singers as Patti, Lillie Lehmann, Jean de Reszke, Emma Eames, and Lillian Nordica in such operas as *Fidelio, Die Meistersinger*, and *Tannhäuser*. How- ever, from the mid-winter of 1891 until the opening of the exposition preparations for the fair prevented there being any opera in Chicago. Of course, one could still go to the Auditorium to hear John Philip Sousa lead the United States Marine Band or Robert Ingersoll deliver his famous address "Why Am I an Ag- nostic?"

Chicago was fortunate in the return of one of the Midwest's prodigal sons, Hamlin Garland, who had gone east to seek his literary fortune but had now returned at the urging of William Dean Howells. Garland believed that the West would give birth to a genuine American literature and that Chicago would be the center and fountainhead of the arts in America. He made this bias clear in his collected essays *Crumbling Idols* (1894). Garland conceded that New York was the art center of the nation, but he rejected its leadership. The scene must and would shift because the literary figures of the day were from the West and South. Then too, there was Chicago itself. What made Chicago such a promising literary center, Garland contended, was its uniquely American flavor. "Chicago is much more American [than New York], notwithstanding its foreign population. Its dominant population is splendidly American."[39] It seems a curious argument, but apparently Garland was infected with Chicago's enthusiasm. He argued that even Chicago's foreign population was a positive influence through its Scandinavian and German elements. In spite of the strained nature of his argument, there was some cause for Garland's optimism. Perhaps the writer he had most in mind was Joseph Kirkland, whose two works of the late eighties, *Zury* and *The McVeys*, portrayed rural western life. These works were of sufficient virtue to earn Kirkland mention in literary histories along with Harold Frederic, Edward Howe, and Garland as influential practitioners of rural realism. In fact, Kirkland influenced Garland, who was at work in Boston at the time on some of the stories that would appear in *Main-Traveled Roads*, whose second and larger edition was published in the year of the fair. The third promising realistic writer in Chicago was Henry Blake Fuller, whose Chicago-inspired novel *The Cliff-Dwellers* (1893) was probably the first significant American city novel. His writings would influence the man who culminated the Chicago literary achievement, Theodore Dreiser. In fact, Dreiser considered Fuller the leading realist of his time.[40] Another Chicago writer who influenced Dreiser was the poet-columnist-epigrammist, Eugene Field. His "Sharps and Flats" column in the *Daily News* "was the outstanding newspaper feature in Chicago."[41] Indeed, Field had earned a national reputation. Among Field's fellow journalists were cartoonist John T. McCutcheon, satirist George Ade, and Finley Peter Dunne, with his famous sayings of Mr. Dooley. Thus Chicago was extraordinarily fortunate in her newspapermen and in some of her newspapers, primarily the *Tribune* and the *Daily*

News. But besides Field the only poet of whom Chicago might be justly proud was Harriet Monroe, and her greatest service to the art was yet to come—the founding of *Poetry* in 1912. It was Harriet Monroe who deplored the lack of attention given literature in preparations for the exposition.[42] For in spite of the development of Chicago as a literary center, writing did not enjoy the kind of patronage wealthy Chicagoans bestowed upon music, architecture, and painting. "The new plutocracy of Chicago found little use for the traditional role of the man of letters. Direct support of him added little to reputations which were not made in the drawing room, but in the market place." What Chicago tycoons wanted as patrons of the arts was the prestige that is evidenced in conspicuous consumption.[43] That might be fine for the architect or the painter, but the man of letters was on his own. Even so the man of letters provided Chicago with a significant literary output.

Along with its budding literary ascendancy Chicago had become a significant publishing center. Though she would never match New York, Chicago was, as usual, determined to try. Prominent publishing firms included Rand, McNally & Company; A. C. McClurg & Company; Belford, Clark & Company. To these, at the end of the exposition year, would be added the distinguished firm of Stone & Kimball. Then too, there was the Literary Club, with more than 200 members, and McClurg's Bookstore, the literati's watering hole. McClurg's was one of the largest booksellers in the nation. Its sales indicated, concluded F. B. Smith, partner of General McClurg, that Chicagoans read mostly fiction; then history, biography, travel, science, philosophy. The primary interest in fiction was the work of modern writers. But the most popular sellers included Charles Dickens, Sir Walter Scott, Oliver Wendell Holmes, William Dean Howells, and Mark Twain—the last most of all. Others whose works sold well were Frances Hodgson Burnett, Thomas Nelson Page, Mary E. Wilkins, and General Lew Wallace. The works of Walter Besant and Arthur Conan Doyle, and those of Robert Louis Stevenson especially, were in demand. But Rudyard

Kipling's nasty comments about Chicago had cost him his local readership. As for poets, their work was largely ignored, although Shakespeare, Longfellow, Tennyson, and Browning continued to sell.[44] Thus Chicago's literary taste fairly well mirrored the taste of the nation at large.

It was perhaps in the leading literary journal of the time that Chicago was most fortunate. The *Dial*, founded in 1880 by Francis F. Browne, was by the time of the exposition an independent magazine, since Browne refused to have it influenced by potential advertisers. Its associate editor, William Morton Payne, was an energetic booster of Chicago. He rightly called attention to such phenomena as the Newberry and Crerar libraries, the new University of Chicago, the Art Institute, as evidence that Chicago was "passing to a higher and maturer stage of civic existence."[45] And it did seem as if events were conspiring on the eve of the exposition to fulfill his prophecy. Chicago lawyer Edward G. Mason called attention to the city's libraries as evidence that the city "has developed intellectually in a ratio not disproportionate to its material growth."[46] Though Chicago boosterism underlies his statement, his claims had foundation. The Chicago Public Library, containing 175,000 volumes and adding 20,000 more annually, ranked seventh in the nation; the Newberry Library already contained 80,000 volumes; and the library of the University of Chicago "takes rank in a single day as the third of our great libraries by the purchase of three hundred thousand volumes at Berlin," paid for through the subscriptions of wealthy Chicagoans.[47] And the libraries were used, as even the Frenchman Paul Blouet (Max O'Rell) attested with awe: whereas there were only 620 daily readers in the British Museum in 1888, the figure for Chicago's Public Library, with one-fifth the population to support it, was 1,569. He concluded, "The activity in Chicago is perfectly amazing."[48] Chicago's pursuit of "high culture" was corollary to her strivings in other areas.

One of the circumstances which created and intensified those cultural and material strivings was Chicago's cosmopolitan population. "By 1890, 77.9 per cent of the city's population was of foreign parentage derived from almost every civilized quarter of the globe."[49] The Germans and the Irish were the leading European contingents, accounting for over 35 percent and 15 percent each of the foreign-born population of Chicago in 1890.[50] But there were also sizable numbers of Scandinavians, Poles, Britons, Italians, and Bohemians—over three times as many of the last, curiously enough, as there were blacks.[51] It was such a conglomerate population, contributing to the sense of diversity verging upon chaos that visitors remarked upon, which led one post-exposition English visitor to a characterization of the city in rhetoric as extravagant as any that a Chicagoan could muster. Wrote G. W. Steevens, "Chicago, queen and guttersnipe of cities, cynosure and cesspool of the world! . . . the most American of American cities, and yet the most mongrel; the second American city of the globe, the fifth German city, the third Swedish, the second Polish, the first and only veritable Babel of the age."[52] Babel it might have been, since each ethnic group congregated in its own area of the city and spoke its native tongue. Each had its own newspaper, theatre, social organization. But in just such ways each contributed to the cultural vitality of Chicago. The Germans, larger in numbers than the native-born, gave to the city a brewing industry, Socialist-oriented labor organizers, an emphasis on quality education in public schools. The Irish contributed strong ward politicians. The Scandinavians provided lake captains and seamen and an emphasis upon Americanization. The Poles and their fellow mid-Europeans brought such skills as bricklaying and painting and an emphasis upon religion. The Jews helped to establish and promote Chicago's garment industry. The Italians contributed restaurants. The Negroes contributed benevolent societies, a budding civil rights movement. Such diversity of population also, of course, contributed problems. Italian residents already were obliged to protest that they had no Mafia. Though Roman Catholic, the Poles and the Irish were mutually hostile. Blacks were, as elsewhere, victims of segregation and discrimination. Crowded tenement dwellings, smoky air, unemployment, poverty, ignorance took their toll. One account, having duly taken note of Chicago's multiethnic populace, moved on to a subject whose morbidity even attested to Chicago's eclat: "Even death must be called in to testify to the greatness of a city, and he points his bony finger to a record of 790 violent deaths that occurred during the six months ending June 30, 1892, all requiring the investigation of a coroner."[53] It seems Chicago was to be outdone in nothing. This apparently violent and lawless atmosphere, reflective of a society barely removed from the frontier climate, led Congregationalist clergyman and espouser of the New Theology, Washington Gladden, to fear for the safety of visitors—especially youthful ones—to the fair and the city. "We want her [Chicago] to make her streets safe and orderly while they are there," he wrote. "We call upon her to restrain and suppress those classes of her population who thrive by the corruption of their fellow men. Chicago is burning to show us her tall buildings and her big parks. It is a thousand times more important that she show us a city well governed."[54] Gladden was asking a lot.

With violence so rampant—a rate four times as great as Chicago's murder statistics for recent years—it might appear that institutions of enlightenment and preservation were somehow ineffective or malfunctioning. And to some extent that was precisely the case with respect to Chicago's schools. "By the year 1891-92 teachers and principals numbered 3,520 to care for the needs of 166,895 [a ratio of about 1 to 50].... The salaries paid the instructional staff did not parallel other signs of urban growth.... At times ... all teachers got only scrip, and in 1877 and '78 their pay was suspended. Building also lagged far behind needs, and as late as 1893 enrollment exceeded seats provided for pupils by 14,000."[55] Clearly, though Chicago's phenomenal growth was most impressive, it caused formidable problems in areas of social need. And it is questionable whether the churches, the most durable and most prevalent of American institutions, guardians of both secular and religious values, were effective in uplifting Chicago's citizens. As in other matters, an obvious problem for the churches was too rapid expansion of the population. "By 1889, during a decade of phenomenal growth, the city could count one Protestant edifice to every 315 Protestants, one Roman Catholic church to every 2,202 Roman Catholic communicants, and one synagogue to every 919 of the Jewish faith."[56] The Lutherans were the largest single Protestant denomination, though the Methodist, Baptist, Presbyterian, Congregational, and Episcopal churches had sizable followings. The Roman Catholics numbered over a quarter of a million, so that Chicago was the "second largest Catholic center in the country."[57] In 1890 the Jewish populace affiliated with synagogues totaled 9,187, which was about one-fourth the number of Lutherans.[58] Protestant and Jewish groups suffered from the same divisive stresses that pertained elsewhere: Protestants from the struggle between orthodoxy and the idea of biological evolution, and the inroads of secularism; Jews from the Reform and the Ethical Culture movements. Missionary societies, so numerous in the nineteenth century, found fertile ground in Chicago, as did the YMCA and the YWCA. And in 1885 the Salvation Army had come to Chicago and stayed to save souls for the Protestant faith. Any form of religious activity was welcome in Chicago—Christian Science, Buddhism, Theosophy—in addition to the established denominations. And the people appeared to be very religion-centered, as the usually skeptical Charles Dudley Warner concluded, "for Chicago, which does everything it puts its hand to with tremendous energy, is a church-going city. . . . Religious, mission, and Sunday-school work is very active, churches are many, whatever the liberality of the creeds of a majority of them."[59] Nevertheless, theatres and taverns were open on Sunday in Chicago, and one of the most controversial questions for organizers of the fair was whether it should be open on the Lord's day. The Lord lost. Consequently some distant observers of the city seemed to think that Chicago was a modern-day Sodom. Had they known the truth, their suspicions would have been confirmed.

The flesh-pots and sin centers of Chicago were both prodigious and renowned. In his famous study of vice—*If Christ Came to Chicago!*—the English editor William T. Stead judged the city to be "the *cloaca maxima* of the world."[60] Here especially sins thrived in conjunction. Saloons, gambling halls, and bordellos existed in amiable proximity in over a dozen locales with such colorful names as Black Hole, Little Cheyenne, Satan's Mile, Hell's Half Acre. Probably the best known of all the vice areas was the Levee, the principal red-light district, which was part of Satan's Mile— South State Street. Stead, however, regarded the nineteenth precinct, which included the Levee, as merely rather typical of the city as a whole—doubtless he exaggerated somewhat. "In the nineteenth precinct there are 46 saloons, 37 houses of ill-fame and 11 pawnbrokers. This is an underestimate of the places which are commonly regarded as the moral sore spots of the body politic."[61] For Chicago as a whole, there were from six to seven thousand saloons and ten thousand prostitutes.[62] Chicago's brothels were especially notorious, some of them because of their vicious, slovenly, and thieving whores; but others more deserving— with sumptuous furnishings, voluptuous girls, and excellent wine cellars. The best brothels were found in the nineteenth district. Here, for example, one could visit the house of the famous Negro madame Mrs. Vina Fields, well liked and widely respected, who nearly doubled her staff to sixty during the year of the exposition—business was good. Her house and others, with commentary on their qualities after the fashion of a modern restaurant guide, was described in Chicago's Baedeker of brothels, *Sporting and Club House Directory*. The reader could learn therein of the irresistible enticements of Lizzie Allen's House of Mirrors, which later, at the turn of the century, accrued to two ladies from Kentucky—the renowned Everleigh sisters—who transformed it into the most prestigious, most splendid brothel in American history, a house of not only ill but international repute.[63] At the time of the exposition, though, Carrie Watson's, at 441 South Clark Street, was the finest bordello in the United States: a three-story brownstone mansion with five parlors, over twenty bedrooms, a billiard room, and, according to legend, a bowling alley in the basement. The furnishings were luxurious: furniture upholstered in damask, posh carpets, paintings, and tapestries. A three-piece orchestra played daily. Wine costing ten dollars per bottle was brought to the parlors in solid silver buckets and served in golden goblets. The girls serviced their customers atop sheets of linen. Carrie Watson's house, so revealing of the extreme energies and contradictions of Chicago, was a house of impeccable discrimination, with no red lights, no red curtains, and no hustling. "The only advertising of the resort, so the story goes, was done by a parrot trained to say: 'Carrie Watson. Come in, gentlemen.' This ornithological pimp spent its waking hours in a cage outside the door."[64] Its spiel must have been hard to resist.

In other respects also Chicago gave herself up to appetites. As Chicago was a brewing center it is understandable that, true to their robust nature, her citizens consumed enormous quantities of malt liquors. It was reported in 1890 "that for every man, woman, and child in Chicago forty-nine gallons were consumed, more than twice as much as the per capita for Germany. At any rate, in 1890 Chicago was credited with drinking up 1,673,685 barrels and in the World's Fair year something over a million more."[65] And there was eating. Tales of comestibles available to diners in Chicago are enough to make a gourmand salivate. Carter Henry Harrison, son of Chicago's mayor and later mayor himself, described dining at John B. Drake's Grand Pacific Hotel, famous for its game dinner in the 1880s and 1890s. The menu for 1893, Harrison recounted, presumably with tongue in cheek, "shows a distinct falling off in the game available. A mere 32 items appear in the list of roasts and of these 22 are of feathered fowl. Moose, elk, antelope, several varieties of deer, coon, opossum, squirrel and jack rabbits were the animals offered." But it is true that in 1880 the bill of fare offered nineteen mammals and fifty varieties of birds.[66] Harrison spoke of the zest with which his father and his political cronies feasted—a fact which might suggest the conclusion that Chicago's energy manifested itself in every aspect of life.

Carter H. Harrison, Sr., a descendant of Kentuckians, was probably the dominant political figure in Chicago, and as his son has it, he was none too pleased about Stead's early exposes of gambling, the liquor trade, and prostitution. Nevertheless, these were activities which he regarded with a certain benign tolerance. That tolerance derived most likely from Stead's insight that such activities formed the very bedrock of Chicago politics, which, like those of other American cities, depended upon ward bosses who made alliances with both innocent immigrants and traffickers in vice. As Stead had it, "Bribery, intimidation, bull-dozing of every kind, knifing, shooting, and the whole swimming in whiskey!"—such was the nature of ward politics. "Yet here, even in this nethermost depth, was the principle of human service, there was the recognition of human obligation." Perhaps the ward bosses' humanitarianism derived from a desire to control votes; yet, Stead concluded, the political party organizations were doing the work the churches should have been doing, the work of serving the people's needs.[67] Harrison apparently understood as much. He was a "reform" mayor, a supporter of Grover Cleveland in 1892, and a candidate for governor in 1884. He was reelected mayor for the third time in 1893 over the opposition of his fellow Democrat DeWitt C. Cregier. Harrison was not one to reject the support of any constituency. In fact, Harrison's primary supporter and the real power behind his throne was Michael Cassius McDonald, the dominant figure in Chicago's gambling empire with his four-story brick casino known as "the store."[68] Men like McDonald and the ward leaders he kept in his back pocket augmented Harrison's power base, which was widespread. "Above all others in the local Democracy towered the figure of Carter Harrison. . . . he demonstrated an astute leadership unexcelled in municipal and county struggles."[69] He made effective use of his popularity with voters of all types and with his ownership after 1891 of the *Times*. Harrison was able to appeal to both millionaires and immigrants. He was a most suitable mayor for a most American city.

The most American city and yet unique, Chicago finally both defies and invites summation. As a microcosm it may explain the values, concerns, problems, and expectations of the urban-centered culture of America that rose to dominance in the nineties. But even as a microcosm it resists analysis. Often it is easier for poets or novelists to evince succinct interpretation than it is for historians. And it is certainly true that, whether they were patronized or not, Chicago writers of the 1890s and the years leading up to the World War, distilled from the city's atmosphere a new kind of literature that was at once distinctly American, prophetic of the dominant subject-matter of our modern literature, and revelatory of our society's commercially dominated, urban-centered values. It was in Chicago that the view of the city in our literature became that of the city-dweller rather than that of the writer of rural prejudices. "The creation by the Chicago writers of a common perspective on urban life was a major achievement in American letters."[70] Subjects for this city literature were the Great Fire, money, social classes, commerce, politics. The exposition would provide still another subject. Since rebuilding after the fire made architecture so prominent, architects were frequent heroes of Chicago novels. But the prevailing hero, the hero discovered and interpreted by Chicago writers, was the businessman. "A new hero type in American culture, the 'business man,' emerged in Chicago. . . . Chicago writers faced the task of creating a 'society' life based on business because business was the main concern of Chicagoans."[71] As the exemplary American city Chicago revealed with a vengeance the new commercial ethic. Though Stead's view was somewhat skewed, it nevertheless contained a large kernel of truth, when he wrote, "It is impossible to describe Chicago as a whole. It is a congeries of different nationalities, a compost of men and women of all manner of languages. It is a city of millionaires and of paupers. . . . This vast and heterogeneous community, which has been collected together from all quarters of the known world, knows only one common bond. Its members came here to make money. They are staying here to make money. The quest of the almighty dollar is their Holy Grail."[72] Again, it is a judgment that must be taken with a grain of salt—even Stead would admit that there were many in Chicago, like Jane Addams of Hull House, who labored selflessly and praise them for that fact. But it is true that Chicago was heterogeneous, that she owed her present fate and her future to commerce, upon which everything from her fine arts to her politics depended. Chicago was, after all, a genuine Horatio Alger city—enterprise was her gospel.

Probably no other writer has been more enthralled by nor written more evocative paeans to the spirit of American enterprise that Chicago symbolized than Theodore Dreiser. One of his most ebullient evocations of the city which so fascinated him appeared in *The Titan*, the second volume of his trilogy based upon the life of Charles T. Yerkes—the Cowperwood of the novels. Cowperwood came to Chicago in 1873 to seek a new life and immediately relished the spirit of the place. Returning in 1913 to study the city while writing his novel, Dreiser recollected the lure of Chicago: "This singing flame of a city, this all America, this poet in chaps and buckskin, this rude, raw Titan, this Burns of a city! By its shimmering lake it lay, a king of shreds and patches, a maundering yokel with an epic in its mouth, a tramp, a hobo among cities. . . . Take Athens, oh, Greece! Italy, do you keep Rome! This was the Babylon, the Troy, the Nineveh of a younger day. . . . Here hungry men, raw from the shops and fields, idyls and romances in their minds, builded them an empire crying glory in the mud."[73] If such extravagant words were appropriate to the Chicago of 1873, when Cowperwood arrived, then they became doubly appropriate to the Chicago of 1893, when the World's Columbian Exposition opened.

It was ironic but certainly apt that one of the members of the board of directors of the World's Columbian Exposition Corporation was that rapacious businessman Charles T. Yerkes. For it was he and his fellow titans of commerce who made possible the creation of the exposition, a world that for millions of visitors would make tangible the poetry and energy of Chicago's spirit. Within the reclaimed miry wastes of Jackson Park on the shore of Lake Michigan near the heart of her teeming, striving commercial empire, Chicago would build for herself and for the world a smaller but more harmonious empire. And the White City would cry forth a still more eloquent glory in the mud.

3

THE GREATEST FAIR
IN HISTORY

In its scope and magnificence the Exposition
stands alone. There is nothing like it in all
history. It easily surpasses all kindred
enterprises. . . .

Congressional Committee report,
May 20, 1892

ONCE CHICAGO had secured the honor of being host city for the
fair, the promoters, the World's Columbian Exposition Corporation specifically and a host of citizens generally, necessarily
focused their attention upon such questions as where in Chicago
was the best locale for the fair, what the nature of the architecture
and exhibits should be, who should be in charge of what. The
board immediately named Lyman Gage as president of the corporation, with Thomas B. Bryan and Potter Palmer as vice presidents.[1] The officers demonstrated sound judgment. They appointed numerous committees—finance, grounds and buildings,
legislation, national and state exhibits, foreign exhibits, transportation, fine arts—which in turn performed surprisingly well, given
the brief time, a mere three years, in which they had to work.
Their first chores were choosing the site, the architects, the builders. They decided, first of all, that the site of the exposition
should be on the Lake Front. Next three singularly good choices
were made: F. L. Olmsted & Co. as consulting landscape architects, Abram Gottlieb as consulting engineer, and Burnham &

Root as consulting architects.[2] It was James W. Ellsworth, member of the Committee on Fine Arts, who persuaded a reluctant Olmsted to join the enterprise by inspiring him with the vision of the fair's potential.[3] Frederick Law Olmsted, after surveying the possibilities, proposed that the exposition be located at the northernmost possible site on the lake shore because it would be simplest and cheapest to provide with drainage and transportation, it would enhance the fair as spectacle through the comings and goings of the lake traffic, "an arrangement of buildings simpler and much grander than elsewhere would be practicable; and the buildings would have a much better setting and framing of foliage provided by standing woods."[4] The directors thought this locale would present too many transportation problems, and so the landscape architects chose Jackson Park. After some adjustments, the inclusion of additional areas, approval of the National Commission which had favored inland Washington Park, and the raising of money, the Committee on Grounds and Buildings was ready to proceed. Chaired by E. T. Jeffrey, president of the Illinois Central Railroad, the committee drafted a plan for the layout of the site, including the main buildings, lagoons, a canal, landscaping, that would largely remain the plan carried to fruition. And they appointed Daniel H. Burnham as chief of construction. "The duty of the Chief of Construction . . . was, broadly stated, to select, organize, and control all forces needed to prepare the grounds and erect the buildings for the Exposition. These forces were those of surveys and grades, landscape works, architecture, sculpture, decorations, general superintendence, sewers, water and fire protection, steam plant and other machinery, electrical plant, transportation of persons and goods, guard and secret service, fire department, medical department, construction accounts, purchasing, attorneys."[5] Thus Burnham became the field marshal of the entire project. He shared his authority.

"The general scheme of land and water for the Exposition was suggested by Mr. Olmsted. The arrangement of the terraces, bridges, and landings was made by his partner, Harry Codman. The size and number of the buildings was determined by Olmsted, Codman, Burnham, and Root."[6] But at this early stage of the planning nothing was determined about the architecture. At the recommendation of Burnham, Root, Olmsted, and Gottlieb the Committee on Grounds and Buildings, after some debate, agreed that the architects of the fair should be chosen by selection rather than by the traditional means of competition. Thereupon Burnham selected five firms to confer upon plans for the fair and its major buildings: Richard M. Hunt of New York; McKim, Mead, & White of New York; George B. Post of New York; Peabody & Stearns of Boston; Van Brunt & Howe of Kansas City.[7] Van Brunt & Howe accepted Burnham's invitation immediately; but the eastern architects were not fully persuaded until Burnham dined with them in New York just prior to Christmas 1890 and converted them to enthusiasts. Upon his return to Chicago, Burnham was authorized to choose five Chicago firms to design five other major structures at the fair.[8] He made the obvious choices: Burling & Whitehouse, Jenney & Mundie, Henry Ives Cobb, S. S. Beman, Adler & Sullivan. They all accepted. All the architects assembled for the first time on January 10, 1891, in the office of Burnham & Root. Burnham took them on a visit to Jackson Park. That night they were treated to dinner by the Grounds and Buildings Committee with Lyman Gage presiding. And Burnham himself evoked the cause, extolling the World's Columbian Exposition as the third great event of American history, comparable to the Revolution and the Civil War, and calling for self-sacrifice and cooperation. "There was a fine response. The Chicago men promptly responded to the old appeal of the Spirit of Chicago on which they had been brought up. From that night the spirit of cooperation never failed."[9]

The rest would be hard work. In less than two and a half years the architects had to design and oversee the erection of an entire city. They began their consultations immediately. But tragedy intervened, for on January 12 John Wellborn Root contracted pneumonia. He died on January 16, leaving Burnham and the others devoid of his excellent counsel. Burnham insisted later that Root's "unerring artistic instinct, his fertility of invention, and his vigorous enthusiasm left indelible traces on the work carried on . . ., and the large lines of the general design, which were due as much to him as any one else, were, practically, never altered."[10] Nevertheless, alterations were made and it remains debatable how Root's death affected the final plans. But Root's sister-in-law, the poet Harriet Monroe, insisted that had the architect lived and his designs been carried out, the buildings of the exposition would have been more festive and colorful.[11] In the wake of Root's death the architects changed the arrangement of the buildings around the Court of Honor and reestablished the plan's axes to extend the vistas and to enhance the effects of the buildings and lagoons. But the most important of their agreements concerned design. "It was not considered judicious to impose upon the designers any conditions in regard to style or proportions which might tend to hamper them in the free exercise of their artistic skill and invention; but, as harmony was an essential element of the composition of the Grand Court, it was suggested that the adoption of the classical style in that group of buildings would secure the desired result. Acting in the direction of this suggestion the Board [of Architects] agreed to fix the height of the cornice of these buildings at sixty feet from the ground."[12] Thus the legacy of the Beaux-Arts intruded itself; harmony triumphed over inventiveness. With these matters settled, Burnham designated who should design which buildings: Hunt, Administration; McKim, Mead & White, Agriculture; Van Brunt & Howe, Electricity; Cobb, Fisheries; Jenney, Horticulture; Peabody & Stearns, Machinery; Post, Manufactures and Liberal Arts; Beman, Mines and Mining; Adler & Sullivan, Transportation; Olmsted, landscaping.[13] These were the major assignments. Burling & Whitehouse were charged with designing the Venetian Village which was to stand near the great pier, but this project was finally abandoned. Somewhat later Holabird & Roche were chosen to design the Live Stock Exhibit and, by means of an architectural competition, Sophia G. Hayden of Boston won the opportunity to design the Woman's Building. Later still Charles B. Atwood, whom Burnham brought from New York to take Root's place and to be designer-in-chief, was made responsible for several small structures and the Terminal Station, the Art Building, and the Peristyle, an arcade of columns originally proposed by Augustus Saint-Gaudens, the consultant on sculpture.[14] The original group of architects met on February 22, 1891, with Lyman Gage presiding and spent the entire day presenting, discussing, and revising their plans which in their ultimate form Gage called a dream. Saint-Gaudens, who had sat by quietly listening, expressed his enthusiasm to Burnham: "Look here, old fellow, do you realize that this is the greatest meeting of artists since the fifteenth century!"[15] Thus was the Dream City envisioned. The National Commission accepted the plans a few days later and the stage was set for construction to begin.

The onset of activity inspired tremendous public interest with some noteworthy effects. "A curious epidemic of invention raged in all classes of society . . . while the plans were in course of study and while the public mind was still unsettled as to the probable character the Exposition would assume." This epidemic brought forth proposed "projects for towers, novel structures, and ingenious entertainments."[16] Some proposals were bizarre, some were quite prosaic. Architect Bruce Price's suggestion that the fair be all under one roof became inspiration to a Chicago architect named E. S. Jennison, who designed a much-discussed structure to house the entire exhibition. This structure was to be tentlike and 3,000 feet in diameter (or seven city blocks square); it was to have a central pole or tower over 1,000 feet high which would serve both as a roof support and an observatory.[17] Jennison's novel and astonishing conception elicited from the editor of *Architecture and Building* the comment that everyone would concede that this was a gigantic project and that, though Chicago could not expect to rival Paris in architectural beauties, "it may still be left to it to surpass that city and all others by the erection of a building four times larger than any exposition building the world has ever seen."[18] Although Jennison's proposal never reached fruition, the fair builders would erect structures of unparalleled size.

The precedent of the Eiffel Tower at the 1889 Paris Exposition led to numerous proposals for huge towers. One such scheme was that of the Columbian Tower Company, formed solely for the purpose of raising a great structure in the city of Chicago as a private enterprise. The plans supposedly called for a tower 1,500 feet high (the Eiffel rises to 984 feet), with a diameter at the base of 480 feet. The main entrance would be eighty feet wide. Inside, in the center of the tower, there would be a dome 237 feet in diameter to be used as a music hall, the largest in the world. The tower would contain a hotel with over 5,000 rooms.[19] Even today the immensity of the whole scheme seems quite staggering. Another proposed structure, not nearly so sizable but in its own way quite imposing, was described as being "truly American in its conception." Called "Freedom Raising the World" by its designer, F. S. Ingoldsby, this allegorical structure took the form of a giant rising on one knee while holding the world on his back. It was to have been 450 feet in height; the equator circling the globe at a height of 380 feet was to have been a balcony from which visitors could observe the fair. The base of the giant would have housed an assembly hall capable of seating 10,000 to 15,000 persons. The globe itself was to be made of glass except for the spaces representing the continents, which would be metal.[20] Its designer argued that as an attraction it would be the Eiffel Tower of the American fair. Burnham attested that this proposal was highly popular. Also popular, he said, was the so-called Water Palace, which was accepted until it proved to be impracticable. The Water Palace would have been a large circular structure, topped off with a steel and glass dome, on which would be mounted replicas of Columbus's three caravels and over which would tumble an enormous volume of water which would plummet into a moat around the base of the dome that would harbor a historical exhibit of naval architecture—all to be illuminated by electric lights. Still another proposal was the creation of an underground palace to simulate a mine. Fortunately, as Burnham noted, a high standard prevailed among the architects and no wild schemes reached fruition.[21] One bizarre proposal was that put forth by a group of enthusiasts who planned to buy the Colosseum at Rome and reconstruct it stone by stone in Chicago. As one editor wryly suggested, why not just bring over Saint Peter's with the pope intact upon his throne?[22] Such proposals, and many more of similar nature, indicate what was the prevailing sentiment regarding the exposition—that it must be unprecedently huge and grand, with at least one attraction that would belittle all attractions at all previous expositions. This must be the greatest fair in history. Public and Directors both agreed on that point.

The grandeur of the endeavor having been agreed upon, the pressing need was a master plan for the arrangement of the grounds and such necessary services as transportation, sanitation, and lighting. The architects had already devised the appearance of the formal part of the fair surrounding the Grand Basin, but the entire site was much vaster. As matters evolved the nature of the rest of the site was decided upon as need required, a fact which in itself makes still more impressive the success of such an enormous undertaking. The final plan designated seven distinct areas. These were the Basin and the canal determined by the original corps of architects; the wooded islands and lagoons where more freedom was allowed in architectural style while essential harmony was still demanded; the Government location, locale of the buildings of the United States and foreign governments; the Federal State site consisting of the Fine Arts Building and various state structures; the Midway Plaisance containing model villages of various nations, the buildings of the concessionaires, the Ferris Wheel, the Ice Railway, and other amusements; the area for livestock, outdoor agricultural exhibits, Convent of La Rabida, Leather, Forestry, Dairy, and Anthropological Buildings, and anthropological exhibits; and finally the railway yards, storehouses, warehouses, and workshops.[23]

The first order of business was the clearing, filling, and grading

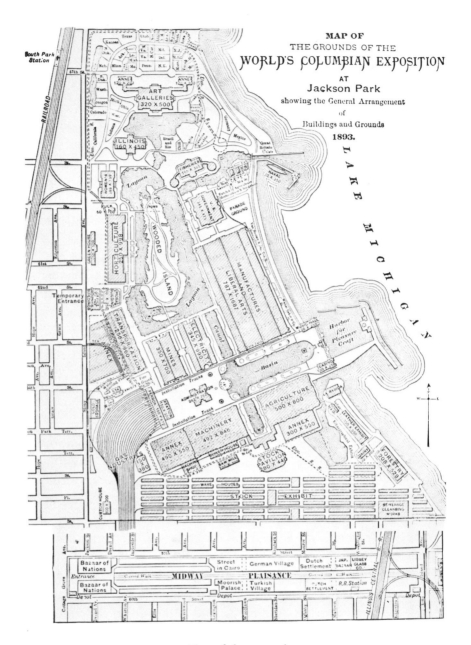

Map of the grounds

Courtesy of the Chicago Historical Society

of the grounds. This activity drew thousands of spectators in the unusually mild winter months of February and March 1891. Their interest was understandable. For Olmsted's complaints about the original locale had led to its expansion to include the Lake Front, all Jackson Park, and the Midway Plaisance leading to Washington Park, an area totaling almost 650 acres; with the addition of Washington Park the total was 1,037 acres—"nearly *three times* the space of any previous exposition."[24] Its giant size made landscaping a problem. In addition, Jackson Park, which had originally been planned by Olmsted and his earlier partner Calvert Vaux in 1870 but never developed, was, as Olmsted's partner Henry Sargent Codman reported, "swampy, the surface of a large part of it not being materially above the surface of the lake at high stages of the water."[25] The huge dredging and filling operation necessitated by this condition was begun on February 11, 1891, and resulted in a total cost of over $615,000.[26] The unimproved area of Jackson Park, consisting of 469 acres of the total site, was leveled upward by six and a half feet and interspersed with waterways, while the demand of the South Park Commissioners that the black earth there must be initially removed and then replaced over the filling to preserve the ground for park purposes "required the handling of 400,000 cubic yards of earth twice."[27] Such monumental endeavor foretold the nature of the construction and every other aspect of the fair. The excavating and filling was completed in May. Erection of the buildings followed.

"By June 1, 1891, the first building site—that of the Mines Building—was raised to the level on which foundations could be begun, and in July that building and the Woman's Building were started."[28] By the end of August most of the major buildings were under way. The Machinery Hall and the Fine Arts Building were the last to be started. Delays in constructing the former resulted from Burnham's concern for the proper operation of the power plant and for the security and stability of the structure, whose strains he thought had been miscalculated. This latter concern led to a dispute with Gottlieb, who decided to resign; thus

Burnham also assumed the burden of general supervising engineer with the added title of director of works. Burnham did, however, place Edward C. Shankland, with the title of chief engineer, in charge of the designs and structures of all the great buildings.[29] The holdup in constructing the Fine Arts Building derived from public sentiment that it should be a permanent structure and from a proposal that it be erected on the Lake Front separate from the rest of the fair, so that it might become the property of the Chicago Art Institute. This proposal was finally abandoned after lengthy consideration.[30] It was decided, however, to make this building the one permanent structure of the exposition. Consequently, it was constructed of different materials from the other structures at the fair, most of which, sculpture included, were made of a combination of plaster of Paris and fibers, which was called staff, superimposed upon lathe. "The Art Building was constructed chiefly of brick and steel [actually cast iron], with exterior covering of staff, and was practically fireproof." One reason for this mode of construction was concern for the safety of the artworks loaned for exhibit, which were valued at $3 million. Fortunately no losses did occur, ostensibly because of the precautions taken by Halsey C. Ives, chief of the Department of Fine Arts.[31]

Construction of the buildings entailed a prodigious effort. To bring materials to the scene a spur track of the Illinois Central Railroad was laid out, with offshoots in various directions to encompass the area. Up to July 11, a total of 36,407 carloads of structural materials, coal, and supplies, were transported to Jackson Park.[32] "To afford some faint conception as to the proportions of the Fair, it may be stated that, in the construction of the main buildings there were used nearly 20,000 tons of iron and steel and 30,000 tons of staff, many thousand tons of glass, and about 70,000,000 feet of lumber."[33] Such statistics are imposing certainly, but also nearly unfathomable. What may, in fact, provide a more meaningful idea of the size of this feat of construction is the number of men involved. Though the job of excavating had required only a few hundred men, the construction work required several thousand; and in the final months before the fair opened "from 12,000 to 14,000 workmen were busily employed within the inclosure."[34] Naturally, there were some problems. There was a demand that the directors employ only union men, set minimum wages, and accept an eight-hour day. The directors agreed to the last stipulation and to overtime pay in return for a guarantee that there would be no strikes. But there were strikes by the iron setters, electricians, and, most importantly, the carpenters. Such problems inflated the cost of constructing the exposition— probably by more than $1 million.[35]

In addition there was a problem of dual authority between the National Commission and the Board of Directors. Lyman Gage retired as president of the board in March 1891; he was succeeded by William T. Baker. Then in August 1892 H. N. Higinbotham assumed the job. The directors managed to secure agreement on the appointment of George R. Davis of Chicago as director-general of the exposition; a conference resulted in organizing the exposition under fifteen departments, with Davis having the right to appoint heads of each, subject to approval by both the commission and the directors. Then too, a Committee of Conference was established to referee disputes between the two bodies. But these arrangements were cumbersome. The relationship between the commission and the directors "was characterized by constant concessions to expediency, and differences were continually arising which hampered the work and lessened the efficiency of the organization."[36] This difficulty might have exacerbated the problem of finances. An estimate of the exposition's total cost drawn up in February 1891 amounted to over $17 million; it proved woefully inadequate. The figure was $6 million short of the cost of construction alone. (These and other cost figures should be multiplied by at least ten for an idea of their 1972 equivalence.) The total costs to "the Exposition company to June 1, 1894 amounted to $27,245,566.90."[37] The company sought help from the federal government. In December 1891 each house of Congress appointed a committee on the exposition, a bill was introduced to appropriate $5 million, and an investigative committee was sent to Chicago to study the matter; the result was a report of 689 pages.[38] The report, presented in May 1892, did little to expedite matters. The exposition's needs got sidetracked by the approaching presidential election. It was advised that Congress might agree to a loan, but the directors rejected this idea—after all, Chicago herself had put up $10 million. Finally, the matter was handled by the passage of a bill authorizing the Treasury to mint $5 million worth of Columbian half dollars; the amount was subsequently halved and after much haggling the bill passed in August 1892. Unfortunately the bill provided that the exposition must remain closed on Sundays, a stipulation which would lead to still another problem; but its passage saved the day by aiding the corporation to issue $5 million worth of bonds.[39] Still numerous other financial crises followed. With the onset of a recession in the early summer of 1893 and low gate receipts, it appeared that the corporation was headed for disaster. But finally the crowds came and the corporation emerged solvent.[40]

Besides these problems there was the question of how to transport visitors to and from the exposition. "The transportation question was like the stone of Sisyphus. . . . This problem might be formulated as follows: How to move 300,000 people from their lodgings and residences in the city to Jackson Park within a reasonable time in the morning, and return them to their homes at night."[41] It was decided that the job could be done by providing facilities that could move 150,000 persons per hour for three hours each in the morning and afternoon. But a study indicated that extant rail, traction, and water facilities in October 1891 could move only 39,000 persons per hour. A number of proposals, such as the elevation of the Illinois Central Railroad and the improvement of the Chicago City Railway Company's tracks, solved the problem. One difficulty remained. On the grounds of the exposition accommodation in the terminal yard allowed for the reception of over 41,000 persons at a time, apparently more than could even be delivered by rail; and neither the railroads nor the visitors found the Terminal Station acceptable. The Illinois Central even refused to bring its trains into the station. "The station was a beautiful and costly building, a model in its way, and the yards and terminal tracks leading to it were perfect . . ., but it never received business enough to give it an appearance of activity."[42] The terminal's nonsuccess was a sore disappointment to the builders of the exposition.

There were still other problems, such as damages and delays caused by high winds or foul weather, and the mundane but vital question of sanitation and water supplies. The fairgrounds were patroled nightly to collect all refuse, which was burned. For the fairgoers' comfort ample provision was made. "Within the Exposition grounds there were 3,116 water closets, as against 250 at the Paris Exposition of 1889, and 900 at the Centennial Exposition of 1876 in Philadelphia. . . . In addition . . . there were 895 closets belonging to the various concessions and the offices of the Exposition."[43] Thus the fairgoers who boosted Chicago's annual beer consumption to an all-time high in 1893 had no need to worry. Since water had to be supplied for drinking, fire protection, mechanical devices, and fountains, it was needed in great quantities which came from a well beneath the Machinery Building where two huge Worthington pumps, each able to pump 12 million gallons daily, were located.[44] The amateurishness of the Columbian Guards who were hired to police the grounds and protect visitors created some difficulties. But such problems as these were either unavoidable or manageable. One problem at least would prove unmanageable: fire in the buildings. On July 10, 1893, after the fair had been opened for several weeks, a catastrophic fire destroyed the Cold Storage Building, a private enterprise erected by the Hercules Iron Works Company to serve exhibitors and concessionaires. The chimney, centered in the building and rising to a height of 250 feet, was the fire's source. Firemen trying to haul hoses up the inside of the tower surrounding the chimney became trapped when the flames spread beneath them. Some slid down hose lines, others jumped to the building's roof, where they perished. Thirteen firemen died, along with four workmen; and over a score of others were injured. Thereafter visitors were forbidden access to the roof of the Manufactures Building and to the domes of other buildings which had been open to the public.[45]

Far less menacing than fire, but problematic nonetheless, were troubles with promotion and publicity. Europeans had assumed, on the basis of demeaning reports in New York newspapers—a matter of jealousy—that the exposition was to be little more than a local trade fair. "Ignorance prevailed abroad and skepticism at home."[46] The commission did a splendid educational job by sending representatives to the governments of nations throughout Latin America, Europe, Africa, and Asia. The story of their labors is long, though they received impetus from a belated proclamation of President Harrison issued on December 24, 1890, which invited foreign governments to participate in the fair.[47] The representatives finally managed to dispel the effects of damaging reports, to overcome doubts about Chicago's capacity to transport and house guests, and to evoke the enthusiasm of foreign politicians, especially in Europe. Promotion was administered by Moses P. Handy, director of the Department of Publicity and Promotion. "No other Exposition ever held was so widely advertised. For nearly two years scarcely a day passed on which less than 2,000 to 3,000 mail packages, freighted with information, were not distributed from this department. The circulars, pamphlets and books issued were in every modern language." Newspapers here and abroad were supplied with information. Chicago newspapers, with special stories on the fair, were sent everywhere. "The result was that the people of all countries were made perfectly familiar with the scope and magnitude of the Exposition a year before its opening."[48] The organization and endeavors of this department were herculean; they attested the exposition's promotion as the first example in American history of full-scale international advertising, a harbinger of Madison Avenue. The advertising succeeded. Its extravagant success created another problem: foreign nations and exhibitors requested far more space for exhibitions than could be provided. "The Exposition received exhibits from sixty foreign nations, states, and colonies. These exhibits consisted of 162,629 packages, valued in the statements of the exhibitors at $14,797,693 and required about 8,000 cars to transport them."[49] An exceptional number of nations exhibited at least something somewhere at the fair. "Eighty-six nations, colonies and principalities exhibit . . . and the moneys appropriated by all for the purpose of exhibits and buildings amount to over $8,000,000."[50] Nineteen foreign nations—Great Britain, France, Germany, Russia, Italy, Austria, Canada, Ceylon, China, Colombia, Costa Rica, Ecuador, Guatemala, Haiti, Japan, Nicaragua, Norway, Sweden, and Turkey—had their own buildings at the fair, which marked the first time in the history of expositions that all the colonies of England and France were represented by exhibits.[51] "Previous to this time no exposition projected upon an international basis had received the support of more than one-third of the governments of the earth." Chicago provided the first opportunity ever offered for all nations to exhibit their goods and resources on neutral ground.[52] The result was the most international of all world's fairs. "The true magnitude of the World's Columbian Exposition can only be realized when it is stated that . . . the space allotted to foreign nations alone exceeds the *total space* of any previous World's Fair."[53] Thus a certain degree of success was assured.

But public relations offered other problems. The difficulties over jurisdiction between the commission and the directors led to a visit in November 1890 by a committee from the House of Representatives to investigate and report upon the fair's progress. The astute Benjamin Butterworth of Cincinnati managed to ameliorate the Congress, a contribution which earned him appointment as solicitor general for the directors.[54] There remained perhaps the most controversial of all the exposition's public relations problems, the issue of Sunday closing. Clergymen argued that if the exposition were open on Sundays it would distract people from churchgoing. But at least one Protestant minister, John W. Chadwick, pastor of the Second Unitarian Society in Brooklyn, argued that there was nothing in scripture or tradition that demanded the Sunday closing of fairs and that this exposition certainly was more deserving than the museums, art galleries, and libraries that remained open on Sundays. He expressed the standard argument: "Sundays are the only days on which the poorer people of Chicago and the surrounding country can visit the Fair." The poor would benefit greatly from the fair's appeal to the imagination and the satisfaction it gave.[55] The liberal Roman Catholic theologian John Lancaster Spalding, bishop of Peoria, went one step further. "None can live without pleasure," he wrote, "and the overburdened toilers of our commercial and manufacturing cities feel most intensely the need of diversion and recreation." The city was the seat of our social problems, he continued, and if we were to save its toilers, its poor and degraded, then we must provide them with innocent and uplifting recreation. The exposition did so. It was an opportunity for self-improvement and it would set an example for all American cities. Close the saloons and places of vice, yes; but do not let "the clamors of the narrow-minded, who would make the Sunday a rabbinical Sabbath" deter us from pastimes that ennoble, elevate, and enlarge human life.[56] The feminist leader Elizabeth Cady Stanton entirely agreed. Closing the fair, she argued, would not bring people to church, nor should the state have the power to impede such a great popular enterprise as the exposition. The exposition might, in fact, serve the same purposes as more traditional Sunday observances. "If we would lift the masses out of their gross pleasures, we must cultivate their tastes for more refined enjoyments." The exposition was exceptionally well suited to do just that—with its splendid setting, its beautiful architecture, its international exhibits, its orchestral music. The exposition would both entertain and instruct.[57]

The Board of Directors felt much the same way. They also thought the fair would keep out-of-town visitors from swelling the crowds of the native lawless if kept open—which might also, of course, enhance the corporation's profits. But the issue became muddled through court suits and congressional artifices. One condition Congress had stipulated and the directors had agreed to with the issuance of the Columbian coin was Sunday closing. But Congress had abrogated this agreement by retrieving over $570,000 of the original appropriation to spend on other projects and the directors decided to ignore the Sunday closing condition. Attendance on Sundays was significantly less than on weekdays, though the directors provided ministers for services. Finally contending sides in the issue brought court proceedings. Jurisdiction over the matter fell to the Superior Court of Cook County after a decision by the United States Circuit Court of Appeals, and the Superior Court determined that the fair remain open on Sundays. But the controversy had been so belabored that the public was never quite certain about its outcome. The directors ceased to provide clergy for services and many of the exhibits were closed, so that it was not until the early fall of 1893 that Sunday attendance became substantial. Thus the courts helped to promote the success of the fair and to save the company from the financial disaster that threatened as a result of congressional inconsistency.[58]

In the meantime, while problems occupied the directors and controversies occupied public attention, the architects and artists of the exposition, under the guidance of Burnham, pushed forward its construction. They labored assiduously. "The life of the Director of Works and his staff was like that of soldiers on the field. They seldom went home, their entire energies were put into the work, and there was no cessation day or night."[59] The work on the buildings and sculptures preoccupied both the exposition staff and the city of Chicago for over two years. Indeed, sometimes it must have seemed to both Chicagoans and visitors that the exposition was the city. In early 1892 Barr Ferree, who was professor of architecture at the University of Pennsylvania, editor of *Engineering Magazine*, and an astute critic, wrote that to visit

Chicago without going out to the fairgrounds was like "seeing Rome without visiting St. Peter's, or Paris without a glimpse of the Louvre." Ferree was quite amazed and impressed by the rapidity of the exposition's construction.[60] But it should be remembered that the growth of Chicago itself was amazing and that the city was also on exhibit and saw itself in that light. The city was an exposition that should easily have rivaled the attractions of the fair. Julian Ralph said straightforwardly, "Chicago will be the main exhibit at the Columbian Exposition of 1893. No matter what the aggregation of wonders there, no matter what the Eiffel-tower-like chief exhibit may be, the city itself will be the most surprising presentation. Those who go to study the world's progress will find no other result of human force so wonderfully extravagant, or peculiar."[61] He was quite right. Of course, many of the Americans who came as visitors had already seen Chicago, and many more found the exposition so time-consuming that they never managed to examine the city. It would be left largely to Europeans to make note of the marvels of Chicago. A French marquis, for example, reported to some of his countrymen that "No description can give an exact idea of the immense American city . . . covered with an immense net of wires, cut by numbered streets, encumbered with vehicles of every kind, sprinkled with elevated railroads, which pass riotously over lofty structures of wrought-iron. How . . . picture to you the singular aspect which the houses of Chicago offer with their sixteen, eighteen and even twenty stories?"[62] Still, the main purpose of a visit to Chicago in 1893 was seeing the exposition. And, as the Marquis noted, the country of P. T. Barnum was not about to be outdone by France, so that it could be assumed everything about the exposition would be more grand than was the case in Paris in 1889. So it went, for the men who were responsible for Chicago's elevated railways and her many-storied buildings were now devoting their energies to preparations for the celebration of the discovery of America.

Their prodigious efforts created an exposition that well compensated for financial and other problems. Certain features of the

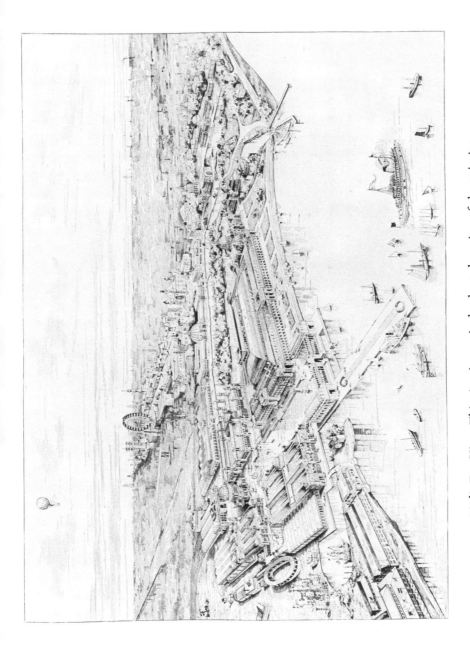

Bird's-Eye View. This view is a revised, adapted version of the painting.

Courtesy of The Bancroft Company, Publishers

Manufactures and Liberal Arts Building

Courtesy of the Chicago Historical Society

construction were novel, imposing, and instructive. The publication in early 1891 of a bird's-eye view painting of the exposition designed to enhance its promotion led the editors of the *Inland Architect* to conclude that the view had given "to the world some conception of the magnitude of the enterprise and its probable scope. To no other profession is this exposition so interesting as to the architectural, and from it can no other tradesman learn so much as the builder." For the exposition would reveal the development of architecture and of construction methods; it would demonstrate new uses for materials and new labor-saving techniques; and it would provide the opportunity for comparative study of methods and materials.[63] Indeed, though most of the later commentary on the exposition would be devoted to architecture, exhibits, and other matters, perhaps the most impressive achievement was the magnitude of its construction—in itself an extraordinary feat of engineering.

That construction involved far more than the buildings and their appurtenances. The landscaping of the exposition alone must have constituted one of the most superhuman efforts in the history of landscape architecture. "Altogether," Olmsted reported, "we have planted on the shores of the lagoons one hundred thousand small willows; seventy-five large railway platform carloads of collected herbaceous aquatic plants, taken from the wild; one hundred and forty thousand other aquatic plants, largely native and Japanese irises, and two hundred and eighty-five thousand ferns and other perennial herbaceous plants. The whole number of plants transplanted to the ground has been a little over a million."[64] Still the laurels for most colossal effort must go to the erection of the buildings. The largest structure at the fair, the Manufactures and Liberal Arts Building, was a project of unprecedented nature. Commentators delighted in recounting the various statistics relating to its size and erection. The Manufactures Building cost $1.5 million to build; its floor alone consumed over 3 million feet of lumber and five carloads of nails; it contained 44 acres of floor space; one thousand houses measuring 25 by 30 feet

Steel trusses of Manufactures Building

Courtesy of the Chicago Historical Society

could have been placed within it; the trusses of the central hall constituted 12 million pounds of steel.[65] These three-hinged arched trusses were thought to be the largest in the world. They had a clear span of 386 feet. To raise these trusses into place a derrick over 250 feet high had to be built—the largest traveling derrick in the world. Carl Condit has judged that "The Manufactures Building revealed the most extensive and elaborate system of hinged-arched framing ever undertaken in the United States. The framing of the central part of the roof followed the precedent of the balloon trainshed, while that of the sloping ends was an extraordinarily complex but perfectly articulated array of two- and three-hinged arches. . . . Along with the Galerie des Machines at the Paris Exposition (1889), it marked the triumph of steel arched framing in the nineteenth century."[66] As a professional observer of the time opined, "Altogether, the construction of this roof is the greatest engineering feat on the whole grounds," but, as he surmised, fairgoers would pass by unheedful of the achievement.[67] What would not escape their notice was the awesome size of the Manufactures Building. They were prepared to be impressed by the propaganda issued from Moses P. Handy's Department of Publicity which informed readers that the building was three times larger than Saint Peter's, four times larger than the old Roman Colosseum; that it could seat 300,000 people, each having six square feet to himself; that the entire army of Russia could be mobilized on its floor; that six games of baseball might be played here simultaneously.[68] The architecturally knowledgeable might have been more impressed by a diagram produced by one of the trade journals which showed plenty of room to spare in the Manufactures Building even after serving as an enclosure for these structures: the United States Capitol, the Great Pyramid, Winchester Cathedral, Madison Square Garden, and Saint Paul's Cathedral.[69] Or perhaps it was enough just to know that the Manufactures Building was the largest roofed structure ever erected.

Another engineering feature of the exposition whose nature and novelty could not have escaped notice was the extensive use of electricity. The exposition comprised the largest electrical exhibit and the greatest employment of electrical energy in the nineteenth century. The lighting of the interior of the Manufactures Building alone should have been awe-inspiring, had it not unfortunately been attempted from such a great height as to lose its effectiveness. The building was lighted by "five coronas, aggregating 315 lights, of a total capacity of 630,000 candle power. These lamps . . . were supposed to illuminate a space of 434,000 square feet. This was impossible." Light was dissipated in the upper part of the building and heavy shadows were cast in the lower part by exhibition pavilions. Only the Electrical Building was sufficiently well lighted to be a nighttime attraction.[70] But the fairgrounds were a different matter entirely. After much haggling over prices and apparently some chicanery in the bids of the General Electric Company, contracts were finally awarded to the Westinghouse Company as primary supplier, and to several lesser companies. Westinghouse established its central plant in Machinery Hall, "which included sixteen generators, giving an aggregate product of 8,955 kilowatts, driven by fifteen engines aggregating 13,000 horse power. The station was capable of lighting simultaneously 172,000 16-candle-power incandescent lights."[71] Westinghouse agreed to create this electric power plant at an enormous savings to the corporation, since the cost was estimated at about $400,000, about one-fourth of earlier bids, a rather striking sum, as Westinghouse thus committed itself to building a plant with a capacity "two or three times as great as that then in existence in the business district of the city of Chicago."[72]

Considering the giant scale of the exposition, it is little wonder that construction suffered delays and that not all was in readiness by the time of its actual opening. The process of decoration itself was monumental and it had to await completion of the buildings, as did the installation of exhibits. Up to the time of his resignation in the spring of 1892, William Pretyman, the first director of color, had witnessed only meager achievement in his area. He resigned because of a dispute over decoration. He wanted to use variegated colors on the buildings—apparently following the early wish of his friend Root—whereas Burnham insisted upon a uniform white or off-white. Pretyman's resignation was therefore significant. Had he remained the exposition might have been gayer, more festive; it would certainly never have become known as the White City. He was replaced by the famed and redoubtable Francis D. Millet, who came to Chicago from New York and remained for the duration of the fair. Millet was an early associate of John LaFarge; he was an artist trained in Holland, a writer, and a designer of stage costumes. "He had charge of all coloring inside and outside the buildings, the flags, banners, and woven-fabric effects of the processions and ceremonies inside of the grounds, and later of all the music and illuminations and fireworks; directed and controlled the sculpture and mural paintings, and was the friend and adviser of the Chief of Construction in everything."[73] Fortunately for Millet and his band of muralists and sculptors the chief of works' department concluded that money, time, and energy forbade finishing the interiors of the great buildings. With the exception of the Administration, Art, and Woman's buildings, and the Terminal Station and Peristyle, it was decided to treat the buildings "as great shelters for the housing of exhibits, and they were accordingly planned to satisfy the conditions of economy, of protection from the weather, and of convenience of installation. . . . The buildings would therefore be little more than great architectural sketches, carried out with sufficient elaboration and finish to give an effect of solidity and magnificence."[74] Nevertheless, there was enough work to occupy an army of decorators for well over a year. Under Millet's direction were a veritable *Who's Who* of American painters and sculptors. The painters included muralists J. Carrol Beckwith, Edwin H. Blashfield, Charles Reinhart, J. Alden Weir, Edward Simmons, Kenyon Cox, Walter MacEwen, J. Gari Melchers, Walter Shirlaw, who worked on the Manufactures Building; the Impressionist Mary Cassatt, who worked on the Woman's Building; Charles Coleman, who worked on the Horticulture Building; and George Maynard, who worked on the Agriculture Building. Among the sculptors were Karl Bitter, Richard W. Bock, John J. Boyle, Frederick MacMonnies, Philip Martiny, Edward C. Potter, Bela L. Pratt, Daniel Chester French, Edward Kemeys, Alice Rideout, Lorado Taft, Augustus Saint-Gaudens and his student Mary B. Lawrence—in short, every significant American sculptor except J. Q. A. Ward.[75] Architects, engineers, artists, sculptors, and construction workers labored cooperatively with sufficient impetus to have the fairgrounds essentially ready by opening day.

In anticipation of the opening and to commemorate Columbus's historic discovery, official dedication of the World's Columbian Exposition was set for October 12, 1892, when many of the buildings and exhibits remained incomplete. However, since New York City had planned an elaborate celebration honoring Columbus on that day—a celebration President Harrison wished to attend—Chicago graciously postponed her affair until October 21. Preparations for the dedication had been arranged by the committees on ceremonies of the corporation and the commission, the former including Edward F. Lawrence, chairman, Charles H. Schwab, William D. Kerfoot, Charles T. Yerkes, Charles H. Wacker, Charles Henrotin, and Alexander H. Revell. It is difficult to conceive of a more grandiose ceremony than the one these men elaborated. The celebration was to be preceded by Columbian religious services in all Chicago churches on Sunday, October 16. Then on the following Wednesday there would be Columbus Day ceremonies in all the schools; and that night was to be held a reception and ball at the Auditorium, under the sponsorship of Major General Nelson A. Miles, Marshall Field, George Pullman, Philip Armour, and N. K. Fairbanks.[76] On Thursday would occur a civic parade in the morning reviewed by the president, followed by a reception and a dinner given for the president and other distinguished guests. Then on Friday, the twenty-first, there would be a military parade to Jackson Park, reviewed by the president in Washington Park; dedication of the exposition buildings at the Manufactures Building; dedication of the World's Congress Auxiliary at the Auditorium in the evening; fireworks displays in various parks. During the dedication would occur the "Procession of the Centuries," a series of floats in the lagoons designed to illustrate the progress of civilization throughout American history. Though plans for this "Procession" were virtually fulfilled, it had to be canceled finally because of dangers of fire and accident and a problem of motive power. It was an expensive failure. In addition, and quite unfortunately, "President Harrison was prevented from attending the dedication by Mrs. Harrison's severe illness, which soon afterward proved fatal. Vice-President [Levi P.] Morton represented the President."[77]

These disappointments seem not to have diminished the grandeur of the ceremonies. The civic parade on October 20 set the tenor of events for the following day of actual dedication. "Almost every European nationality resident in Chicago, a division of colored citizens, and even the Indian boys from the Government school at Carlisle, Pa., all joined in marching under the flag of our country. The column was in platoon front of sixteen and twenty abreast, close order, music in quick time. It was over ten miles long, and occupied three hours in passing the northern portal of the Customhouse."[78] Dedication day itself became an astounding spectacle. Following a sunrise salute, there was a military parade. "It had been estimated that five hundred thousand people witnessed the civic parade, and, . . . fully eight hundred thousand people witnessed the military parades."[79] Thereafter a light luncheon and the dedication took place in the Manufactures Building, the world's largest structure being decorated with the flags of all nations. "The size of the great Liberal Arts Building was more than ever impressed upon one on this day than it can ever be on any subsequent occasion," wrote one observer.[80] For it was on this day the scene of an incomparable assemblage and pageant. Officials of most of the nations of the world, of the federal government, and of all the state governments; church dignitaries, business leaders, the great and the famous and the unknown, swelled a crowd of perhaps 140,000 persons who witnessed the ceremonies.[81] A platform at the east side of the building seated 2,500 people; another at the south end, capable of holding 5,500, was filled with a great choral group which had been trained for a year by director William L. Tomlins to render songs for the occasion. "Before the chorus was placed the Chicago Orchestra, augmented to 190 pieces and 50 drums, and led by Theodore Thomas." So handily did the Manufactures Building accommodate the huge invited crowd that corporation president H. N. Higinbotham ordered the gates opened to allow the crowd outside to enter. "The scene in the Manufactures Building will never be forgotten by those who witnessed it. . . . The eye and brain could scarcely comprehend the vastness of the audience stretching out before the platform. . . . There was little motion, but the air was resonant with an indescribable hum of voices." Every one of the notable guests was escorted to his seat by both soldiers and cavalry.[82]

With everyone in place, the ceremonies began. They were opened with the Columbian March, composed by Harvard Professor John Knowles Paine and performed by the orchestra and chorus. The benediction was delivered by Bishop Charles H. Fowler of the Methodist Episcopal Church of California. Then came the introductory address of the commission-appointed director general of the exposition, Colonel George R. Davis.[83] Davis was apparently a trifle overwhelmed. "In a presence so vast," he intoned, "on an occasion so pre-eminent in the progress of universal affairs, I am moved by emotions that can sweep a human heart but once in a life. Awe overmasters inspiration, and both are lost in gratitude that I am permitted to inaugurate these ceremonies."[84] He proceeded to deliver a sermon on the bountiful blessings of America. And he reserved his chief eloquence and laudation for Chicago. "The ceaseless, resistless march of civilization, Westward, ever Westward, has reached and passed the great lakes of North America, and has founded on their farthest shore the greatest city of modern times. Chicago, the peerless, . . . And that this city was selected as the scene of this great commem-

Opening ceremonies in Manufactures Building

Courtesy of the Chicago Historical Society

orative festival was the natural outgrowth of predestined events. Here all nations are to meet in peaceful, laudable emulations on the fields of art, science and industry . . . and to learn the universal value of the discovery we commemorate; . . . the nearness of man to man, the Fatherhood of God and the brotherhood of the human race."[85] With such lofty aspirations was the World's Columbian Exposition sanctified.

Davis's address was followed by a welcoming speech by the mayor of Chicago, Hempstead Washburne, who, quite naturally, voiced paeans of praise to his fiefdom. Addressing the congressmen and other officials who had awarded Chicago the honor of hosting the exposition, he said of his city, "She needs no orator to speak her merits, no poet to sing her glories. She typified the civilization of this continent and this age; she has no hoary locks, no crumbling ruins. . . . Her liberality to all nations and all creeds is boundless, broad as humanity and high as the dome of heaven."[86] Then, still in keeping with such high-mindedness, New York actress Sarah C. LeMoyne read selections from the *Columbian Ode*, written for the occasion by the poet Harriet Monroe, who was paid $1,000 for her efforts. The dramatic reading was interspersed with renditions of the *Ode*'s lyric passages by the orchestra and the Columbian Chorus, 5,000 voices strong. These passages had been set to music by George W. Chadwick of Boston. The *Ode* invoked the spirits of various nations and of heroism and exploration. Above all it invoked the spirit of Columbia, gem of the oceans, heiress of history, hope of the future:

Columbia, my country! dost thou hear?
Ah! dost thou hear the song unheard of time?
Hark! for their passion trembles at thine ear.
Hush, for thy soul must heed their call sublime.
Across wide seas, unswept by earthly sails,
Those strange sounds lure thee on, for thou shalt be
Leader of nations through the autumnal gales
That wait to mock the strong and wreck the free.[87]

Harriet Monroe would leave the dedication believing that her ode at least "had a chance of longer life than any other word we had listened to," but she was rather dismayed to learn it was not so, as she used the unsold pamphlet editions of her *Ode* for fuel throughout that winter.[88] Fortunately she was wealthy and wrote poetry as a service to art, not as a means of livelihood.

Following the delivery of the *Ode*, Daniel Hudson Burnham presented the buildings and the artists of the exposition to President Higinbotham. Burnham described the event as an "epoch" and spoke of its significance as an act that had freed the allied arts for the first time since Columbus's discovery. In response Higinbotham praised the buildings and awarded each of the architects a medal that had been designed by Elihu Vedder. While the medals were being presented the chorus sang Mendelssohn's "To the Sons of Art."[89]

At the end of Higinbotham's presentation, Mrs. Potter Palmer was called forth to report upon the work of the Board of Lady Managers, of which she was president. Less florid and more incisive than the others, Palmer delivered an inspired feminist speech. The exposition itself, she said, would not so vividly represent modern progress as would the fact of woman's participation in it. "The provision of the act of Congress, that the Board of Lady Managers appoint a jury of woman's peers to pass judgment upon her work, adds to the significance of the innovation, for never before was it thought necessary to apply this fundamental principle of justice to our sex." Here was a milestone in the history of the sexes. The Board had helped to establish women on the world's fair boards of every state and territory and in many nations abroad—a unique organization of women that would seek to enhance their material progress. For, as Palmer informed her listeners, machinery had liberated woman from the drudgery of household work; she was in turn liberating herself from the misconceptions of medicine, science, and society about her role and ability. The federal government was to be heartily commended for its liberal assistance in furthering woman's role at the fair. Palmer concluded with a judgment that might have sent some ripples of disquietude among the assemblage, but which was certainly refreshingly straightforward: "Even more important than the discovery of Columbus, which we are gathered together to celebrate, is the fact that the General Government has just discovered woman."[90] Not all the governments of foreign nations were pleased by that discovery—some Asian and Arabic nations tried to discourage female participation—but at least Bertha Honoré Palmer had sounded the clarion call.

Higinbotham resumed the podium in order to present the buildings to the president of the World's Columbian Commission, Thomas W. Palmer. In so doing Higinbotham bespoke a concept of the fairgrounds that would become an idée fixe in the minds of many visitors. Only recently the grounds had been a morass, he said. "To-day they stand transformed by art and science into a beauty and grandeur unrivaled by any other spot on earth."[91] Palmer reiterated Higinbotham's view in acknowledging that there were no new continents to discover; but that much remained to be done in uplifting man in both hemispheres, and that expositions could be material aids to that end. He expressed these ideas in presenting the buildings, in his turn, to Vice President Levi P. Morton. It was the vice president's function, at last, to dedicate the buildings themselves. In so doing, Morton delivered a remark which also came to be typical of responses to the fair. "As we gaze upon these magnificent erections, with their columns and arches, their entablatures and adornments, when we consider their beauty and rapidity of realization, they would seem to be evoked at a wizard's touch of Aladdin's lamp." But Morton, a rather erudite man, went on to evoke the names and works of numerous great men of many nations, ending with a quotation from Milton. He viewed the exposition buildings as "worthy shrines to record the achievements of the two Americas, and to place them side by side with the arts and industries of the older world, to the end that we may be stimulated and encouraged to new endeavors."[92] This great exposition, then, was considerably more than hail, Columbia!

It was, in addition, a measure of the spirit of internationalism.

When Morton had finished dedicating the buildings the orchestra and chorus performed the "Hallelujah Chorus" from Handel's *Messiah*. Henry Watterson, renowned editor of the *Courier-Journal* of Louisville, was introduced to deliver the Dedicatory Oration. Watterson quickly scanned history, referred to the discovery of America as the most significant event since the birth of Christ, and advised his listeners that he would confine his attention to the character of the Americans as a people. "We are a plain, practical people," he said. "We are a race of inventors and workers, not of poets and artists. We have led the world's movement, not its thought. . . . Let us consider ourselves and our conditions . . . with a candor untinged by cynicism and a confidence having no air of assurance." With this admonition Watterson began to discuss the right of suffrage, the 1892 presidential election campaign, the Civil War, the end of slavery, the illusion of the Confederacy—he fought for it in the Civil War—and the attainment of union. America was moving toward true fraternity. All over the Union people were commemorating Columbus's discovery. And from there, in a confessedly overwrought moment, Watterson proceeded to extoll American children and womanhood, and finally God.[93] It was a stellar performance. The listeners might justifiably have felt that by now they had heard ample fine rhetoric. But no. When Watterson finished, the chorus and orchestra performed the "Star Spangled Banner" and Chauncey DePew, the famed lawyer, orator, and president of the New York Central and Hudson River Railroad, was introduced to deliver the "Columbian Oration."

Depew wasted no time in citing the prime meaning of the exposition. "This day belongs not to America, but to the world," he began. "The results of the event it commemorates are the heritage of the peoples of every race and clime. We celebrate the emancipation of man. The preparation was the work of almost countless centuries; the realization was the revelation of one. The Cross on Calvary was hope; the cross raised on San Salvador was opportunity." He proceeded to yoke Jesus Christ and Columbus, to outline a popular history of monarchy and the birth of printing, to paint a portrait of Columbus as hero nonpareil. Having finally got Columbus to the New World, he then recounted the high points of American history and invoked the memory of the founding fathers. He extended good wishes to all the nations of the world. Finally he reverted once again to the heroic figure of Columbus and concluded, "All hail, Columbus, discoverer, dreamer, hero, and apostle! . . . Neither marble nor brass can fitly form his statue. Continents are his monument, and unnumbered millions, present and to come, who enjoy in their liberties and their happiness the fruits of his faith, will reverently guard and preserve, from century to century, his name and fame."[94]

Harriet Monroe would recall Watterson delivering his speech "in the old-school orotund gesticulatory style" and Depew offering his with "conventional eloquence," " both orators waving their windy words toward a vast, whispering, rustling audience which could not hear."[95] Perhaps that was just as well. For, as the poet observed, there was nothing said that day which could compare in eloquence or lastingness to the Gettysburg Address. But in scope, length, and grandiloquence the speeches were appropriate to the giant scale of the World's Columbian Exposition. With the oratory at last ended, "The ceremonies were concluded with prayer by his eminence, Cardinal Gibbons, Archbishop of Baltimore; the chorus, 'In Praise of God,' by Beethoven; and the benediction, by the Rev. Henry C. McCook of Philadelphia."[96] And the vast assemblage dispersed from the Manufactures Building. Or, as one account nicely phrased it, "While the great audience was passing out, a national salute was fired by the artillery."[97] And so the site and the structures of the World's Columbian Exposition were officially dedicated.

The show had awed or pleased most everyone, though it left at least one member of the audience, however deeply moved as he confessed, a little skeptical. The prominent American black leader, Frederick Douglass, commissioner from Haiti to the exposition, wrote, "In contemplating the inauguration ceremonies, glorious as they were, there was one thing that dimmed their glory. The occasion itself was world embracing in its idea. It spoke of human brotherhood, human welfare and human progress. It naturally implied a welcome to every possible variety of mankind. Yet, I saw, or thought I saw, an intentional slight to that part of the American population with which I am identified."[98] Douglass was right. Although there were 8 million blacks in the United States, not one was invited to join the dignitaries on the main platform for the ceremonies. And after all, as Douglass intoned, it was labor that had made possible the march of civilization in America—labor by Africans perhaps more so than by anyone. The blacks had witnessed, enhanced, and endured the entire history of America. They deserved to be included in the celebration. Though he was indisputably right and though his demurrer was recorded, what Douglass said could hardly have been expected to make a ripple within the tidal wave of self-congratulatory and hyperbolic rhetoric that characterized the ceremonies. The dedication was a star-spangled success.

With six months more of construction intervening, the next great moment in the life of the fair was its official opening. The interim months had witnessed a presidential election which returned Grover Cleveland to the White House and a mayoralty election which returned Carter Harrison to the City Hall of Chicago. And so the cast of characters in that next great drama was different. The opening ceremonies were set for May 1, 1893. The king and the queen regent of Spain were invited to attend, but had to refuse because the Spanish Constitution prevented such a sojourn. Hence the chief dignitary at the opening was the duke of Veragua, lineal descendant of Columbus. In addition, Eulalia, the infanta of Spain, would attend the exposition. The opening day was marred by a severe rainstorm; but it diminished to the merely threatening circumstance of dark clouds, which allowed for a dry assemblage of nearly 200,000 people in Jackson Park. A procession of carriages was led by the Committee on Ceremonies; then

Colonel Davis and Daniel H. Burnham; President Cleveland, General Palmer, and H. N. Higinbotham; the duke of Veragua, and Ferdinand Peck and Thomas Waller, vice presidents of the corporation; the duchess of Veragua and Mrs. Potter Palmer. These were followed in turn by cabinet officers, senators, ambassadors, foreign commissioners, officers of the armed forces, Governor John Peter Altgeld of Illinois, Mayor Carter H. Harrison—all accompanied by military escorts. They made their way to the fairgrounds, where the ceremonies were held in the open before the Administration Building in the Court of Honor. Here was a platform to seat 3,000, where the dignitaries gathered, among them Vice President Adlai Stevenson, justices of the Supreme Court, governors of the states, and congressmen.[99]

"The ceremonies, which were simple, earnest, and impressive, were opened with the Columbian March, rendered by the orchestra." The chaplain of the House of Representatives, William H. Milburn, gave a prayer, which was followed by a poem—even less memorable than Harriet Monroe's *Ode*—on the subject of Columbus's discovery written by William A. Croffut. The orchestra played Wagner's overture to *Rienzi*. Director General Davis had another chance to experience once-in-a-lifetime emotions as he delivered another lengthy speech. In it he praised everybody— builders of the fair, foreign nations, Chicago, exhibitors. He voiced again the lofty sentiment: "It is our hope that this great Exposition may inaugurate a new era of moral and material progress, and our fervent aspiration that the association of the nations here may secure not only warmer and stronger friendships, but lasting peace throughout the world." Then it was President Grover Cleveland's turn. The president was politic: he was brief. He waved the flag of the democracy as he expressed the belief that the American faith promised a "proud national destiny" and that Americans exhibit "the unparalleled advancement and wonderful accomplishments of a young nation, and present triumphs of a vigorous, self-reliant, and independent people. We have built these splendid edifices; but we have also built the magnificent fabric of a popular government, whose grand proportions are seen throughout the world." The exposition, then, was presumably symbolic of the attainments of a free people. Grasping the electric key that would set in motion the machinery of the exposition, the president intoned, "As by a touch the machinery that gives life to this vast Exposition is now set in motion, so in the same instant let our hopes and aspirations awaken forces which in all time to come shall influence the welfare, the dignity, and the freedom of mankind."[100] And with that the World's Columbian Exposition came alive. Amid the "Hallelujah Chorus," the president pressed the key, a great 2,000 horsepower engine sprung to life, the Worthington pumps pulsed water into every fountain at the fair, and all flags burst unfurled. "Amid the enthusiastic cheers of the vast multitude, the shrill whistling of the lake craft, and the deep diapason of booming guns, the formalities were complete."[101]

What this affair certainly had in surpassing measure over the dedicatory ceremonies was the virtue of brevity. It was soon over. It was not, however, all happiness. The surging crowd that had come to witness the proceedings experienced some troubles. The *Tribune*'s reporter wrote that at least twenty women fainted in the crush of bodies, and the ambulances could not reach them till the cavalry cleared a pathway. Higinbotham and Davis urged the teeming thousands to keep calm—easy enough for them to advise, since they were safe on the platform, as the reporter commented. Others had a problem. "One elderly lady who was caught in the crowd held on to the barricade as long as she could, but finally fainted. She was dragged over the rail and laid out on one of the reporters' tables." Apparently the jostling and pressing angered some of the spectators. "A few fights occurred to relieve the monotony and Col. Rice's Columbian Guards, who stood hard by, drew their swords and began flourishing them about wildly."[102] Mostly, however, order was maintained until the ceremonies had concluded. Thereafter the great crowd dispersed throughout the grounds, while President Cleveland, his entourage, and other dignitaries were given a conducted tour of the exposition.

And so began what was probably the greatest world's fair in history. The opening ceremonies were simple, brief, a trifle disorderly, but nonetheless imposing. "It was impossible to behold the scene unmoved," wrote H. N. Higinbotham; "the occasion was the climax of a grand drama."[103] No comment could have been more apt. For the dedication, the opening, the construction, the exposition itself, constituted a dramatic triumph. The exposition was a stage spectacle worthy of David Belasco and Augustin Daly and embellished by the machines and marvels of Steele MacKaye. It was produced on the largest stage ever constructed, with monumental use of electric lighting, a host of huge buildings for its sets, and a cast of nations. On some days nearly three-quarters of a million people were in the audience, and by the time it ended its run over 27.5 million theatre-goers would have passed the box office. The World's Columbian Exposition was the greatest theatrical production of the century.

It was, by one account, "the grandest Exposition this planet has ever witnessed."[104] With respect to size alone the statement was assuredly true. Not only were the fairgrounds nearly three times greater in area than those of any previous fair, but also "the number of square feet under roof—over 5,000,000—is nearly twice as much as the greatest exposition of the past."[105] The hugeness of the exposition overwhelmed visitors. Some were even awestruck by their anticipation of the fair. One observer wrote, "Everywhere talk of the fair is big. . . . In fact, the unit of measure in this enterprise has been set so large that one is in danger of forgetting that the Yankee nation was established for any other purpose."[106] Such a thought was exaggerative of course; but then just as exaggeration was the nature of Chicago, so it characterized the exposition. Visitors of all temperaments were struck by that fact. For the bigness of the fair imposed itself upon the imaginations of most visitors as their first and enduring impression. The English novelist Walter Besant cited the exposition's great size as mind-boggling. "The Bigness of the World's Fair first strikes and bewilders,—one tries in vain to understand it—and then it saddens," he wrote. "I observe that most people . . . set down their tears to the evanescent nature of the show. 'Three months more,' they say, 'and it will be gone like a dream. The pity of it!' Nay, dear friends, but the Vastness of it!"[107]

Former President Benjamin Harrison, who finally made it to the fairgrounds, spoke of the exposition as having "surpassed all its predecessors in size, in splendor, and in greatness both of conception and of execution." He avowed that the impression he most liked to keep in mind was "the indefinite sense of vastness which one gets as he ascends towards the high roof of the building dedicated to manufactures and liberal arts."[108] The fair was an American triumph, Harrison opined. It was also a world triumph. But only Chicago, among all the cities of the world, could have created such a vast and glorious exposition as this. The *Chicago Tribune* proudly drew that conclusion: "It is a World's Fair so far as its commemorative purpose and its exhibits are concerned. It is a Chicago Fair so far as energy, public spirit, enterprise, courage, and determination are concerned. . . . Chicago deserves the credit."[109] The World's Columbian Exposition was a consummation of Chicago's spirit and energy. In it Chicago created a small world that radiated beauty and pleasure. Even the stolid Andrew Carnegie concluded, "First, then, the grandest thing about the exhibition was the scene from without. The frame was finer than the picture, and more valuable. . . . This is high praise."[110] It was impossible to speak of the exposition without using superlatives. No doubt the ultimate superlative was the assertion that those who had transformed Jackson Park into a world peopled with great buildings "must have been very near to God."[111] The artist W. Hamilton Gibson even went so far as to say that the exposition was a realization of what the sons of Adam had fancied as the "Heavenly City," or the "New Jerusalem."[112] Its designers must indeed have been very near to God.

4

A WORLD'S FAIR
OF THE ARTS

Greatest of all the exhibits at the Fair are the
palaces which contain them, forming of
themselves a display more superb and imposing
than any of their contents.

Hubert Howe Bancroft

THE WORLD'S COLUMBIAN EXPOSITION was many things to many people. Some were intrigued by exhibits of machinery, others by the pleasures of the Midway Plaisance. Some were attracted chiefly by the transportation exhibit, others by the art exhibit. But in one response nearly everybody agreed—they felt that the most beautiful, most imposing exhibit at the exposition was its architecture. Commentators on the fair concentrated upon the buildings. Journals of every sort contained lengthy articles upon the architecture written by people from all walks of life— from the experts to the amateurs—in an avalanche of comment. Had nothing existed at Jackson Park but the buildings, most visitors would still have considered the fair a great success. Many felt, in fact, that the architecture was the exposition. As Chicago architect Peter B. Wight expressed it, the architecture "alone will take this down to history as *the* Great Exposition."[1] To those students of architecture who were interested in new departures or in the development of a native style, the fair buildings were disappointing; but to those desiring only the pleasure of beauty, they seemed Olympian. The former were disappointed for the same reason that the latter were pleased: the buildings were mostly in classical or Renaissance styles. They were retrospective, but they were also elegant.

Anyone wishing to see the expression of current design and achievement in American architecture was well advised to tour Chicago, not the fair, as Henry Van Brunt and others pointed out. A tour of the exposition, however, said Van Brunt, had the value of awakening a visitor to a consciousness of architecture's role as a fine art, a diversity of quality in design, and, as a consequence, an obvious cooperation among the architects.[2] Any architect, whether preferring classical design, as Van Brunt did, or modern design, would have to appreciate these general qualities, which resulted from agreement among the fair's architects to work essentially within classical guidelines and to maintain a uniform height (sixty feet) for all building cornices. Thus any conspicuous caprice on the part of an architect was precluded. Then too, nearly every building was complemented by statuary designed and made by sculptors working closely with the architects. It was the resulting harmony that people would find most striking, once they had absorbed their first impression of the great size of the buildings, the perceptive critic Mrs. Schuyler Van Rensselaer said. "And because of the harmony thus revealed on so grand a scale and with such richness of decoration, because the items of beauty and impressiveness are so many and varied yet so concordant . . . you will behold a sight which . . . has not been paralleled since the Rome of the emperors stood intact."[3]

Rome was the analogy that so easily came to mind for many people. Others likened the appearance of the exposition buildings and grounds to Venice. For some visitors even the splendors of ancient Rome or Venice were insufficient metaphors. As one commented, on the erstwhile swamp of Jackson Park had risen "the Venice of the Western World" which, when lighted at night by its myriad electric lights, presented "a fairy scene of inexpressible splendor reminding one of the gorgeous descriptions in the Arabian Nights when Haraun [sic] Al Raschid was Caliph."[4]

Great Basin, looking east

Courtesy of the Chicago Historical Society

Others saw the exposition as a fairy kingdom created by the touch of Aladdin's lamp, as President Cleveland had suggested. Thus on the shores of Lake Michigan one could experience a world of Venice, Rome, Aladdin, and the Arabian Nights in magic combination. As Van Rensselaer coyly observed, the fair was not really as imposing as imperial Rome; it merely seemed so. For probably nowhere before in history had such a magnificent panorama of buildings presented itself with such unity of purpose, such unalloyed splendor and beauty. The buildings were in truth ephemeral structures, but as a whole their splendor was undiminished. They were magnificent. They were huge. Bigness may not be the most noble of effects; but it is among the most telling, and even the critical observer cannot escape its influence. For, as Montgomery Schuyler wrote, in this country "mere bigness counts for more than anywhere else, and in Chicago, the citadel of the superlative degree, it counts for more, perhaps, than it counts for elsewhere in this country." In Chicago, after all, the very highest form of praise was to say that something was the "greatest" of its kind in the world and the underlying critical assumption was "that the biggest is the best."[5] In such terms Chicagoans would readily have judged the World's Columbian Exposition architecture as the greatest in the history of expositions. For once most Americans would have agreed with the Chicagoans.

But the impressiveness of the exposition's architecture was not merely a matter of bigness. Nor was it dependent upon romantic critical visions. It was gigantic, yes, and it was of classical style; but certainly just as important—indeed more important—was its group harmony, as Van Rensselaer suggested. It was that harmony which elicited unparalleled public approval. Talbot Hamlin has concluded that "it was the compelling effect of its formal plan, rather than the accident of its superficial style, which was largely responsible for this popularity. For the first time, hundreds of thousands of Americans saw a large group of buildings harmoniously and powerfully arranged in a plan of great variety, perfect balance, and strong climax effect. This vision of harmonious

Great Basin, looking west

Courtesy of the Chicago Historical Society

power was such a contrast to the typical confusion of the average American town that the visitors were almost stunned, and the enthusiasm of their admiration bore witness to the success of the plan."[6] First of all, there was the appealing layout of the building site, essentially the fulfillment of John Wellborn Root's vision, but finally the achievement of Frederick Law Olmsted. As Charles Eliot Norton observed, "the arrangement of the buildings according to the general plan produces a superb effect in the successful grouping in harmonious relations of vast and magnificent structures."[7] Here was a singular achievement in landscape architecture. Norton was referring specifically to the arrangement of the Court of Honor, but the comment might have applied overall. Halsey Ives wrote, "The great exhibit buildings of the Fair will stand unrivalled in the history of the century as the most complete architectural work produced. So much has been written and said of the beauty of the individual buildings that many have lost sight of the work as a whole. The real art work—the design—was the ensemble."[8] It is emphatically true, nonetheless, that the main focal point of the fair was its very heart, the Court of Honor.

It would have been impossible, or at least cynical, to deny the marvelousness of the court. At its center was the Great Basin which could be approached from Lake Michigan via the Park Haven or Casino Pier, which measured 250 by 2,500 feet and whose length was traversed by a movable sidewalk. The lake end of the pier was planned to have a restaurant where over 5,000 persons could be served—a plan never completed. At the pier's inland extremity stood the Casino. The Casino was connected to the Music Hall by Charles B. Atwood's Peristyle. The Peristyle was a series of forty-eight Corinthian columns, one for each of the American states and territories, with an immense triumphal arch at the center. The Peristyle itself was 500 feet long and 150 feet high, its top being a broad promenade populated by eighty-five allegorical figures in heroic scale. Upon the great arch, which stood twenty feet higher still than the Peristyle, was the *Columbus Quadriga*—the work of sculptors Daniel C. French and E. C.

Potter—depicting the discoverer standing fourteen feet high in a chariot drawn by four huge horses led by women.[9] Such was the lakeside portal to the World's Columbian Exposition—the initial view for visitors who arrived by boat. Beyond this imposing portal rested the Great Basin, wherein rose the statue of the *Republic*, also the work of the eminent sculptor D. C. French. The *Republic* was a colossal work, reminiscent, as one comment observed, of the ancient heroic statues of Phideas or the more modern work of Bartholdi. "This statue is sixty-five feet high. . . . The face is fifteen feet long, the little fingers a yard. The total height from the water is one hundred feet."[10] (As a means of comparison, Bartholdi's *Statue of Liberty* is a little more than 151 feet high and stands upon a base that is 100 feet high.) The great size of the *Republic* was not its only accomplishment. Years later, Lorado Taft said of the *Republic*, "That crowning feature of the Fair was more than a big feature; it was a great one. Some did not like it, but that was their misfortune. . . . Such a union of personality with sculptural generalization is rare. To convey the impression of a soul so great yet so far removed is a remarkable achievement."[11] That being its achievement, it was perhaps unsuitable or pretentious that the *Republic* was completely gilded. Van Rensselaer, however, found the statue beautiful, dignified, reposeful, and perfectly suited to its setting.[12]

At the opposite end of the Basin from the *Republic* was the elaborate *Columbia Fountain*, designed by Frederick MacMonnies. The concept represented in the *Fountain* was the apotheosis of modern liberty. Here was Columbia enthroned upon a triumphal barge rowed by eight standing figures which represented the Arts, Science, Industry, Agriculture, and Commerce. The barge was guided by Time and heralded by Fame. It was preceded by eight sea horses all mounted by young men representing modern commerce. The base of the fountain was circular and measured 150 feet in diameter. Water for the fountain flowed by way of a great half circle of dolphins at the rear of the barge and by a system of jets surrounding the barge and its various allegorical figures. The

The Peristyle

Courtesy of the Chicago Historical Society

entire fountain was flanked by two fifty-foot columns surmounted by eagles. At night the fountain became breathtakingly illuminated. MacMonnies, a student of Saint-Gaudens and only thirty years old, had created in this spellbinding work one of the greatest crowd-pleasers of the fair. One guide book acclaimed the fountain's beauty in stating that, "Certainly no more striking, and perhaps no more perfect a work of art can be found among the groups and figures of sculpture which adorn the grounds. . . . It arrests attention even among the wealth of attractive objects which are visible in that portion of the park, and grows upon the admiration as one observes and comprehends the exquisite detail in which the artist has executed a design of bold and large conception."[13] Lorado Taft's judgment was straightforward. "The fountain was intended to be, and was," he wrote, "the finest sculpture on the grounds. The artist saw at once that it would be useless to attempt to compete with the enormous buildings which were to surround it; he could not make it look big. So he wisely chose the better part, elaborating a wonderfully chiseled jewel instead."[14] Nevertheless, in retrospect the *Columbia Fountain* appears to have been overblown. For here too the proportions were of grand scale; the smallest figure in the fountain was twelve feet high. The *Republic* and the *Columbia Fountain* were the most conspicuous works of sculpture at the exposition and certainly the dominant attractions within the Great Basin itself. But this area, as the guidebook mentioned, contained "a wealth of attractive objects." For circling the Great Basin like the glittering diamonds of a huge necklace were the giant structures of the Court of Honor, the most monumental architectural features of the White City, their freshly painted exteriors gleaming with monochrome whiteness in the summer sun.

Directly behind the MacMonnies fountain towered the Administration Building, the western gateway to the exposition. It was the main entrance to the fair and perhaps the dominant building there—quite appropriately the work of the dean of American architecture, Richard Morris Hunt. The Administration Building

Columbia Fountain

Courtesy of the Chicago Historical Society

was 262 feet square. The dome surmounting it rose to a height of 277.5 feet (57 feet higher than the dome of the Capitol at Washington) and was thus the highest feature of any of the exposition buildings. The portal of the Administration Building measured 50 feet in height by 37 feet in width. The Administration Building, Van Rensselaer observed, "serves many practical purposes, but its chief purpose is symbolical—is to proclaim the Fair's immensity and dignity, and its builders' regard for beauty; to proclaim that our Fair has been organized for the glorification of art even more than for that of science and industry."[15] Van Brunt wrote that in its dimensions the Administration Building was inferior only to the work of Michelangelo—Saint Peter's itself.[16] Like Saint Peter's, the dome was its primary component. Van Rensselaer thought it one of the most beautiful domes ever designed and she judged it the chief feature of the fair. Van Brunt felt the building was rather reservedly decorated, as it relied for richness of effect upon three colossal groups of statuary on each of the administrative pavilions, two groups flanking the main entrances, and eight others crowning the gallery around the dome. Each of these groups measured from twenty to thirty feet in height. All were produced by New York sculptor Karl Bitter. Van Brunt paid them high tribute, describing them as "characterized by great breadth and dignity of treatment, and by that expression of heroic power and fitness which is derived from knowing how to treat colossal subjects in a colossal way," and as a fine complement to the architecture of the building.[17] Internally the Administration Building was divided into four grand pavillions. It housed all the exposition administrative offices. The Administration Building was, by all accounts, an appropriate, imposing, and magnificent entranceway to the White City.

Through this entranceway passed visitors who came to the fair by train, for directly behind the Administration Building was the Terminal Railway Station, said to be the largest depot in the world with its thirty-five tracks—the largest but perhaps the least used, as H. N. Higinbotham lamented in his report. The station's lack of

Administration Building on Chicago Day

Courtesy of the Chicago Historical Society

use was not a comment upon its design which, rendered by Charles B. Atwood in Corinthian style, was pleasing. To the south of the station and the Administration Building sprawled another chief structure, the enormous Machinery Building officially called the Palace of Mechanic Arts. This palace measured about 492 feet in width by 846 feet in length, and its immediately adjacent annex extended this length by another 551 feet. Peabody and Stearns of Boston were the architects. They had designed the building in an essentially classical style and modeled its details upon designs of the Renaissance period in Spain. Barr Ferree considered it the best of the buildings in the Court of Honor. Van Brunt noted that Machinery Hall was larger than the Houses of Parliament by a ratio of five to two, about the same size as the palace of Diocletian at Spalatro, and substantially larger than the Capitol at Washington (a mere 680 by 280 feet by his figures).[18] Evidently once such comparisons were drawn, however, there was little more to be said in praise. Van Brunt disliked the building because it was too literally imitative in design. Van Rensselaer, on the other hand, found Machinery Hall imposing, magnificent, "festal looking, while the Spanish-American character of its tall pavilions gives it a peculiar appropriateness."[19] These tall pavilions, actually towers, were certainly the unique feature of Machinery Hall. They resulted from the desire to make the building prominent without competing for attention with the dome of the Administration Building. The most famous of the towered entrances to the hall was its eastern facade, which emphasized the building's iron arches and which, like those of the Manufactures Building, represented a singular engineering achievement. "On the pediment above the fine Corinthian porch . . . was a bas-relief personating Columbia enthroned, with a sword in her right hand and a palm in her left, and surrounded by Honor, Genius, and Wealth." Above this pediment appeared "five heroic female figures, the central one representing Science, and the others Air, Earth, Fire, and Water. These figures, which were modeled by M. A. Waagen, of Chicago, were notable for their grace and beauty."[20]

Machinery Building

Courtesy of the Chicago Historical Society

To the east of Machinery Hall across the South Canal lay the somewhat smaller Agricultural Building, whose main northern facade extended nearly the length of the Great Basin. The work of McKim, Mead & White, the Agricultural Building measured 500 by 800 feet, and it had an annex at its south facade which was 30 by 500 feet. In keeping with the custom of its famous designers, the building was in classical style, with the noteworthy feature of a sixty-four-foot wide entranceway flanked by mammoth Corinthian columns fifty feet high and five feet in diameter. Most observers were favorably impressed by the Agricultural Building. Van Rensselaer judged it the most beautiful building on the fairgrounds, except for the Fine Arts Building, and in addition "the most interesting and satisfying when one studies its features and the manner in which they are combined, and much the most successful as regards its sculptural adornment."[21] Van Brunt was of like mind. He especially admired the decorative sculptures; of the building itself he said that "it presents not only in scale and extent, but in its serious beauty, in its splendor of enrichment and refinement of detail, a model of imperial luxury and pomp."[22] Of its kind the building clearly was a sumptuous and splendid example. The popular historian Hubert Howe Bancroft deemed it a "well-nigh perfect work of art," and he concluded, "In none of the homes of the Fair has sculptural . . . embellishment been more happily blended with architectural design."[23] No doubt he was right. Crowning the gilded dome of the building was Saint-Gaudens's "brazen Diana."[24] First created for Stanford White's exquisite Madison Square Garden, the *Diana* proved out of scale when placed there, but here it appeared in good harmony atop such a gigantic structure. Furthermore, it was Saint-Gaudens's pupil Philip Martiny, certainly one of the better sculptors at the fair, who was responsible for the decorative figures. These included representations of the various ethnic types, rendered in four groups of giant female forms at the four pavilions; representations of a shepherd and shepherdess atop the pediments of these pavilions; the signs of the zodiac and emblems of abundance; an

Agricultural Building, north facade

Courtesy of the Chicago Historical Society

Making sculpture for Agricultural Building

Courtesy of the Chicago Historical Society

allegorical personification of agriculture. Over the main entrance of the Agricultural Building was a statue of Ceres designed by the Florentine-based artist Larkin J. Mead, who wished through this work to "reveal to our American artists what sculpture really is."[25] How well he succeeded is difficult to say. But it is notable that he was an expatriate from New Hampshire, brother-in-law of William Dean Howells, and brother of William Rutherford Mead of the architectural firm, so that his connections were good. In any event, though woman might not yet have come into her own, it was clear through all these figures and others at the fair that she was the model and motif par excellence of the art of American sculpture.

To the northwest across the Great Basin and directly opposite the Machinery Hall and Administration Building were the two Lilliputians of the Court of Honor, the exhibition halls for mining and electricity. The Mines and Mining Building, as the sixth building in the Court, had been awarded to Chicago architect S. S. Beman. The structure he designed was a mere 350 by 700 feet. But it was distinguished by being the first building at an international exposition to be devoted entirely to mining products. Beman modeled it after early Italian Renaissance designs. Though this and the Electricity Building were overshadowed in size, one observer at least felt of the Mines and Mining Building that it "seems particularly to impress its size on the beholder, because of the heaviness of its details and lesser architectural features."[26] The effect created by these details was not particularly attractive at close range, but from a distance it at least helped prevent the building from being dwarfed. The building was not a success. Van Rensselaer did not even comment. One generally enthusiastic commentary damned the work with faint praise: "The architect ... very properly sacrificed imposing style to strength and adaptability, and the result was gratifying to a degree."[27] Perhaps the building failed partly because of its dearth of sculpture. It bore only one work, a large half-reclining allegorical figure representing mining—again a female—with a lamp in one hand and a pick in the other. It was designed by Richard W. Bock. Somewhat more successful was this hall's mate, the Electricity Building, which was nearly identical in size, its dimensions being 690 by 345 feet. It shared a distinction with Beman's building, since it was the first building in the history of expositions to be devoted completely to displays of electricity and electrical contrivances. The Electrical Building had the further distinction of containing more window panes—40,000 in all—than any other structure at the fair. It sported both Corinthian and Ionic columns and otherwise adhered to the prevailing classical style of the exposition, but it bore no decorative sculptures. Henry Van Brunt, who had designed it, described the building's style as conventional Italian Renaissance. Van Rensselaer commented, "Greater variety, greater picturesqueness have been sought in the Electricity Building than in any of its neighbors, not everywhere with entire success, yet still in a way which does not seriously mar the harmonious effect of the great Plaza and Basin."[28] Ferree demurred. He had nothing good to say about either of these adjacent structures. He felt that neither did justice to its architect's true talents, and he dismissed both with the comment that they "are comparatively small buildings, and hence are necessarily without the interest attaching to the larger ones."[29] In other circumstances that might have seemed a curious comment; but given the exposition's stupefying size, it probably made perfect sense.

Next to these relatively small structures on the Great Basin extended one that suffered not at all from lack of size. This was the giant of the giants, the Manufactures and Liberal Arts Building. Designed by New York architect George B. Post in the Corinthian style, the Manufactures Building measured 787 feet in width and stretched to a length of 1,687 feet. Not only the largest building at the fair but also the largest roofed building ever constructed, it inspired far more comment than any other fair building. The Manufactures Building was the unrivaled star of the show. It was the exposition's challenge to the Eiffel Tower. The south facade of the building fronted upon the Great Basin and was

Mines and Mining Building

Courtesy of the Chicago Historical Society

only slightly shorter than the length of the Agricultural Building which faced it directly across the water. Its longest facade looked eastward over Lake Michigan. The mere bulk of this structure was inevitably impressive. The appropriate question was whether the Manufactures Building was aesthetically pleasing. At least that would have been the appropriate question if critics could have overlooked the building's mammoth size. But few could see beyond that attribute.

Those who did try to judge the Manufactures Building as a work of architecture invariably allowed its bigness to obtrude upon their critical assessments. One writer admired the simplicity of the building's exterior because he felt that profuse ornamentation would have detracted from its great size. "The motive in its architectural inspiration," he wrote, "was undoubtedly to impress the beholder with its solidity and grandeur, and not to subordinate these to considerations of mere beauty." Had the sight been broken by carved balconies, arabesques, or other details, he added, then the immensity of the building would have become indiscernible to the spectator. "As it is, the eye takes in at a glance its chaste, plain exterior, and the mind is thrilled by the idea of its stupendous size, solidity, and strength."[30] That thrill was clearly preferable to the admiration of mere beauty. Indeed, it might be pointless to attempt the aesthetic when one can have the gigantic. Ferree had to agree in large part, though not in principle. He felt that the Manufactures Building's exterior was rightly kept simple. But he added that, though the building's great size meant it "must be, by the usual American standard, the best building on the grounds, if not the best in the world—[it] is one of the least successful."[31] It was unsuccessful, however, partly because its tremendous size was obscured. The roof was too high, as Ferree saw it, and so were its arches, fine though they were; and these faults served to hide the building's true proportions. Furthermore, by including in the design a series of segmental arches carrying an arcade of round arches—two series of two different arches in juxtaposition—Post had ruined the facades. The truly remarkable

Electricity Building

Courtesy of the Chicago Historical Society

thing about the Manufactures Building, Ferree said, was not its design but its construction. But he concluded rather dispiritedly that few people would note this engineering aspect. They would instead be content to leave the fair feeling that the Manufactures Building was the best because it was the biggest.

Henry Van Brunt chose to admire those very features of the building which Barr Ferree depreciated. He admired the curved roof which "arose like a mountain" high above the structure's base; the arcade of windows which vanished into the distance "in endless perspective"; the "infinite monotony" of the long facade that was broken only by the entranceways; the elegant Renaissance style of the round arches as well as the grandeur of the Roman-style segmental arches.[32] Van Rensselaer was inclined to agree. "The simplicity of its exterior," she wrote of the Manufactures Building, "is in true artistic accord with its vast size, for when a building is very large indeed no architectural device is effective as the extended repetition of similar features." In addition, she regarded the huge interior trusses as equally worthy aesthetically as they were structurally.[33] It was left to Montgomery Schuyler to have the last words, and they were plentiful as they were final. He said it would be impossible for anyone to be apathetic in the presence of a structure of such great size, that even a pile of barrels as big as the Manufactures Building would be striking. Thus the art of such a building, he argued, consists in the development of its magnitude, in the carrying out of effects that will inspire the spectator to appreciate this magnitude. "That is to say, the art consists in giving it scale. It is a final censure upon the treatment of a piece of architecture which aims at overpowering the spectator by its size that it does not look its size, as is the current and accepted criticism upon St. Peter's."[34] Scale in the Manufactures Building, as in all the buildings at the fair, was readily discernible from the details—pillars, arches, windows—and by the nearby bridges and wharves with their parapets and railings, which forced upon the spectator's senses an awareness of the giant size of the buildings. Sculpture might also provide scale, as it did admirably on the Administration and Agricultural buildings. And the Manufactures Building did contain sculptures—eighteen-foot high eagles atop each of the four main portals and figures in bas-relief at the entranceways, all the work of Austrian-born Karl Bitter. But the impression of magnitude in this structure depended less upon its scale than upon succession and uniformity—"an interminable repetition of the unit."[35] In other words, as Van Brunt had observed, the impression depended upon endless perspective and infinite monotony. If the major purpose of the Manufactures Building was to overwhelm the spectator by its transcendent immensity, then it was a singular success. As a memorable account had it, "For vast extent, boldness of conception, wonderful engineering, faultless proportions, and impressive grandeur the Manufactures building is easily the greatest of them all, and the greatest building on earth."[36] George P. Post had done his job well.

Such were the jewels that composed the necklace about the Great Basin. And such was the Court of Honor. "Whether we look upon this spectacle by day, under a blue sky that is clarified by the reflection of the limpid waters of Lake Michigan; or by night, when fretted with fires that out-spangle the vault of heaven, with flying fountains bathed in floods of rainbow lights, and overlooking domes bejeweled with glittering crowns . . . we feel that the dream of hope has come true. . . . Nowhere else in the modern world have the skill and genius of sculptor and architect been so prodigally bestowed."[37] The Court of Honor was clearly an amazing spectacle, a wondrous composition of water, esplanades, sculpture, and architecture. Even that most level-headed of critics, Barr Ferree, admitted in his understated fashion that "in more ways than one the visitor is dazzled by the grandeur of the scene now on view in Jackson Park."[38] Imagine, then, what a spellbinding impression the Court of Honor made upon the average fairgoer.

Anyone might have been forgiven for lingering at the Court of Honor, feasting upon its beauty, during his visit to the White City. But beyond that Court lay still other, and in some ways better,

Transportation Building

Courtesy of the Chicago Historical Society

more interesting, structures to beguile the senses. Perhaps the finest architecturally of all the buildings at the fair, the Transportation Building was situated across the lagoon from the Manufactures Building and to the northwest of the Mines and Mining Building. It was designed by Adler and Sullivan. No mean structure, it measured 256 by 960 feet. It was surmounted by a quite original cupola 165 feet high. But the features which made the Transportation Building of such great interest were its polychromatic decoration and its so-called Golden Door. The building was bright with red, orange, and yellow colors. This polychrome coloration made it distinctive among the fair's major buildings, with their white monochrome, and elicited high praise from Barr Ferree, who wrote, "It is not too much to say that, without any exception whatever, this is the most ambitious and successful example of polychromatic architecture in America. For in this building, unlike any of the others, the color decoration has been carried out on a most elaborate scale, and . . . it is the color decoration that gives it its character and its beauty, lifts it out of the rut of classicism, into which the other Fair buildings drift, and makes it the most remarkable and interesting structure upon the grounds."[39] He added that no bolder scheme had ever been undertaken in American architecture and that no more notable lesson than the one this great building afforded could be learned at the fair. The "Golden Door" alone was a masterpiece. Ironically, Sullivan had designed two small portals originally; it was Burnham who proposed the single large one. This immense portal contained a series of five receding arches, all overlaid with gold leaf— reminiscent of the proscenium in the Auditorium. It was extraordinarily rich with carvings, bas-reliefs, and entablatures, the work of Philadelphia sculptor John J. Boyle. The architect contended that the portal's effect was Wagnerian.[40] So impressive was the "Golden Door" that it earned Louis Sullivan the medal of the Société des Arts Décoratifs, the only French award given for any building or building feature at the fair; indeed, the only instance of international acclaim for any of the architecture there, except for a later award to Hunt by the Royal Institute of British Architects, made partially in recognition of the Administration Building. The Comte de Soissons wrote of the Transportation Building that, in the midst of the whiteness of the other buildings, its multicolored attractiveness was compelling. But more compelling still was its architecture. " 'It was architecture of a primary character, of studied roughness; a cyclopean and barbarous conception, but certainly not a common one,' wrote the Comte. 'One could see in it a seeking after the strange and enormous, a dream of new forms which would harmonize with the tumultuous and brutal genius of the human collectivity acting in Chicago, that monstrous city.' "[41] For the comte the source of appeal in the building's architecture—of a novel modified Romanesque style— appears to have been almost spiritual and certainly elemental. Not everyone agreed. "Close at hand the building is an entertaining salad of styles," wrote one critic. ". . . altogether, a pleasant building to pass the time with; but seen at a distance, all these details [including the 'Golden Doorway'] fail of effect, and the epithet 'shabby' applied to it by the London *Times* seems justified."[42] But such criticism reflected a minority view. The Transportation Building, and its "Golden Door" especially, won wide critical approval and public popularity. "For forty years the structure was the best known of Sullivan's designs and the one that was generally felt to be the most representative of his peculiar genius."[43]

Near to Sullivan's building and facing the Wooded Island in the lagoon rose the Horticultural Building, assumed to be the largest hothouse ever built, which had been designed by the dean of Chicago architects, William LeBaron Jenney. This was the last of the giant buildings on the fairgrounds. It measured 250 by 998 feet. In appearance it was completely different from all the other buildings, for its plan consisted of a large central pavilion connected with two end pavilions by front and rear screens. This central pavilion was roofed by a huge crystal dome, 187 feet in diameter and 113 feet high. Running between this and end pavilions (117 by 250 feet each) were the four curtains, two on each

The Golden Door

Courtesy of the Chicago Historical Society

Horticultural Building, main entrance

Courtesy of the Chicago Historical Society

side, which formed interior courts each measuring 270 feet in length and 90 feet in width. The two rear curtains were in fact huge greenhouses. The whole was designed in a Venetian Renaissance style with Ionic columns and motifs. The *American Architect* wrote of the Horticultural Building that it "declares itself as a 'fair' building and an extremely good one, too, not too light in form to be substantial, but lively in treatment and joyous in general air. The great dome is architecturally the most successful feature of its kind on the grounds."[44] The main facade of the building contained a decorative frieze with some cupids at play; a pediment on each side of the arched entrance, one bearing a farmer, the other a milkmaid; and two huge columns, one with a sculptural group symbolizing a *Battle of Flowers* and the other with a group called the *Sleep of the Flowers*—all the work of Lorado Taft of Chicago. One description considered Taft's sculptures to be like the genius of the man: "smooth rather than notable—rich, pleasing, but conventional, although on the best models."[45] The approach to the Horticultural Building was most appealing. At a landing on the lagoon visitors might arrive by gondola and ascend a broad stairway flanked on either side with low rows of vases overflowing with flowers and plants.

At the north end of the lagoon stood the Woman's Building. In size it was one of the lightweights, a mere 199 by 388 feet. Its architect, Sophia G. Hayden, had been selected by competition as a result probably of the fact that a woman was wanted and there were only three known female architects in the nation. Most people agreed that the Woman's Building was undistinguished. Nevertheless, since it had been designed by a woman and built primarily for women, it aroused much interest, especially among women. Some of the attention the building received it might have happily been spared. The *American Architect*, for example, commented ruefully and rather sarcastically, "The Woman's Building is neither worse nor better than might have been expected. It is just the sort of result that would have been achieved by either boy or girl who had had two or three years' training in an architectural school, and its thinness and poverty of constructive expression declares [sic] it to be the work of one who had never seen his or her 'picture' translated into substance."[46] Van Rensselaer, on the other hand, did not find the building all that bad; but rather "refined and pleasing."[47] And Candace Wheeler, who had been in charge of its interior decoration, spoke of it as "the most peaceably human of all the buildings. . . . It is like a man's ideal of woman—delicate, dignified, pure, and fair to look upon."[48] The Woman's Building was at least in keeping with the nature of the other main buildings, since it was modeled upon Italian Renaissance types. It was decorated with numerous sculptural groups created by Alice Rideout—all of them representative of woman's various attributes and roles. Overall, however, the Woman's Building was probably the plainest of the major buildings at the fair. Perhaps that in part explains its lack of critical acclaim. For, Van Rensselaer's brief comment notwithstanding, the Woman's Building was largely and probably rightly deemed mediocre.

Directly across the lagoon was a building that charmed and delighted: Chicago architect Henry Ives Cobb's Fisheries Building. Comparatively small though it was, it still elicited tremendous popular approval. Even the *Official Guide* referred to its accreditation as "an architectural poem" and asserted that, although the building was large, it was so designed that the general effect "is rather one of delicacy than of grandeur."[49] Actually, the building itself was not large when contrasted with the other major structures. The main building was only 365 feet long and 165 feet wide. But this length was extended by arcades at each end of the building connecting it with two polygonal structures which each measured over 133 feet in diameter. The entire distance covered was 1,100 feet in length. The Fisheries Building was described as of Spanish-Romanesque design. It lacked the imposing scale of many of the other buildings and it was quite different from all of them because its ornamentation consisted of myriad representations of marine life sculpted by many of the sculptors who took time out from their larger projects to indulge in this enjoyable

Fisheries Building

Courtesy of the Chicago Historical Society

Doorway of Fisheries Building

Courtesy of the Chicago Historical Society

task. Its ornamentation was the Fisheries Building's singular virtue.
The great double rows of columns on the facades of the building
were covered with fishes and their capitals contained thousands of
marine forms, crabs, lobsters, frogs, shells, water snakes, and algae.
Since the Romanesque of southern France and northern Spain is
"distinguished by a semi-barbaric humor expressed in grotesque
and caricature," as Henry Van Brunt had it, then there appeared in
Cobb's building "no unnecessary audacity of imagination in the
playful treatment of the details . . .; it not only brings it into
harmony with the spirit of the style, but serves to make it joyous
and festive without loss of dignity, grace, and fitness." Here was a
building well suited to the proper celebrative spirit of an exposition. As one caught sight of the Fisheries Building rising above the
shrubbery and trees of the shores, with its towers and belvederes
and its whimsical ornamentation, one thought, Van Brunt said, of
"the hidden luxuries of a 'stately pleasure house,' decreed by some
Kubla Khan of oriental romance."[50]

North of this romantic building devoted to sea creatures rested
the North Pond, overlooked by the Art Building, which was
approached from the pond by an immense flight of steps. The Art
Building was a sizable art museum or gallery. Its dimensions were
320 by 500 feet. It was topped by a dome 125 feet high, which
was originally surmounted by a heroic statue of *Victory* (later
removed) standing fourteen feet high, the work of Philip Martiny.
Behind the main building and connected to it by arcades were two
annexes, each 126 by 200 feet in dimension. Charles B. Atwood
had designed the Palace of the Arts in a Greek-Ionic style, with the
addition of the dome, that was exemplary of the most refined
neoclassical architecture. Of all the buildings at the fair this one
was alone in being universally praised as a work of art. Van Brunt
thought it an excellent structure. Van Rensselaer said, "It is the
finest thing on the Fairgrounds, and the finest building of so
classical a sort which the modern world has constructed. It is not
just like any building which classic nations themselves constructed;
it is much larger and more varied in mass, and its dome is a distinct

innovation. But we feel it just such a building as the Greeks might have built had they known about domes and had they wanted something of this size for a similar site and purpose."[51] It was perhaps such praise that moved Barr Ferree to declare that the critical acclaim had been overdone: it was a fine building, but its dome was marred by its base and the annexes detracted from the main design.[52] But in his opinion Ferree stood virtually alone. The summit of tribute came from author Julian Hawthorne, who declared the Fine Arts Building "the most beautiful piece of architecture in the world."[53] Views of the Art Palace were so laudatory that its sculptural features suffered by neglect. In addition to his *Victory*, Martiny had sculpted the frieze of the Art Palace, which contained female figures representing Architecture, Painting, Music, and Sculpture; flanked by winged female figures and caryatids at each of the two pediments of the entranceway. At the south entrance were two large lions, one on either side, modeled by Theodore Baur and A. P. Proctor; at the north entrance stood two more modeled by Edward Kemeys. On the stairway leading up to the south entrance from the lagoon was a large statue done by Olin L. Warner. All this sculpture presumably enhanced the building itself, eliciting one view that, "This entrance was very impressive, and set forth well the character of the details and of the building."[54] But the building alone was obviously imposing enough.

One other building at the fair drew nearly unanimous critical judgment: the United States Government Building, located between the Manufactures and Fisheries buildings with one facade overlooking the lagoon and the other facing Lake Michigan. Rather typical of federal government architecture at Washington and elsewhere, it was crowned by the ubiquitous dome, this one being an immense octagonal construction 120 feet in diameter and 150 feet high. The building itself covered an area of 345 by 415 feet. The entire building was pretentious. It earned the dubious honor of being the only major building at the fair which was unanimously condemned. Perhaps it failed because it was designed

Art Building

Courtesy of the Chicago Historical Society

by government architects, the pariahs of the profession. While conceding that the Government Building was "monumental in magnitude," the *Architectural Record* disdained it as a totally ineffective architectural effort, a gross aberration. In every other case the architect had chosen some dimension—the height of the dome, the expanse of a facade—for emphasis and architectural development; in the Government Building alone there was no suggestion of such a purpose. The dome was too lofty to be the crown of a sprawling building and it failed as well to command attention. The building's length, rather than being properly developed, was merely "deviled up."[55] Evidently the building's only attribute was size. As Van Rensselaer viewed it, however, the Government Building provided at least a worthy lesson. It was, she wrote, "as bad as, in these days, nothing but one of our government buildings is likely to be. It is bad in design, and bad in treatment and finish; its only virtue is as an object-lesson, pointing the fact that a general reform is needed in the matter of our official architecture."[56]

There were numerous other examples of government architecture. Thirty buildings were erected by state and territorial governments. Of these probably only two deserve mention. These were the two largest state buildings, those of Illinois and California. Both were central to the exposition, being located in the vicinity of the Art Palace, on or near the North Pond. It was apt that the Illinois building was large, since Chicago was hosting the exposition. The state legislature appropriated $800,000 for the building, exhibits, and accessories. For this generous sum they got the most pretentious of the state buildings. Chicago architect W. W. Boyington designed this neoclassical structure in the form of a Greek cross whose main axis measured 450 by 160 feet, making it larger than the main Fisheries Building. Towering above the building's center was a great dome 72 feet in diameter and 235 feet in height—the tallest dome at the fair, except for the one atop the Administration Building. The entrances to the Illinois Building were fronted by splendid terraces with balustrades, statues, fountains, and stairways. It was an imposing work, but not satisfying. Perhaps its major failing was that it occupied "a very conspicuous position in the north part of the park," as the official Illinois catalog said.[57] Van Rensselaer, for example, quite succinctly damned the Illinois Building as "too big for its place because it shuts off the view of the Art Building, . . . and also unsatisfactory in mass and crowned by a very ugly dome."[58] Had its site been less dominant, the building might have proved less objectionable.

Most successful of all the state buildings, and in fact one of the best structures at the fair, was the California Building. As with the Arts Building, everyone seemed to admire it. Its dimensions were 144 by 435 feet. The California Building, designed by A. Page Brown of San Francisco, imitated a Moorish style; it was modeled after the mission architecture of California, especially the church at Santa Barbara. Its south front and its tower replicated those of the old mission church at San Diego. Its roof was a garden well stocked with semitropical plants. The south portal of the building was classical in style—a curious anomaly—but viewed from either of its lengthy east and west sides, the California Building seemed quite unified and impressive. Montgomery Schuyler found it a thoroughly admirable structure. Its great size, he wrote, had the advantage of "giving an ampler scope than is elsewhere among the state buildings to be found for attaining picturesqueness and variety without losing mass, sobriety and repose." Furthermore, the material of which it was made was happily like adobe and allowed for an unusual depth, "giving again an effect of massiveness exhibited by strong contrasts of light and shadow."[59] The California Building, unlike some of the neoclassical structures, was an imaginative and successful adaptation of an antique style. Schuyler also admired the New York State Building, and probably rightly so. It was the work of McKim, Mead & White. Other state buildings were largely ignored in critical commentaries.

The material known as staff, to which Schuyler referred when discussing the California Building, was perhaps especially suited to stucco buildings, but it was also particularly appropriate to an exposition intended to be both grand and temporary. The staff used at the fair was a combination of powdered gypsum and fibers, with alumina, glycerine, and dextrine—a plaster of Paris with fibers mixed in. Without staff the magnificence of the exposition would have been unattainable. It allowed for the designs of the architects and sculptors to be executed with minimal expense, maximal facility, and adequate permanency. Staff freed the architects to pursue their greatest aspirations. "It permitted them, in fact," wrote Frank Millet, "to indulge in an architectural spree . . . of a magnitude never before attempted; it made it possible to make a colossal sketch of a group of buildings which no autocrat and no government could ever have carried out in permanent form; it left them free, finally, to reproduce with fidelity and accuracy the best details of ancient architecture, to erect temples, colonnades, towers, and domes of surpassing beauty and of noble proportions"; and to present to the public the huge realization of this sketch so attractively as to make it of great educational value.[60] Without staff the great buildings could never have been. With it they could not endure. They were merely models. Even before the fair had ended some of the buildings showed signs of decay. But for the summer of 1893 at least the great White City was a reality. The buildings were splendid. And their splendor was enhanced by the work of sculptors and painters.

The architecture of the World's Fair was not only ennobled externally by sculpture, but in some cases it was decorated internally by both sculpture and mural work. With the exception of a few isolated instances of cooperation between architect and sculptor—for example, Hunt and Bitter working together on the Vanderbilt house—the World's Columbian Exposition was the first occasion in America when the two arts, combined with their sister art of painting, had joined in mutual endeavor to produce works of great scale and of correspondingly great interest. The three arts had united to effect a single work of art, not simply the individual buildings, but the exposition as a whole. There has never been such a large-scale common undertaking of the arts before or since.

California Building

Courtesy of the Chicago Historical Society

The major impact of that undertaking was clear from one's first impression of the exposition. But to secure its full impact one needed to enter the buildings themselves. There one could witness the work of the painter. Though born to early extinction like the buildings they adorned, the interior mural and fresco works were important because of their scale and singularity, their generally good quality, and the eminence of the artists. The amount of decorative painting was necessarily limited by the huge number and size of the buildings. It would have been both impractical and economically impossible to have decorated some of the interiors. Furthermore, since the buildings were purely functional in nature, genuine interior finish was largely superfluous. Thus decorative painting was confined to a few domes and panels in certain pavilions, to wall spaces under colonnades and porticos, and to those few interiors which were of sufficiently high finish to allow such work.[61]

Originally William Pretyman had been in charge of mural work and sculptural decoration as director of color; but he resigned in May 1892 and was replaced by Francis D. Millet, artist, author, journalist, war correspondent, costume designer. A man of many talents, Millet worked well with both artists and architects. His task was Herculean. "He is to turn the Columbian Exposition into a brilliant picture—a vast stage effect," wrote Julian Ralph.[62] To accomplish this task he had to guide not only the sculptors already mentioned but also the most impressive array of talented painters ever brought together in this country to do mural work. They included J. Gari Melchers, Edwin H. Blashfield, Will H. Low, C. C. Coleman, Kenyon Cox, and a host of others. The question of whether any of them achieved the highest possible quality in his work was subordinate to the reality that for virtually the first time in history American painters had the chance to do original mural work of heroic scale. They were freed from the confines of the easel. Their canvases were expanded to the seemingly unlimited size of the walls, domes, and panels of the largest buildings in existence. It was cause for awe and rejoicing. As Will H. Low observed, to have been a follower of the arts, to have noted the alternate ebb and flow of the public's desire for art, and "to have seen that our artists as they grew in strength and numbers claimed the right to do something larger and finer and better than the private house, the portrait statue, or the *genre* picture; and then to come here, where for the first time they have found opportunity, and where the alliance of architecture, sculpture, and painting has produced its first work, to find that first work surprisingly good," was to feel proud of the craftsmen, of the nation at large which supported them, and especially of the men of Chicago who had planned the fair.[63] The artists approached their work with justified enthusiasm and cooperation.

Since it was generally regarded as the central structure of the exposition, the Administration Building was quite appropriately the most thoroughly finished of all. Its interior was decorated with sixteen huge bronze plates on which were inscribed in gilded letters the names of those nations represented at the fair. These plates were set in the wall about forty feet high in panels that extended between the pillars of the great arches in the central gallery. Encircling the dome at the top of these arches was a carved white molding worked in gilt. Upon this molding were eight panels each bearing a gilt slate supported by two winged female figures. These slates recorded various events in the world's history. Above these was a row of light terracotta panels with small latticed windows. Still higher was another molding bearing the names of discoverers and inventors. Thereafter was a row of plaster medallions, heads of the world's different types of women; and at the summit of the inner dome were eight more panels with groups of statuettes. At the very apex of the building's crown, the outer dome, was a skylight—"a great Cyclopean eye"—275 feet above the floor, through which the sunlight might flood the entire rotunda and the 250 foot high walls.[64]

Embellishing this kaleidoscope of ornamentation was the prodigious mural of W. L. Dodge, *The Glorification of the Arts and Sciences*, which decorated the outer dome. The mural was a representation of Apollo enthroned and bestowing honors upon victors in war and leaders in the arts and sciences. A warrior bowed before him; other men approached the throne by a broad stairway, their procession extending entirely around the dome, their ranks containing figures representing music, poetry, the arts, sciences, and industries. Four winged horses drew a model of the Parthenon behind them. Over all this horde were angels drawing back the canopy from the amphitheatre in which such an assemblage would have gathered in ancient times. The whole effect must surely have been grand enough to rival the palaces of Europe. Indeed, the well-known art critic Royal Cortissoz found Dodge's work rather awe inspiring. The painter, he wrote, had been privileged to create this great crowd of more than life-size figures, privileged because "I fancy there can be nothing pleasanter for a painter with a feeling for mural decoration, nothing more eagerly desired by him or more highly prized when secured, than an opportunity to cover a space of fairly unstinted dimensions. Then there need be no limit to his vivacity in respect to composition. He has *carte blanche* both as a matter of fact and of art."[65] Such was Dodge's opportunity and he had risen to it. His work was good in both draftsmanship and construction, and its virility was stirring, Cortissoz wrote.[66] The composition was assuredly enormous, since it covered a surface area of 35 by 300 feet; and apparently it was truly successful as a painting. For Millet also liked Dodge's mural. He termed it "bold and imposing not only in magnitude but in line."[67]

Supplementing this mural decoration were the sculptural works of Karl Bitter, who was responsible for the profusion of figures adorning the various entrances to the Administration Building. In the uppermost part of the dome Bitter had created a bas-relief representing Columbia seated on her throne. She was lavishing laurels, as symbols of recognition, upon various representative industries which appeared beneath her in allegorical bas-reliefs. Here too was a circle of winged genii holding tablets inscribed with the names of famous inventions. Upon the columns at the entrance to the dome—the gallery, that is—were placed figures symbolizing Victory. On the ground floor Bitter had added decorative sculptures in each of the four pavilions. As he described the pavilions: "They are decorated by twelve groups, each pavilion having three, allegorizing the elements, their capacities, inclinations, and dispositions which nature renders to man. Strength, patriotism, religious sentiment, diligence, charitableness, love of liberty, satisfaction by pleasure, respect for traditions, etc., are thus symbolized. Special regard is thus paid to the character and the principles of the American nation." There was still more. At the sides of the four small domes surrounding the large one Bitter had placed other groups symbolizing such things as art and science, war and peace, theology and justice.[68] Bitter's labors outside and inside the Administration Building were manifold. "Mr. Bitter was fully equal to the task and knew it; nor did he hesitate to add to this great undertaking the further responsibility of decorating the Liberal Arts building at the urgent request of its designer, Mr. George B. Post." He thus became "the most conspicuous decorator" of the exposition, in Lorado Taft's words— and probably the most tired.[69] His achievement, however, may not have been all that grand. Bancroft, who echoed Cortissoz's judgment on Dodge's mural work, remarked simply of Bitter's twenty-eight sculptured groups and numerous bas-reliefs that they "relieved the severity of the structural design."[70] Still, the Administration Building was satisfyingly replete with ornamentation.

None of the other buildings at the west end of the Court of Honor—that is, Mines and Mining, Electricity, and Machinery— contained any mural decorations. All three were finished in simple flat tones. The Agricultural Building, by contrast, was richly decorated. The murals here were the work of George W. Maynard, with the help of H. T. Schladermundt and other assistants. Maynard was one of America's foremost muralists. It is not surprising, therefore, that the murals he painted on the walls of the Agricultural Building's porch were praised by Cortissoz as "the finest decoration of all that enters into a bird's-eye view of the Court in its color significance."[71] What made Maynard's work so praise-worthy was its having been treated chiefly as part of the architectural design. Thus Maynard's mural had that quality most rare in decorative painting: a sense of relation with the structure, a balance between the needs of the subjects he was illustrating and the spaces allotted to him for decoration. The interior spaces consisted, first, of the walls of the two pavilions at either end of the building which had large entrances that broke each wall into two panels. Each panel contained an elaborately ornamented dado, a border of Indian corn down its sides, and garlands of fruit on top that framed an oblong red-colored rectangle which bore a colossal female figure representing one of the seasons. Above these panels, which were connected by a band of color, was a frieze containing rearing horses, bulls, oxen drawing an ancient cart, and other small groups of agricultural subjects. The main portal, as the entrance to the rotunda, was the focal point of the decorative painting; it was known as the Temple of Ceres. A plan similar to that used in the side pavilions was carried out here, with one significant difference. Millet wrote, "as it [the rotunda] provides a much greater area of wall surface, Mr. Maynard has been able to introduce a richer combination of colors and a greater variety of figures."[72] Here could be seen his murals of *Abundance* and *Fertility*, two huge female figures which filled great flat niches on either side of the entrance. These in turn were flanked on the side walls by the figures of King Triptolemus, mythological inventor of the plow; the goddess Cybele, symbolical of earth's fertility. The former rode in a dragon-drawn chariot; the latter was leading a pair of lions. "These figures, as well as those in the four porticos, are treated in a broad, simple manner, so that they carry perfectly to a great distance and at the same time lose nothing by close inspection," Millet concluded.[73] Will H. Low also had high praise for Maynard's work. Of all American painters Maynard was best suited by past experience to treat great wall spaces. His project in the Agricultural Building had been vast in scope. Apparently he performed according to expectation.

As the largest structure on the grounds, the Manufactures and Liberal Arts Building quite naturally engaged the labors of the largest number of painters and therefore displayed the largest number of murals. There were two tympana in each of the four corner pavilions of the Manufactures Building. Those at the Basin, or south, end of the building were assigned to J. Gari Melchers and Walter MacEwen. They were painting almost up to the day the fair opened. MacEwen painted compositions representing Music and Manufactures or Life. In the foreground of the former composition were satyrs piping tunes to a group dancing about the Muse Enterpe; the rest of the panel showed females playing instruments and a baby with a tambourine. *Manufactures*, intended to illustrate manufactures and textiles, contained two men shearing a sheep at the left, a group of females at center, and a man weaving at the right. Both compositions had in their backgrounds processions in honor of Athene, who was supposed to have invented spinning. Melchers's panels were *The Arts of Peace* and *The Chase and the Arts of War*. Each contained eleven or twelve figures. In the former there were figures of men representing Exploration, Medicine, Politics, and other societal functions. The *Arts of War* boasted a central figure on horseback followed by several warriors with spears and shields. These were preceded by men carrying a slain deer and accompanied by another man restraining two dogs—*The Chase*. Critic W. Lewis Fraser was more interested in these murals than in any others because he had observed them in progress. He wished to avoid the mention of bigness, Fraser forewarned, "but the bigness of these pictures, and the studios in which they were being painted, were not without their effect."[74] The pictures were colossal—forty feet in length. Melchers and MacEwen worked closely together in the same gallery, counseling each other frequently, and yet producing murals of distinctively different quality. "MacEwen's work has led him to the gentle, the poetic, to the more feminine of the arts," Fraser observed. His murals were filled with women and children. "Melchers, on the contrary, has been impelled toward the grand, the heroic."[75] Men dominated his compositions. Though such comments might now be regarded as sexist, at the time the murals of both artists were generally well received.

The mural works that inspired the most attention were those created in the eight domes that surmounted the side arches of the four grand central portals of the Manufactures Building. Each dome was painted by a different artist. The domes on the south front bore the work of J. Alden Weir and Robert Reid. Though their compositions were quite distinct, the two artists had tried to harmonize their designs. Weir's murals were allegorical figures of women representing Decorative Art, the Art of Painting, the Goldsmith's Art, and the Art of Pottery. Each figure was seated on a balustrade. Flowing draperies and capitals of the four orders of architecture connected the lines of the painting, which also contained a cupid holding a tablet that bore the inscriptions of the different arts along with a decorative wreath. "The figures are large and simple in line," Millet wrote, "and the general scheme of color is pale blue varied with purple and green, a combination suggested by the evanescent hues of Lake Michigan."[76] Reid's allegorical figures were also seated; but they were complemented by the addition of four youths, one on the keystone of each arch, holding above their heads wreaths and palm branches which met and crossed to create a band of decorative forms around the upper part of the dome. A seminude man with an anvil and shield represented Iron-Working. A girl in white with an arm resting on a pedestal and the hand of her other arm touching a carved stone was Ornament. Another figure dressed in purple and drawing on a scroll was Design. And the fourth represented Textile Arts.

E. E. Simmons and Kenyon Cox were responsible for the two domes at the east portal. Simmons painted the single figure of a man in each pendentive of his dome as symbols of Wood Carving, Stone Cutting, Forging, and Mechanical Appliances. Quite obviously the genders employed in Simmons's decorative paintings presumed precise distinctions about sex and occupation. Of these murals as art Millet commented rather tersely, "The composition is bold in line, firm in outline, and original in conception."[7] No doubt as a complement to Simmons's work, Cox painted a female figure against a background of balustrade and foliage in each of the pendentives of the adjacent dome. Banderoles over the heads of the figures made each pendentive into a shield-shape and bore the titles of the subjects the figures were meant to portray. Steel Working was a woman holding a sword; Ceramic Painting, a graceful girl in blue and white drapery holding a vase; Building, a tall girl in green robes standing beside an uncompleted wall; Spinning, a stately girl in rose-colored drapes with a spider web.

In the domes of the north portal could be seen the murals of J. Carroll Beckwith and Walter Shirlaw. Here again the figures were female, this time representing inventions and material objects. Beckwith's females, one in each pendentive, symbolized the Telephone and the Indicator, a woman holding a telephone to her ear while tape from a ticker was piling up about her; the Arc Light, a kneeling woman holding aloft a light; the Morse Telegraph, a woman reading a book at a table which was the operating machine; the Dynamo, a woman seated on a magnet with a belt and a wheel at her feet. At the very apex of the dome radiating lightning was the Spirit of Electricity—a boy. This last representation seems a curious departure, if not an inappropriate image, from the prevailing female forms. In the neighboring dome Shirlaw had painted allegorical female figures entitled *Gold, Silver, Pearl,* and *Choral* which represented the abundance of land and sea. The striking feature of his dome was that he had connected the figures with a spider-web pattern. The dominant colors of white, green, and gold also enhanced the flavor of this group. It seems clear, however, that there was little or nothing about these compositions that was distinctly imaginative. All contained huge male and female figures as symbols. All were confined to spaces that were the same in size and shape. The only real distinction possible in such circumstances was that of execution rather than of conception.

The works in the domes of the west portal apparently did have such distinction of execution. C. S. Reinhart's painting in the southern dome here was far more elaborate than any of those previously described. It contained a white marble terrace which circled the dome just above the arches. Above this terrace appeared a vibrant blue sky with tints of salmon pink. The four pendentives were occupied by seated female figures which represented the arts of Sculpture, Decoration, Embroidery, and Design. Between these figures were urns bearing cacti and trailing vines and flowers that bound together the entire composition. "The treatment is mural—broad, flat tones within the severe contours," wrote Frank Millet. "Above, in the sky, faint in color . . . , four cherubs are having a merry-go-round with pale ribbons."[78] Reinhart was not going to be outdone in quantity of figures or motifs at least. His dome was well filled.

The same might be said of its twin to the north which had inspired E. H. Blashfield to do some of his best work. Blashfield filled the pendentives of his dome with four winged genii that represented the Arts of Metal Working. There was a helmeted figure to personify armor making. Two half-naked youths, the one holding a trencher and the other a hammer, symbolized the Brass Founder and the Iron Worker. A maiden, clad in a clinging gown and holding a statuette in her hand, was the Art of the Goldsmith. The extreme points of the pendentives exhibited a pair of gauntlets, a brass worker's tools, a horseshoe, and a medal. Above and behind the heads of the figures extended a frieze of scrollwork. The entire composition was unified by flying banderoles and by the sweep of the genii's wings. Two cherubs bearing a shield occupied the dome's center. The background was a sky of pale blue. Peacock blues, greens, and purples and bright white tones were prominent in the coloration. Royal Cortissoz was especially impressed with this work. He considered it a good example of mural design. "The ceiling retains its architectural character, the proprieties of construction are not violated, and at the same time the painting has flexibility in the composition, and a certain amount of the pictorial interest which is characteristic of easel-painting that comes quite as much within the province of artists working on larger surfaces. Indeed, the larger the surface the wider the possibilities of thoughtful, even imaginative, composition."[79] There were, he added, degrees of largeness that for the purposes of genre painting might just as well be restricted. But those artists who painted the murals in the domes of the Manufactures Building had used their spaces properly. That was Will H. Low's major premise in judging, like Cortissoz, that Blashfield's work was probably foremost among the murals in the domes. "Tried by the standard that the space allotted to a decoration should be filled, and filled by a composition which could not serve within any other shaped space than that for which it is devised, Mr. Blashfield's [mural] seems the most successful," Low wrote.[80] Blashfield had most assuredly filled the space. What he had filled it with evidently was also admirable as art. Certainly the praise of Royal Cortissoz, not only a respected critic but also a friend of John LaFarge, the nation's finest muralist, must be credited. Nevertheless, in retrospect, it might fairly be said that the murals here and elsewhere suffered from the absence of that superior talent and inspiration that LaFarge's work always revealed.

There were no murals in the Transportation, Horticultural, and Fisheries buildings. The United States Government Building was profusely decorated under the guidance of an obscure artist named Emil Phillipson. The rotunda of the Government Building was embellished with such a plethora of pilasters, arches, and murals that it appeared gaudy. The murals consisted of scenes of famous natural wonders, cities, and symbolical groups. Although Bancroft succinctly referred to Phillipson's murals as "all in the highest form of decorative art," no one was especially interested.[81] The Woman's Building, however, contained several decorative paintings that did arouse interest not so much because they had a special quality or felicity but because they were the works of notable women and because they were in the Woman's Building. Everything in or about the Woman's Building was noteworthy, whether excellent or mediocre, because never before at any exposition had woman received such salient recognition. Women artists, architects, writers—women of all sorts—had been honored, or at least acknowledged, by the creation of the Board of Lady Managers and the Woman's Building and by the director general's grant in March 1893 that the Woman's Department should be equal in status, scope, and features to all the other departments. Perhaps such unprecedented attention to the sensibilities of women contributed to the fact that a majority of the visitors to the fair were women. Quite naturally they flocked to the Woman's Building. They would enter a central hall which opened into a large rotunda topped by a skylight and surrounded on its first and second stories by open arcades. Once there they could view murals created by Mary MacMonnies and Mary Cassatt, most notably, and by some artists of less renown—Dora Wheeler Keith, Lydia Emmett, Amanda Sewell, Emma Sherwood, and numerous others.

Unfortunately critics found even the works of Mary MacMonnies and Mary Cassatt not very distinguished or memorable. MacMonnies had painted a mural entitled *The Primitive Woman* at one end of the building's court, and Mary Cassatt had painted *The Modern Woman* at the opposite end. *The Primitive Woman* contained at the right one male, a hunter, just returned from the kill, whose wants were being cared for by a group of women and children. In the center of the mural woman as burden bearer was represented—here were girls carrying water-jars and a mother with two babes. And at the left were girls sowing grain. *The Modern Woman* offered a distinct contrast. The right area of Cassatt's panel showed one woman playing a string instrument, with a second woman listening, and a third dancing. The central part of the panel depicted women gathering apples. And in the left portion a group of girls followed by ducks were pursuing Fame, who was flying heavenward. As comments on woman's changing roles the two murals were quite direct. As art they were less notable. A female critic observed, "Both decorations are too high to be effective, and the space is too small in which they are placed." She described MacMonnies's work as "reverent in tone and dignified in

Interior of Woman's Building

Courtesy of the Chicago Historical Society

treatment. . . . if hung where it could be seen to better advantage, [it] would be the most successful example of mural decoration in the building. Miss Cassatt's panel is 'cynical,' and is the one note of discord in the harmony of color."[82] Will Low seconded this admiring view of MacMonnies's work, but he felt one had to take the excellence of Cassatt's work on faith—the figures were so small in scale that they could not be accurately discerned.[83] Low obviously was a gentleman. Maud Howe Elliott, feminist and daughter of Julia Ward Howe, said of *The Primitive Woman* that it was a work "of a high order; it shows a true decorative sense, a sure hand, and a fresh, joyous imagination. Artistically and intellectually it is a composition which commends itself to all those who understand and honor the idea for which our building stands."[84] She was content merely to describe *The Modern Woman*. Certainly it is interesting that *The Primitive Woman,* which appeared above the inscribed name of Bertha H. Palmer, elicited warmer regard from male and female critics both than did *The Modern Woman*, which appeared above the name of the Woman's Building architect, Sophia G. Hayden.

Although these two murals highlighted the decoration in the Woman's Building, they actually represented only a very small part of that decoration. The interior of the Woman's Building was probably the most profusely ornamented of all the building interiors. The great rotunda alone contained four more mural panels, along the side walls. These were the work of Lucia Fairchild, Amanda Brewster Sewell, Rosina Emmet Sherwood, and Lydia Emmet. Their subjects were the Pilgrim mothers and daughters; *Woman in Arcadia;* the Republic; and music, art and literature (all female figures). The vestibule entrance to the rotunda also contained murals on the walls and ceiling. Part of the decoration consisted of 150 portraits of famous women. Various rooms in the building bore mosaics, inlaid woods, and marble polished panels. Throughout there were the sculptural works of Alice B. Rideout, depicting such subjects as the three Fates, family groups, woman's virtues, sacrifice, charity, maternity, love; and, perhaps most telling of all, *Woman as the Spirit of Civilization*. But, by all accounts, next to the MacMonnies and Cassatt murals, the most significant decorative work in the Woman's Building was the mural painted by Dora Wheeler Keith upon the ceiling of the library. Keith was Candace Wheeler's daughter. The outer edge of her mural was a frame of scrollwork. Within this frame appeared a drapery, embellished with bunches of lilies which effectively formed a garland separating the four medallions of the mural, each of which contained a symbolical figure. Central focus of the mural was a group of three figures: a male representing Science enthroned with Literature, a graceful woman, beside him; between them stood Imagination, who bound them together. As Maud Howe Elliott conceived of this work, Keith had undertaken "the most difficult branch of decoration, and the artist is to be congratulated that she has painted what is perhaps the rarest thing in the whole range of art, a successful ceiling."[85] It may have been so.

About the qualities of the mural works and sculptural ornamentations in the various buildings no final judgment can be made—perhaps none is desirable, in fact—because all these works perished along with the temporal structures they adorned. Considering the enormous effort and the innumerable hours that went into the design and execution of these huge murals, their brief existence does seem sad. As W. Lewis Fraser lamented, "It was to me most melancholy . . . that so much excellent art had been put upon raw plaster, that up to date the greatest efforts of so many of our leading painters must in a few months pass out of existence."[86] That was a melancholy fact. But it was a fact which prevailed over the entire creation at Jackson Park. Nevertheless, while it lasted, the creation that had resulted from this unprecedented conjoining of the arts was lacking in neither glory nor merit. For the artisans the exposition had provided the opportunity of communal effort and achievement. For the public it had provided a unique visual experience. Candace Wheeler, herself an artist, wrote, "As artists, as painters, as sculptors, and as lovers of the arts, we owe to that great enterprise . . . that the field of artistic effort has been so greatly enlarged by examples of good painting and good sculpture as accessory to architecture."[87] That was the real value of the enterprise: it opened the way for future cooperation among the arts. As Candace Wheeler emphasized, however, it had to be understood that here painting and sculpture were not independent creations, but only accessories to architecture. Architecture was unquestionably the predominant art of the World's Columbian Exposition. Its primary accessory was sculpture. Painting, given the vicissitudes of the bigness and uses of the buildings, was of tertiary note.

It was the arts of music and literature, however, that became the real foundlings of the exposition. The slighting of music was not intentional. In fact, it was planned from the beginning that music should be integral to the exposition. Nothing less would suffice in a city that boasted the orchestral leadership of Theodore Thomas, musical director of the fair. The exposition chorus and orchestra were conspicuous at the dedicatory ceremonies. They were to have remained so throughout the duration of the fair. First of all, the corporation was pledged to the erection of the Festival (or Choral) Hall, where choral and orchestral concerts would be performed. "Plans for this building were made by F. M. Whitehouse, and a site was assigned to it on the west side of the park, facing the Wooded Island, between the Transportation Exhibits Building and the Horticultural Building." It cost nearly $90,000 to build and it could seat 5,200 people.[88] A simple Doric-style building, it was circular and 250 feet in diameter. Its front entrance was a Doric portico. Its interior consisted of a parquet surrounded by tiers of seats. The hall was equipped with a grand organ of sixty stops, located behind the seats for the chorus. The hall was quite plain and since its acoustics were satisfactory, it was more frequently used than the Music Hall which formed the north end of the Peristyle. The Music Hall had been designed in Corinthian style by Charles B. Atwood. Its interior was quite sumptuous.[89] It contained a circular auditorium with a stage that could seat an orchestra of 300, while 2,500 seats were provided for the audience.[90] Both the Music Hall and the Festival Hall were decorated with mural paintings and bas-reliefs representing the progress of music and various famous composers. Music Hall was in readiness when the exposition opened; Festival Hall was finished in early June. In addition to these music halls, three ornately decorated bandstands were put up; two in the plaza east of the Administration Building and one on the Lake Shore in front of the Manufactures Building. Other temporary musical facilities were arranged from time to time.

As musical director, Theodore Thomas planned a full and continuous schedule of serious and light concerts. In fact, Thomas envisioned "a gigantic plan for an exposition of music beyond anything that had so far been known."[91] The Bureau of Music intended to provide three kinds of music: symphonic recitals by the orchestra under Thomas's direction; choral presentations under the direction of William L. Tomlins; popular band and orchestra music performed throughout the fairgrounds. The symphony concerts were to be held at least twice a week in Music Hall—admission $1.00. The popular music recitals would occur daily at noon, free of charge. The orchestra was also to accompany the choral concerts given in Festival Hall.[92] The programs Thomas arranged presented "opportunities never before paralleled—in this country, at least, if in any—for a liberal musical education."[93] Unfortunately this great exposition of music ran into some snags and had to be abandoned before the fair ended. First of the snags was a fatuous controversy. Ignace Jan Paderewski had consented to play at the first concerts given in Music Hall on May 2 and 3. He chose as his instrument a Steinway piano, and Steinway had refused to exhibit at the fair because of dissatisfaction with the rules of the exposition. This refusal had led the National Commission to forbid the use of Steinway pianos on the grounds. Theodore Thomas got involved in the controversy. He upheld Paderewski's right to choose his own instrument and the directors of the corporation upheld Thomas.[94] A nasty dispute ensued in which Steinway's rival piano manufacturers who were exhibiting at the exposition harried Thomas and tried to undermine his position. This trifling dispute, exemplary at best of petty commercial rivalries, resulted in a storm of abusive editorial comment in newspapers throughout the nation. Thomas, a resolute and veracious man, was deeply affected by attacks upon his integrity. The World's Fair became his Waterloo. The National Commission asked for his resignation.[95] The directors continued to support him but ensuing weeks brought the second of the two snags to the fore.

That snag was the onslaught of the recession of 1893, one of the worst in American economic history. Since attendance at the fair was below expectations during June and July, the directors, fearing a staggering deficit, searched for ways to save money. Musical performances seemed a most likely activity to eliminate or at least to curtail. The free concerts of light music were well attended, but the performances by the orchestra and chorus "were poorly attended, and the programs were criticized as of a character too severely classical to suit the holiday surroundings and the tastes of people exhausted from sightseeing."[96] Accordingly the directors decided to discontinue the orchestra in early August and Theodore Thomas, disillusioned and disappointed, submitted his resignation. Abandoned were such events as two series of early autumn concerts, one to be directed by A. C. Mackenzie and the other by Camille Saint-Saëns, and other special programs. Thomas's plans and efforts had not been by any means entirely in vain, though. "From the inaugural concert held in Music Hall on May 2 to August 12, when Mr. Thomas closed his connection with the Exposition, there were eighty-eight working days, during which the orchestra of one hundred and fourteen assisted in one hundred and six performances. The enlarged orchestra of one hundred and fifty appeared in eight performances."[97] No one could deny that in the three months of its existence the World's Columbian Orchestra had performed mightily.

Some of those performances were noteworthy. One of the stellar events in Festival Hall occurred at the behest of H. N.

Higinbotham and Bertha Palmer, namely, a concert in honor of the infanta. Contributing to the program were Edward Lloyd, an English tenor, the exposition's children's chorus of one thousand voices, the chorus of Chicago's Apollo Music Club, and the exposition orchestra, all under the direction of Thomas and Tomlins.[98] Even before this event, Music Hall had been the scene of a gala honoring foreign dignitaries. Officers of the fleets of the major European nations and of Brazil and Argentina, which had participated in a combined naval review at New York in late April, traveled to Chicago, where they were joined by the exposition's foreign commissioners and prominent Chicagoans. They all converged upon a sumptuously decorated Music Hall for a reception featuring national hymns and orchestral music, followed by breakfast.[99] In addition to such special celebrations, there were several invited guest performances or compositions. Distinguished American orchestras performed at the exposition, outstanding among them the Boston Symphony Orchestra conducted by Franz Kneisel and the New York Symphony Orchestra conducted by Walter Damrosch.[100] The distinguished sopranos Amalia Materna and Lillian Nordica presented programs. William Tomlins secured concert appearances by choral groups from a dozen major American cities including Minneapolis, Saint Louis, Pittsburgh, and Cleveland. Among these was the famous Old Stoughton Musical Society. American ethnic choral societies, such as the German American Woman's Chorus, the United Scandinavian Singers, and the United Polish Singers, made appearances. The Bohemian Singers performed on October 12, with Antonín Dvořák, then director of the National Conservatory of Music in New York, as their honored guest.[101] Besides the specially commissioned compositions by John Knowles Paine and George Whitfield Chadwick rendered at the dedicatory ceremonies, the works of other leading American composers were aired. "Later programs brought works by Edward MacDowell (1861-1908), Arthur Foote (1853-1937), Harry Rowe Shelley (1858-1947), and the expatriate Arthur Bird (1856-1923)." The official opening of the Woman's Building included a program of music by women composers, most notably Mrs. H. H. A. Beach of Boston.[102] The Woman's Building was the scene of numerous additional concerts.

Along with these serious musical endeavors the exposition offered popular music. The orchestra itself was not entirely forsaken. It was partially reformed under the direction of Max Bendix and continued to give light music concerts—twenty-nine in all—for the remainder of the fair.[103] And certainly the fair was a bandmaster's heyday. There were two bands in service in May; by September there were six, all employed by the directors. They were presenting up to fourteen concerts a day in September. Among the bands were Sousa's New Marine Band, Liesegang's Chicago Band, Innes's Thirteenth Regiment Band, Gilmore's Band, the Iowa State Band, and the bands from Elgin and Pullman, Illinois.[104] Fairgoers thus had the chance to hear every major band in the United States. No wonder the bands drew larger crowds than attended Thomas's orchestral concerts. They were free, they were everywhere, and they played what Americans liked to hear. Every day John Philip Sousa's musicians regaled audiences with Charles K. Harris's most popular *After the Ball*.[105] Elsewhere, in the Midway Plaisance, fairgoers could listen to any number of foreign bands—for example, Ziehrer's Royal Austrian Band, the imperial German cavalry and infantry bands, the Coldstream Guards Band, the Royal Hungarian Band. Here also could be heard the exotic music of the Orient.[106] And so although Thomas's grand plan was dismantled, his energies had proved redoubtable.

That other foundling of the exposition, the art of literature, was far less in evidence than music. Literature's degree of interest to the fairgoing public must have lain somewhere between that of the corn exhibit in the Iowa State Pavilion and the Diamond Match Company exhibit. Considering the fact that even those who were deeply interested in the arts, and in literature especially, were constantly enticed by hundreds of industrial displays, scores of exotic foreign exhibits, the delights of the Midway Plaisance, and the relief of resting, it is hard to imagine that many found sufficient energy to rouse themselves to inspect some first editions; for there is not much else that literature can be at an exposition but a display of books. The organizers of the fair had wanted all the arts to be represented. Architecture, sculpture, and painting were clearly present in diverse abundance. Music at least had its own buildings and featured daily concerts. But what could the literary profession have done with a separate building? Nevertheless, though not effectively fostered with its own edifice, literature was present.

The visitor with a literary passion would certainly have been attracted to the Manufactures and Liberal Arts Building and to the Woman's Building. Within the gigantic structure that dominated the fairgrounds he would have discovered somewhere beyond galleries of photographs, engravings, and displays concerned with the reproduction of color and form, that the publishing industry in the United States had its wares on exhibit. There the visitor could have found original illustrations of artists and original manuscripts of authors. In Harper's pavilion, for example, was a recent edition of *She Stoops to Conquer*, with original illustrations by Edwin A. Abbey, along with the original manuscript of *Ben-Hur*. Other publishers displayed manuscripts of Thomas Bailey Aldrich, Henry James, and William Dean Howells. One could peruse the last manuscript sheet of Frank R. Stockton's *The Lady or the Tiger?* as well as some of the copy of Frances Hodgson Burnett's beloved *Little Lord Fauntleroy*. Also here for examination were manuscripts of Mark Twain, Bret Harte, Richard H. Stoddard, Edman C. Stedman. There was a historical collection of dictionaries.[107] The American Library Association exhibited its recommended 5,000 volume popular library. This library ranged from the *A. B. C. of Finance* to the zoological works of Louis Agassiz and Charles Kingsley. It contained the works of such American luminaries as Mark Twain, Howells, and Irving and American magazines like *Nation* and *Century*. Here too were listed Henry Adams's histories and the voluminous historical works of Hubert Howe Bancroft.

Also included were myriad entries of foreign authors. It was a seemingly exhaustive compendium.[108] French and German publishers displayed extensive collections. And over in the Woman's Building was the literary attraction of a 7,000 volume library, with one cabinet that contained forty-seven different translations of *Uncle Tom's Cabin*. Here one could see some of the works of Julia Ward Howe, "the foremost literary woman of to-day." And here also were books and manuscripts of the great English writers: Mrs. Gaskell, Jane Austen, the Brontes, George Eliot.[109] The publishers' exhibits and the exhibit in the library of the Woman's Building were complemented by portraits and busts of famous writers.

Aside from such conventional displays, literature asserted its presence in dramatic form at least once on the exposition grounds. To honor literature the fair provided a special day, August 30, 1893, known as Poets' Day, thus giving literature equal standing with such other special recognitions as Confectioners' Day, Utah Day, Nebraska Fete Day, Missionary Day, and College Fraternity Day. The Committee on Ceremonies, which assigned such occasions, was at least well intentioned. On Poets' Day *As You Like It* was performed on an outdoor stage in the Sylvan Dell, which was near the German pavilion. Rose Coghlan and Otis Skinner, erstwhile members of Augustin Daly's troupe, were cast in the roles of Rosalind and Orlando, while E. J. Henley played Jacques. Edmund Lyons was Touchstone. "Sylvan Dell became, for the time being, the enchanted forest of Arden."[110] About 2,500 people witnessed this transformation. The stage, sodded with real grass and surrounded by real trees, was perhaps of more interest than the play. A reviewer for one of the Chicago newspapers commented, "But this wonderful spectacle in the midst of the marvelous White City, complete in itself, was a dream to be inclosed within the memory like a pearl without a flaw."[111] Recalling this precious dream years later, Otis Skinner dismissed the occasion with a terse depreciatory comment: the play was a failure and the Sylvan Dell was merely three scrofulous willows and a sickly oak.[112] In any event it could hardly be argued that Poets' Day—with no parades, no speeches, no poets, no writers of any kind—was a glowing tribute to literature. And surely the most ironic comment of all was that the organizers of the World's Columbian Exposition, the epochal celebration of the New World's discovery and progress, offered not an American play as their sole homage to literature but a Shakespearean comedy.

Although music and literature were not fully integrated into the celebrative scheme, music certainly enhanced the fairgoer's experience of the exposition and the minimal representation of literature could hardly have been said to distract from that experience. It would have to be conceded, however, that no matter how much music and literature might have been emphasized, there could never have been any doubt that the real artistic achievement of the exposition inhered in the marriage of architecture, painting, and sculpture. William LeBaron Jenney, dean of Chicago architects, asserted that the policies of the Committee on Grounds and Buildings "have paid the highest compliments to the professions of architecture, sculpture, and painting, and have given them opportunities that they never enjoyed before in this country."[113] That Jenney, father of the steel frame skyscraper, should have admired the achievement of an alliance of the arts at the fair is indicative of the White City's superlative beauty. It is quite understandable, then, that an architect favorable to neoclassical styles should find the results of the cooperative endeavor both an inspiration and a lesson. To millions of people of varying intelligence "the architecture of Jackson Park, with its subsidiary sculpture and painting, was a revelation of the power of art, and millions of lives were made larger and fuller by the experience," wrote Henry Van Brunt. "The Exposition of 1893 apparently restored this art to the people, and rehabilitated it as one of the acknowledged agencies of civilization. Indeed, it has perhaps restored architecture to architects, in giving to them a memorable object-lesson of the immense impressiveness of loyalty to those established types of art which were . . . expressive of the greatest eras of human history."[114] If it was indeed the case that the exposition helped to civilize many and that it purified the ranks of architecture, all well and good. But Van Brunt's view is rather worrisome. Montgomery Schuyler, for example, expressed some misgivings that the exposition might lead to direct imitation which would ignore the White City's genuine merits. The success of the exposition was threefold, Schuyler wrote: success of unity, of magnitude, of illusion. "What the World's Fair buildings have to tell us, and what they tell equally to a casual glimpse or a prolonged survey is that they are examples . . . of holiday building, that the purpose of their erection is festal and temporary, in a word that the display is a display and a triumph of occasional architecture."[115] That triumph should be sufficient in itself, Schuyler argued; it should not be deemed to have made a useful contribution to the development of architecture. In principle and in fact, Schuyler was quite right.

Nevertheless, outstanding lessons were to be learned from the exposition, even within the limitations of Schuyler's succinct and admonitory summation that "The White City is the most integral, the most extensive, the most illusive piece of scenic architecture that has ever been seen."[116] Illusive and scenic it was, as Van Brunt agreed, but nonetheless compelling as achievement, as art, as spectacle. Engineer, novelist, diplomat Arthur Sherburne Hardy suggested the reason for the exposition's exultant success when he asked, "Were ever composition, arrangement, variety, unity—those principles invoked by the artist in the creation of his canvas, and by the architect in the erection of his building—were ever these principles applied on so gigantic a scale?"[117] The answer is, no, they never were. That was the undeniable glory of the World's Columbian Exposition: it manifested on an unprecedentedly gigantic scale the aesthetic principles of ensemble and unity. The painter William Anderson Coffin commented, "It did not seem so remarkable that the principal buildings were architecturally good and beautiful—that the ornamentation, the fountains, sculptured groups and statues, were so excellent, for we might have expected that they would be, as that all were so fittingly placed that each component part formed such a well-balanced factor in the whole."[118] There was mediocre work and some of the attempted novelties were failures, but such weaknesses in individual detail were trifles within an impressively unified artful achievement.

Most observers saw this achievement of harmonious integration among the fine arts—always granting architecture primacy—as a singular advancement upon the Centennial Exposition. Benjamin Harrison, for example, argued that the contrast between the Philadelphia exposition and Chicago's, "gives a glorious vision of the growth in power, wealth, invention and art, which sixteen years have brought to the world."[119] Philadelphia novelist and journalist Thomas A. Janvier expressed the view most concisely when he said that in contrasting the Philadelphia and Chicago expositions point by point, we could "arrive at a just appreciation of the prodigious advances which we have made on the lines of intellectual development." Projecting the same rate of progress into the future left him groping for mental security over the potential for change by 1910.[120] Some observers believed that the achievement of the World's Columbian Exposition surpassed not only the rather grotesque buildings of the Centennial, but also those of the often touted Paris exposition of 1889 and therefore constituted an artistic declaration of at least equality. Chicago architect Peter B. Wight said straightforwardly that both the buildings and their sculptural adornments were superior to those at Paris.[121] The editors of the *Architectural Review* argued that the Chicago architecture was better than its Parisian predecessor.[122] There was ample justification for such argument: photographs of the buildings at Paris show them to have been frivolous and perhaps even absurd. But Frenchmen were most likely to find fault with the American exposition as imitative. The Marquis de Chasseloup-Laubat said Chicago's fair showed no uniform general plan— revealing surely a remarkable lack of perception on his part—and that its derivative architecture implied America's failure to attain a native style.[123] There was justification for his thoughts on the native style at least. Paul Bourget, a famous French traveler in

America and author of *Outre Mer*, acknowledged this apparent shortcoming; but he emphatically defended the Americans' feverish quest after culture, and he concluded that the national conscience of the United States "feels its work to be the creation of a personal ideal. . . . That is the promise the White City leaves."[124] The White City's legacy, he rightly discerned, was the promise of the ideal. Such demurrers and protestations were understandable. Many native Americans held similar misgivings and hopes.

At least one foreign visitor, however, called the attention of his fellow Europeans back to the primary impression. Edmund Mitchell, a Briton, spent eight months in Chicago in 1893. He spoke with numerous European visitors who had visited the London Exhibition of 1851, the various Paris expositions, the Viennese and the Philadelphia fairs. He concluded that among these visitors there was a consensus that "the City of White Palaces in Chicago has never had a compeer as regards architectural magnificence. . . . it was universally allowed that never before had there been such a massing of glorious palaces, such exquisite grouping of noble buildings amidst an unrivalled setting of lake and lagoon, . . . statuary and stately colonnades, islands and avenues, landscape designs and floral effects."[125] As Mitchell noted, the White City was the accomplishment of Chicago. Furthermore, from a visit to the exposition a foreigner might have imbibed the nature of Chicago itself, "this young giant city of the West, with its striking architectural features that mark a distinct epoch in building engineering, with its teeming and polyglot population, with its phenomenally rapid commercial growth, with its web of concentrating railways, with all its feverish energy and enterprise."[126] Here was an insuperable city. The White City might have been an inspired architectural achievement, but the entirety of the World's Columbian Exposition was the achievement of Chicago. Chicago was the real glory. Thus English novelist Walter Besant rapturously concluded, "the people dream epics; Art and Music and Poetry belong to Chicago; the Hub of the Universe is transferred from Boston to Chicago; this place must surely become, in the immediate future, the center of the nobler world—the world of Art and Letters."[127] Many had worried over whether this exuberant and youthful city could produce a fair worthy of the occasion and of the nation. Their fears had proved groundless. Chicago had secured the honor as host city and Chicago had determined the unparalleled magnificence of the World's Columbian Exposition. "History will call it the Chicago World's Fair," wrote James P. Holland. "It is useless to expect otherwise."[128] The fair authorized as a splendid tribute to the discovery of America actually honored Chicago. That was most fitting.

5

EXHIBITS, PASTIMES, & PLEASURES

Sell the cookstove if necessary and come.
You *must* see this fair.

Hamlin Garland

THE MAIN EXHIBIT at the World's Columbian Exposition was the buildings—the White City itself. But a feature that enhanced and ennobled that city's vistas, the approaches to the buildings, the expansive esplanades, and the arched bridges was the outdoor sculptural work. Referring to all the statuary on the grounds and buildings, one account declared with exuberant hyperbole, "In the zenith of its achievements Venice was never so statuesque as Jackson Park. Nor Rome, nor Athens in their haughtiest epochs, could point to so many inspiring effigies."[1] Though mistaken about their quality, the observer was quite right in touting the quantity of the statues. Nearly every thoroughfare of the exposition was populated by immense statues of animals—buffalo, moose, bear, elk, antelope, jaguar—the works of Edward Kemeys and A. P. Proctor. The most conspicuous placement of these animal statues was on or near the bridges of the lagoon and in the area of the court. "Copies of these designs were placed at almost every advantageous place in the balustrades that bounded the waters of the park. The effect ... was gratifying to the lover of nature, and offered one of the distinct artistic triumphs of the Exposition."[2] Actually as art most of these statues were dubious,

180

but the crowds found them pleasing. Before the Agricultural Building were two huge bulls, one accompanied by Ceres, that had been modeled by E. C. Potter. Across the basin stood a farmer beside his plowhorse, both symbolizing Labor, as Proctor conceived it. Near these at the end of the South Canal stood the Obelisk and Lion Fountain. Elsewhere there were statues of Indians and other human subjects, the most prominent being Proctor's *The Cowboy* and *The Indian*, situated in front of the Mines and Mining Building. Around the Great Basin there towered six *columnae rostratae* bearing figures of Neptune and other free-standing columns topped with such figures as Victory—all the works of Johannes Gelert. All these sculptural works, like the buildings and thoroughfares they augmented, were heroic in scale. Candace Wheeler found them awesome indeed both in scale and numbers. "Gigantic inhabitants of a city of a dream, they people it so abundantly," she wrote, "that the small human element is almost an impertinence, or, at most, something unnoticeable in the grand company of its own creation."[3] The statuary dwarfed the fairgoers.

That was especially true of some of the heroic works in the Court of Honor and at entrances to buildings, such as the statue of *Columbus* which stood on a pedestal fourteen feet in front of the Great Basin entrance to the Administration Building. The original statue had been started by Augustus Saint-Gaudens's brother Louis, who was unable to finish it. It then passed to Saint-Gaudens's pupil Mary Lawrence, with the master serving as critic and adviser while she molded the *Columbus* into a finished work. It was to her, Saint-Gaudens said, that all the credit was due for its "virility and breadth of treatment."[4] One view had it that the statue was "One of the grandest pieces of statuary art that was seen at the Exposition. . . . And it is significant of woman's future, as it is of her ability to rise to the noblest conceptions, and to create forms of her brilliant fancies, that a woman should design and execute this chief monumental figure at the Fair."[5] Other views were not so generous. Many disparaged the work. Another

Statue of *Columbus*

Courtesy of the Chicago Historical Society

heroic statue whose subject was also of historic interest appeared in the entranceway to the Electricity Building. This was Carl Rohl-Smith's *Benjamin Franklin*. The sculptor had depicted Franklin, head back gazing heavenward with his kite in hand, waiting for the opportune moment to begin his electrical experiment. Without doubt the oddest of the outdoor sculptures was a work by Theodore Baur of New York which reclined near the Art Palace. "This incompleted group is named 'The Secret,' of which a meaning may be gathered from the Cupid whispering into the ear of a curious sphinx, apparently half woman and half lioness in form. The pleased and yet sinister radiance of this creature's face, though it be wellnigh as brutish as her feline body, is considered by many to be a masterpiece of sculptural expression."[6] Just what the secret may have been is a little hard to surmise. But certainly this group constituted a bizarre admixture and the sphinx was an interesting metamorphosis of the original, since from its chest sprouted two sizable breasts.

All such sculptures served as complements to the elegance of the fair's buildings and grounds—and in some cases, no doubt, as distractions. Just so, they were festal and ephemeral, all made of the staff material. Thus the fairgoer who wished to study genuinely substantive works of sculpture, and of painting especially, would have hastened by Baur's sphinx and into the rooms of the Art Palace. Here he would have been confronted with a superabundance of galleries: "In the main building alone there are seventy-four galleries, varying in size from 30 x 30 feet to 36 x 120 feet." The wall space was so immense that it was exceedingly difficult to hunt out individual paintings.[7] For, although the Fine Arts Building was frequently criticized for having too-small rooms, into its galleries were compacted "a better general representation of the world's art than has been made at any exposition in the past."[8] French expositions had slighted German works, and German expositions had slighted French art. Scandinavian artists had been slighted in all previous expositions and Russian art was barely known outside of Russia, whether in galleries or at expositions.

Since the United States had friendly relations with all nations at that time, political considerations prevented none from exhibiting. Hence in the Fine Arts Building was on view "so comprehensive and brilliant a showing of modern works of art" as was ever assembled.[9] The amplitude of the exhibits created problems. First of all, nations asked for far more space than was available and even after the submitted works had been winnowed to manageable numbers, they still constituted a bewildering array upon the walls and floors of the galleries.

Space was allotted according to the assumed significance of the various participants in the field of art. For example, in square feet of hanging space France was the forerunner, with an allotment of 29,201 square feet. The United States, as host nation, was second, with 23,324 but in actuality, given other sections of the galleries, it was first. Then followed England with 21,325. Germany had 20,340 square feet of wall space; Austria and Belgium each had about 11,500; Italy and Holland each had over 9,000. Russia and Spain were each awarded nearly 7,800 square feet. Even sparsely populated Norway had 8,282. At the bottom of the list, with the least space of all, was Mexico, given 1,500 square feet of wall space.[10] The official groupings of the artworks by the various countries were sculpture; oil painting; watercolors; painting on ivory, enamel, metal, porcelain, etc., including frescoes; engravings, etchings, and prints; chalk, charcoal, pastel, and other drawings; antique and modern carvings, engravings in medallions, cameos, etc.; exhibits of private collections.[11] Loan collections were placed in the United States section, regardless of the painters' nationalities. The Art Palace contained a total of 10,040 individual exhibits. The full catalog of works, listing everything by name and number, is 506 pages long.[12]

The American exhibit contained 1,075 oil paintings alone—325 from New York, 139 from Boston, 112 from Philadelphia, 75 from Chicago, and 250 from American artists living abroad—not to mention engravings, etchings, watercolors, and sculpture. Of primary interest to fairgoers and critics were the oil paintings. Halsey

C. Ives was responsible for the choice of paintings, though committees of artists from each nation assisted. Believing that the nature of the American exhibit, as compared with exhibits of other nations, would determine the general evaluation of our art by both Americans and foreigners for many years to come, Ives deemed it extremely important that the paintings should be of "the highest quality obtainable; that each example shown represent the highest achievement of the artist, and that the collection as a whole present in a dignified manner the best productions of our native art."[13] Ives was carefully selective. For example, New York alone submitted 1,350 works, from which Ives chose 325. Still what Ives selected amounted to an immense exhibition, with the walls of the American galleries smothered by the works of painters whose talents varied from great to mediocre to worthless. The density of the hangings was fatiguing to contemplate. It was quite impossible to see everything and barely possible to digest what was seen.

Visitors made the attempt, nevertheless. They scrutinized the art exhibits with interest and curiosity and they were sometimes rather severe in their critical judgments. In his study of the exposition, *The Book of the Fair*, Hubert Howe Bancroft asserted that American criticisms of the American paintings were more often than not partly or fully unwarranted. "First of all," he wrote, "it was objected that the pictures were too large; that here was not art in its essence but art by the acre, the average dimensions of the canvases rising far above the usual standard." This was erroneous criticism, Bancroft insisted, because of the extensiveness of the galleries; for "while size is not itself a merit, the general effect of a series of large galleries, permitting a focus of long range, is better when filled with paintings proportioned to their dimensions."[14] Bancroft's point forms the basis of what seems a curious aesthetics, but it might be noted that art students at the École des Beaux-Arts were instructed on this point; they were to paint large because of the size of the galleries at the French Academy. Still, in this case, Bancroft's point is conditional at best. After all, the majority of these paintings were not done specifically for these galleries or even for this exhibition. It is not surprising, though, that many of the paintings were huge, as large canvases had been customary since the days of the Hudson River school and certainly they had long been customary in France and other European art centers. What was surprising was that some critics objected.

Some visitors also complained that there were too many commonplace portraits and that too many of the paintings were imitative of French methods. Bancroft was dubious of these criticisms too. The only major shortcoming he found, in fact, was that there were so few paintings of historic persons or events, a judgment which might be expected from a historian. It would have been more suitable probably to have deferred to the criticism. Since the time of Gilbert Stuart and the Peales, American portrait work had been in decline; it had devolved mostly upon itinerant painters. G. P. A. Healy, then resident in Chicago, was the current master, but he was no match for the expatriate John Singer Sargent. In other words, native American portraiture of superior quality was rare. Furthermore, our artists, like our architects, were still largely French-trained. Probably it was rather delusive to think that the American works chosen for exhibit would declare the creation of a distinctly native art. Nevertheless, there were some exceptional works and some curious ones.

As a whole Bancroft's judgments were fairly discerning regarding both the exceptional and the curious. His views on the American works were generally in agreement with popular attitudes or artistic good taste or both. For example, he greatly admired the portraits done by Sargent and the canvases of James A. M. Whistler, even his more impressionistic efforts and especially the *Nocturne, Valparaiso*, which certainly qualifies Bancroft as an art critic of some superior insight. As for portraiture, Sargent may have stood alone. William A. Coffin believed that he and Winslow Homer carried off "the honors of the exhibition," with Sargent especially well represented by the *Portrait of Ellen Terry as Lady*

Macbeth.[15] Bancroft concurred. There were other works worthy of some praise. Bancroft found appealing some works done by Abbott H. Thayer, paintings of a lady, and of a brother and sister together; "but his best and largest painting is the 'Virgin Enthroned,' where the subject is treated with tenderness and spirituality."[16] This kind of commentary is rather typical of Bancroft, for he was most susceptible to paintings of a religious nature. He spoke highly of George de Forest Brush's *Madonna*. He liked Walter Gay's works, all of them devoted to religious subjects. J. Gari Melchers's canvases elicited extended and enthusiastic response from him. " 'The Communion,' by Gari Melchers is a painting of remarkable individuality and strength. Worship is its theme, pure and reverent worship, a simple and trusting faith unclouded by the faintest shadow of doubt."[17] This was a large painting which attracted much favorable attention. But then most paintings with religious or sentimental motifs were well received. Bancroft's prejudices were widely shared.

It might be thought, then, that paintings whose contents were suggestive or harsh would ensnare few viewers. Yet of the American paintings that were most popular with fairgoers, one that attracted the largest crowds and earned unqualified admiration was certainly fearsome: Carl Marr's *The Flagellants*. Its subject was a huge procession of medieval flagellants, scourging each other, wailing, groaning, as they passed a cathedral in northern Italy. William Walton described *The Flagellants* as the "largest and most historical composition in the American section and one of the largest and most important in the Exposition." Walton said this ghastly procession epitomized the Dark Ages, when, fearful of God and the plague, zealots sought atonement through self-persecution. "The painter has reproduced all the characteristics of this terrible march with great artistic intelligence," Walton concluded.[18] Marr, a Milwaukean, had exhibited his painting in 1889 in Munich, where it was seen by European art critics who hailed it as one of the best pictures exhibited in fifty years; it was awarded a Munich Exhibition gold medal.[19] Bancroft noted that the painting was mammoth and yet crowded with figures. Indeed, the canvas was crammed with figures—two hundred in all—among them old men and children whose naked backs and shoulders endured the frenzied and lusty lashings of harrowing maidens. This repulsive composition was so studded with human figures, the church architecture so imposing, and the subject so bizarre, that curious crowds remained to study and finally to admire.

Much different was the subject of that painting which probably was most popular of all in the American exhibit, Thomas Hovenden's *Breaking Home Ties*, which told a sentimental story. It was a simple and touching representation of a son leaving his New England country home to make his way in life. Standing in the middle of the living room, the youth was saying farewell to his mother, and both looked sad indeed. Nearby waited the son's dog and his sisters, while his father moved toward the doorway carrying a carpetbag. On the table appeared the dishes and remnants of their last meal together. The painting had no particular merit except sentiment, and perhaps a superficial empathy. As one account summed it up, Hovenden's painting revealed the "influence of romanticism"; hence the choice of a subject from American life.[20] The scene depicted was familiar to most families. Certainly the fairgoers loved it. Bancroft said nothing about the painting's artistic quality—it pleased him simply because it was descriptive of American life.

Walter MacEwen's *Witches*, depicting the execution of a witch and a girl in old Salem, also was admirably invested with an American theme. Unfortunately MacEwen's other paintings dealt with foreign subjects. Frank Millet contributed eight paintings which were representative of his highly finished and scholarly style. George Maynard's oils included a portrait of Millet and some other works of rather symbolic nature, among them *Pomona* and *Civilization*. Judgment on the works of both men might be reserved, however, because Millet was a thoroughgoing product of the Dutch school and Maynard invariably chose alien or allegorical themes. Foreign influence, Bancroft may well have thought, was also too discernible in the impressionistic works of John Henry Twatchtman. Bancroft did not find impressionistic painting inherently objectionable, but Twatchtman's works he depreciated as examples of "impressionist paintings of the purple and lilac school which disfigure the walls of these galleries."[21] He did concede that Twatchtman's landscapes had a certain attractiveness. He found more striking examples of Impressionism, though, in the paintings of William T. Dannat and Robert Reid.

Like most Americans, Bancroft was especially fond of landscapes, so that he had a great deal to say about those which he deemed superior. Landscape was, as all agreed, the American form of painting. In William Coffin's view landscapes demonstrated more conclusively than any other works that American artists were "making steady and rapid progress in individual expression. . . . the landscapes in the American section are extremely good, and one has but to walk through the galleries of the other nations after looking at them, to feel how good they are."[22] Coffin highly regarded the landscapes of George Inness, Alexander H. Wyant, and R. Swain Gifford. Landscapes that Bancroft admired included some of the canvases of the popular painter Dwight W. Tryon, of Frederick Vinton, and of Thomas Allen— painters whose reputations have proved of limited durability, though Tryon's work probably merits renewed attention. All were sons of Massachusetts. John J. Enneking, also of this group, probably deserved praise. Though himself a native of Ohio, Bancroft clearly was biased in favor of New England painters. He was careful to call attention to their work, even though at the time many of these painters were of limited repute, in keeping with their talents. Bancroft liked Charles H. Woodbury's *North Sea Dunes*, a wilderness of sandhills. "Here," wrote Bancroft, "is the very genius of desolation, the sketch being taken from the landward side, and with Lilliputian figures of peasant women contrasting with the gigantesque proportions of the dunes."[23] He liked also the marine paintings of Walter L. Dean, in particular the ironically named *Peace*, which showed the white squadrons of the

American navy anchored in Boston Harbor. They were ominous looking ships, but Dean's skill "has given to these frowning leviathans of war an element of the picturesque, grouped as they are in placid waters and under a summer sky. This picture, it may here be mentioned, is the largest of its class, nine feet in length by more than six in width."[24] By the usual American standards, then, as Ferree or Schuyler might have commented, the painting must have been excellent.

Such works seemed attractive because they were somehow distinctly American and they were large enough to command notice among the thousands of paintings. Indeed, so myriad were the works on exhibit that any canvas less than six or eight feet in width was likely to go entirely unnoticed. Still there were American works that were impressive for more reasons than their dimensions. Numerous gold medals were awarded for genuinely worthy art. Among the recipients was Winslow Homer's *A Great Gale*. The award was Homer's first gold medal and therefore the ostensible beginning of his recognition. How creditable to Chicago that it should have been the first to honor this giant of American landscape painting, and for one of his large seascapes specifically. Homer, who visited the fair and did some sketches of it, was represented by fifteen canvases in the Art Palace galleries. Walton had special praise for Homer's seascapes. Some of them, he wrote, "are complete works of art,—theme, design, color and human interest, all being present. . . . all are marked by that robustness and un-grossness of painter's talent which makes his works conspicuous among those which have caused the wonder of the foreign visitors at the American display."[25] Walton's strangely worded comment was well taken. It is noteworthy, for example, that in the French exhibit appeared not a single canvas from the Impressionists—at that time the most innovative and most truly native of French painters—whereas in the American exhibit could be found not only some of the best works of the native school, like those of Winslow Homer, George Inness, Thomas Eakins, and Thomas Moran but also the works of American students of Impressionism, like Mary Cassatt, William Merritt Chase, Childe Hassam, Theodore Robinson, and John Twatchtman. Thus the American oils were more deserving, as both distinctly native and creative works, than those in the exhibit of France, the presumed fountainhead of the painterly art.

Other kinds of artwork were plentiful in the American exhibit. There was a copious display of watercolors, containing works by W. Hamilton Gibson, Edwin H. Blashfield, John LaFarge, R. Swain Gifford. Here were the well-known paintings of mosques by Samuel Colman, some of Edwin Abbey's illustrations for Shakespeare, Frederick Church's *Pandora*, and Childe Hassam's *Fifth Avenue*. In the section of etchings Whistler's work was prominent, with fifty-nine examples in all. There were some engravings and even a few pastels, notably those of Chase and Twatchtman. A large collection of pen, charcoal, and other drawings was displayed: more Shakespearean illustrations by Abbey, architectural studies by Joseph Pennell and Harry Fenn, landscapes by Howard Pyle, a charcoal drawing of Charles Dudley Warner by C. S. Reinhart, animal and military sketches by Frederic Remington. There was an exhibit of historical works dating back to 1729 and one of drawings and watercolors by American architects, among them Louis Sullivan, R. M. Hunt, Stanford White. There were private collections containing works by American luminaries: Washington Allston, George Caleb Bingham, George Catlin, Thomas Cole, Asher B. Durand, John Singleton Copley, John Kensett, Gilbert Stuart, and James, Rembrandt, and Charles Wilson Peale. Many of these works were interesting and some were highly significant. But it was the oils that won the fairgoer's pleasure and attention. In the end, after all, having examined the yards upon yards of oil paintings that bedecked the seemingly infinite galleries of the Fine Arts Building, what spectator could have had the strength needed, let alone the inclination, to study hosts of smaller works? The succinct judgment of Lew Wallace might suffice: "With respect to conclusions, enough that Americans had reason to be proud of the merit conspicuous in the canvases of their countrymen."[26]

The display of American sculptural works, on the other hand, left something to be desired. Among American sculptors who were true sons of the native school, there were some singular omissions. It was not a matter of the absence of some representative works by such deceased American sculptors as Horatio Greenough, for this was a modern show. But there was not a single work of America's greatest living artisan, Augustus Saint-Gaudens. Furthermore, "Mr. J. Q. A. Ward does not appear among the sculptors, and the best of the animal groups here suggest Barye and Cain rather than any fresh, truly American, inspiration."[27] Nor were there works by Lorado Taft, E. C. Potter, Karl Bitter, or Frederick MacMonnies. But Edward Kemeys and Olin Warner had several works in the display, and John Rogers, America's most popular sculptor, was represented by a single work, *Statue of Abraham Lincoln*, seated.

There were 148 pieces of statuary in the American exhibit. Of these, works that received some especial comment from critics or were pleasing to the crowds included H. K. Bush-Brown's *The Buffalo Hunt*, an Indian killing a bison; F. Edwin Elwell's *Charles Dickens and Little Nell;* and Daniel Chester French's *The Angel of Death and the Sculptor*. The latter was a plaster cast of a monument erected in a Boston cemetery in memory of sculptor Martin Milmore which depicted the angel of death interrupting a sculptor who is intently chiseling a sphinx. The cast supposedly displayed "Conception of a high order and masterly plastic treatment" of the sort that infused French's *Minute Man* and *Republic*.[28] Overall the sculpture lacked the appeal of oil painting. Lew Wallace observed, "Two pieces left impressions—one a nude female-figure, large as life; the other an essay in the line of portraiture; it being a Dickens seated upon a high box pedestal, with little Nell standing at his feet. . . . These two were up to standard; but the others . . . were nearly all faulty in some particular. Those which might have claimed originality were grotesque; a few were indecent. Not that nudity implies indecency; but that the idea of the piece must be high enough to save it from gross suggestions."[29] Alas, we shall never know what nude female figure stirred Wallace's admiration, but his comment raises an interesting point. Regarding what they would accept in art, Americans were supposed to be prudish. Kenyon Cox complained of not being able to paint nudes. Eakins lost his teaching position because he used nude male models. Exemplary of such apparent prudery was a comment upon an education exhibit in the Manufactures Building that appeared in a photographic work on the exposition and referred to two nude figures representing the typical American male and female. "It may seem a little shocking, at first blush," ran the comment beneath the photo, "to affirm that the above statues are those of American college students. They are not portrait figures, however, nor must it be inferred that any living student ever posed to the gifted sculptor who modeled them."[30] The statues simply represented the findings of Harvard Professor D. A. Sargent, who measured 20,000 students to determine the contours of the typical male and female American students. The comment was not nearly so timorous as the illustration, which judiciously revealed only the backsides of the figures. Such fastidiousness suggests priggishness; yet as a whole the American exhibit of artworks implied no such attitude. Among the paintings, for example, was Kenyon Cox's full-length frontal rendering of a haughty naked *Diana;* John Singer Sargent's rear view of a half-turned seductive *Egyptian Girl* wearing naught but her hair; F. A. Bridgman's *Day Dreams*, a frontal view of a reclining, suggestive nude; Alexander Harrison's *In Arcadia*, depicting three naked girls in various poses within a sunlit woodland beside a stream. American sculpture, both within the Art Palace and on the buildings and grounds, was replete with nude female figures or male seminudes with uncovered genitalia. Public display of such works might belie American prudishness, especially since there was minimal adverse comment upon these and similar works among the art exhibits of other nations.

Some of those foreign works must be mentioned, even though our focus is upon the American experience of the fair. The World's

Columbian Exposition afforded millions of Americans their first experience, and for many of them their only experience, of the art of foreign nations. And it is interesting that the French and British works were more likely to reveal prudery, that is, strategically placed draperies or grape leaves, than were the American. It is also instructive that one of the foreign works most frequently commented upon by Americans was *The Five Senses* by Austrian artist Hans Makart. This was an enormous screen of five panels, each panel containing a naked, or nearly naked, female figure symbolic of one of the senses. Walton found it undistinguished. But a historian of the fair referred to it as the "most striking work in the [Austrian] collection."[31] One of the photographic collections popular with fairgoers included the observation, "If not very sensitive, the scantily draped or half-averted figures are at least of much sensual fleshiness."[32] In any event, the distinctive quality of some of the foreign art exhibits is of more moment than the question of prudery. For the Americans the exhibition of French art should have been especially interesting, because so many of our own artists had studied in France and because French art had an exalted reputation. As William A. Coffin viewed the exhibit, in sculpture at least, only the Americans and French were represented. "The other nations, it may be noted here, present scarcely anything of value." Though the exhibit of French paintings fell below the merit of the retrospective exhibit at Paris in 1889, Coffin found their sculptural works redeeming.[33] Yet the French exhibit largely proved a disappointment.

The list of painters whose works hung in the French section contains only a handful of durable names. For the exhibit represented chiefly the attitudes of the French Academy. France displayed oil paintings that were technically proficient, grandly executed, and broadly sterile. Considering that this exhibit had educative significance for the American public and especially for native painters who had not studied or traveled abroad, France here provided a lesson that was probably better not learned. "The paintings were thoroughly representative of the different methods and manners of the French school, but in quality they were not as good a representation as the English and German."[34] The latter conclusion was apt, but the former was quite mistaken and certainly reveals how uninformed the American public was regarding French Impressionism. Moreover, John C. Van Dyke, critic and art historian at Rutgers, observed, "Parisian ideas and notions of art may be better than our own, but the point is, they are not our own, and if we repeat them, we are . . . imitating, and not creating." Gallicisms would only impede the creation of distinctly American art of the sort best represented in the works of Homer, Inness, Homer Martin.[35] In this instance Van Dyke's warning, however chauvinistic it may sound, was deserved. The French display of sculpture was, happily, more valuable, as it contained works by Rodin, Cain, Barrias, Gérôme, the latter represented by his famous *Pygmalion and Galatea*, which actually belonged to Charles T. Yerkes and appeared in the American loan collection. Walton found most of the remaining sculptural works not very deserving. For one thing, "The nude figures of the size of life are bewildering in number and somewhat monotonous in their uniform technical excellence."[36] None of them, he argued, could surpass Houdon's *Diana*, seen in the historic collection. He concluded, rather enigmatically, "The development of a culture for art in these United States owes so much to France, so very many of those painters and sculptors who strive to contribute to the building up of the American school have derived both their training and their enlightenment from those hospitable shores, that it will not be without a certain grief that the passing of the sceptre of Art from her hands will be viewed by the younger nation."[37] Apparently Walton anticipated a future American supremacy in art. Given the contrast in quality between the American and French exhibits, his anticipation was understandable.

Numerous other nations were well represented in the Art Palace—Austria, Belgium, Brazil, Great Britain, Italy, Spain, Norway, Sweden, Denmark, Holland. Probably the most unusual exhibit for Americans was Japan's. Though parts of America were familiar with oriental arts or crafts, it is doubtful that many citizens had seen such a representative collection of Japanese work assembled in one place. So alien was this art to Western tradition that many commentators only gave it passing reference. But its presence was of obvious significance. "Japan, whose people never made a display in the art section of an exposition before, gives one of the most unique displays in Chicago. It includes paintings in oil and water-colors on canvas, wood and silk, metal work, wood and ivory carving, tapestries, embroidery, lacquer work, enamel, and porcelain wares." Since the Japanese art was so different from Western art, Halsey Ives had graciously exempted it from the requirements of the classifications. "The result is that the Emperor permitted a display of works never seen out of his country before. In delicacy, coloring and novelty these works are unexcelled and attract constant interest."[38]

Of the other exhibits probably that of most interest was the Russian one. The Russians shared with the United States, France, and Germany the distinction of being among the largest exhibitors at the fair. The Russians had been scarcely evident at previous expositions. Here they ranked third, after France and Germany, in the amount of funds appropriated. Czar Alexander III had decreed that all expenses of the exhibitors—transportation, insurance, installation, management—should be paid out of imperial funds.[39] Russian exhibits throughout the fairgrounds constituted what Walton termed a contribution that "is one of the most worthy of an international exposition that may here be seen."[40] The catalog of Russian artworks is twenty-three pages long, with comments on what were considered subjects needing explanation. The exhibit contained over 100 paintings but only sixteen sculptural works. "Many of the finest paintings of the exhibition were in this section, notably those of Makovsky and Verestchagin, as well as the scenes from the life of Columbus by Awazovosky."[41] Russian works were almost entirely given to what was known in some circles as storytelling. They were largely hieratic, imitative, stylized. As Walton concluded, it was in their industrial and decorative arts, rather than in their fine arts, that the traditions and native art of Russia could best be seen.[42] Modern Russian artists were trying to recover a naturalistic quality while preserving the traditional, and the results were not very inspiring. "It is very possible," Walton said, "that the period of unrest and transition through which the whole nation is believed to be passing may be also characteristic of its art, and that these camera-like studies of man and nature may be but the precursors of a somewhat higher and more imaginative art."[43] That was not to be the case, for in 1894 the last Czar of all the Russias, Nicholas II, would come to the throne. But here at the exposition at least the emperor managed a beneficient, if not very imposing, display of Russian artistic achievement. That display provided Americans with some meager insight into the enigma of Russia. The potential virtue of such insight, and of exposure to the artworks of so many other foreign nations, was that "not only school predilections, but even those innate predispositions which inhere in race and temperament, relax their grasp upon our spirits, and, freed for the moment from their own tyranny, the universal in them, more than the Anglo-Saxon or the individual, speaks."[44] If this international exhibit could serve the purpose of revealing the catholicity and universality of art, then, however mediocre parts of it may have been, its causes and effects would be unqualifiedly worthy.

Anyone who had absorbed the impact of the White City and had traipsed the many galleries of the Art Palace could justifiably have felt that he had seen enough of the fine arts to last a lifetime. It might have been with a sense of relief that he thereafter sought out the seemingly more mundane exhibits of machines, electrical contrivances, and agricultural products found in other buildings. Yet which exhibit the earnest fairgoer might have journeyed to next would involve a difficult decision. There were, besides the fine arts, eleven classifications of exhibits: agriculture; horticulture; livestock; fish and fisheries; mines, mining, and metallurgy; machinery; transportation; manufactures; electricity; liberal arts; ethnology, archaeology, etc. But within each of these there were numerous subclassifications—118 altogether in Department A, Agriculture; 122 in Department E, Mines, Mining & Metallurgy; 213 in Department H, Manufactures.[45] Artist J. A. Mitchell sighed, "To visit the Fair with profit or comfort you must leave your sense of duty behind. . . . Where other exhibitions have been satisfied with a display of an hundred cubic feet of any special article, Chicago must have at least an acre. . . . This means for the visitor more steps, more fatigue, more confusion, more time, and more money."[46]

As with our own brief overview of the exhibits, the fairgoer could not see everything; but he might choose at least to see the big things. In that case he would visit the Agricultural Building where "one is reduced relatively to about the size of a rat before a monster cheese weighing 22,000 pounds." The cheese was made in Canada. Nearby the rat-perspective could be reinforced by standing beside "a temple thirty-eight feet high, made of 30,000 pounds of chocolate." Having savored these two exhibits, the fairgoer would certainly want to see, in the Mines and Mining Building, "the largest nugget of gold in existence, the Maitland Bar nugget, which weighs 344.78 ounces, contains 313 ounces of fine gold, and has a value of $6,000." In Machinery Hall he could examine the Westinghouse electric lighting plant, the largest such installation in the world. And over in the Forestry Building, designed by Charles B. Atwood and located on the Lake Front well to the south of the Agricultural Building, the fairgoer might rub a thumb along "the largest plank in existence . . . a finely finished piece of California redwood sixteen feet five inches wide, twelve feet nine inches long and five inches thick." Here also was a cross section of a redwood tree whose rings revealed it was six and a half feet thick when Columbus discovered America. Northward from here along the Lake Front, past the Leather Exhibit Building, the fairgoer would come to one of the most popular exhibits at the fair. Here stood the building of the Krupp gun works, reminiscent of a feudal castle with its turrets, towers, and bartizans. And in this building the visitor could see "the much-talked-of greatest gun of the age, a 120-ton rifled gun, sixteen inch calibre and forty-six feet in length. . . . It is said to be able to throw a projectile weighing one ton a distance of twenty miles."[47] This was the largest cannon in the world and its projectiles were able to pierce the heaviest armor of any extant ship. The Krupp ordnance display, a collection of cannons, armor plates, and shells so large as to require this special building, was worth $1.5 million.[48] This menacing exhibit, so popular with the crowds, was surely an anomaly in the midst of the White City.

If the fairgoer still remained perplexed about what exhibits to devote his time to, he could refer to guide books. One was *The "Time-Saver"; A Book Which Names and Locates 5,000 Things at the World's Fair*. This convenient pocket guide provided a simple critical key: 1 Interesting, 2 Very Interesting, 3 Remarkably Interesting. Thus the fairgoer might simply choose to see only those things awarded a 3. He would have been spared much walking. For example, not a single painting in the American exhibit in the Art Palace was "Remarkably interesting." Even *The Flagellants* received a mere 2. On the other hand, the great Krupp cannon was among the threes.[49] With or without such a guide in hand, the fairgoer was quite likely to have entered the Manufactures and Liberal Arts Building, if only to say he had been inside the largest building in the world. There he would have found exhibits sufficient to do justice to any average international exposition. Varied structures representing nations, manufacturers, and other exhibitors lined the walkways within the building. The great length of the Manufactures Building, running north and south, was traversed by Columbia Avenue, a fifty-foot wide thoroughfare. At the middle of the building this avenue was crossed by another one fifty feet wide which connected the east and west portals. If a fairgoer were to enter from the south entrance, "his impression will be that he is . . . visiting a city of palaces, temples, castles, arches, monuments, and hanging gardens. But his eye will necessarily be drawn toward a beautiful structure in the center of the building. . . . The great central landmark, looking like the spire of a cathedral in alabaster, is the clock tower, 135 feet high." The tower clock contained a face and dials on each of its Columbia Avenue sides and a chime of nine bells. "When they ring it sounds like the music of heaven reverberating through the immense spaces of the building."[50]

Along Columbia Avenue were display areas for the United States, Japan, Austria, Germany, Great Britain, Canada, Denmark, Brazil, Switzerland, Holland, Italy, Spain, Norway, Russia, Belgium, and France. Smaller areas off of the avenue were reserved to Jamaica, India, China, Mexico, Persia, the Argentine Republic, Ceylon, Korea, Monaco, Siam, Turkey, New South Wales, Bulgaria, and Portugal. Towering over the exhibition sites at the north end of Columbia Avenue was the gigantic Yerkes Telescope, the gift of Charles T. Yerkes to the University of Chicago. Overhead in the gallery surrounding the building were still other areas for exhibits of some of the same nations, book publishers, architectural firms, schools, and universities. The United States section occupied the entire northeast quarter of the ground floor and a large part of the northwest quarter. Its exhibits included chemical and pharmaceutical products; paints, colors, dyes, and varnishes; typewriters, paper, stationery; furniture; ceramics and mosaics; art metal work; glass and glassware, stained glass; jewelry; clothing; rubber goods; toys; leather goods; lighting appliances; hardware; plumbing materials; refrigerators; and enough other items to fill an entire page.[51] Perhaps the most interesting display was that of decorative furnishings, which had wide popular and aesthetic appeal. As one account said of the entire American section, "The most striking exhibit here is the pavilion erected by Tiffany, the jeweler, and Gorham, the silversmith, both of New York."[52] It contained the incomparable ornamental pieces and stained glass objects of the famed Louis C. Tiffany, such as the golden, luxuriant Magnolia Vase. The most remarkable work was a complete chapel designed by Tiffany in a Romanesque style. Its various parts—altar, reredos, retables, arches—were composed of hundreds of thousands of colorful mosaic glass particles. "During the Exposition one million four hundred thousand persons visited this chapel, which won the encomiums of all American and foreign art critics and ecclesiastics."[53] The Tiffany Pavilion was without doubt the highlight of the American exhibition of manufactures.

Other nations having large exhibition areas in the building were Germany, Great Britain, France, and Russia. The German pavilion was noted for the elaborate wrought iron which, in sections, formed the pavilion's boundary. Some thought it a more fitting subject for pride than the monster Krupp cannon, since "it is an admirable exhibit, and in perfection of workmanship, flowing lines, graceful curves, and . . . high art, is probably on a par with the best specimens of iron-work that have ever been forged."[54] The pavilion of Great Britain was attractive to fairgoers because it contained an exact reproduction of the dining room at the famous Elizabethan-era Hatfield House and because it exhibited England's famous chinawares—Royal Worcester, Doulton, Wedgewood, Minton. The French pavilion sported a large archway entrance under which stood the statue *La France* and above which was a decorated half dome. Its much admired facade was flamboyant with columns, entablatures, terms, moldings. One commentary, referring to Hippolyte Taine's belief that a nation's characteristics are always seen in its artworks, remarked, "In no exhibit at the Exposition is his theory more plainly shown than in the beauty of the exterior of the French pavilion which is a triumph of Aesthetic Art. . . . In comparison how cold and gloomy seems the Russian pavilion beyond, with its round arches, suggestive of prostration and prayer."[55] Even so, a visit within the Russian pavilion was rewarding. Unable to construct a log structure in the area of foreign buildings as planned, the Russians had contented themselves with a massive Byzantine-style pavilion in the Manufactures Building. Into it they compressed an elaborate display of manufactures. The most enticing was a series of bronze miniatures. "The Russian bronzes," wrote one observer, "were an unending source of wondering delight. They were rustic groups and animal pieces, telling stories of Russian outdoor life and rural toils, hardships, humor, and pleasures with perfect naturalness, accuracy, and interest."[56] There were items of curiosity, artistic merit, or mechanical ingenuity on display within the exhibition sections of each of the other nations represented, but their manifold numbers forbid mention. Suffice it to say that wherever an American visitor might have wandered among the exhibits in the Manufactures Building he would willy-nilly be experiencing, if not a revelation, at least an education. Never before had "such an opportunity been presented of comparing the relative progress of manufacturing industries among European, American, and Asiatic nations, together with their inventive genius, whether in the direction of labor-saving appliances or of improvements in quality and design."[57]

Any visitor who was interested in progressive industries would most certainly have paid a visit to the Electricity Building. In the words of one observer, "there is no place where the crowds go so early and so often and linger so long" as to this building.[58] The purpose of the exhibit here was not merely to demonstrate the working of electrical apparatus, but to present a facile history of electricity, including inventions of Thomas Edison: the phonograph, incandescent light bulbs, the kinetograph. All the exhibitors were private firms, some of them archrivals. The major part of the exhibit was the machinery and devices for generating and using electrical power; "but probably the most interesting, certainly the most beautiful, exhibit in the building is the Edison Tower of Light, built by the Phoenix Glass Company. From a colonnade thirty feet in diameter rises a shaft seventy-eight feet high studded with thousands of electric lamps. . . , with different colored globes arranged so that they will flash in various designs and colors." This tower was a reproduction of the German Tower of Victory in Berlin. It was topped off by a huge incandescent lamp made of pieces of cut glass.[59] The General Electric Company was responsible for the lighting. Demonstrations of the tower's lighting effects were greeted with enthusiasm. Not to be outdone, the rival Western Electric Company had erected an Egyptian temple, with

German gates in Manufactures Building

Courtesy of the Chicago Historical Society

friezes and other decorations, in which to display its wares: annunciators, drill presses, telephone and telegraph apparatus.[60] It was, however, in mechanisms such as electric motors, convertors, transformers, voltmeters, and dynamos, largely the products of General Electric and Westinghouse Electric, that the true significance of the harnessing of electrical energy lay. It was generally impossible for visitors to comprehend that significance merely by studying the machines. But the outdoor displays of lighting generated from this building made the point. "To the majority of Exposition sight-seers," wrote Bancroft, " . . . the illumination of grounds and buildings, of fountains and waterways . . . [forms] a more striking illustration of the wonders wrought by this science than any mere collection of machinery could."[61] Part of that illumination was provided by the largest searchlight in the world, a ten and a half foot high, 6,000 pound behemoth manufactured by General Electric.[62] Of this illumination primarily and the many uses of electricity generally America's Minister to Russia, Murat Halstead, wrote, "The Fair, considered as an electrical exposition only, would be well worthy of the attention of the world. . . . It is all an electrical exhibit. . . . The energy that drives is stored electricity."[63] Nearly everything that glowed, that sounded, that moved at the fair was powered by electricity. The man in charge of this department, John P. Barrett, declared rightly that at this exposition "electricity seems undoubtedly to have made a stride almost suddenly, that placed it at least abreast of the sister sciences, arts and industries, and demonstrated at once that for all time it was to take precedence of, when not ministering to, all the other commercial industries."[64] Electrical power at the World's Columbian Exposition was the largest, most imposing, most eloquent expression of energy in the entire Age of Energy. It foretold the coming supremacy of electricity in American life and industry.

Electricity in large part made possible the contents of Machinery Hall. The *Official Guide* to the fair pointedly stated, "The Centennial exposition created an epoch in Machinery exhibits at International Fairs. Compared with the Centennial the Columbian exhibit is full of surprises." Star of the Centennial had been the great Corliss engine. In 1876 Corliss was America's only manufacturer of engines. In 1893 there were sixty such firms.[65] The vast extent of the exhibits in Machinery Hall was, then, less of a surprise than it was a testimonial to rapid and monumental change. "In 79 groups and nearly 200 classes of exhibits is here represented almost every mechanical device fashioned by the ingenuity of man. There is machinery for the transmission of power . . .; there are machinery and appliances for the manufacture of textile fabrics, for the preparation of various articles of food, for type-setting, printing, binding, stamping, embossing, and other branches of book and newspaper work; there are machines, apparatus, and tools for lithography, color printing, photo-mechanical and other mechanical processes of illustrating; for working metals, minerals, and woods. Finally there is a collection of fire engines and fire extinguishing appliances."[66] No thoughtful person who wandered among the rows of mechanical devices in Machinery Hall could fail to comprehend that the age of the machine was consummated. Cornell professor Robert H. Thurston declared, "at Chicago, the product of the inventive genius . . . was made shrine as well as monument; and all the world went there to admire, if not to worship, the material evidences of the culmination of an era of triumphs in every department of invention, construction, and engineering achievement."[67]

It is probable that these various exhibits were the most significant of all in their reflection of or influence upon popular and critical values, tastes, and expectations, although certainly, by the same token, the displays in the Transportation Building were significant. After all, here too one could see the evidences of man's rapid material progress, for here was exhibited the history of transportation from the invention of the wheel to the steam locomotive. And no one would dare gainsay the profound impact of the locomotive upon nineteenth-century American life. This was the railroad age. Nor could anyone deny the popularity of the transportation exhibit. "The displays in this building seem to come closer to the interests of everyone than do most of the others, and the greatest crowd is usually found herein."[68] This exhibit, moreover, held a special lesson for American visitors. The effect of transportation upon our lives "should always be in mind, and it should never be forgotten that America has been the leader in the invention and improvement and adoption of appliances to be utilized for these purposes."[69] One might very well have learned here the true import of America's ready adaptation to new means of transport and her rapid expansion of railroads. "How Darwin would gloat over the transportation exhibit! . . . Whether or not the doctrine of evolution applies to man, there is no question that it applies to the works of man. . . . From the original 'Rocket' and 'Meteor' locomotives with their stove boilers and barrels of water on wheel-barrow tenders to the 130-ton locomotives capable of a speed of 100 miles an hour is an object lesson seen here in a moment, but it compasses the experiences and best work of hundreds of thousands during their lifetime."[70] In a matter of a mere forty years the locomotive had developed from primitive beginning to high-speed steam propulsion. It was a prime example of mechanical progress telescoped.

Similar innovations might have been witnessed in some of the exhibits of the Mines and Mining Building and the Agricultural Building. It seems likely, however, that mining, here honored for the first time at any exposition by having its own building, was actually being thus recognized as a vitally important adjunct to the other and more immediately important enterprises of machinery, electricity, and transportation—none of which could have existed without the products of mining. The mining exhibits were infrequently visited. It is hard to muster enthusiasm for large collections of ores, minerals, and fuels, though diamonds and gold nuggets have their appeal. Visitors might have been discouraged, though intrigued, by the heavy-handed morality inherent in an unusual life-size representation of "Lot's Wife" carved from a huge block of rock salt.[71] The truth is, however, that the single exhibit in the Mines and Mining Building to receive the most comment had only a secondary relation to mining. The famous statue of *Justice* in Montana's exhibit, seven feet high and astride the back of an eagle, was made of pure silver—hence its relation to mining. But the reasons for its fame were two, and neither referred to mining or its products. This rendering of Justice was the first one in history to show that admirable lady with her eyes open and the model who posed for sculptor R. H. Park was none other than the famous actress Ada Rehan of Augustin Daly's company.[72] As for the agricultural exhibits, though they encompassed four separate buildings—Agricultural, Forestry, Dairy, and Live Stock—and though agriculture's significance to the welfare of America was thereby duly recognized, they were not nearly so appealing as the beautiful palace that formed their main exhibition hall. Typical were displays of sugar, canned goods, bee culture, food products, farm implements, tobacco, and various cereal grains. There were also some curious exhibits. Among them was a huge columnar construction of bottled beer from Denver which was rather strikingly suggestive of the future Empire State Building. Maybe beer manufacturers had learned something from the "Chicago style."

Exhibits in the other major buildings at the fair merit some reference. The luxuriant floral and botanical displays in the Horticultural Building provided a welcome refuge for fatigued fairgoers; the Fisheries Building contained exotic forms of marine life; the United States Government Building provided the largest government-sponsored exhibit at any exposition, an exhibit of national and historical interest. But the remaining major building whose exhibits commanded unusual attention was the Woman's Building. In this case the importance inhered not so much in the nature of the exhibits themselves, about which there was little that was extraordinary, as in the significance of both the building and the exhibits to American women and to the general public. "The one essential point of vantage possessed by the present World's Fair," wrote Bertha Honoré Palmer, "has indeed been from the beginning the prominence of women in the making of it. Not merely as contributors to the marvelous display of genius and skill in its

207

many grand divisions, but as a recognized executive factor."[73] Women took personal interest and pride in this recognition and achievement.

The significance and honor bestowed upon woman's roles and achievements were clearly revealed in the special ceremonies that marked the official dedication of the Woman's Building on May 1. The occasion unfortunately created some ill will. A few malcontents were upset that Bertha Palmer had not chosen them for the Committee on Ceremonies because they were thereby excluded from joining the illustrious ones on the platform. Bertha Palmer was supported by all the members of the Board, except Phoebe Couzins, "who is a hopeless case." Palmer endured some shrewish remarks with dignity and precluded further challenges to her leadership.[74] The episode became a *succès de scandale* in the press. But Bertha Palmer had triumphed and she took her place with the other distinguished women on the platform: the duchess of Veragua, Lady Aberdeen, Princess Mary A. Schakovsky from Russia, Mrs. Adlai E. Stevenson, Mrs. John P. Altgeld, Mrs. Linchee Suruja of Siam, Baroness Thornburg Rappe of Sweden, Frau Professor von Kasetowsky from Germany, and others. Theodore Thomas and the orchestra and chorus provided music—a grand march composed by Frau Ingeborg von Brousart of Weimar. An ode was read. Then Palmer incisively and stirringly advocated the liberation of woman. She also extolled the exposition as a benefit to women, "not alone by means of the material objects brought together, but there will be a more lasting and permanent result through the interchange of thought and sympathy from influential and leading women of all countries, now, for the first time, working together with a common purpose and an established means of communication."[75] The means of communication were the boards of lady managers in the various nations participating in the exposition. The common purpose was summarized by Palmer: "The absence of a just and general appreciation of the truth concerning the position and status of women has caused us to call special attention to it, and to make a point of attempting to create, by means of the Exposition, a well-defined public sentiment in regard to their rights and duties, and the propriety of their becoming not only self-supporting, but able to assist in maintaining their families when necessary."[76] Thus the building and the exhibits, however beautiful or interesting, were really adjuncts to the furtherance of woman's status.

They should have fulfilled that purpose well. The Woman's Building contained thousands of artworks, handicrafts, and other products of woman's industry from nations throughout the world. Bancroft may have best defined the overriding meaning of these various exhibits in speaking of one of them which he felt thoughtful visitors would find most interesting: "a retrospective collection, from pre-historic eras to the age in which we live, the contributions made by women to the huge workshop of which this world so largely consists, their contributions not only to the industries of the world but to its sciences and arts. Thus it is hoped in a measure to dispel the prejudices and misconceptions, to remove the vexatious restrictions and limitations which for centuries have held enthralled the sex."[77] Such an exhibit clearly revealed that women had actually originated most of the industrial arts, had developed the construction and maintenance of homes, had prepared all kinds of edibles, invented sewing and textile devices, initiated the molding of pots and the making of baskets, and been responsible for numerous other inventions. These exhibits, the Woman's Building, and the involvement of women in all phases of the fair meant that this exposition marked a recognition of woman's rights. At the time, however, it was advocated, even by Bertha Palmer, that woman's primary role was as mother and homemaker. The point was underscored by the fact that the Board of Lady Managers secured the erection of a Children's Building adjoining their own building. Though it was intended mainly as a nursery, the Children's Building included a series of exhibits, "displaying the best of our nineteenth century methods of rearing and training children."[78] Thus was confirmed woman's presumptive major role as mother.

Other special days of celebration similar to the ceremonies that marked the opening of the Woman's Building were held during the fair. There were, for example, fete days devoted to Norway, Denmark, Maine, Nebraska, Germany, Massachusetts, Brooklyn, France, the Irish, designed in large part to acknowledge the contributions of various countries and ethnic groups to the development of the United States. One such day, notable as a tribute to America's most ignored minority, was Colored People's Day, August 25. "The dignified observance of this day, and the high standard of music and oratory with which its celebration was distinguished did honor to the Afro-American race." Afternoon exercises in Festival Hall included recitations, musical selections, and a speech by Frederick Douglass on "The Race Problem in America." Paul Dunbar delivered a poem, the Jubilee Singers presented plantation songs and Negro melodies, and selections were given from Will M. Cook's opera of *Uncle Tom's Cabin*.[79] Other special days which, in effect, honored blacks were those devoted to Liberia and Haiti. These, however, were no more resplendent than the days honoring butchers and grocers, the merchant tailors, the foresters, and amateur athletes. The day devoted to Chicago, October 9, was the grand climax of the exposition, attracting over three quarters of a million people to the fairgrounds. If anything Chicago Day was more elaborate, with music, speeches, fireworks, floats, than the dedicatory ceremonies of the fair.[80] But no city or segment of the populace could claim such honor as was forthcoming from the mere existence of the Woman's Building.

In the environs of the Great Basin near the Agricultural Building was another structure that attracted many fairgoers. It was an exact reproduction of the Convent of La Rabida, where Columbus had taken refuge before finally securing from Queen Isabella the sponsorship of his voyage of discovery. "Inside the Convent are found some of the most valuable relics of the Exposition, comprising illustrations of the life history of Columbus, with relics of the court of Ferdinand and Isabella."[81] This building and exhibit were under the jurisdiction of the Ethnology Department whose central locale was the Anthropological Building, but its exhibits were spread throughout the grounds and included such things as a reproduction of a cliff-dwellers village, an Eskimo village, and a Viking ship which floated in the South Pond. But for students of Columbus, who after all was supposed to be the central figure in this great celebrative affair, the Ethnological Department exhibits most worthy of attention, besides the Convent, were the reproductions of Columbus's three caravels, the Niña, the Pinta, and the Santa María. These reproductions, built in Spanish naval yards, were moored on the Lake Front near the Convent. By this time, however, rather than walk another step, the fairgoer might have preferred to circle the fairgrounds riding on the Intramural Railway or to treat himself to a non-stroll upon the movable sidewalk, which could carry him and 5,609 other persons to the end of the Casino Pier at a rate of six miles per hour, at the cost of a five-cent ticket.[82] More restful still would have been a trip around the Wooded Island in a canopied gondola. That trip would have brought the fairgoer to the vicinity of the state and foreign buildings.

Most of the state buildings were primarily intended simply as managerial headquarters, but some of them contained impressive exhibits. The most lavish and extensive of these was the Illinois State Building, which dominated the north end of the lagoon. At its entranceway stood a whimsical sculpture depicting the child's game of blindman's buff. The exhibits within the building constituted a miniature exposition, given up to such things as horticulture, geology, education, agriculture, archaeology, fisheries, and women's works.[83] Naturally the city of Chicago was prominently featured. In one of the halls, for example, the city was represented with 125 canvases painted by the women artists of the Chicago Palette Club.[84]

Other state buildings that justified at least a brief visit included those of California, New York, Florida, Pennsylvania, and Virginia. The Virginia State Building contained a replica of Mount

Vernon furnished with antiques and eighteenth-century relics. The Florida State Building had a reproduction of Saint Augustine's famous Spanish fortress, Fort Marion. The central architectural feature of the Pennsylvania State Building was a replication of the clock tower of Independence Hall. Inside were various old documents and the Liberty Bell. (In commemoration of the exposition, the New Liberty Bell was cast, its cost paid through gifts, and placed near the Administration Building. It was rung on special occasions.) Perhaps to assuage their disappointment that New York City was not chosen as the site of the exposition, New York erected one of the largest and most expensive of the state buildings. Measuring 214 feet in length and 142 feet in width, this modified replica of the old Van Rensselaer house was replete with sumptuous decorations. The entrance contained sculptures, two of them representing Henry Hudson and Christopher Columbus, done by the well-known Olin Warner. The interior contained a large loggia with a grand staircase and mural decorations. The second floor was also decorated with murals, the major one, a ceiling panel, having been painted by Frank Millet. On the building's roof was an attractive garden. The California State Building, next in size to Illinois's, also had a roof garden. And its interior was filled with exhibits of the products of California: minerals, canned goods, fruits. Perhaps the most curious of these exhibits was Santa Barbara's fifty-foot high obelisk of bottles of olive oil, which was even more strikingly reminiscent of the Empire State Building than Denver's beer bottle tower. Here also was an exhibit of wines, but the most spectacular of such exhibits was a large fountain that gurgled real wine which California provided to the viticulture section in the Horticultural Building.

In the same general area, on the Lake Shore near the North Pond, rose the buildings of various nations. Of these some were more enticing than others. Primary among the former was the German Government Building, "the most substantial and much the handsomest on the lake shore."[85] It was an extraordinary hodgepodge of eclectic designs, "none of which, however, contrast too violently."[86] According to one description the German Building represented the architectural transition from the renaissance to the Columbian period and it was a composite of Gothic, Nuremberg, and modern German styles. The center of the building was in the form of a richly decorated chapel.[87] Americans apparently found the building beautiful and its interior, rich with pillars, balconies, and ornamentation, even more so. Here could be seen exhibits of the German publishers and of relics of Bismarck and Von Moltke. Equally charming, it seems, and certainly idiosyncratic, were the buildings of Norway, a peaked and gabled model of an old Viking Stavkirke, and of Sweden, a large picturesque edifice in that nation's sixteenth-century style. Both of these buildings were originally erected in their native lands and then dismantled and shipped to Chicago for reconstruction. Both also contained arts and manufactures of their native artisans and at the Swedish building a visitor could rest at an outdoor table beneath the trees and sip a beer from "the Venice of the North," Stockholm.

Of the other European buildings at the fair the two most notable were those of England and France. England was represented by the Victoria House. This was a substantial structure, "the first story being of red brick and heavy terra cotta trimmings, and the second of interlaced timbers of a style that was common in the time of Henry VIII."[88] The sumptuous interior was reserved mostly for the use of England's commissioners. Near to Victoria House was the pretentious neoclassical beaux-arts style French Building. It consisted of two pavilions connected by a semicircular colonnade which enclosed an attractive lawn and a bronze fountain. In one of the pavilions were exhibited relics and mementos of Lafayette. And in the other, the south pavilion, "were displayed objects that interested the largest number of visitors, as it was a veritable rogues' gallery, wherein were shown portraits of famous criminals, and the methods employed to identify them by Paris police authorities."[89] The Spanish Building, as befitted the occasion, was a replica of a section of the silk exchange at Valencia which had been begun in 1492. "The section shown represents the column hall and the tower wherein all defaulting and bankrupt merchants were confined." It contained few exhibits and was occupied mainly by members of the Spanish commission.[90]

Perhaps the most interesting of all the foreign buildings, and certainly the most exotic, were those of the Asian nations. Primary among these was the Japanese Building. Japan expended more funds for her participation at the fair than most of the other foreign lands. Central to her participation was the Ho-o-den, facsimile of a celebrated temple built in 1052. It presumably sparked Frank Lloyd Wright's lifelong interest in Japanese architecture. "The structure takes the form of a great temple in three parts, a main body and two wings, symbolizing the phoenix." Nothing could have been more appropriate to the city that had arisen out of the ashes of its own Great Fire of 1871. Japan had arranged that the Ho-o-den be given to Chicago, subject to the provisions that the building and its gardens be maintained and that one room be set aside for displays of Japanese art.[91] Chicago was pleased and obliged. Tiny Ceylon sent her own workmen, as Japan did, to erect a pavilion that proved to be a popular attraction. This was a Dravidian style building, after the architecture of Ceylon's ancient temples. It contained a large central hall whose ceiling was supported by two dozen elaborately carved pillars. "Colossal figures of Buddha and Vishnu were placed on opposite sides of the hall, while those of a Buddhist priest, of a Veddah and his wife, and of a Kandyan chief were placed at intervals." Elsewhere throughout the building were exhibits of teas, minerals, and various products.[92] The novelty this building afforded, of introducing fairgoers to the culture of a distant and non-Christian land, might well explain its appeal. In similar fashion, visitors could imbibe some of the flavor of the Ottoman Empire's culture in the Turkish Building, which was filled with samples of nearly all that nation's products and resources. This structure was "in imitation of the Hunkhar Casque, or fountain, of Sultan Ahmed II, in Constantinople." Unlike most of the other foreign buildings, which were designed by native architects, the Turkish Building was

Building of Sweden

Courtesy of the Chicago Historical Society

the work of an obscure Chicago architect named J. A. Thain.[93]
Nearer to the American consciousness and significant to Columbus's discovery, were the nations of South and Central America.
Brazil, Colombia, and Venezuela had their own buildings filled
with exhibits, as did Costa Rica and Guatemala. Representative of
the West Indies was the building of the Republic of Haiti, which,
since Haiti supposedly had no native style of architecture, was
designed in a southern colonial style. The building was dedicated
on January 2, 1893, the nineteenth anniversary of Haitian independence. It contained paintings, portraits, and busts—among the
latter, one of Frederick Douglass—mementos of Toussaint L'Ouverture, and one of the anchors lost from the Santa María, which
was shipwrecked off the north coast of the island during Columbus's second voyage in December 1493. Otherwise central to
Haiti's exhibit was coffee.[94]

Such were the exemplary foreign and state buildings which
completed the main environs of the fair. They could hardly have
been expected to arouse people's interest quite to the extent that
the Court of Honor did, and yet they were integral to the grounds,
purposes, and nature of the White City as a whole. The desired
international flavor that they contributed to the exposition was
enhanced by the pleasures and atmosphere of the Midway Plaisance. The Midway Plaisance was an avenue 600 feet wide and a
mile in length which connected Jackson Park with Washington
Park; it lay between Fifty-ninth and Sixtieth streets and extended
westward from a point directly behind the Woman's Building.[95]
Its features were privately sponsored, though they constituted a
sanctioned part of the exposition. The character of the Midway
was distinctly exotic, polyglot, cosmopolitan, festal. Regardless of
the weather, the Midway was always crowded. It was "a side show
pure and simple. But side shows are interesting, and to many
hundreds of thousands of people who have not been afforded the
opportunity of seeing how other hundreds of thousands live, the
Midway Plaisance is amusing, interesting and instructive."[96] It was
a phantasmagoria of Irish villages, a South Sea Islands village, a

The Midway Plaisance

Courtesy of the Chicago Historical Society

Java village, German and Turkish villages, a Street in Cairo, a Moorish Palace, a Vienna cafe, an Algerian and Tunisian village, an Austrian village, a Dahomey village, and a score of other attractions.[97] "Here was an opportunity to see these people of every hue, clad in outlandish garb, living in curious habitations, and plying their unfamiliar trades and arts with incomprehensible dexterity; to listen to their barbaric music and witness their heathenish dances, their acrobatic feats, and curious theatrical spectacles. There were three thousand of these denizens of the Midway gathered from all quarters of the earth, many of them led thither by the hope of gain, and many influenced still more by the desire to visit this wondrous land."[98] In short, here from forty-eight nations of the earth had assembled men and women who desired to visit the United States and to huckster goods and gull Americans on the very soil where Barnumism flourished.

Upon entering the Midway, the fairgoer saw to his left the Blarney Castle erected by Irish industries and to his right the building of the International Dress Costume Company which housed the so-called Beauty Show where girls paraded in the costumes of their native lands. Though the Beauty Show was quite respectable, those familiar with burlesque might have suspected otherwise from the wording of the marquee: "40 Ladies from 40 Nations: World's Congress of Beauties."[99] Inside, however, the forty ladies kept their clothes on; the show was the clothing, not the ladies. Still, one observer had it that the American girls at least were "boldly genuine, and their good looks and big eyes have in them memories of that district that New York calls the Tenderloin. But the costumes are handsome, picturesque, and geographically correct."[100] That peculiar admixture of the dubious, the picturesque, and the handsome characterized most of the Midway exhibits.

Further along the Midway one passed the Irish Village, the Japanese Bazaar, and the Hagenbeck Animal Show. Of these the Irish Village seemed most appealing, as it featured a half-size reproduction of Donegal Castle, filled with Irish art, a reproduction of a tenth-century round tower, and a restaurant and beer garden. Beyond the Japanese Bazaar, where goods from that nation could be purchased, one approached the intriguing Javanese Village—eighty dwellings inhabited by three hundred natives from Java, Sumatra, Borneo, Samoa, Fiji, New Zealand, and the Sandwich Islands. The village had two theatres, featuring "dancing girls, jugglers, medicine men and acrobats."[101] Immediately above this site was the large German Village. It consisted of "a moated castle called the Wasserburg, of the style of the fifteenth century, surrounded by examples of urban and rural architecture of different provinces."[102] It was a place where fairgoers could bide a while listening to a band from the Berlin Philharmonic or one from the German army, while dining on Berlin-style cuisine and quaffing flagons of Bavarian beer. "One feels that he is in Germany every time he visits the German village," said one account.[103] For the confirmed Germanophile there was directly across the Midway a Viennese restaurant and theatre and further up the avenue the Austrian Village. Known as Old Vienna, this village was a replica of part of the Austrian capital as it had appeared in the eighteenth century, with restaurants, theatres, concert gardens, shops. It was "one of the most popular places in the Midway."[104] Less frequented than these attractions were the Lapland, Chinese, Turkish, and Dahomey villages. Doubtless the most curious of these to the American fairgoer was the Dahomey village, described as "the most exclusive and independent of all the exhibits." It contained three buildings, one of them a museum, and a series of huts to house its forty women and sixty men. "The various dances and other ceremonials peculiar to these people are exhibited, and their songs, chants and war cry are given. They also sell unique products of their mechanical skill, such as quaint hand-carved objects, domestic and warlike utensils, etc." In the later months of the fair a placard was placed outside the entrance to the Dahomey village requesting visitors not to ask the villagers about their former custom of cannibalism, since they found such questions annoying.[105] Americans were perhaps still inadequately cosmopolitan,

Coverplate of "Cairo Street Waltz"

Courtesy of the Chicago Historical Society

even with the experience of seeing here what seemed to be the whole world in one locale.

Though the customs of the Dahomey seemed a little bizarre to Americans, they swarmed to another recreation from North Africa—the Arab section of the Midway. "The greatest attraction of all, undoubtedly, is the 'Street of Cairo,' with its 180 men, women and children, theatres, camels, donkeys and dogs."[106] The Street was a generalized representation of the architectural nature of the old city of Cairo. Its charm was its atmosphere. "A glorious achievement in its entirety, a matchless triumph in detail. It is a restored Cairo, in the days of its unimpaired splendor. Its mosque and fountain are transcendently beautiful; the balconies . . . are veritable gems, ornamented as they are with antique Meshrebieh." But what secured the aura of "the liveliest and most picturesque city in the world," here reproduced in miniature, was the throng of native people—Egyptians, Arabs, Nubians, Soudanese—imported to inhabit it.[107] These inhabitants twice daily presented a characteristic street scene, either a wedding procession or a birthday festival, for the visitors' delight. Some of them kept shops where they sold Arabian jewels, brasswork, cloth, perfumes; others served as drivers for camels and donkeys which fairgoers could ride through the teeming street.[108] Fairgoers with religious inclinations could visit the mosque, highlighted by an ornate minaret. Those with an ethnological or historical interest could visit the archaeological exhibits that illustrated Egyptian art: the Tomb of Thi, a monument of the Fifth Dynasty (about 3800 B.C.), the Temple of Luxor of the age of Amenophis III and Rameses II (1800 to 1480 B.C.), the mummies (1700 to 1070 B.C.), and the Tomb of the Sacred Bull, built under the Ptolemies (260 B.C.).[109] Here obviously one could find a profitable education in antiquity.

But most of the visitors to the Street in Cairo were not interested in education so much as they were in entertainment. For within this most popular of all Midway sites nestled a voluptuous theatre, "where are given the wild, weird performances peculiar to the race. . . . The sword dancers, candle dancers, those who perform the *Dans du Ventre* [*sic*], are the bright particular stars of the Egyptian firmament, while the musicians who accompany them are as weird and picturesque as the dancers themselves."[110] Weird, perhaps, but irresistible in ways that created extreme responses, from exuberance to disgust. Some enthusiasts pictured the dancing girls as "splendid specimens of oriental beauty" and their dances as peculiar but skillful and natural.[111] Other spectators had grave doubts about the rhythmic gyrations of Egyptian dance. "No ordinary Western woman looked on these performances with anything but horror, and at one time it was a matter of serious debate in the councils of the Exposition whether the customs of Cairo should be faithfully reproduced, or the morals of the public faithfully protected."[112] The debate seemed anomalous in the city of Chicago; nor was it clear just how the highly skilled artistes were corrupting the morals of America. The source of dispute was the *danse du ventre* performed by an Arabian beauty known as "Little Egypt." "When western officials came to gaze on her rendition of the act by which John the Baptist lost his head, they were sorely perplexed. This dance was undoubtedly the style in Cairo, where our own Western Black Crook amazons would be instantly suppressed. Notwithstanding the indignation of the Board of Lady Managers, the *danse du ventre* proceeded, and though thousands went to see it, they did not go often, for the music was too irritating."[113] Evidently the board did not appreciate either the *danse* or the fact that they need not have witnessed it. Plenty of other visitors welcomed the opportunity to spectate in the Cairo theatre.

For those wearied of the Egyptian theatre by the irritating music, there was similar but more resplendent dancing in the theatre of the Algerian Village next door. Here performed one remarkable girl, the theme of whose dance was love, "but it is the coarse animal passion of the East, not the chaste sentiment of Christian lands. Every motion of her body is in the illustration of her animalism." Prudish American women left the performance outraged, young girls left giggling, men left seeming "to think they had the worth of their money."[114] If they had their doubts, then they might have pursued yet a third chance to exchange money for the privilege of ogling. For nearby was the "Persian Palace of Eros" with its theatre. Here came exclusively male audiences to gape at an Arabian odalisque giving a performance that "should not be permitted in any place of public entertainment." It was, again, the notorious *danse du ventre*, but the girl was quite handsome. "Now she revolves and turns, her face assuming a dreamy smile, her painted eyes half closed, her white teeth showing between lips made redder and fuller by art. Now she begins the contortions that mark all the Oriental dances; her movements are snake-like and vulgar, and she sinks lower and lower, wriggling, twisting, jerking, her face half veiled with her handkerchief, until she almost touches the stage."[115] Perhaps the Board of Lady Managers had cause to fear that John the Baptist lost his head for good reason. The chief Algerian dancing girl was beautiful, mysterious, and popular, "but she was less fascinating to young men visitors . . . than Fatima, of the Persian theatre, who . . . was more lithesome, and executed the *danse du ventre* with a wild abandon that called for repression by the authorities."[116]

Nothing else in the Midway could possibly have competed with the dancing girls or the Street of Cairo, of which it was said, "When the Columbian Exposition shall have become a thing of the past . . . there shall be one spot which will remain brighter than all the rest, . . . its beautiful Cairo Street."[117] That spot has not lingered in memory so long as the White City itself, though it was memorialized in song with William B. Gray's *She Never Saw the Streets of Cairo*, which incorporated the *Hoochie-Coochie*.[118] And it also inspired the *Cairo Street Waltz*. Probably of more enduring historic interest was the exhibit in the Zoopraxographical Hall, just outside the Street of Cairo, where one could examine Eadweard Muybridge's famous and original photographic studies of locomotion, which had influenced the work of Thomas Eakins. But of more immediate interest, and a feature of the Midway that has endured, in one form or another, was that great structure which dominated this entire area of the exposition—the Ferris Wheel. George W. G. Ferris had envisioned his famous wheel years before; but it was not until the Exposition Corporation granted him a concession that he had the chance to recreate his idea in steel. The giant spider web of the Ferris Wheel, facing east and west along the Midway, was modeled after the structural principles of the bicycle wheel and run by two 1,000 horsepower reversible engines. It was 250 feet in diameter, 825 feet in circumference, and 30 feet wide and was raised another 15 feet above ground.[119] The wheel contained 36 pendulum cars each able to hold 40 passengers, so that it could carry a total of 1440. Each of these cars was 27 feet long, 13 feet wide, 9 feet high; constructed of wood and iron; paneled with plate glass windows; furnished with swivel chairs. The entire structure weighed 1200 tons and was supported by two pyramidal steel towers each rising to 140 feet.[120] "Great as are the achievements of engineering in the Exposition buildings in Jackson Park," the manufacturing company stated, ". . . they sink into insignificance when compared with the Ferris Wheel. It has been favorably compared with the Eiffel Tower . . . , and yet the latter has no claim for comparison with this gigantic achievement. The Ferris Wheel stands alone; it is without precedent, and while it is doubtful if ever a greater wheel will be constructed, in such an event, Mr. Ferris' name will always be coupled with it."[121] They were quite right on all counts. The Ferris Wheel was a singular engineering achievement. For the majority of fairgoers, however, its importance lay not in engineering but in pleasure. For them the Ferris Wheel was a relished plaything. "Nowhere else could this gigantic toy belong but to the World's Columbian Fair."[122] For fifty cents the fairgoer could enjoy two revolutions of the Wheel, with six stops on each revolution. On one of those stops, 250 feet in the air, he would have a commanding bird's-eye view of the exposition.

There were other vantage points from which to obtain a bird's-eye view: the roof of the Woman's Building, for example. But best of all was the extensive roof of the Manufactures and Liberal Arts

The Ferris Wheel

Courtesy of the Chicago Historical Society

Building—a half-mile long promenade. The Manufactures Building had four elevators with a capacity of 600 persons per hour, which carried fairgoers 200 feet upwards to a platform leading to the promenade.[123] From this vantage point they had a spectacular view. As one account had it, "that person must indeed be a dullard, a veritable clod of earth, who would not be moved to his inmost heart by the magnificence and suggestiveness of the views obtained from the roof of Manufactures Building."[124] This obviously would have been a desirable spot from which to view the illumination and fireworks which provided the fair's nighttime gala entertainment. The initial fireworks displays were staged around the Great Basin. They proved so popular that, beginning on July 1, they were moved to the Lake Shore. From the roof of the Manufactures Building huge searchlights flashed their beams skyward while pyrotechnic displays were shot aloft from the lake. A most memorable night apparently was that of July 4 when 200,000 fairgoers awaited the display. A balloon sailed out over the lake and as it ascended over the heads of the crowd "a shower of sparks and the American flag was revealed in brilliant flame suspended in midair" from the balloon.[125] Unfortunately after the tragic burning of the Cold Storage Warehouse on July 10 the hazard of fire forced closing of the roof of the Manufactures Building. That roof had also presented another hazard which afforded a bizarre comment on the fair. "The great national vice of spitting was never more repulsively exhibited than at our splendid Exposition. Placards mildly requested visitors not to spit from the elevator-landing in the Liberal Arts Building, but to remember the human insects below! . . . Everywhere men were spitting. I saw women indulging in the same vulgar vice. But it was not only Americans born: Germans and Turks, Russians and Samoans, Irishmen and Zulus, with equal effrontery, left their traces on corridor and rug, on sidewalk and car."[126] It seems that quite literally everything about the Chicago exposition was superlative. But the exercising of this particular offensive vice at least revealed the internationalism of the fair.

However breathtaking the exposition was when illuminated after dark, it is likely that individual fairgoers would not have paid it many night visits, since few of the exhibits were open then. Thus the fairgoer was likely to choose on most nights either to rest or to seek out the pleasures of the city of Chicago itself. Of the latter there were many. Some were created as adjuncts to the exposition with the tacit but not financial support of the Exposition Corporation. Among these adjuncts by far the most impressive was Steele MacKaye's ill-fated Spectatorium, which must easily have been the most monumental undertaking in the history of the theatre. The Spectatorium was the grandest project of MacKaye's mercurial career. For years Steele MacKaye had mulled over the idea of a "National Theatre" which by virtue of its size, its mechanical and electrical devices, and its usage of his own stage innovations, would be the center of panoramic and dramatic arts in this country. While in London in 1891 he realized that the World's Columbian Exposition was a logical place for such a theatre to be born. So he traveled to Chicago, where he would devote the last years of his life to the achievement of his greatest dream. Initially he presented his idea to the directors and artists of the fair. All were enthusiastic. Frederick Law Olmsted said, " *This is the noblest artistic scheme I have ever heard of.*' "[127] H. N. Higinbotham was entranced. D. H. Burnham requested Charles Follen McKim to prepare plans for the construction of the Spectatorium on the fairgrounds. Everything seemed propitious. Then a detractor appeared who doubted the Spectatorium's practicability and forced MacKaye to undergo the expense of making models of his schemes. Delays plagued the planning and finally it was too late to erect the Spectatorium at the exposition. But George Pullman, Lyman Gage, A. C. McClurg, and other Chicago businessmen came forth to sponsor the project as a private enterprise. These entrepreneurs, unfortunately, saw the Spectatorium not merely as MacKaye's grand theatre, but as a more elaborate and more expensive structure with restaurants and roof gardens. Their vision probably foredoomed the project in the depression of 1893.

MacKaye's project was a generation ahead of its time in stage-craft. So grandiose was his vision that discussion of the mechanical devices, stage effects, and novel lighting would in itself merit a book. MacKaye envisioned the Spectatorium as an entirely new kind of theatre devised expressly for an entirely new kind of production, the spectatorio. MacKaye's leviathan of a theatre, designed by Jenney and Mundie in a blending of Spanish Renaissance and Romanesque features, overlooked the fair, towering 270 feet in the air just to the north of the state buildings. The Spectatorium was 480 feet long and 380 feet wide. Its staging area, known as the Scenitorium, would contain twenty-five telescopic stages designed by MacKaye. The frame of the stage picture was 150 by 70 feet, with the full range of vision before the audience (a potential crowd of 9,000) exceeding 400 feet. Vastly larger than the Auditorium stage, the Scenitorium was clearly a predecessor of the present-day panoramic cinema. MacKaye designed a new system of lighting to create the closest possible reproductions of various kinds of natural light. An innovative curtain of light would replace the ordinary drop curtain. Cyclone machinery would produce simulated land and water effects and all sorts of weather.[128]

The noble play that Steele MacKaye created for his Spectatorium was *The Great Discovery, or The World Finder*, a six-act production of the life of Christopher Columbus. Each of the scenes was to be an elaborate spectacle in itself, with carefully reproduced architectural features, constellations of stars, swarms of supernumeraries. MacKaye planned to compound the spectacle with complementary music. There would be three full-scale choral groups accompanied by an orchestra of 120 pieces. Antonin Dvořák was commissioned to compose the orchestral works and out of his efforts sprang at least some parts of the *New World Symphony*. As MacKaye envisioned the staging of *The World Finder*, the story would be "*told in pantomime*, with orchestral accompaniment of the action, explanatory of the sentiment of each actor as it occurs ... also of the great elemental cosmic movements, presented with amazing realism by the spectacle. In addition, there is a grand overture and two great entr'acts [*sic*]."[129] The grandeur of MacKaye's conception was awesome. But his dream was never to become reality. A few weeks before the projected July completion of the Spectatorium, MacKaye's financial backers withdrew. By November the Spectatorium was already being razed. MacKaye would convert a Chicago theatre into a small-scale Spectatorium and incorporate his innovations into a small-scale Scenitorium where *The World Finder* would finally be presented for the first time on February 5, 1894. But he was never to recover from the debilitating efforts and profound disappointments of his great failed venture. He died on February 25, 1894. Though an erratic genius, so noble were his conceptions that his death was a significant loss to the American theatre. The failure of his grand Spectatorium deprived Chicago and its fairgoers of what promised to be the city's greatest attraction.

Chicago had other attractions, less grand perhaps than the Spectatorium, but certainly plentiful. "There are thirty-two first-class theaters and places of amusement in Chicago." Among these were the Auditorium, McVicker's, and Schiller theatres; the Grand and Chicago Opera Houses; and the Central Music Hall.[130] At the Schiller Theatre, which had been designed by Louis Sullivan, fairgoers could see performances of David Belasco's original company of *The Girl I Left behind Me*. Devotees of vaudeville could hear Haverly's Minstrels at the Eden Musee. Better still the World's Fair attracted to Chicago Ziegfield's famous vaudeville review, housed at the Trocadero. At the Columbia fairgoers could hear Chicago's own Lillian Russell, while the Coliseum featured Buffalo Bill's Wild West Show and Congress of Rough Riders of the World.

Chicago had fine examples of that favorite American diversion, the panorama. On Wabash Avenue at Hubbard Court one could see the Battle of Gettysburg Panorama and directly opposite it the Panorama of Niagara Falls. At Michigan and Madison was the Chicago Fire Panorama. (The Midway Plaisance boasted two panoramas: one of Kilaueau and one of the Bernese Alps.) There was also the Hardy Subterranean Theater where one could experience the simulated sensation of descending over 1,000 feet into the earth. There were dime museums and dance halls. And there were innumerable beer gardens and barrooms, some of them quite respectable, others a trifle shady. "To those of cosmopolitan taste, who desire beer and tobacco, and do not draw the line at abbreviated dress, Engel's Opera Pavilion . . . will appeal. As to the rest, 'dive' is the only correct definition of dozens, and Chicago 'dives' will be well avoided by any strangers."[131] The advice was sound. The visitor who ignored that advice might very well have been sorry later.

For Chicago lived up to its reputation as "the wickedest city in the United States." It was not simply the business district that had risen phoenixlike from the ashes of the Great Fire; no part of Chicago was rebuilt more rapidly than the saloons, gambling houses, and brothels. And they flourished for the rest of the century and well beyond. "[Carter] Harrison had promised during his campaign that he would give the World's Fair crowds a wide-open town, and he more than kept his word. . . . Chicago was the most wide-open town that America had ever seen. . . . And it was also, with the possible exception of New York in the days of Boss Tweed, the most corrupt, and . . . had been for a decade." That corruption, in Carter Harrison's mayoralty at least, derived largely from the mayor's friendships and dealings with Chicago's gamblers. Of these the most notorious was one Michael Cassius McDonald, "bounty-broker, saloon and gambling-house keeper, eminent politician, and dispenser of cheating privileges." He was a close friend and adviser of Harrison; he was the boss of Chicago, which he ruled with an iron hand. The only venal traffic in the city he did not control was prostitution—a matter of distaste, not of incapacity. It might have been McDonald who coined the classic line, "There's a sucker born every minute." Plenty of suckers who came to Chicago to see the exposition were fleeced of their cash at McDonald's famous gambling establishment, the Store, located at the corner of Clark and Monroe streets. Elsewhere Chicago's notorious bunco man, Tom O'Brien, "perhaps the most expert of all American swindlers," with the aid of his associates, made $500,000 during the five months the fair ran. Then too, there was abroad on the dark streets of the city a rogue who came to Chicago in the year of the fair to rob drunken men in the infamous districts known as the Bad Lands and Little Cheyenne. His name was Mickey Finn. As a Chicago saloon-keeper Finn would later give his name to the lexicon of American slang as administrator of the original knockout drinks.[132]

But to lose his money was not the worst of perils confronting the fairgoer. Far more unfortunate were those fairgoers who, while staying in the city, presumably fell prey to Herman W. Mudgett, alias H. H. Holmes, the most diabolical murderer in Chicago history. He had first appeared in the area in 1885 and in 1892 he built at Wallace and Sixty-third streets an enormous building known as Holmes's Castle which contained eighty or ninety rooms. In this house, which featured trapdoors, labyrinths, concealed rooms, a crematory, a dissecting plant, and numerous other ghoulish features, the monstrous Holmes seduced and murdered untold numbers of women and performed ghastly experiments. Holmes operated his castle as a boardinghouse during the World's Fair, at a time when hundreds of visitors to Chicago, come to see the fair, disappeared forever. It is assumed that many of them were Holmes's victims.[133]

Avoiding such a pitfall, the male fairgoer who sought nighttime sport in Chicago could have made his way to Custom House Place, the brothel district. There he might have fallen into the clutches of the vicious madame Mary Hastings who boasted that no act was too depraved for her girls; or he might have entered one of the panel houses, where the rooms contained hidden panels allowing one girl to rob his trousers while he was abed with another; or if he visited the very depths of perdition he might have encountered the twin holy terrors among black madames, Big Maud and Black Susan. Had he been more discerning, however, he would have made his way to Carrie Watson's, "the finest bordello in Chicago," or to the house of her primary rival Lizzie Allen, whose pander at the time was the aptly named Christopher Columbus Crabb. These ladies ran brothels that were at the opposite end of the spectrum from such depraved places as Mary Hastings' house or others where one could observe sodomy and similar venalities. Perhaps nicest of all the brothels was the largest, that of black madame Vina Fields: "there were never fewer than forty boarders in her place, and during the World's Fair her staff of harlots numbered between seventy and eighty. All of her girls were Negroes, but only white men were allowed in the establishment." No one ever filed a complaint against her, she was never raided, and she never paid protection.[134]

The White City, quite obviously, existed in stark contrast to Chicago's infamous red-light district with its associated evils of prostitution, gambling, drinking, and crime. And it was the fair, not the city itself, which attracted the general public, artists, dramatists, writers. Some who came had ironic, prophetic, and exultant experiences. Mark Twain, for example, traveled all the way from New York to see the exposition; but upon arriving in Chicago he fell ill and spent eleven days in his hotel bed. He left Chicago without ever having been to the fairgrounds. The young journalist Theodore Dreiser journeyed to Chicago from Saint Louis as a reporter for the *Republic*, which paid for an excursion of twenty Saint Louis schoolteachers whom he accompanied. One of those teachers would eventually become Dreiser's wife. He met her on the train. He wooed her in the Arabian Nights dreamland of the White City, which charmed them both. Dreiser also visited his father and took him to the fairgrounds. Hamlin Garland, recently become a resident of Chicago, was more fortunate than Mark Twain or Theodore Dreiser in that he had five months in which to satiate his avidity for the exposition. He too induced his father to visit the fair, sending him a letter which amounted to an unequivocal recommendation of circuses ahead of bread: " 'Sell the cookstove if necessary and come,' it read. 'You *must* see this fair.' " Garland himself was so "amazed at the grandeur of 'The White

City' " that he implored all his friends and relatives to see it. He led his father and mother on expeditions to the fairgrounds which left them exhausted and bemused.[135] The White City, which attracted so many artists, became one cause of Garland's belief that Chicago was to become the literary and artistic center of the nation. The exposition evidenced Chicago's artistic coming of age, Garland argued in *Crumbling Idols*.

It was left to William Dean Howells, foremost among American writers, to draw the obvious moral of the White City, which he visited in the guise of the Altrurian Traveler. As a visitor from utopia the Traveler's sentiments revealed a more enlightened and objective attitude than that of the ordinary visitor. He saw Chicago as only "the realized ideal of that largeness, loudness and fastness, which New York has persuaded the Americans is metropolitan."[136] Nevertheless, the harried Chicagoans could take heart from the Traveler's view that the exposition revealed a glimpse of the future. He visualized a time when all the capitals of the East and West would be White Cities and such metropolises as New York would have receded. So impressed was he with the White City that he deemed it "a bit of Altruria: It is as if the capital of one of our Regions had set sail and landed somehow on the shores of the vast inland sea [of Lake Michigan]."[137] The Traveler spent his happiest days in America there; when he visited the fair tears filled his eyes. "In grandeur of design and freedom of expression" the buildings were "perhaps even nobler" than those of the Regionic capitals of Altruria; and when he saw the "vast lateral expanse of the Liberal Arts building" lighted at night he was reminded of "our national capitol, when it shows its mighty mass above the bosks around it, on some anniversary night of our Evolution."[138] No visitor, architect, artist, or whatever, had expressed higher praise of the exposition. "An immortal principle, higher than use, higher even than beauty, is expressed in it," wrote the Traveler, "and the time will come when they [Americans] will look back upon it, and recognize in it the first embodiment of the Altrurian idea among them, and will cherish it forever in their history, as the earliest achievement of a real civic life."[139] Although as reality the White City would pass into dust, as ideal it would remain imperishable. For both ordinary visitors and astute critics alike the White City was the most international, most extensive, and most beautiful exposition in history. And for that fulfillment the city of Chicago could take full credit as catalyst and consummator. That modern American version of Sodom, urban center of vice, corruption, and chicanery, inland capital of industry, commerce, and the arts, Chicago was, ironically and paradoxically, the progenitor of the great White City. Ever afterward her creation would be known as the Chicago World's Fair.

6

THE WORLD'S CONGRESS AUXILIARY

The progress made in the World's Congresses
of 1893 will not be lost. The movement of
which they are a part holds the whole world
in its embrace.

Charles C. Bonney

AS AN INTERNATIONAL exposition the Chicago World's Fair
had one feature which made it more truly international and more
catholic than all previous fairs: the World's Congress Auxiliary.
The congresses were a series of meetings attended by people who
represented virtually every conceivable spectrum and activity of
humanity. There was precedent for such meetings at an exposition—for example, there was a congress at the Paris Exposition of
1889—but there was nothing to compare in scope or inclusiveness
to the World's Congress Auxiliary. It was held in Chicago from
May 15 to October 28. It included twenty departments and 225
general divisions. "These Congresses embraced Woman's Progress,
The Public Press, Medicine and Surgery, Temperance, Moral and
Social Reform, Commerce and Finance, Music, Literature, Education, Engineering, Art, Government, Science and Philosophy,
Social and Economic Science, Labor, Religion, Sunday Rest, Public Health, and Agriculture."[1] Within these general categories were
subsumed many other topical subjects which made the congresses
all-inclusive.

The congresses had been first proposed by Chicago judge

Charles C. Bonney in September 1889 and had received immediate and enthusiastic support. Bonney was placed in charge of a committee to organize the congresses and one of their first endeavors was to circulate an announcement of their intention to convene a parliament of nations in conjunction with the World's Columbian Exposition. Their announcement began with a statement of philosophy: "The crowning glory of the World's Fair of 1892 should not be the exhibit . . . of the material triumphs, industrial achievements, and mechanical victories of man, however magnificent that display may be. Something still higher and nobler is demanded by the enlightened and progressive spirit of the present age."[2] The proposal to convene the congresses was received as favorably abroad as it had been at home. And so the Exposition Corporation formally established the World's Congress Auxiliary of the World's Columbian Exposition of 1893, whose motto would be "Not things, but men."[3] The formal organization, designated on October 30, 1890, consisted of Charles C. Bonney, president; Thomas B. Bryan, vice president; Lyman Gage, treasurer; Benjamin Butterworth, secretary. The Woman's Branch of the Auxiliary was headed by Bertha Honoré Palmer, with Ellen M. Henrotin as vice president, and a large committee including Frances E. Willard, Mrs. Henry Wilmarth, Mrs. O. W. Potter, and Dr. Sarah Stevenson. These officials set to work in earnest, secured recognition for their endeavor from the United States Congress, and sent invitations to the various nations of the world. Those invitations declared the purposes of the World's Congress Auxiliary to be a convening in Chicago of leaders of human progress from all nations in order to establish mutual acquaintances and fraternal relations; to review in the congresses progress already achieved in the various subject areas; to define the still outstanding questions of the era; "and to receive from eminent representatives of all interests, classes, and peoples, suggestions of the practical means by which further progress might be made and the prosperity and peace of the world advanced."[4] Thus the auxiliary was a noble undertaking, its purposes transcending those of the festive White City. Its potential seemed more meaningful than any exhibit, however beautiful and grand, of ephemeral buildings and material objects. The World's Congress Auxiliary was the most promising feature in the life of the White City.

The various congresses of the auxiliary convened in the Art Institute of Chicago. This massive three-story building, designed by Shepley, Rutan, and Coolidge, contained thirty-three halls. In the area between its two giant wings two large audience rooms were arranged, the northern one called the Hall of Columbus; the southern one, the Hall of Washington. Though the directors contributed $200,000 to the construction of the Art Institute (one-third of its cost) with the understanding that it would be completed and furnished in time to accommodate the auxiliary, the building actually was not finished until July 1, 1893. Nevertheless, in May the auxiliary moved in.[5] The opening session of the World's Congress Auxiliary occurred on May 15. Bonney presented the formal opening address. His ideas were most appropriate to the beginning and goals of such an undertaking. The auxiliary was organized, he declared, as a means of serving peace; of eliminating ignorance, misunderstanding, prejudice, animosity; and restoring in their place intelligence, charity, industry, and happiness. "We would unite in international associations the devotees of every branch of learning; the disciples of every virtue; the friends of every charity; the supporters of every reform."[6] Men need not adopt the views of other men, but only try to serve the truth which transcends all views to understand their fellow beings. Citizens of each nation must be granted equal rights and privileges in all other nations and brotherhood must be effected, Bonney said. And having thus expressed the philosophic nature of the auxiliary, he proceeded to outline its history and organization. He spoke eulogistically of those men who were to have contributed to the auxiliary but had died beforehand: Rutherford B. Hayes, Henry Edward Cardinal Manning, Alfred Lord Tennyson, John Greenleaf Whittier, George William Curtis, Phillips Brooks. Bonney extolled the peaceable pursuits of art, science, and poetry over those of warfare. He foresaw the coming twentieth century as the culmination of 700 years of human progress—if their cause could go forward. The World's Congress Auxiliary, formally opened, was ready to begin its work.[7]

The work undertaken was prodigious. By the time the various congresses completed their deliberations they would have held a total of 1,283 sessions aggregating 753 days. The printed programs of the congresses revealed that 5,978 speeches or papers were delivered: "But these are much less than the actual number, for many papers and addresses were admitted after the programmes were printed."[8] Participants in the congresses represented all the continents, ninety-seven nations, provinces, or colonies, and the fifty states and territories of the United States. They listened to 3,817 speakers. But they were not allowed to debate with those who addressed them. "On the contrary, strict regulations were made and enforced for the exclusion of volunteer addresses, and of every form of random talk. The entire time at disposal was allotted to those who were supposed to be most competent to instruct and advise. Controversy was prohibited, and the passing of resolutions of approval or of censure was forbidden. The writers and speakers were asked not to attack the views of others, but to set forth with as much cogency as possible the merits of their own." It was assumed that those who spoke to the congresses would reach a larger audience through discussions of their addresses in pulpits, newspapers, magazines, and private conversations—a justified assumption. Each speaker was carefully selected by the Committee of Organization.[9] Thus the World's Congress Auxiliary did not present an open forum for public debate; its very size prevented such openness. But it did provide an enormous pulpit upon which was focused the attention of a large part of the world. The correctness or truculence of the responses to preachments from that pulpit were questions left to the nonparticipants whose numbers were inestimable. Though not free, the discussions at the auxiliary were nonetheless widely known, influential, and provocative.

The first of the congresses was also one of the three or four most significant. The Congress of Women under the auspices of the Department of Woman's Progress convened following Bonney's opening address and remained in session throughout the first week of the auxiliary, until May 22. During that time nearly two hundred women addressed the congress. Their speeches dealt with an extraordinary range of subjects: from art to agriculture, from cookery to Assyrian mythology, from Islam to the industrial revolution, from women as pioneers to women as financiers. Many of the speeches generally shared two viewpoints: pride in the achievements of women and an insistence upon the humanity and individuality of women. Most of the speakers avoided controversy in their choices of subjects, which was easily done, since the congress was set up in sections dealing with education, literature, science, religion, government, occupations, social reform, philanthropy. But many speakers took their cue from Bertha Palmer. Only two weeks prior to the beginning of the auxiliary she had spoken out during the dedication of the Woman's Building. It was her larger desire to be conciliatory. Thus she temperately conceded woman's role as housewife in saying, "We advocate . . . the thorough education and training of woman to fit her to meet whatever fate life may bring; not only to prepare her for the factory and workshop, for the professions and arts, but, more important than all else, to prepare her for presiding over the home. It is for this, the highest field of woman's effort, that the broadest training and greatest preparation are required."[10] Though she may have thus placated some male listeners, she did not hesitate to excoriate idealists who placed woman on a pedestal and advocated home-confinement or political economists who voiced fears over economic competition from women. She asserted straightforwardly, "Of all existing forms of injustice, there is none so cruel and inconsistent as is the position in which women are placed with regard to self-maintenance—the calm ignoring of their rights and responsibilities, which has gone on for centuries."[11] Not all women were or could be homemakers. Were such women to be forever denied the right to earn their own livelihoods?

Plenty of lesser known women furthered Palmer's theme. One of them was a forthright lawyer from California, Laura DeForce Gordon. She had some definite ideas about the "woman question," as feminism was then known. A notable feature of that entire question, Gordon advised, "is the zeal and persistence with which men of all classes and conditions have from time immemorial been defining and explaining woman's natural sphere." Man's persistence in this effort had led to atrocious effects. Gordon attacked with impressive zeal: "The rational man evolved from savagery could not estimate worth save by use. This environment made war a necessity, and prowess in arms was his whole standard of merit or superiority. Hence woman, the mother of the race, the builder of the home, was the conservator of peace, and perforce, was relegated to the position of inferior; but with the advance of civilization . . . there is no excuse for this relic of barbarism to exist." There is some reason to believe that the relic referred to here was war-making man, but presumably it was man's attitude toward woman, which Gordon rather succinctly defined: "All through the ages there has been a system of repression, suppression and oppression practiced toward women that is incomprehensible." An example of such oppression in her own life was that a mere fifteen years earlier, women were not allowed to practice law in California; after a court suit led to a constitutional amendment which remedied that situation, another court suit was required in order to open the doors of the state's law schools to women. Thus the institutions of the state had been used to effect oppression—and not only the institutions of the state, but also of the home and the church. As Gordon saw it, "The conservative repressive training of the home has been supplemented and emphasized by the religious teachings of the church." But this vast conspiracy of institutions was no longer cause for despair. A new era had come. "The woman of the nineteenth century has discovered herself," Gordon declared. "She has discovered that she has a distinct objective existence." This discovery was of far greater import than Columbus's. The new woman, her building at the fair, and her participation in all the works "of this beautiful 'White City' demonstrate the fact that henceforth and forever 'woman's sphere' in life will be defined and determined by herself alone. Her place in nature, no longer fixed by masculine dogmatism, shall be as broad and multifarious in scope as God shall decree her capacity and ability to accomplish."[12] With her fate now in the hands of God, woman's future seemed inevitably brighter. If Gordon's view did not prevail, it at least defined the issue. Woman's sphere should be determined by woman and by nature, certainly not by man.

A few women at the congress would find such sexist-oriented distinctions a little hard to accept. There were some who favored the idealist view of woman referred to by Palmer—woman as mother and homemaker. For example, Madame Hanna K. Korany of Syria, while arguing the need for education of women, nevertheless insisted that learning was needed only to make women better in what she believed was their appointed role: "I believe that woman should have a liberal education to fit her for the responsibilities of wife, mother and general educator. Woman should be thankful and happy in her place in creation."[13] That place was in the home, not in the office or factory. Similarly Juliet Corson said, "So far as women are concerned, if the test of their advancement be the degree of influence they exercise upon their age and the part they play in culture and progress, we may seriously ask ourselves in what respect we have raised the standard of womanly usefulness? And whether we are not in danger of losing sight of the homely virtues of wifehood and motherhood in our strife for public equality with men?"[14] Thus even an unmarried woman staunchly defended the supremacy of woman's role in the home. Of course it might be argued that Corson had a vested interest in homemaking, since she was the founder of cooking schools in America and author of several books on cooking and household management. In any event, there were views of woman more damaging than that of housewifery.

A Chicago lawyer, Charlotte C. Holt, perhaps laid bare some raw nerves in arguing her case for the ideal woman. She wanted to see men and women judged as equals, not as sexually distinct entities, because she saw the ideal woman as intensely human: "She is conscious that whatever else she may be, she is first of all a human being, with all the desires and limitations, with all the faults and aspirations, with all the virtues and failures that are common to the human family. She asks for herself only that which she is willing to concede as right for everyone else." This ideal woman, then, existed without illusions. Certainly she had no sentimentalism about humanity, and hence none about her own sex, as Holt envisioned her. "She has ceased to complain about the cruelty of man to her sister woman, for she knows that doubly refined is the cruelty of women to those of her [sic] own sex. It is impossible for any man to inflict upon a woman the bitter injustice; the intensity of suffering that is possible for a woman." Apparently Holt had had some unfortunate experiences with other women. Thus, though advocating compassion toward all persons, she disclaimed the rule of women. "The tyranny of woman would be as oppressive as the tyranny of man," Holt concluded. She even disputed the role of woman as homemaker. Whereas, she insisted, a woman must have a home of some kind, reasonable people would have to admit that some women were bad mothers and worse homemakers and might better spend their time elsewhere.[15] Holt was clearly an open-eyed advocate of sexual equality and a balanced view of life. Furthermore, she believed that the time of her ideal woman had already come.

That belief at least was widely shared by Holt's fellow participants in the congress. Another Chicagoan, Caroline K. Sherman, who also took a dispassionate view of life, agreed that the age of the new woman was here, but did not see the new era as a revolution or a fulfillment of progress. "That woman's influence will radically change the character of public affairs is not to be anticipated," she said, "since the intellect of woman does not differ essentially from that of man. . . . The greatest changes and the greatest advantage arising from the new order of things will be to woman herself. The enlarged opportunity of the present time means for her, first of all, the privilege of gaining an independent livelihood, or, in other words, of deciding for herself the direction of her life."[16] Sherman was doubtless right. What the new conditions really meant was an altered status for women, not a reformation of society. But woman's altered status would in turn effect significant changes in the social and economic patterns of America. It is interesting that Chicago women were among the most rational and disingenuous of commentators on the "woman question." Perhaps their composure derived from the nature of the city itself, whose sins, incidentally, were fervently outlined before the congress by Isabel Wing Lake, who had worked for six years with Chicago prostitutes. The challenge was formidable—over 31,000 women and children had come under the care of the police matron in 1892 alone—and Lake could muster no help from the Christian women of the churches to eradicate evil from "our sin-sick city of Chicago."[17] She properly called this sinfulness to the attention of the congress, for it certainly reflected upon the oppressed status of American womanhood. Still, the new day was come, the new woman was here, the major struggle seemed past.

Even militant laborers for women's causes agreed that women had attained a new status. That fact was perhaps most dramatically attested by the statement of Helen L. Bullock, a national organizer of programs on narcotics and the rescuing of girls for the Woman's Christian Temperance Union. Her speech began, "We are all doubtless aware ere this that Columbus discovered America. America's uncrowned queen, Miss Frances E. Willard, once said, 'The greatest discovery of the nineteenth century is the discovery of woman by herself.'" Bullock proceeded to extoll woman's moral and religious superiority over man—hence her power. But what was to be done with woman's new status and her power? Bullock advocated their enhancement through suffrage.[18] Ellen M. Henrotin prescribed financial independence for women. "The keynote of the relation of the sexes is really a financial one," she said; "this may appear a very materialistic view to take of the situation, but the readjustment now in progress between the relative position of the sexes is largely of that character." Hence to effectuate that readjustment, women must learn more of financial affairs.[19] Others held similar views. Mary A. Greene, another lawyer, argued in favor of women entering the professions, since in the previous thirty years professional schools had at last been opened to them. She advocated suffrage, new laws to protect the personal and property rights of women, and she foresaw the coming of legal equality. "Thus we are more and more closely approaching the time when woman shall be recognized as the full legal and social equal of man," she concluded.[20] Cara Reese, a Pittsburgh newspaperwoman, adopted, like Henrotin, what was perhaps a peculiarly American view that the source of equality was financial. "The new era finds women divided into two great classes, wage-earners and home-makers," she said. "Upon the proper adjustment of these depends future serenity. . . . Relations have been strained to the utmost. Surface indications prove the wage-earning class the stronger. The flaunted dollar is proving the magnet to draw the wife from the husband, the mother from her children, and fair young girls from the safe shelter of the home. Nay, more. The signs of the times prove that husbands, fathers, sons and brothers are not averse."[21] So it was the acquisitive instinct that would finally bring about woman's emancipation. Someday men and women would stand equal in the sight of the almighty dollar. Money would answer the "woman question" and assure the new era.

There was, indeed, considerable cause for optimism. Feminism was, after all, of recent origin and in its brief history it had made enormous gains. That grand old lady of the feminist movement, Lucy Stone, who would be dead before the Columbian Exposition ended, described the progress of American women for the congress. "The commencement of the last fifty years," she said, "is about the beginning of that great change and improvement in the condition of women which exceeds all the gains of hundreds of years before." The beginning of the new epoch actually preceded that fifty years; it was the founding of Oberlin College, for the education of both sexes, in 1833. That and other schools which followed established the right of women to higher education. Then, through their efforts in the antislavery movement, for which they were condemned by many men, women won the right of free speech. With these two rights established, other improvements were certain to follow. "Half a century ago women were at an infinite disadvantage in regard to their occupations," continued Stone. "The idea that their sphere was at home, and only at home, was like a band of steel on society. But the spinning-wheel and the loom, which had given employment to women, had been superseded by machinery, and something else had to take their places. The taking care of the house and children . . . could not supply the needs nor fill the aspirations of women." But of course when women tried to seek employment men resisted; when they advocated women in the professions men reviled them. Nevertheless, courageous women had opened up business and the professions one by one to their sex. Fifty years before, women had been discriminated against by the laws; marriage, for example, deprived them legally of their property. Now there were laws to secure those rights. And so Stone might justly draw her conclusion: "The last half century has gained for women the right to the highest education and entrance to all professions and occupations, or nearly all." Now there were numerous women's organizations, educational and industrial unions; there were women in medicine, law, education, journalism, the ministry. Without recounting the anguish and travail by which women had secured such great improvements Stone declared, "These things have not come of themselves. They could not have occurred except as the great movement for women has brought them out and about. They are part of the eternal order, and they have come to stay. Now all we need is to continue to speak the truth fearlessly, and we shall add to our numbers those who will turn the scale to the side of equal and full justice in all things."[22]

The representativeness of this first congress is briefly suggested by the names of those involved in these discussions of feminism, which retrospectively must be deemed the most interesting and memorable of the many speeches before the Congress of Women. Besides women whose names are since lost to history, there appeared at the congress the luminaries of the feminist movement—Julia Ward Howe, Susan B. Anthony, and Elizabeth Cady Stanton. The first spoke of the moral initiative of women; the second read an address prepared by the third on the civil and social evolution of women; and Stanton delivered a speech on suffrage. Elsewhere in the meetings of the congress Jane Addams spoke on domestic service, and outstanding women from various fields extolled the contributions and distinctions of women in sundry human endeavors: religion, medicine, science, the arts, literature, education, social reform. There was a heavily attended session on women in the drama, in which Madame Helena Modjeska traced woman's history in the theatre, the American actress Clara Morris adulated the theatre as the origin of female employment, and the English actress Julia Marlowe declared that woman was better understood for having been faithfully portrayed on the stage. There was also a significant discussion of the progress of black women since emancipation. Certainly the remarks of Mrs. A. J. Cooper of Washington, D.C., contained in one of the two speeches presented on the subject, are worthy of remembrance. Her cause was not merely to recite the history of developments, but to espouse an ethos. Cooper declared that throughout the darkest periods of her oppression in this nation, the black woman's history "is full of heroic struggle, a struggle against fearful and overwhelming odds, that often ended in a horrible death, to maintain and protect that which woman holds dearer than life. The painful, patient, and silent toil of mothers to gain a fee-simple title to the bodies of their daughters, the despairing fight . . . to keep hallowed their own persons, would furnish material for epics." Such truth put the oppression of women in proper perspective; for if women had been oppressed, then black women had been doubly oppressed. But Cooper's intent was not to prove superior suffering. In fact, it was she who stated most succinctly and eloquently the lofty principles of humanity: "The colored woman feels that woman's cause is one and universal; and that not till the image of God, whether in Parian or ebony, is sacred and inviolable; not till race, color, sex, and condition are seen as the accidents, and not the substance of life; not till the universal title of humanity to life, liberty, and the pursuit of happiness is conceded to be inalienable to all; not till then is woman's lesson taught and woman's cause won . . . the cause of every man and every woman who has writhed silently under a mighty wrong."[23] Such a cause was obviously worth patient and laborious struggle over centuries of time.

Quite appropriately, it was Bertha Honoré Palmer who gave the final speech of the Congress of Women. She reiterated the point she had made in her speech at the opening of the Woman's Building. It was a fact, she insisted, that the direction of life in modern times was increasingly to remove woman from the home. That fact could be blamed largely upon men who failed to provide adequately for their wives and children. "We have heard for years of the incompetent wife and mother," said Bertha Palmer, "but it occurs to me that we have heard singularly little of the incompetent husband and father." Women were entering the job market not because of a revolution on their part against their role as wife and mother, but rather because of pressing financial needs. If men could adequately fulfill those needs, then women would presumably be happy to return to the home. But such an achievement by men seemed unlikely. So the facts of life must be accepted. "We are not able to see how far-reaching may be the result of this period of change and experiment. We feel urgently impelled to follow the highest law known to us, that of evolution and progress. We must abandon ourselves blindly to the instinct which teaches us that individuals have the right to the fullest development of their faculties, and the exercise of their highest attributes." For better or worse woman was no longer to be deterred from self-fulfillment. In that respect the congress and the exposition itself had been extremely helpful. "No attempt has been made [in the congress] to demonstrate any theory, or to realize Utopian ideals which we would wish to see prevail," said Palmer. "Our only desire has been to present the actual conditions existing, which will give us a basis to build upon for future improvement." Such a conservative approach in the congress, she conceded, had disgruntled both some of the more militant women and some of the willing prisoners of conventionalism. But anyone reading the many papers delivered to the congress must concede in turn that Palmer was right to assume that the facts in the case of the "woman question" had been rather thoroughly aired. Furthermore, the work of women in the exposition must have its influence. "That we have been successful in creating an organization through the world, and in interesting the governments of the world in the condition and position of their women, is of incalculable benefit. A community of interests has been created among women in every part of the world, such as has never heretofore existed, and women delegated by their respective governments have visited the fair, and carefully studied not only our country and our customs, but those of every other part of the world," Palmer argued.[24] The ultimate results of such experiences might be impossible to prophesy, but it is fair to say that the three-year labor of the Board of Lady Managers and participating women throughout the world had made significant impact at least upon women and probably upon some societies in their entirety. Though it did not signal a revolution, the Congress of Women served several worthy purposes: those of education, organization, and aspiration. It is for that reason that one of Palmer's final statements seems so bizarre. She spoke of how much the organizational work had meant to everyone, how well all the women had worked together, how splendid had been the exchanges of views and the receptions at the Woman's Building, how kindly were the feelings expressed on all sides. "It was the proudest moment of my life," she revealed, "when I was told last Saturday, with a heartfelt hand-shake, and with accents of deepest sincerity, by one of our visitors, that seeing me had given her more pleasure than anything at the fair, except the Ferris Wheel."[25] What did she mean by such a revelation? Was it tongue in cheek? Was it an ironic suggestion that machines, which freed women from their bondage to the home, would soon subordinate both women and men? One can only speculate. But Palmer's curious statement may in fact have been the most cryptic but pregnant of all the statements in that entire impressively educational experience officially known as the World's Congress of Women.

This most inspired and important congress was followed by that of the Department of Medicine and Surgery, which also lasted for a week. Here the speeches were devoted to history and developments of dentistry, anatomy, pathology, bacteriology, and related fields. Perhaps the most interesting event in this congress was the focus of its final session—the World's Congress of Homeopathic Physicians and Surgeons. In his address to the meeting, the president of the American Institute of Homeopathy, spoke of the tremendous growth of this branch of medicine in America. He said, "Homeopathy has passed the stage of controversy; it is now a firmly established science."[26] Its apparent promise has long since been eclipsed. Philadelphia, site of the famous Hahnemann Hospital, is one of the few places in the United States where some vestige of homeopathy's principles of medication survive. This congress was followed by still others in specialized medical fields: obstetrics, gynecology, otology. And then, in perhaps most suitable sequence, came the Temperance Congress.

The chairman of the committee on the Temperance Congress was Archbishop John Ireland; the woman's branch was headed by Frances E. Willard, leader of the WCTU. As with all the other congresses, Charles C. Bonney appeared to deliver the opening speech on June 5. Among other things, he said, "The temperance reform, properly understood, does not unduly interfere with personal liberty, but arises from the instinct of self-preservation, by which society, which is only a larger man . . . seeks to protect itself against drunkenness, insanity, and crime."[27] The way was prepared for participants in the Temperance Congress to inveigh against the evils that the demon rum inflicted upon society. Ireland pleaded for uplift, enlightenment, and litigation. We must have laws, he said, but we must also instruct people on the dangers of intemperance, for the laws will not be served by doubters. "We need moral suasion, we need religion, we need that moral strength which comes only from the skies to build up the poor, wrecked, trembling victim of intemperance. We need laws . . . to ward off the fatal hand of the enemy from individual and social virtue. We need laws as a protest against iniquity."[28] It is doubtful that such virtuous declarations found a credulous audience in many regions of Chicago. But here assembled in Chicago's new Art Institute were delegates and speakers of one mind—members of the United Kingdom Band of Hope Union, the Order of Royal Templars of Temperance, the Non-Partisan National Woman's Christian Temperance Union, the American Medical Temperance Association. Their day of triumph was yet to come. For the moment their work at the congress was to proselyte and to educate. They considered that their purposes had been fulfilled, "that the Congress revealed in clearer light than ever before the universality of the drink habit, and [provided] . . . conclusive testimony . . . that it curses all nations alike." Delegates almost universally accepted the need for total prohibition of the manufacture and sale of alcoholic beverages and they emphasized the absolute need to inform people of the adverse effects of alcohol. They took encouragement from reports of work being done with young people, especially the establishment of coffee houses in Great Britain, and from the renewed interest of the medical profession in the problems of drinking. Though their forces in attendance at the congress were considerably fewer than 1,000, the temperance advocates found cause for optimism in their mutual reassurances.[29]

Next came the Congress on Commerce and Finance, whose organizational committee was chaired by the indefatigable Lyman Gage. In his introductory address Charles C. Bonney expressed either a naive optimism or a prophetic insight. "We have reached a stage in the evolution of the business world," he said, "in which the fierce and deadly strife for supremacy, called competition, in which the stronger build up prosperity on the ruins of the weaker, and that next natural development, the substitution of gigantic combinations for competitive strife, are giving place to a third advance, the one of all destined to be enduring, the stage of co-operation."[30] He predicted an age of honest, peaceable, and moral enterprise, while sounding like an advocate of Edward Bellamy's utopian Nationalism. But it is hard to believe that Bonney's peculiar view of how Spencerian principles applied to modern economic evolution was widely shared by his audience. Lyman Gage opened the section on banking and finance with an inspirational discussion of a subject dear to American hearts: money. He was rather hard-pressed to be optimistic, since the western world as a whole had already entered a severe depression. He was followed by other speakers who discussed the history and nature of banking and finance in various nations, among them Ellen M. Henrotin, wife of prominent Chicago banker Charles Henrotin, who spoke on woman as an investor. There were talks on the gold standard, on bimetallism, and on free coinage of silver. In their final meeting the delegates indulged in an open discussion of the current financial situation, highlighted by the opinions of such participants as David Wells and William Jennings Bryan.[31]

The subsequent Congress on Literature consisted of sections devoted to philology, folklore, history, libraries, and literature proper. Chairman of the organizational committee was William F. Poole, librarian of the Newberry Library; the seemingly ubiquitous Ellen M. Henrotin chaired the woman's committee. They set up what was widely regarded as one of the most significant of all the congresses. It opened on July 10. Welcoming remarks were delivered by Bonney, Charles Dudley Warner, Richard Watson Gilder, George W. Cable, Walter Besant, and Max Richter.[32] Warner seems to have been the real star of the show. He was rhapsodic over the exposition itself: "I fear all the time that the Fair will disappear, and I grudge every moment spent away from it. . . . And when it has gone these poor scribblers who have not money enough to create it, and many of them not imagination enough to put it into poetry or into romance even . . . will have to take up the task of perpetuating this creation of beauty and of splendor, . . . the great achievement of this city of Chicago in 1893."[33] As a curious blend of acidity and vision, Warner's speech was certainly a suitable keynote for the Congress on Literature.

The first business session of the congress was devoted to the subject of copyright, a sensitive issue for American and European authors. The history of literature in the nineteenth century on both sides of the ocean had been a tale of mutual piracy. American dramatists, for example, stole virtually all their plots and themes from European playwrights, and European publishers distributed unauthorized editions of American literary works. Losses in royalties were sizable. The copyright session was presided over by George E. Adams, who as a congressman had been primarily responsible for passage of the Copyright Law of 1891. It was generally agreed by the discussants that, although this law was beneficial, much more needed to be done to protect the rights of authors. (A more substantive law was passed in 1909, but the 1891 law did bring relative financial security to American authors for the first time.) In conjunction with this discussion of copyright, one session of the congress was concerned with the question of the rights and interests of authors. Walter Besant presided. He pointed out, among other things, the startling consideration that an author writing in English could draw upon a world readership of more than 100 million people, the largest potential audience in history. With such an audience Dickens would have had 20 million readers. Thus there was need to further the independence and nobility of authorship.[34] Others who addressed themselves to this question included Charles C. Coffin, Mary Hartwell Catherwood, and Daniel Lothrop.

But the most important session of all on literature proper centered on the subject of criticism and literature. Charles Dudley

Warner read the opening paper, "The Function of Literary Criticism in the United States." He deplored the fact that American literature had not been subjected to sound criticism, full of scholarship and comparative references, which would establish its validity as a contribution to world literature. "It seems to me that the thing American literature needs just now," said Warner, "and needs more than any other literature in the world, is criticism."[35] He referred to the critical judgments of Matthew Arnold, and borrowing from Arnold's terminology, he leveled a scatter-gun blast at prevailing literary standards: "Now, we have not in the United States the Philistine, or Philistinism, at least not much of it, and for the reason that we have no tradition. We have thrown away, or tried to throw away, tradition. . . . We have not Philistinism, but we have something else. . . . Some say it is satisfaction in superficiality . . .; the French say that it is satisfaction in mediocrity. At any rate it is a satisfaction that has a large element of boastfulness in it, and boastfulness based upon a lack of enlightenment, in literature especially a want of discrimination, of fine discerning of quality."[36] In speaking of boastfulness, Warner could not have chosen a better site than Chicago, the original home of boosterism. His subsequent castigation of the content of American literature was probably also a denunciation of the business motifs of the city novel of Chicago, for he said, "literature in national life never stands alone—if we condone crookedness in politics and in business under the name of smartness, we apply the same sort of test, that is the test of success, to literature. It is the test of the late Mr. Barnum. There is in it a disregard of moral as well as of artistic values and standards. You see it in the press, in sermons even, . . . the lack of moderation, the striving to be sensational in poetry, in the novel, to shock, to advertise the performance. . . . No, this is not Philistinism. I am sure, also, that it is not the final expression of the American spirit, that which will represent its life or its literature. I trust it is a transient disease, which we may perhaps call by a transient name,—Barnumism."[37] Such excoriation from the man who coauthored *The Gilded Age* was hardly surprising, but its loftiness revealed a certain intractable disdain for even those legitimate literary efforts to render the world of business, politics, and finance in fiction. Barnumism might have been an apt term for such aspects of American life. Barnumism might even have been a disease. But it was not a merely transient manifestation of the American spirit.

Other subjects under discussion in this same session included the relationship between literature and journalism, the future of English drama, and children's literature. But for American literati the more interesting of the discussions was probably that on aspects of modern fiction. The presiding author was George Washington Cable. In speaking on "The Uses and Methods of Fiction," Cable revealed the artistic man's view that the era of two cultures—science and humanism—had already arrived. He acknowledged science's successful search after truth but cautioned that facts are not the only vehicles of truth. "The world will do well to let its storytellers be . . . ambassadors of hope," Cable advised. "The fealty they owe is not a scientific adherence and confinement to facts and their photographic display, however benevolently such an attitude may be inspired, save in so far as they may help them the more delightfully to reveal the divine perfections of eternal truth and beauty." The service of fiction was to a higher truth than that inherent in objective fact. Thus fiction ministered to the human soul through depiction "of human passions, wills, duties, and fates. . . . Or, more briefly, it is the contemplation of the *truths* of human life as it ought to be, compared with the facts as they are."[38] The service of such truth obviously was more vital than the service of facts. With more precise focus than Cable's talk afforded, Catherwood spoke on "Form and Condensation in the Novel." She was in turn followed by Alice French, who discussed the genre of the short story. Hamlin Garland spoke about local color and Joseph Kirkland discussed the "Ebb Tide in Realism."

These sessions on literature proper were regarded as eminently successful. "It is true that there were disappointments, but, with allowance for all mishaps, the Congress achieved a distinct success;

its sessions were dignified and inspiring, it attracted the serious attention of a considerable and influential public, and it is to be hoped that it has paved the way for a better organization of authorship and a better understanding of literature both in its commercial and in its artistic aspects."[39] A part of the success of this venture was its very uniqueness. Walter Besant advised that some of the conference's failings had to be viewed within the light that "it was the first gathering of the kind ever attempted by an English-speaking people." That being the case, the organizers of the congress were not fully aware of the possibilities, nor even of the materials available to them; nevertheless, they had prepared their programs with the right objectives. "Much was learned that could hardly have been learned in any other way. The discussions were free from heat and passion; prejudices were frankly met and overcome; misconceptions were set right. It is not too much to say that the writers who assisted at the conference, as well as the mere audience, left the meeting far wiser as to their own craft than when they came."[40] One conspicuous failing was the sparseness of outstanding writers among the conference's participants. But that did not discredit the efforts of its organizers—Francis F. Browne working in Chicago; George Woodberry and Oliver Wendell Holmes working nationally at the head of the Committee of Co-operation.

Concurrent with the sessions on literature ran the conference arranged as part of the Congress of Literature by the American Philological Association, the Modern Language Association, and the American Dialect Society. Many of the papers read at this conference were merely sent in and, since philology is a rather esoteric subject, the discussions were sparsely attended. Nevertheless fully sixty papers were delivered. "The Congress assembled, as a whole, what was probably the most important gathering of philologists that ever met in the United States."[41] The Folklore Congress was more successful, despite its having been discouraged by officials of the American and English societies. "This was the third International Congress of Folklore, and really the first to which all nations were invited. More than thirty nationalities were represented, one hundred persons actively participating in the literary exercises, and more than a hundred in the concert." There were twelve sessions of the Folklore Congress which heard sixty-eight papers and forty-seven songs, all as a result of the labors of the chairman of the committee on arrangements, navy Lieutenant Fletcher S. Bassett.[42] Stewart Culin reported in the *Journal of American Folk-lore*, "The Columbian Exposition at Chicago afforded the greatest opportunity to the student and collector of folk-lore that has ever been presented upon this continent." Culin called attention especially to the folk music at the congress, while ignoring the speeches, and to the impressive collections of artifacts in various buildings, notably those of toys and games—some of which had been chosen by Culin himself and by Franz Boas. "The chief points of attraction, however, for the student of folk-lore at the Exposition, were to be found in the Midway Plaisance."[43] Culin referred to the wealth of native peoples and simulated habitats in the Midway. He had a folklorist's discerning eye. Less ambitious than the folklore conference was the Congress of Librarians, augmented by the annual meeting of the American Library Association, which heard papers on such subjects as an overuse of books, the relation of libraries to education, and library science.

Of all the conferences that formed parts of the Congress on Literature none proved more significant than the World's Congress of Historians held in conjunction with the ninth annual meeting of the American Historical Association. It attracted fair-sized audiences during three days of meetings and "was regarded as a complete success." Thirty-three papers were read; their contributors included three university presidents and seventeen professors. Of the remainder, ten were historical writers and four were women, "whose papers were among the most interesting."[44] Given the cause of the celebration of the World's Columbian Exposition, there was a surprising dearth of papers on Columbus. The majority of speakers discussed subjects from more recent American history. There were papers on the relation of history to politics, the

Constitutional Convention, the Missouri Compromise. Of curious interest was a paper delivered by James Schouler of Boston which took to task Hubert Howe Bancroft, the popular historian of the West and preeminent chronicler of the exposition. Schouler spoke on methodology. He argued that the efforts of an individual scholar doing systematic research were preferable to those of Bancroft, who hired legions of assistants to examine his library of 20,000 volumes. "The trained assistants which one employs with only a mercenary interest in the study can accomplish little, after all, compared with one mind inspired for its task and concentrating its powers."[45] There was virtue in Schouler's argument, but there was also no gainsaying the prodigious list of publications under Bancroft's name. Though his work still evokes controversy because he employed some 600 assistants and perhaps a dozen writers, Bancroft did focus historiography upon some areas and subjects that had been previously ignored. His contribution was valuable.

The paper that secured the significance of the Congress of Historians was delivered by Frederick Jackson Turner of the University of Wisconsin on "The Significance of the Frontier in American History." His talk itself has been a subject of American historiography ever since. Though at the time of its delivery Turner's speech elicited only moderate attention, it was soon to become the cause of a fundamental change of focus, bias, and intent in American historiography. Precisely what Turner meant in his "frontier thesis" still is arguable, but the nature of his historical bias was and remains clear. Turner began with the startling assertion, "The existence of an area of free land, its continuous recession, and the advance of American settlement westward, explain American development."[46] Certainly this was a distinctly novel and indigenous approach to defining the growth of American social and political institutions. It constituted in effect a declaration of independence from the concept that America was merely an extension of European civilization. "The growth of nationalism and the evolution of American political institutions

257

were dependent upon the advance of the frontier," Turner said. Americans' response to the frontier promoted the growth of our democracy and also our distinctive traits of national character: inquisitiveness, practicality, inventiveness, restlessness, individualism, exuberance.[47] There were other and newer factors that would need to be taken into account—for example, the rise of industries and cities—if Turner's thesis was fully to explain four hundred years of American history. But the propounding of such a thesis could have occurred in no setting more appropriate than the World's Columbian Exposition.

The succeeding educational congresses were nearly exhaustively inclusive. They dealt with institutions of higher learning, fraternities, students, administration, kindergartens, manual training, agricultural education, education of the deaf and blind, and numerous other fields. William T. Harris, United States commissioner of education, headed the Committee on Arrangements. He and his cohorts arranged "the largest international educational congress that has yet been held."[48] It is noteworthy that no part of the congress received more attention than the sessions on kindergarten education. Two congresses were devoted to psychology, one on experimental psychology presided over by G. Stanley Hall, president of Clark University; the other on rational psychology led by James McCosh. The latter heard a paper submitted by Josiah Royce. Probably most momentous because of the number and prestige of the participants were the congresses on higher education. Chairman of this department was the renowned president of Johns Hopkins University, Daniel Coit Gilman. Other university presidents or professors who contributed to the discussions included James B. Angell of Michigan, Mary A. Jordan of Smith, William Gardner Hale of Chicago, Martin Kellogg of California, Woodrow Wilson of Princeton, David Starr Jordan of Stanford, Seth Low of Columbia, and others from various European nations—an impressive list of educators. Most of their sessions concerned such issues as the nature and goals of universities, whether Latin and Greek should be humanities requirements, the "Problem of Excessive Specialization in University Studies," and "The Relation of Our Colleges and Universities to the Advancement of Our Civilization." Ernest Fenollosa, professor of the Boston Art Museum, was on hand to pursue his interest in "The Influence of Japanese Art" which had so impressed Henry Adams and John LaFarge. E. L. S. Horsburgh, speaking on "The Universities and the Working-men [*sic*]," flailed the exclusiveness of the universities and the narrowness of some of their products. "Our universities, too, have proved a favorable soil for the production of a narrow, exclusive, and priggish character," he concluded. "Men pass from their undergraduate days to fellowships, tutorships, and professorial chairs. Thus they have spent their days in an unnatural and hothouse atmosphere. They have mixed little with the world. ... they know nothing of lives of incessant toil in mine or factory ... they become purblind."[49] Obviously it would have been far better, Horsburgh might have argued, had professors and university presidents been personally familiar with such work as formed the subject matter for the Congress of Social Settlements that was organized by committees under Charles Zeublin of the University of Chicago and Jane Addams of Hull House. Among its speakers were Florence Kelley, Helena Dudley, Ellen G. Starr, and Henry Demarest Lloyd. Their papers were noticeably more pointed and worldly than many of those on higher education.

In August occurred the congresses of the Department of Art, which embraced architecture, painting, sculpture, decorative arts, ceramics, and photography. The General Committee for the department was headed by Charles L. Hutchinson. Daniel H. Burnham was in charge of the Committee on Architecture, Lorado Taft chaired the Committee on Sculpture, and Candace Wheeler headed the Woman's Committee. The congresses heard papers concerning decorative arts, English porcelain, wood engraving, photography. The highlight of the Congress on Painting and Sculpture was thought to be the address by the popular writer-artist F. Hopkinson Smith, who lectured on "The Illustrative Arts of America." The American Institute of Architects (AIA) met in conjunction with the Congress on Architecture, probably the most noteworthy of the art congresses. The congress was chaired by Burnham, who presented a paper on "The Organization of the World's Columbian Exposition." Alfred Stone, secretary of the AIA, read a paper submitted by Frederick Law Olmsted on "The General Scheme and Plan of the World's Columbian Exposition." During the five days that the congress was in session there were several other papers on the fair, among them discussions of its construction by E. C. Shankland and on its electrical plant by R. H. Pierce. But there were also speeches devoted to traditional architectural concerns: professional ethics, government practice, acoustics, competitions, fireproof construction. Louis Sullivan spoke, quite appropriately, on "Polychromatic Treatment of Architecture."

But as an expression of a professional philosophy, Henry Van Brunt's paper "The Growth of Characteristic Architectural Style in the United States" stood out. He deplored professional enslavement to correct archaeological styles and critics' lack of "sympathy for those contemporaneous experiments in form, in which the architect of today is more or less ingenuously seeking to adapt the underlying principles of the historical styles to modern materials, modern methods, and modern usage." Modern America could not reproduce the architecture and the cities of former eras, Van Brunt insisted, even though it could learn from those eras. The intelligent appreciation and support of the public was vital to the future of our architecture, and the public "will not submit to inconvenience for the sake of a theory of design . . . , but they will rejoice to see useful things made beautiful, practical ideas elevated into the domain of art, and common sense made consistent with grace and elegance, without being unnecessarily embarrassed or sophisticated in the expression by a pedantic affectation of Greek, Latin, early Christian or mediaeval archaeology." Hence the value of the Chicago exposition, which would create in the public more exacting standards of judgment. It seemed an uncharacteristic argument to come from a man who admired classical styles, but Van Brunt was espousing what he perceived to be the truths of current American conditions in architecture. And one of the most important of those truths was that, "in the absence of patriotic traditions, the most potent element in the development of form as a fine art is evidently the science of economic building."[50] Van Brunt was not alone in his advocacy.

Among the speakers was Barr Ferree, who read a most perceptive paper on the influence of economic conditions upon American architecture. He pointed out that if our city architecture was to be properly understood, one must first be aware that "current American architecture is not a matter of art but of business. A building must pay or there will be no investor ready with his money to meet its cost. This is at once the curse and the glory of American architecture." The merit of this circumstance was as impetus for the "marvelous development of the commercial building in America, with its consequent benefit to the architect financially and to the community at large in affording visual and external evidence of prosperity, wealth and intelligence." The benefits of such a financial state were therefore greater than its harm, because commercial buildings had given to American cities a grandeur which could not be obtained with low-storied structures. Nevertheless, financial considerations were also responsible for many unartistic and unpleasant features in some of the architecture. Ferree also called attention to the contrast between the commercial city and the White City. "The World's Fair buildings," he said, "and the business buildings of Chicago offer the most admirable and useful lesson of the possibilities and achievements of American architecture that could be imagined. On the one side we have its highest achievement in free monumental architecture; on the other its greatest work in commercial buildings." But, Ferree warned, the differing conditions under which these two kinds of architecture were erected must be fully appreciated if the buildings were to be properly evaluated.[51] Architects should rightly have kept that distinction in mind.

The congresses on art were followed by those on philosophy and science. Philosophy was under one chairman, R. N. Forster, but science was divided into departments—geological, chemical, meteorological, electrical, astronomical, psychical, evolution—each of which had its own chairman. The philosophers heard William T. Harris speak on the errors of Kant's philosophy. They heard papers on teleology, immortality, and synthesis. Josiah Royce, the celebrated Harvard professor, spoke on "The Twofold Nature of Knowledge." He had a good deal to say about ego, consciousness, the discoveries and limitations of psychology. He ended his speech on a quite religious note by referring to "a perfect knower," "a timeless knower," in whom finite knowers could find their true selfhood.[52] Other papers were mostly of very learned and esoteric nature. But among them was one read by John Dewey of the University of Michigan, who addressed the subject of the "Reconciliation of Science and Philosophy."

Of the various congresses on science, that devoted to evolution was conspicuous. It was, curiously enough, an adjunct of the World's Parliament of Religions. A letter from Thomas Henry Huxley, explaining that illness prevented his traveling to Chicago, was read to the Congress on Evolution, as was a paper by Herbert Spencer on "Social Evolution and Social Duty." Spencer addressed his remarks to correcting an error, as he saw it—the view that as evolution applied to society it was fatalistic. Self-aggrandizement had created the industrial society, but that did not negate altruism. The theory of evolution, Spencer contended, "implies that for genesis of the highest social type and production of the greatest general happiness altruistic activities are essential as well as egoistic activities, and that a due share in them is obligatory upon each citizen."[53] That must have come as good news to Chicago's beleaguered social reformers. Spencer's paper was followed by a variety of others, some dealing with Spencer's ideas, some with Darwin's. Women were participants in this congress, as in all the others. One of them, Sara A. Underwood, provided one of the meeting's curiosities—an essay entitled "The Poets of Evolution," in which she discussed the literary works of Lucretius, Erasmus Darwin, Goethe, Emerson, George Eliot, and others. One participant spoke on "Evolution and the Fair." And Florence Griswold Buckstaff, speaking on "The Evolution of the Modern Family," called attention once more to that question of the double standard which so grated upon woman's sensibilities. "The development of the family," she lamented, "is sadly slow so long as society and mothers permit the pure young woman to marry the impure young man, while casting into outer darkness his victim or the partner of his crime."[54] But she was optimistic about the future development of both male chastity and sympathetic family relations. One of the most topical features of the congress was the session on the relationship of evolution to economics. Among its noteworthy participants were John Fiske and Lester Ward. A session devoted to the influence of evolution upon philosophy was highlighted by the reading of a paper submitted from Germany by Ernst Haeckel. Clergymen had their say at the sessions devoted to ethics and evolution and to the effect of the theory of evolution upon religion. But there were no prominent names among the speakers.

These various congresses—even the well-attended Congress on Women—were all overshadowed by the largest of all the congresses which was planned to convene during the last month of the exposition. The World's Parliament of Religions "was the crowning event of the World's Congresses of 1893."[55] It was the longest, most ambitious, most visited, most admired of the many congresses; and it evoked the most extensive comments in books, newspapers, and magazines. The probable source of excitement over the parliament was its all-inclusive scope. That scope is suggested by the General Committee which was set up to organize the parliament. It was headed by John Henry Barrows, the remarkably liberal pastor of Chicago's First Presbyterian Church, and it contained fifteen other members representing the Episcopal, Roman Catholic, Baptist, Lutheran, Methodist, Unitarian, Universalist, and other churches, as well as Judaism and the Society of Friends. But that was merely a beginning. Separate committees were established to arrange for the congresses of each participating denomination. Then the General Committee issued invitations to representatives of all faiths in the world. These representatives were asked to prepare papers or be discussants on a variety of themes: "the triumphs of religion in all ages, the present state of religion among the nations and its influence over literature, art, commerce, government, and the family life, the power of religion in promoting temperance and social purity, and its harmony with true science, its dominance in the higher institutions of learning, and the value of the weekly rest day on religious and other grounds."[56] There was to be no proselytizing, no discrimination, no controversy. Frankness and fidelity to one's creed were encouraged. The archbishop of Canterbury declined the invitation on behalf of the Anglican church on the grounds that such a parliament amounted to tacit recognition of the equality of all religions, whereas Christianity was the only true religion; he implied that the Church of England was its only true and catholic church.[57] His Grace Edward White Benson was clearly not in an ecumenical mood. Nor was the sultan of Turkey, who discouraged the Greek and Armenian churches in the Turkish Empire from attending. But otherwise the responses to the invitation from throughout the world were overwhelmingly favorable. Subsequently, through the aid of the State Department, under James G. Blaine and his successor John W. Foster, and its network of embassies and consulates; by means of letters; and through the efforts of world-traveling scholars and clergymen, the Parliament of Religions gained sponsors and participants from all areas of the world.

The World's Parliament of Religions was officially convened on September 11. The ceremonies began with chanting of the doxology, singing of the hymn "Before Jehovah's Awful Throne," and reciting of the Lord's Prayer led by James Cardinal Gibbons.[58] Bonney then delivered his welcoming address. Perhaps a little awestruck by the occasion, he was at first hyperbolic. "The importance of this event cannot be overestimated," he said. "Its influence on the future relations of the various races of men cannot be too highly esteemed." Then he became efflorescent. "If this Congress shall faithfully execute the duties with which it has been charged, it will become a joy of the whole earth, and will stand in human history like a new Mount Zion, crowned with glory and marking the actual beginning of a new epoch of brotherhood and peace." Finally, citing the occasion as the beginning of a new era of religious peace and progress, Bonney welcomed all the delegates to the parliament in the name of this new era of the "Brotherhood of Religions."[59] Bonney's welcome was followed by one from Barrows. Responses to these statements were delivered by the archbishop of Chicago, Patrick A. Feehan, and by Cardinal Gibbons as representatives of Roman Catholicism. Then the Reverend Augusta Chapin offered a welcome on behalf of the Woman's Committee. She expressed the view that such a parliament could not have been held fifty years earlier; and had it been held twenty-five years earlier fully half of the religious world could not have participated. "Woman could not have had a part in it in her own right for two reasons: one that her presence would not have been thought of or tolerated, and the other was that she herself was still too weak, too timid and too unschooled to avail herself of such an opportunity had it been offered."[60] That woman was represented was ample evidence of the importance of this first major worldwide meeting on religious faiths. There followed addresses or statements from Harlow Higinbotham; Alexander M'Kenzie of the Shepherd Memorial Church of Cambridge speaking on Puritanism as an influence on American character; Dionysios Latas, archbishop of Zante, Greece; P. C. Mozoomdar of Calcutta, representing the Brahmo-Somaj faith; Pung Kwang Yu, first secretary of the Chinese Legation in Washington; Prince Serge Wolkonsky from Russia; Reuchi Shibata representing the Shinto religion; four Buddhist priests from Japan; Count A. Bernstorff of Germany; M. Bonet-Maury of France; H. Dharmapala, a Buddhist delegate from Ceylon, who gave the closing address.[61]

With the international nature of the parliament thus clearly manifested, delegates were ready to proceed with the programs. These consisted of four distinct groupings. First was the general program in which numerous nations were directly represented—England, Scotland, Sweden, Switzerland, France, Germany, Russia, Turkey, Greece, Egypt, Syria, India, Japan, China, Ceylon, New Zealand, Brazil, Canada, and the United States—and several other nations had surrogate representation. The general program was devoted to consideration of Theism, Judaism, Islam, Hinduism, Buddhism, Taoism, Confucianism, Shintoism, Zoroastrianism, Catholicism, Greek Orthodoxy, and Protestantism—in short, every major religion in the world, with numerous references made to minor religions. In addition, the general program would deal with such subjects as revelation, immortality, the incarnation of God, the universal principles of religion, the relation of religion to morals, marriage, education, science, music, labor, government, war and peace. Fully seventeen days were given over to the general program and nearly as many to the second program, which was concerned with "presentations of distinctive faith and achievements, by selected representatives of different churches." The third program consisted of separate congresses for each of the denominations which were designed to be informative of the purposes and services of these various faiths. The fourth program featured congresses of religious-related organizations or subjects, such as missions, the YMCA, the Evangelical Alliance, ethics, Sunday rest, evolution. (The latter topic was to have been under the Congress of Science, but as circumstances prevented that, it was added to the Parliament of Religions.)[62]

The speeches that ensued during these various programs were of exhaustive number and content. They were published or reviewed in four full-length histories of the parliament that total thousands of pages. Thus the individual who could not possibly have heard even a major part of the speeches could peruse their contents at home. The World's Parliament of Religions overlooked hardly a single conceivable theme of a religious nature. For the Americans the educative value of speeches by various foreign delegates presenting the histories and beliefs of various faiths only peripherally familiar to the New World was inestimable. Nowhere else in

America could the lay citizen have heard native representatives of their faiths explain Hinduism, Confucianism, Shintoism, Buddhism. Probably, however, American visitors would have been more intrigued by speakers and issues nearer to home.

Though some of the most popular figures in American religions were absent from the list of speakers, there were many prominent names or special advocates. Participating American religious leaders represented most of the denominations and sects. The prestige of the parliament was enhanced by the conspicuous presence of the widely admired Cardinal Gibbons, the sage leader of Reform Judaism Isaac Mayer Wise, and the well-known Congregationalist minister Lyman Abbott; its inclusiveness was demonstrated by the less-publicized attendance of the leader of Christian Science Mary Baker Eddy, the advocate of Theosophy Annie Besant, and the spokesman of the Shakers Daniel Offord, all come to explain and to uphold the tenets of their faiths. Other speakers included Edward Everett Hale, Washington Gladden, Richard T. Ely, Josiah Strong, Thomas Wentworth Higginson, Sephardic Rabbi H. Pereira Mendes, Bishop John J. Keane, Frances Willard, Philip Schaff, Antoinette Blackwell, W. T. Stead. Rabbi Wise chose the high road and spoke on "The Theology of Judaism." Professor Schaff of Union Theological Seminary pleaded his favorite cause of Christian unity in "The Reunion of Christendom." Cardinal Gibbons discussed "The Needs of Humanity Supplied by the Catholic Religion" in a paper read by Bishop Keane who, in turn, spoke on "The Incarnation Idea in History and in Jesus Christ." Edward Everett Hale talked about "Spiritual Forces in Human Progress." Such speeches were noncontroversial. But many of the Protestant clergy and reformers, unlike their Jewish or Catholic brethren, chose the opportunity of this forum to discuss social and moral ills. Their speeches, then, are more revealing of the religious state of the nation—or at least of more immediate interest and greater trenchancy—than any of those concerned merely with the abstruse points of theology. Their involvement in secular questions also more accurately reflected the terrible contradictions and tense

267

struggles that American faiths and society were undergoing. No one could have discerned, in Rabbi Wise's speech, for example, that there was conflict over the meaning of Judaism among Reform, Orthodox, and Conservative Jews, let alone have learned of Judaism's difficulties with acculturation. Nor could anyone have surmised from Cardinal Gibbons's words and his liberal embracement of the parliament that the Roman Catholic Church was afflicted with factions and frictions stemming from profound disagreements over its gradual liberalization. But Gladden, Abbott, Ely, and other Protestant speakers, more concerned with the reform of society than with the fine points of doctrine, were forthright in their indictments and exhortations.

The most concise revelation of the state of religion in America is its actual diversity, which manifested the enormous divergency, and sometimes hostility, of views on the nature of faith and of society. It was appropriate, then, that H. K. Carroll discussed the makeup of the American religious community. He informed the delegates to the parliament—most of whom had come from nations with either one faith, or only a few contending faiths—of the singular variety and complexity of American religions. "There are so many religious bodies in America," Carroll began, "that it is desirable, if we would get a comprehensive idea of them, to arrange them, first, in grand divisions; secondly, in classes; and thirdly, in families. I would specify three grand divisions: 1. The Christian. 2. The Jewish. 3. Miscellaneous. Under the last head come the Chinese Buddhists, the Theosophists, the Ethical Culturists, some communistic societies and Pagan Indians."[63] Some of the sects or groups represented within these three categories numbered comparatively few members; nevertheless, the categories themselves suggest a remarkable pluralism—divisions was certainly the apt word. "We count in all 143 denominations in the United States," Carroll continued, "besides 150 or more congregations which are independent, or unassociated with any church."[64] Carroll was quite forthright in explaining why there were so many faiths: "We may, I think, sum up the causes of division under four heads: (1) Controversies over doctrine; (2) controversies over administration or discipline; (3) controversies over moral questions; (4) ambitious and disputatious persons."[65] This matter of controversy was made quite evident at the parliament by the embarrassing absence of the Baptists, the third largest denomination in America, who withdrew their support in outrage over the Sunday openings of the exposition. The other leading denominations were Roman Catholicism, which had made a fivefold increase in adherents in a mere fifty years as a result of immigration; the Methodists; Episcopalians; Lutherans; and Presbyterians. Given such numerous divisions and controversies, no religious leader could be said to speak for more than a select group. Nevertheless, some of the clergy, especially the Protestant clergy, had nationwide audiences.

Among the most prominent was Lyman Abbott. He drew the equation between the religious sense and society in stating that all human activity is transfused with a search, conscious or otherwise, for the infinite and the divine. "All science, all art, all sociology, all business, all government, as well as all worship, are in the last analysis, an endeavor to comprehend the meaning of the great words: Honesty, justice, truth, pity, mercy, love." Nothing, said Abbott, could extinguish the incentive of this endeavor, which was intuitive.[66] How this incentive to comprehend the meaning of the great words infused the enterprises of, for example, some of Chicago's leading entrepreneurs, madames, politicians was questionable. Apparently Abbott himself was somewhat at a loss to make explanation. In welcoming the congress representatives to Chicago—"the most cosmopolitan city of the most cosmopolitan race on the globe," as he termed it—Abbott disavowed the role of Christian exponent. In Christianity, he said, "have been the blemishes of human handiwork. It has been too intellectual, too much a religion of creeds. It has been too fearful, too much a religion of sacrifices. It has been too selfishly hopeful; there has been too much a desire of reward here or hereafter. It has been too little a religion of unselfish service and unselfish reverence."[67] The apparent contradiction may be merely rhetorical. Abbott's point was that doctrine is irrelevant; it is not Christianity, but the divine and eternal Christ, that matters.

Pursuing the relationship between religion and society that Abbott mentioned, other speakers explored the vicissitudes of society and deplored Christianity's inadequate views and treatment of the sores on the body politic. Advocates of the Social Gospel went right to the point. Harvard professor Francis G. Peabody pushed Abbott's equation a step further and helped to explain the seeming contradiction. "Christ, the great individualist of history, was the great socialist as well," said Peabody. "His hope for man was a universal hope. But how can it be that the same teacher can teach such opposite truths? How can Christ appeal thus to the single soul and yet hope thus for the Kingdom?"[68] Peabody was equating the socialist state with the kingdom of God on earth. The fact that respected persons were able before public forums to advocate socialism without fear of recrimination reveals the extent of the political toleration of the 1890s, but still more revealing was the advocacy of Christian socialism. The possibility of such advocacy remains compelling to this day, but more so because it afforded the opportunity to make religion both divine and secular, to make Christianity both theoretical and applied—as Peabody saw it, at any rate. For, as he said, "We reach here the very essence of the Gospel in its relation to human needs. The two teachings, that of the individual and that of the social order, that of the part and that of the whole, are not exclusive of each other or opposed to each other, but are essential parts of the one law of Christ." After all, Peabody argued, each individual is a part of the kingdom, which exists to free the individual from narrowness and selfishness. The improved soul comes about through knowledge of the common life; and, once improved, that soul can serve to better that common life through the personal painstaking effort of Christian charity. There were, Peabody said, three ways to deal with the business world, which was the real world. You could run away from it or you could deal with it while remaining afraid of it. Or you could believe in the business world; "take it as the test of Christian life in the modern age. . . . In this warfare of industry, which looks so shapeless and unpromising, the Christian sees the possibilities of service. It is not very clean or beautiful, but it can be shaped and molded into an instrument of the higher life. That is the Christian's task in the business world." Thus the Christian soldier must do battle in the wars of business in order to effect the highest form of philanthropy in the changed modern world: better methods in the conduct of business. The battle would not be easy. Peabody at least was not denying the major reality of modern life, that it was an era of commerce, industry, and finance. He summarized the Christian lesson for his times: "Individualism means self-culture, self-interest, self-development. Socialism means self-sacrifice, self-forgetfulness, the public good. Christ means both. . . . The Kingdom of God is not to come of itself, it is to come through the collective consecration of individual souls."[69] Thus was the rhetoric of Lyman Abbott rendered comprehensible and redeeming.

Other proponents of the Social Gospel advocated not merely Christian charity, but precise programs, while underscoring Peabody's views. Richard T. Ely, professor of economics at the University of Wisconsin, declared, "As a social force, Christianity favors private frugality and generous public expenditures. . . . Christianity means social solidarity, or it means nothing. Social solidarity means the recognition of the identity of all human interests, and, truly understood, it promotes the identification of oneself with humanity."[70] Thus Ely too emphasized the collectivist nature of true Christianity. Fraternity, Ely argued, was the essence of Christianity. For that reason the United States could not be called a Christian land. "We do not attempt to carry out the principles of fraternity, and any claim that we do is mere ignorance or pretense," said Ely. "It does not avail us to make long prayers while we neglect widows and orphans in need." Nor did Ely hesitate to provide specific examples of shortcomings. "Shall a land be called Christian which slaughters human beings needlessly by the thousand rather than introduce improvements in railway transportation simply because they cost money?" he asked. "That is exalting material things above human beings. Shall a city like Chicago be called Christian, maintaining its grade crossings and killing innocent persons by the hundred yearly, simply because it would cost money to elevate its railway tracks?" But reference to specific evils might become an endless undertaking, and so Ely reverted to the general. His meaning and his target, however, were quite clear. "Christianity means," he asserted, "a mighty transformation and turning of things upside down, and while it seeks to bring about the most radical changes in peace, it has forces within it which nothing can withstand and resistance to which is sure to result in revolutionary violence." Here was a virtual call to arms if American society did not reform itself. But, as if suddenly fearful that he might have expressed himself too strongly, Ely concluded, "Yet in the end the peace of Christ must triumph."[71]

In accordance with the emphases of Ely's concluding remarks, Washington Gladden pursued that subject of paramount concern to Americans: money. "Religion and wealth are two great interests of human life," Gladden began. "In a perfect social state what would be their relations?" Wealth, Gladden said, was not merely exchangeable goods, as the economists defined it. In popular parlance wealth connoted abundance. Europe and America were gifted with abundance. The wealth of America resulted from the development of the earth's resources. Such development and its resultant abundance were beneficent; those involved in such work joined forces with God. "It is clear, therefore, not only that there can be nothing inherently wrong in the production of wealth, but that it may be, and indeed ought to be, essentially a religious service." Wealth provided not only the necessities of life but also the sources of uplift and recreation—schools, parks, museums, libraries, missions. Religion could not fault such things. What religion must fault was not the production of wealth, but its distribution. "The existing practice is far from being ideal. To everyone according to his power, is the underlying principle of the present system of distribution. Witness the recent occupation of the Cherokee lands." Such a principle of distribution must be condemned as irreligious, anti-Christian. In the divine plan the function of wealth was to perfect character and promote social welfare. "Wealth is the material for character-building; it is the foundation of the Kingdom of Heaven. The divine plan must, therefore, be that wealth shall be so distributed as to secure these great results. And religion . . . must teach that the wealth of the world will be rightly distributed only when every man shall have as much as he can wisely use to make himself a better man and the community in which he lives a better community—so much and no more." Just how much that was, Gladden was not prepared to detail at the moment. But the socialistic overtones of his message were unmistakable. Religion must effect a new economic order. The divine plan was a long way from realization. The work of religion was cut out for it: to bring higher principles to the world of politics and industry.[72]

With such principles and some of the enemy already generally defined, A. W. Small of the University of Chicago narrowed the focus from business and politics to life in the cities. That life, he said, "presents human wants in their most importunate and complex forms. In cities, motives to concrete good and evil are intensified to their maximum." In the city a premium was placed on selfishness, whether gross or refined; economic advantage became all-important; most social contacts were the occasion of the conflict of economic interests; the importance of individual personality was minimized. "Essential values thus tend most strongly to reversal in cities. Instead of appraising goods by their service to manhood, men in cities are under the severest temptation to value manhood according to productivity of goods. Men are measured by the same standard as draught horses and steam engines."[73] In other words, the cities focused and intensified the values and problems of an industrial-oriented society. Quite obviously the White City was an unreality. As much a fairyland as its admirers had said, it bore little resemblance to the environment that Small depicted. He continued the indictment by asserting that cities increased the social isolation of the majority of the populace and created social irresponsibility. As a result occurred those evils which were either peculiar to cities or more evident there: poverty, crime, unemployment, minimal wages, inhuman working conditions, unsanitary housing, drunkenness, unsavory business customs, child labor, boardinghouses, wages determined by sex, prostitution, political betrayals, class distinctions, industrial warfare, materialism, alienation.[74] It was, to say the least, a horrendous recital of evils. And what it meant was that religious doctrines or evocations of duty that did not deal directly with such conditions, some or all of which touched the lives of every city-dweller, were "simply mythologies and riddles." So much for theology. What, then, could the churches do? First, they must talk the language of the urbanites; they must realize that they were becoming class institutions; they must develop explicit policies toward city problems; they must make their mission one of relating man to his fellows as well as to his God. To effect such ends the churches should have concrete programs, more workers, slum missions, mutual cooperation, division of labor. "Let us record the hope," Small concluded, "and the prediction that this Parliament of Religions will promote municipal cooperation of all men who love their fellows . . . each pledging to the other his loyal fellowship toward helping every brother man to achieve life in more and more abundance!"[75] Given the kind of life Small had outlined, it might be wondered why anyone would desire it in greater abundance. In any event, Small's hopefulness seemed shaky and his prediction tenuous. And rightly so, for life in the cities offered a formidable, even a frightening, challenge. Chicago was a case in point.

The Englishman William T. Stead, well-known editor and journalist, who came to Chicago to study the city, to visit the exposition, and to address the parliament, would make that point unmistakably clear. Stead spoke of the need for what he called the

Civic Church, civic referring primarily to cities. "The Civic Church," he said, "is a phrase recalling to the mind of man that religion is concerned not merely with the salvation of the individual man, but with the regeneration of the whole community."[76] It is striking that so many speakers referred to this same duality of the individual and the community, citing the need for their mutual salvation. While asserting that patriotism had given a religious ideal to American life (reminiscent of Josiah Strong's views in *Our Country*), Stead advised "But, unless America is greatly belied, the conception of a divine order in city government is far from being naturalized in the minds of those who run the civic machine. It is here, therefore, that the organization of a Civic Church to redeem civic life seems so urgently needed. In a hemisphere which has given us the City of Chicago, the City of Saint Louis, the City of New York, there is need of the Civic Church to build the City of God."[77] Without becoming categorical and offensive, Stead was saying that American cities were so corrupt that drastic reformation was needed. Nothing short of establishing the millennium could redeem them, though, as Stead argued, there was sufficient work to be done to require the cooperation of all faiths—Christian, Buddhist, Muslim, Hindu. The essential ideal of the Civic Church was, however, Christian. Its objective was nothing less than "the restitution of human society, so as to establish a state of things that will minimize evil and achieve the greatest possible good for the greatest possible number." To accomplish this end the city would require devout and energetic leadership—would require, indeed, an angelic force. "Who is the angel of the Church of Chicago?" Stead asked. "Who is the accredited chief of the religious and moral forces of this great city? For combating sin when it develops into crime you have your chief constable. . . . for combating sin when it takes the form of anything touching the pockets or the bodies of our citizens you have the mayor." What Chicago needed, then, was a central authority to combat sin when it threatened the souls of men—a rather nice distinction. One man or woman must take charge of the restitution of the city. Obviously such a labor would be difficult, tentative, slow. But if persistent and fostered, its growth could be inexorable. Stead was hopeful, for, as he saw matters, "it has been reserved for the close of the nineteenth century to bring us within sight of the realization of the apostolic ideal, which is so essentially democratic."[78] As if determined to assume the role of Chicago's angel that he had called forth, Stead remained after the exposition to begin a reform movement. The spearhead of his effort would be his exposé of Chicago's venality and infamy, *If Christ Came to Chicago!* His intensive study of the nineteenth precinct would leave him somewhat less optimistic about the coming of the Civic Church.

It is not surprising that representatives of America's other two major religions—Roman Catholicism and Judaism—did not join their Protestant fellows in delivering even such guarded indictments of the society, which does not mean they were uninvolved in eradicating social evils. But they were, after all, still concerned primarily with securing their adherents from hostility or factionalism. (Rabbi Joseph Silverman of New York, in fact, called attention to the Jews' problems of assimilation in speaking on "Popular Errors about the Jews.") Nevertheless, there were concerns that all the religions shared. Perhaps the city was the focal point of American society's ills, a locus that magnified the seriousness of those ills; but there were issues of national scope that both included and exceeded the cities. Thus it was quite right that Paul Carus—German emigre resident of Chicago, editor of the *Monist*, and philosopher of science—should speak to the parliament about the relationship of science and religion, a relationship which at the time was fraught with hostile debate over such issues as evolution. The hostility was unjustified, Carus believed. For as he saw it, "Science is a revelation of God." Science revealed the truth which in turn revealed God's will. "A scientific insight into religious truth does not come to destroy religion; it will purify and broaden it," Carus argued.[79] His fervent pleas might not have mitigated the hostility, but at least they pinpointed the issue. Much the same was true of the assertions on "Religion and Labor" by James M.

Cleary, a Roman Catholic priest from Minneapolis. Cleary was walking the tightrope of the issue of labor unions, but his essential sympathies were evident. "Labor has a right to freedom," he argued; "labor has also a right to protect its own independence and liberty. Hence labor unions are lawful and have enjoyed the sanction and protection of the church in all ages. But labor must use its power for its own protection, not for invading the rights of others." As if to avoid too great partisanship, Cleary concluded, "Religion's duty is to teach the rich the responsibilities of wealth and the poor respect for law and order."[80] There was, after all, nothing new about the perennial American struggle between human rights and property rights, between higher morality and law and order. Nor was there anything new about America's racial problem.

Several speakers touched upon the fate of blacks in American society. Benjamin W. Arnett, bishop of the African Methodist Episcopal Church for Arkansas, Mississippi, Oklahoma, and the Indian Territory, called attention to the fact that the slaves had been freed a mere thirty years before the occasion of the exposition. He cited the achievements of blacks during that brief time in the fields of politics, education, industry, medicine, religion, theatre, music, and journalism. He also expressed thanks for the possibilities for advancement that had been opened to blacks. He then paid tribute to Congressman James M. Ashley who had helped to secure passage of the Thirteenth Amendment.[81] His speech, totally lacking in rancor, made no reference to still-prevailing discrimination nor to difficulties yet to be surmounted. Fannie Barrier Williams was not so tractable. She voiced the more militant views of Bishop Henry M. Turner of the African Methodist Episcopal Church, for the uncompromising bishop was not at the parliament. "No class of American citizens has had so little religion and so much vitiating nonsense preached to them as the colored people of this country," she declared. "There is needed less theology and more of human brotherhood, less declamation and more common sense and love for the truth." It was not that religion was valueless

277

to the blacks, but that its efforts were misdirected. Fannie Williams recommended what the proper direction should be. "The home and social life of these people are in urgent need of the purifying power of religion. In nothing was slavery so savage and so relentless as in its attempted destruction of the family instinct of the Negro race in America." Hence it was in family life that blacks needed instruction and assistance—in their homes and not in once-weekly pronouncements from the pulpit. Religion could be of help elsewhere. "In nothing do the American people so contradict the spirit of their institutions, the high sentiments of their civilization, and the maxims of their religion, as they do in practically denying to our colored men and women the full rights to life, liberty and the pursuit of happiness." Blacks had appealed in vain to every source of power in America. The churches themselves were guilty of monstrous error and inconsistency by establishing separate congregations for blacks, whereas blacks needed the helpfulness that could only come from communion and contact with whites. Here was something the churches could do. "I believe I correctly speak the feeling of the colored people," she said, "in declaring our unyielding faith in the corrective influence of true religion."[82] That faith, unfortunately, seems to have been misplaced. The Roman Catholic Church alone addressed itself to the race problem during the parliament. The day before Fannie Williams spoke, J. R. Slattery of Saint Joseph's Seminary in Baltimore had described Roman Catholicism's historic opposition to slavery, its position that all men were brothers, and its belief in helping to form the character of the blacks. Here, piously and perhaps unwittingly, he indulged in stereotype. "His [the black's] temperament, his passions and other inherent qualities, in great measure, also his industrial and social environments, are beyond his control, and he needs the aid of the best men of his own race, but associated with . . . the cooperation of the best of the white race." Such cooperation, stressing moral training and character building, would benefit blacks more than whites.[83] Slattery's advocacy, however well intentioned, was simply patronizing. It was precisely such sermons as his that Fannie Williams deplored.

Fannie Williams's outspokenness provided not only a refreshing interlude but also a reminder of the new-found status and independence of women. Other delegates brought the "woman question" to the fore. Spokesmen for feminism moved over from the Congress of Women to bring their message before the Parliament of Religions. Thus Frances Willard was on hand to discuss marriage, temperance, and equal suffrage. "Woman is becoming what God intended her to be," said Willard, "and Christ's Gospel necessitates her being, the companion and counselor, not the incumbrance and toy, of man."[84] Christian faith, it might be noted, was evoked in support of an enormous array of goals and ideas at the parliament. Elizabeth Cady Stanton saw the parliament as a proper forum for advocating purposes of broader scope than Willard entertained. She joined in the chorus of the Social Gospelers: "It is folly to talk of a just government and a pure religion where the state and the church alike sustain an aristocracy of wealth and ease, while those who do the hard work of the world have no share in the blessings and riches that their continued labors have made possible for others to enjoy." Her plea was for equal rights, eradication of poverty, altruism, social morality, improved environments.[85] Julia Ward Howe also pleaded for high-mindedness, but the plea led her finally to her major theme. "I think nothing is religion which puts one individual absolutely above others, and surely nothing is religion which puts one sex above another. . . . Any religion which will sacrifice a certain set of human beings for the enjoyment or aggrandizement or advantage of another is no religion. . . . Any religion which sacrifices women to the brutality of men is no religion."[86] Howe might very well have pursued her charge and castigated the churches for excluding women from the clergy. For churches still denied or impeded women's attempts to enter the pulpit, as the Reverend Antoinette Brown Blackwell observed. The exclusion stemmed from the same sources as the old double standard, she argued; "the outgrowth of the same basal iniquity." But woman was needed in the pulpit, she contended; woman was "indispensable to the religious evolution of the human race."[87] Blackwell's dismay and her strictures were both understandable. Though also restricted in her religious expressions, the Jewish woman was relatively content with her lot, if Henrietta Szold was to be believed. The Jewish woman's influence was in the home, she said. "She is the inspirer of a pure, chaste family life, whose hallowing influences are incalculable; she is the center of all spiritual endeavors, the confidante and fosterer of every undertaking."[88] That might have been a satisfying life for Szold, but it would certainly not assuage the desires of the woman's movement. As Lydia Fuller Dickinson summed up matters, the woman's movement was "the last battleground of Freedom and Slavery. We are in the dawn of a new and final dispensation." There had been some progress, she admitted, but there was more to come—a new reign of justice and love. "This, as I see it, is the inmost secret of the Woman Movement, a movement that includes both men and women, as partakers alike of the woman principle. We are indeed all feminine to the divine, all receptive to the new impulse toward, the new belief in, the brotherhood of man."[89] Such was the meaning of woman's struggle for freedom. God had assisted feminism. Could the churches do any less?

The declarations of these several speakers reflect the concerns and intentions of some of America's most prominent and outspoken religious and secular leaders. Consequently, they probably also reflect the state of mind of those members of the dominant middle class who were at all religiously or civically oriented. But concentrating on these comments, which are most relevant to the meaning of the exposition for Americans, also serves to focus too narrowly upon only some of the programs and speeches of the World's Parliament of Religions and thus unintentionally to obscure the enormous breadth and depth of its scope and impact. For the meaning of the parliament to Americans was not merely that it provided a forum where religious leaders could air their criticisms and ideals, however undeniably important that meaning was. The larger significance of the parliament was its internationalism, its ecumenism. The assumption of that significance was contained in Charles C. Bonney's closing address, in which he declared, "The influence which this Congress of Religions of the World will exert on the peace and prosperity of the world is beyond the power of human language to describe. For this influence, borne by those who have attended the sessions of the Parliament of Religions to all parts of the world, will affect, in some important degree, all races of men; all forms of religion; and even all governments and social institutions."[90] Though Bonney was clearly overawed and though his expectations were extravagant, he nevertheless had caught the sense of hope and brotherliness that permeated the atmosphere of the parliament and especially its closing session.

The World's Parliament of Religions came to an official but reluctant close on September 27, seventeen days after its opening session. More than 7,000 spectators crowded into the Halls of Washington and Columbus to witness the closing ceremonies. The atmosphere was exceedingly cordial, intimate, fraternal. That Bonney's feelings did not exaggerate the prevailing mood is clear from the remarks of the first of the notables introduced, the Reverend Alfred W. Momerie from London, England. The Parliament of Religions, he said, "is the greatest event so far in the history of the world, and it has been held on American soil."[91] Many of Momerie's Christian colleagues would later express the belief that the parliament was the most important occurrence since the birth of Jesus.

And it was all the outcome of inspired efforts put forth by Chicago. As another of the speakers, also an Englishman and a missionary, said, "By this Parliament the city of Chicago has placed herself far away above all the cities of the earth. In this school you have learned what no other town or city in the world yet knows." What had been learned, declared George Candlin, was that Christianity was not the only or the true religion, that there were many faiths under God and that they could all dwell in peace with each other. "This has been known to a few lonely thinkers, seers of the race, in different parts of the world, but not to the people of any town or city ... except Chicago."[92] This was Chicago's message. It was therefore fitting that Barrows related to the assembled throng, "While floating over the illuminated waters of the White City, Mr. Dharmapala said, with that smile which has won our hearts, 'All the joys of Heaven are in Chicago'; and Dr. Momerie, with a characteristic mingling of enthusiasm and skepticism, replied, 'I wish I were sure that all the joys of Chicago are to be in Heaven.' "[93] Thus did the Occident and the Orient meet in peace and friendliness in Chicago. To some it must have seemed strange that a servant of Mammon like Chicago was the catalyst for such humane socializing. But Barrows invoked the city "not as the home of the rudest materialism, but as a temple where men cherish the loftiest idealism."[94] The thought seemed a suitable end to the World's Parliament of Religions.

It was not, however, the end of the World's Congress Auxiliary, though it might just as well have been. There had been numerous other congresses running simultaneously with those already mentioned—congresses on civil law and government, journalism, public health, philanthropy, social reform, music, brewing, stenography, youth, engineering, political science, inventors, labor, economics, Jewish women, Catholicism. Following the parliament, there were congresses on agriculture and public health. But these were anticlimaxes. There is no question that the high-water mark of the auxiliary was the World's Parliament of Religions. To no other congress did the public respond so enthusiastically; commentary on the other congresses as a whole was a mere fraction of that devoted to the parliament alone.

The World's Congress Auxiliary itself came to a close on October 28, with Charles C. Bonney, the author by this time of multifarious speeches delivered at the opening of each congress, providing the benedictory words. He made a worthy distinction. "That the material exhibit of the World's Columbian Exposition in Jackson Park is the most complete and magnificent ever presented to human view, is generally agreed," Bonney observed, "but a multitude of eminent witnesses have declared, after attendance on both, that the Intellectual and Moral Exposition of the Progress of Mankind presented in the World's Congresses of 1893 is greater and more imposing still." The auxiliary was now to take its place in history, he said, as "an imperishable part of the progress of mankind."[95] Bonney had fallen under the sway of the grandiose and, as time proved, illusory atmosphere of the auxiliary. But he was certainly not alone in that; and euphoric as his pronouncements were, they remain representative of the response to this great occasion. As Bonney pointed out, of even the minor congresses it was said that they were the most important conferences of their kind ever held, with respect to both quantity and quality, and to the representativeness and eminence of the participants. Few things went amiss in the programming. Participation was enormous, despite the fact that delegates received no recompense, except for those few who were supported by subscriptions. And the decorum of the proceedings was impressive: there was virtually no controversy. Of course, as Bonney noted, some groups had been excluded, such as the Freethinkers and the Mormon Church —not invited because they sanctioned polygamy. But all in all the congresses constituted a unique assemblage of variant faiths.

Bonney had special praise for the work of the Woman's Branch of the auxiliary, which functioned well in spite of predictions that it would prove unmanageable. The progress of woman, he judged, would secure for her a position in the world that corresponded to her position in the family. In similar vein he applauded the progress suggested by the auxiliary's alliances between religion and labor, science and social reform, finance and altruism, science and philosophy. "The Parliament of Religions," Bonney declared, singling out that congress, "has emancipated the world from bigotry, and henceforth civil and religious liberty will have a larger and easier sway." Again, it was an extravagant claim, but there is no gainsaying the virtue of its underlying goals and premises. These were also contained in the auxiliary's motto, to which Bonney referred. " 'Not things but men! Not matter but mind!'

will henceforth rank among the commanding watchwords of mankind."[96] That his prophecy went unrealized is not to Bonney's discredit. The loftiness of his aspirations for mankind remains admirable though unrealized. It was on the same lofty plane that his final words climaxed the auxiliary's many weeks of remarkable meetings: "and with an abiding faith that henceforth the armies of learning, virtue, industry and peace will march triumphantly forward till the hosts of ignorance, vice, idleness and strife shall everywhere be conquered and dispersed, and law, liberty, and justice reign supreme, I now declare the close of the World's Congresses of 1893."[97]

With the World's Congress Auxiliary come to an official close, judgments upon its value to the American public and to the world at large were soon forthcoming. Few could have doubted that the auxiliary was a momentous event. Its deliberations had been witnessed by 700,000 spectators, a small number when compared with the millions who visited the exposition itself, but an impressive audience nonetheless. In addition thousands of people throughout the world had read newspaper and magazine reports of the sessions and publication or quotation of some of the papers. Thus although overshadowed in the immediate moment by the exposition, the potential influence and perpetuation of the discussions at the World's Congress Auxiliary were quite large. "Out of the World's Columbian Exposition has come inspiration for many boasts," wrote Thomas B. Bryan, vice president of the auxiliary. But since so many people had been involved in the work, he felt that none could be accused of vanity who expressed pride in the outcome. Hence he had no compunction in asserting, "And when the results of the Fair are measured, so far as they may ever be, it seems certain that of all its features . . . none will deserve more credit than the World's Congress Auxiliary for the benefit and the strength of its influences."[98] He may very well have been right. He was certainly right in his implication that the fair's results might never be measured. Barrows said any historian attempting to review the Parliament of Religions alone would be staggered. In addition to the papers, Barrows said, there was an avalanche of commentary.[99] But that avalanche itself attested the auxiliary's influence. Its most outstanding feature had been the World's Parliament of Religions, which the internationally known scholar of comparative religions Max Müller said was "one of the most memorable events in the history of the world," an event which "stands unique, stands unprecedented in the whole history of the world."[100] The parliament had set a precedent; the auxiliary had set a standard. As evidence of the possibility for cooperation, ecumenism, mutual respect in human affairs, the World's Congress Auxiliary set an example of high-mindedness and beneficence that all nations could well have taken to heart in their dealings with each other. As with the White City, Chicago—and indeed the nation as a whole—could take justifiable pride in the outcome of Charles C. Bonney's inspired idea to convene an international congress.

7

VISIONS OF THE CELESTIAL CITY

Sending rivers of regrets after it, we say,
unctuously, it was the fairest city that ever
the sun shown on.

General Lew Wallace

THE WORLD'S COLUMBIAN EXPOSITION officially ended at sunset on October 30. The formal ceremonies marking the fair's end were to have been nearly as elaborate and certainly as celebrative as those featured at the dedication. They were keenly anticipated. But disaster intervened. On the evening of October 28 an office-seeker, disgruntled over failure to receive a political appointment, shot Mayor Carter Henry Harrison on the threshold of the mayor's home. The assassination shocked and saddened Chicago. What was to have been a suitably festive climax to the great exposition became instead a funeral. The closing ceremonies were austere. They were held in Festival Hall; "representatives of all nations were present; oratory and song gave way to prayer and dirge."[1] Thomas W. Palmer and H. N. Higinbotham eulogized the mayor; John Henry Barrows offered prayer. A resolution of sympathy to be sent to the Harrison family was accepted. Palmer announced that the end of the exposition would be signaled merely by a cannon salute and the lowering of the flag. He declared the exposition officially closed. Though none of the speeches originally prepared was delivered, Barrows did read part of Higinbotham's address. His mood was somber: " 'We are turning our backs on the fairest dream of civilization and are about to consign it to the dust. It is like the death of a dear friend.' "[2] Thus were intertwined the deaths of Carter Harrison and the White City. White flags flew at half-staff throughout Chicago; the solemn spectators of the final ceremonies filed out of Festival Hall to the sounds of Beethoven's Funeral March. And so came to a somber climax "the greatest World's Fair in history."[3]

The violent death of Carter Harrison was an unfortunate prophecy of the fate that awaited the closed exposition. Harrison himself had unwittingly foretold that fate on the very day of his assassination while addressing the final assemblage of the Board of Lady Managers and woman participants in the fair at the Woman's Building. Present to hear him were such stalwart leaders of feminism as Bertha Palmer, Susan B. Anthony, Laura Gordon, Sarah Stevenson, Mary Lowe Dickinson, representatives of the Woman's National Suffrage Association, the WCTU, the YWCA, the Daughters of the American Revolution, the Woman's Press Clubs, and other organizations. Harrison's intent was to argue for the preservation of the exposition buildings, since he regarded the fair as "the greatest educator the world has ever known."[4] He expressed the hope that Congress would provide funds to preserve the buildings for another year, so that the exposition might resume in 1894. But if such could not be done, he agreed with Daniel H. Burnham that the exposition should be set afire—its conflagration would be a great spectacle for Chicagoans, Burnham felt. "I believe with him," said the mayor. "If we cannot preserve it for another year I would be in favor of putting a torch to it . . . and let it go up into the bright sky to eternal heaven."[5]

Art lovers put forth numerous proposals for preserving parts or all of some of the buildings and for making the fairgrounds into a center for the arts, while time and weather ravaged the buildings' exteriors and the appeal of Burnham's idea increased. On January 8, 1894, incendiaries set a fire which destroyed the Casino, the Peristyle, and the Music Hall. Then on July 3 the terminal station caught fire. Flames quickly spread to the Administration, Mines and Mining, Electricity, Machinery, Agricultural, Manufactures, and some smaller buildings, creating a fantastic pyrotechnic display. Burnham's proposal was fulfilled. The grand White City, the glorious creation of men who "must have been very near to God," became the scene of a great Götterdämmerung. There was no choice but to sacrifice the buildings to the wreckers. Their work, like that of the builders before, was prodigious.

The unkind fate that befell the fair was recorded in funereal tones by *Scientific American* in 1896: "The World's Columbian Exposition Salvage Company have completed their task of removing the buildings. . . . It has stretched over a period of two and a half years, during which time an immense amount of labor has been done. A few buildings have been permitted to remain, but they stand only to serve special purposes, and are only faintly suggestive of the architectural glories which once graced Jackson Park." Still standing was the Art Palace, converted into the Columbian Museum; "the once beautiful German Building in dilapidation; . . . the sham convent of La Rabida. The Goddess of Liberty still occupies her lofty pedestal, with her cap gone and several of her fingers missing."[6] Of the rest of the buildings bits and pieces were scattered throughout the world. Steel salvaged from the buildings had gone to the furnaces of Pittsburgh and of the Illinois Steel Company. Parts of some buildings had been removed to Kansas City and Springfield. One building had been made over into flats. The trusses from the annex of the Transportation Building had gone to Milwaukee. Its famed "Golden Door" remained intact in the hands of a Chicago dealer. Nothing was salvaged from the New York State Building; Frank Millet's mural work was dust. The Illinois Building was consumed by fire. The plaster ornaments of the Fisheries Building—frogs, fish, lizards—had been removed and were being sold as souvenirs. Glass panes—500,000 square feet of them—used in the buildings had gone into greenhouses and cornices. Bits of staff had gone to schools, convents, universities as specimens. Fire had destroyed all the decorative ornaments of the Woman's Building, which were stored in the Electricity Building. The four lions that stood at the base of the obelisk had gone to H. N. Higinbotham. "They now lord it over inoffensive ducks and chickens at . . . [his] farm at Elgin." Other statues—Franklin, Columbus, the Cowboy and the Indian—had gone to museums, universities, other cities. The rest was ashes.[7] "The glory and magnificence of the 'White City' has passed away."[8]

Now it would be left to the "poor scribblers . . . to take up the task of perpetuating this creation of beauty and of splendor," as Charles Dudley Warner had foretold in his speech before the World's Congress Auxiliary.[9] The poor scribblers were forthcoming. Some of them wrote simply about the exposition itself. Artist-author F. Hopkinson Smith wrote an essay about his experiences and difficulties in trying to do some paintings of the Art Palace, which he described as a building "whose grandeur, symmetry and faultless decoration will last as long as the memory of the great Exposition itself."[10] Julian Hawthorne, son of the great novelist, wrote an entire book about the exposition. When he had first seen it he thought the fair was "the greatest thing of its kind," and after two months of familiarizing himself with it he thought even "more highly of it than I did at the outset." Hawthorne lauded most of the buildings. He found the exhibits good but resented their presence as interfering with "the impressions of magnitude and majestic spaciousness" which he had found so splendid while touring the empty buildings in February 1893.[11] Richard Watson Gilder was stirred to joyous praise in his eulogistic poem of farewell to the White City:

> *Thou shalt of all the cities of the world*
>   *Famed for their grandeur, ever more endure*
> *Imperishably and all alone impearled*
>   *In the world's living thought, the one most sure*
> *Of love undying and of endless praise*
>   *For beauty only . . . .*[12]

Numerous other poets poured forth tributes. The University of Chicago commemorated the White City in its alma mater. But such works as those of F. H. Smith, Hawthorne, and Gilder were limited both in their intentions and in their scope—not imaginative re-creations of the fair, not real literary works at all, but simply travel memories. Addressed more closely to Warner's point were William Dean Howells's utopian *Letters of an Altrurian Traveler*. But still more evocative and commemorative were the novelistic treatments of the World's Columbian Exposition as setting and theme.

The exposition assumed a major role in thirteen novels published in its aftermath, some as recently as the 1920s. Their predominant theme "is the contrast between the White City and the Black. These novels were addressed to farmers, villagers, and middle class urbanites."[13] Some of the novels were more compelling or more curious than others. The most inspirational of them all, and certainly the most thorough literary adaptation of the World's Columbian Exposition, was *Two Little Pilgrims' Progress* by the highly popular writer of children's books, Frances Hodgson Burnett. For Burnett the White City was an earthly paradise where all problems could be resolved. It was a cosmic ideal. Her little novel stars two orphan children, Robin and Meg Macleod, who live with an austere aunt on an Illinois farm. They work hard, they daydream, and they continually reread John Bunyan's *Pilgrim's Progress*. Talk of the exposition excites their interest. They save their money and hasten away to Chicago, where they board with a poor family in the slums. The mother of the family is a saint and the father is a drunkard. Robin and Meg take the son Ben with them to the fair. Here they continuously encounter John Holt, a wealthy widower, who is so charmed by the Macleods that he adopts them, makes provision for Ben, and thoroughly browbeats the drunken father. All's well that ends well.

This little novel embodies several interesting commentaries. It follows the formula of the Horatio Alger stories, and its protagonists have the same frankness, delicacy, and independence as the curly-haired Cedric Errol, hero of *Little Lord Fauntleroy*, Burnett's best-seller. Hence it was in the best tradition of popular nineteenth-century children's literature. Its potential audience was everybody who had seen the fair, and Burnett had with good purpose laid her scene "in Bunyan's City Beautiful made real in the White City by the Lake."[14] Her intentions were all too clear. Once while reading Bunyan and imagining herself as Christian nearly at the gates of the Celestial City, Meg is interrupted by Robin who brings new word of the fair. " 'I do wish,' " Meg laments, " 'there *was* a city beautiful.' " Robin assures her that there will be and that it will be " 'on this earth and not a hundred miles away.' "[15] Thus we are forewarned that the White City will represent an immediate and miraculous attainment of the Social Gospelers' dream of the kingdom of God on earth. Through a blending of the self-help ethic with the Social Gospel, Burnett effects for her little hero and heroine that miraculous realization. They will share it with Ben, whom they lead to the exposition with his eyes closed, so that "all the entrancement of beauty should burst upon Ben's hungry soul, as Paradise Bursts upon translated spirits."[16] The experience is reminiscent of Hopeful accompanying Christian within the gates of the Celestial City. Any doubt of gaining entry is dispelled when Meg, overcome with joy when Holt informs her in front of the Agricultural Building that he will adopt her and Robin, proclaims to their benefactor, " 'We have got *into* the City Beautiful, and you are going to let us live there always.' "[17] Thus the realization of the Celestial City becomes both achieved and ongoing. Furthermore, poor little Ben's mother appears and punctuates this final triumph of the spiritual by assuring everyone that, through his visits to the fair, her son seems as though " 'he had been born over again.' "[18] Wondrous indeed was the magic of the White City.

It would seem merely curious that Burnett had thus synthesized the sublime spirituality of the Celestial City with the temporal evanescence of the World's Columbian Exposition, had not the testimony of other writers supported her interpretation. That is, in fact, the most singular awareness of Burnett's novel: that so many fairgoers could readily project and believe that the secular kingdom of God was affirmed in the physical reality of the exposition. Burnett's analogy was a popular one. It inhered in the expressions, recorded earlier, that those who built the White City "must have been very near to God"; that they had created the "Heavenly City" or the "New Jerusalem."[19] Another author of children's literature, Tudor Jenks, who was associate editor of *St. Nicholas*, correctly summarized such interpretations of the exposition and hopefully anticipated their outcome in the conclusion of his book about the fair: "the phantom city has taught the American nation that they are a great people, who will some day make true in marble all that was imagined in that short-lived fairy-story of staff."[20] Jenks simply reflected the belief of many fervent reformers that America had the capacity to create a secular paradise. That paradise, as much a matter of money, stone, and steel as of faith and reformation, had been brought to life in the White City.

Just how compelling this vision was is further revealed in still other novels that render the fair into fiction. For example, Samantha, the wry homespun heroine of several popular novels by Marietta Holley, found herself quite awed by the Court of Honor: "never agin will such a seen [*sic*] glow and grow before mine eyes, till the streets of the New Jerusalem open before my vision."[21] It was an impression she would repeat, adding that in hoping to see the New Jerusalem at the fair "I hadn't really expected half nor a quarter nor a millionth part enough."[22] Her simplistic, though rather tongue-in-cheek, views were certain to evoke the responsiveness of many readers who had been there. The White City secured two romances in Samantha's tale. The romance motif reciprocated its fairyland, Arabian nights setting.

That was the secret also of a novel by Chicago's own Clara Louise Root Burnham. The White City is where her one hero and heroine, Harvard-educated Gorham Page and demure impecunious Clover Bryant, find each other. In the White City their love blossoms. Burnham's novel serves as a lover's guide to the allurements of the exposition. Jack Van Tassell, the other hero, and Clover watch President Cleveland throw on the electric switch and "the vast pulses of the stately, statuesque White City began to beat."[23] Of the many sights along the arteries that pulse travels the one that most impresses Clover is the Peristyle. Her accompanying friend Mildred is especially smitten by this enormous colonnade, which she appropriates as a fetish—mystical, perhaps, but curious nevertheless. Still other sights intrigue them. Wealthy Chicagoan Jack Van Tassell foresees the promise of the Celestial City when he first gazes upon the Court of Honor. He is awestruck by the Transportation Building and finds the Agricultural Building a divine vision. But it is left to still another companion, the homely Massachusetts spinster Aunt Love, to summarize these various impressions. She does so by drawing a contrast between the Midway Plaisance and the exposition proper. The Midway, with its carnival atmosphere and suggestive pleasures, is, she believes, a representation of matter, whereas the White City is a symbol of mind. To pass from the former to the latter, Aunt Love decides, must be like dying and passing into heaven. " 'Taint only the quiet and grandeur o' those buildin's compared with the fantastic things you've left behind,' she explains; 'I believe it's just the fact that the makers o' the Fair believed in God and put Him and their enlightenment from Him into what they did; and we feel it some like we'd feel an electric shock.' "[24] Aunt Love thus verifies both the essence of the fair as a heavenly vision, a God-inspired creation, and the stunning impact of the fair's electrical displays. In the midst of such vision and energy the culmination of love seems predestined. Clover and Gorham find their waxing love symbolized in the colossal dimensions of the Manufactures Building. But between Jack and Mildred intervenes her thraldom with the Peristyle, emblematic of something higher than mere heterosexual love. While the Peristyle survives Mildred will not promise herself to Jack. Finally on that January evening in 1894 when fire ravaged the fair, Jack and Mildred rush to Jackson Park in time to see the flames consume her beloved colonnade. Mildred is aghast.

" 'The—Peristyle has gone!' she exclaimed chokingly,—'gone back —to heaven!' "[25] The last barrier to their love is burned away.

Such rapturous views of the White City seem a trifle exaggerative or even ludicrous in retrospect, but there is no doubt about the seriousness of their authors' intentions. Nor is there any doubt that such works reflected a popular response to the fair. That response is implied even in some of the novels of more significant writers whose purposes were quite different from those which infused these romantic tales. Henry Blake Fuller, for example, employed the exposition as a means for ironic commentary in one of his typically depreciatory social satires, *With the Procession*. His protagonist, Truesdale Marshall, son of a prominent Chicago family, returns home from a long residence in Europe which has made him into a cultivated man. He finds that the fair, already closed, is still worth a visit. He wanders about the grounds admiringly. The appearance of the exposition far exceeds his brightest anticipation of it, and he regrets that he had not returned two weeks sooner. "He met half-way the universal expectation that the spirit of the White City was but just transferred to the body of the great Black City close at hand, over which it was to hover as an enlightenment."[26] No city was in greater need of enlightenment, Marshall was sure. The damning picture of a great, hideous monster of a city that he drew of Chicago makes it quite obvious that he (and of course Fuller too) believed that not even the influence of the White City could help to transform soot-blackened Chicago into an objet d'art.

Another Chicago novelist, Robert Herrick, made the fair the scene of the major turn of events in his novel *Memoirs of an American Citizen*. Edward Van Harrington, the protagonist of Herrick's novel, was a robber baron who fought his way up from clerk to capitalist in the meat-packing industry. The president of his company was one of the commissioners for the exposition and in the capacity he spent, in Harrington's opinion, an inordinate amount of time away from the business. But the results earned Harrington's admiration nonetheless. He took his family to the fair many times. On one night visit amidst the beauty of the illuminated buildings and lagoons, Harrington slipped out of character momentarily. "In that lovely hour . . . the toil and trouble of men, the fear that was gripping men's hearts in the market, fell away from me, and in its place came Faith."[27] The economic depression, the threats of his enemies, his financial difficulties, the scourge of commercial warfare all receded, leaving Harrington's mind trouble-free, under the influence of the fair's beauty. In their place came faith. It was decidedly a strange sort of faith, not of religion but of superconfidence in his own ego and ability. On this same night at the fair the wife of the company president, Jane Dround, who admired Harrington's ruthless driving nature and shared vicariously in the drama of his rise to power, committed herself totally to the achievement of his ends. She gave him an envelope to be opened only in the event of dire need. When the time came to open it, Harrington discovered a directive to approach a source who would save him from ruin by availing him of Jane Dround's great capital resources. His economic success was thereafter inexorable. The next step was politics. What had been the vision of the City Beautiful for the Macleod children became the inspiration of Vanity Fair for Harrington.

In another of Herrick's novels, *The Common Lot*, whose hero is an architect, there is fleeting reference to the exposition as the initial source of the heroine's education in the beauty and potential of architecture. What she learned during the fair's run perhaps explained the fact that she was enraptured with the hero's grand architectural plans for the future. "For something earnest and large was the first craving of her soul, something that had in it service and beauty in life."[28] In just such terms the exposition itself could have been summed up. It was, after all, in similar terms that the realist William Dean Howells, temporarily turned visitor from the Altrurian utopia, experienced the fair. It was a setting which brought peace and rest. It was totally reminiscent of the cities of Altruria "in being a design, the effect of a principle, and not the straggling and shapeless accretion of accident."[29] One example of accretion of accident in American architecture was New York; another was Chicago itself. The lesson of the World's Columbian Exposition should not be lost, Howells insisted. In future years Americans would look back upon it and cherish the White City as "the earliest achievement of a real civic life."[30]

Though the view of these realistic novelists is more pragmatic than the kingdom-of-God vision of Burnett, it stems from the same inspiration and it hopes for a similar reformation of America's cities from chaos into order. All this literature indicates a prevailing interest in the fair long after its demise. That interest evidenced a desire to assess the fair's worth and influence. For our novelists, whether idealistic or pessimistic, discerned in common that essential truth since attested by William Jordy: "In its Roman and baroque trappings . . . the imperial flavor of the White City accorded with the imperial flavor of American culture at the end of the century. It was not merely, or even principally, the imperialism of foreign affairs which the symbolism of the Exposition made concrete, but the hegemony of the metropolis over the farm."[31] Sentimental, ironic, or sober, authors perceived in the White City either a benign and elevating fairyland or an object lesson of what a desirable urban environment might be—or both. What they saw was the ideal American city as it might have been or could become. Their focus was upon the exposition architecture and grounds. That was neither surprising nor inappropriate. It was believed at the time, and it has been believed since, that the combined architecture, sculpture, and landscape design of the exposition were its most compelling and influential features. That belief in itself is suggestive of the fair's eminence. Describing the White City as "the greatest thing that ever came into my life," as giving "verity and value to everything," and as a thing of beauty never before equaled and perhaps never to be repeated, William Dean Howells summed up its meaning in saying, "There was no niggardly competition, but rather emulation toward the highest and best. And the result is that the esthetic interest in the Fair has quite eclipsed the industrial, which is a great thing for

America."[32] Previous world's fairs had been produced and regarded mostly as huge industrial exhibits, and certainly the World's Columbian Exposition was that. But its more immediate and lasting impression was its beauty. That beauty resulted from the labors of architects, landscape architects, sculptors, and painters in a combined endeavor that was unprecedented in American history. Whether it was really a great achievement for America remains debatable to this day.

The debate had begun while the exposition was still open to the public. One of the country's leading architectural journals defined the nature of the dispute. The *Architectural Review* editorialized, "The great interest of the foreign architects who came to the Chicago Fair lay in the high buildings of the city, rather than in the somewhat stale—however grandiose—problem in the handling of classical forms. . . . Magnificent as was our accomplishment, and valuable as were its lessons for a nation unaccustomed to concerted action in matters relating to art, it yet lacked that seal of distinctive propriety in the largest sense which the foreigner had hoped to see. They came to see us, and we held up to them a mirror in which they saw themselves reflected." The exposition architecture was undeniably imitative, with few exceptions. To see what was distinctively American in our architecture foreign visitors had to visit that urban wonder that the fastidious Henry Blake Fuller labeled the Black City. "In the tall buildings of Chicago," continued the editorial, "they saw . . . what they recognized as an indigenous product, a truthful revelation of native conditions, and of interest for that reason."[33] And rightly so, for in the commercial structures, the innovative skyscrapers, in the heart of Chicago could be seen a genuinely American architecture ostensibly more reflective of the values, purposes, and "national character than any other type of structure, not excepting the work of colonial times."[34] Exposition buildings in classical style were derivative; the Chicago skyscrapers were unique. To emulate the former would be a denial of the very nature of our society. Thus the issue was joined.

The issue, however, was not quite so simple. There was, after all, nothing novel about classical-style buildings in America. Neither was American classicism merely derivative nor determined by the educative legacy of European training. "In fact, although some of the designers [of the exposition] had been trained in France, the architecture was not the same as that being built in any European country. This is an important point, since most criticisms of the Fair's influence . . . are based on the erroneous idea that American architects, especially those from the East, were merely copying what they had seen abroad."[35] Interest in creating a native style, it must be remembered, was as keen among devotees of classicism as among those of the commercial style. The debate over a national style was by no means ended, and prominent in that debate were many architects who favored the classical style or Renaissance adaptations of it. Among them were men whose achievements cannot be gainsaid: Richard Morris Hunt, Stanford White, Charles Follen McKim, and Henry Van Brunt. Van Brunt expressed the view of the classicists rather well in describing the exposition architecture as the achievement of the rigors of discipline and of loyalty to established art forms representative of the best in human history. He added, "To millions of intelligences, from the highest to the lowest, the architecture of Jackson Park, with its subsidiary sculpture and painting, was a revelation of the power of art, and millions of lives were made larger and fuller by the experience."[36] What were the sources of this achievement that was both artistic and popular? "In the first place, the great creation at Jackson Park was made intelligible to the people by its harmonious unity," Van Brunt asserted. This was not, however, a unity of mere uniformity, which would have been monotonous and would have given neither pleasure nor profit. "It is clear therefore that, in the second place, another quality besides unity,—namely, diversity,—was an essential part of the architectural scheme." But to make diversity consistent with unity is an enormous problem, one not possible on such a large scale for a single person to resolve. "Consequently, in the third place, a cooperation of distinct and sympathetic individualities . . . was necessary, being restrained by the adoption of certain leading conditions of composition, common to all the buildings," with each architect still left to make his own building distinct through giving it his personal stamp.[37] These were the truly momentous achievements of the artists who designed the White City: unity, diversity, cooperation.

Van Brunt was not alone in pointing them out, nor in calling attention to their beneficial public effects. Even Barr Ferree, champion of the skyscraper and admirer of the Transportation Building, acknowledged the cultural and educational benefits of the exposition's classical architecture. "No Roman emperor in the plenitude of his power ever conceived so vast a festival as this . . .," he wrote. "It marks a new epoch in the evolution of American character and American taste, and above all in American architecture. Surely among the final results of this great enterprise its influence upon the future of American architecture must hold the first rank. People who never talked of architecture talk of it now, and the fact that there is such an art—a real art and a true one—will be made manifest to many minds where before the very conception of it was impossible."[38] The influence Ferree spoke of was not toward love of the classical style—certainly he would not have advocated that—but toward discovery, awareness. Architecture had never been a concern of the American public. As a profession it was only forty years old; instruction in architecture was a recent development. But the exposition, Ferree assumed, would make architecture real and interesting to the American public. Surely that was desirable. The father of the Chicago skyscraper, William LeBaron Jenney, went even further and argued, "The lessons taught by the architecture of the World's Fair are valuable and will improve the architecture of Chicago. They may be briefly enumerated as dignity—repose—adaptability to the requirements. . . . A careful study of precedents. Regard for proportions as a whole and in the several parts and in details."[39] If such principles might be learned by architects and public alike through the architecture of the exposition, then its influence should have been welcomed by all devotees of art and beauty. Such an influence might not have pleased everyone, but the popularity of the White City could have been taken as an indication of a public desire. "The wish, that the beauty of the Court of Honor might be perpetuated, is the natural expression of the admiration it excites," wrote one critic. "It is also the protest of the imagination against the ugliness of our cities, their general sacrifice of the aspirations of the educated minority to the supposed wants of the majority; and it is delight in a generous offering to our inner desire for a lovelier setting to our lives." This critic called attention to the contrast between the exposition of 1889, surrounded by the lovely city of Paris, and the present exposition surrounded by "a hideous suburb, whence a train whirls you away to a grimy, workaday city." He believed, nevertheless, that there was an inner and moral harmony between the White City and the Black City and that this harmony prophesied Chicago's future. This concept of harmony was his point, as it was Van Brunt's; nor was this critic advocating a classical style—a burgeoning of that, he said, would be a calamity.[40] Similarly, Chicago architect Peter B. Wight, who wished to see neither a period of emulation of the classical style nor further development of the skyscraper, argued that the exposition buildings should not be criticized individually, because they were temporary and would therefore do no harm. "Their faults may best die with them," he wrote, "but their influence for better architectural effects will live as a potent educator in future years. It will teach us that the beauty of our cities can be enhanced as much by careful consideration of the relation between building and building as by the superior excellence of individual but adjacent structures." He went on to denounce the destruction of perspective effected by the skyscrapers and the architectural travesties perpetrated by state and federal governments.[41] But his denunciation hardly calls into doubt the virtue of his advocacy of harmony and beauty in city architecture.

That is a point which architectural historians, in their haste to condemn the presumed influence of the exposition's classical architecture, have repeatedly and injuriously failed to take into account. They have even skewed the comments of that great critic Montgomery Schuyler in employing his criticisms to uphold their negations of the fair's supposed historic legacy. Schuyler did not deplore the classicism of the exposition buildings. What he deplored was the possibility that their success might be misinterpreted and improperly reproduced by architects of limited talent. It is a fear that, as must be quite obvious, pertains to any style of architecture, whether derivative or unique. We need only recall some of the hideous buildings erected in imitation of Henry Hobson Richardson's designs or some of the sterile and soul-withering structures produced by mediocre practitioners of the "International Modern School." The real point at issue was in fact well clarified by Montgomery Schuyler's final words about the exposition.

Schuyler referred to the White City as "the most admired group of buildings ever erected in this country"—an unequivocal statement, to say the least. He then cited Burnham's own conclusion that the fair would inspire the erection of classical-style buildings. Schuyler did not find that prospect pleasing to contemplate, but his doubts did not arise from a feeling that classicism was an aberration. He assumed that the exposition would result in classical buildings whose quality would depend upon the ability of the architects; but, he said, "it is not likely that any of these will even dimly recall, and quite impossible that they should equal the architectural triumph of the Fair." The problem was, he argued, that imitation would ignore the conditions that had made the fair's architecture so successful. The point that needed to be made, then, was what were those conditions. "In the first place," Schuyler asserted, "the success is first of all a success of unity, a triumph of *ensemble*. The whole is better than any of its parts and greater than all its parts, and its effect is one and indivisible. We are speaking now of the Court of Honor," which was, as he said, what everyone was referring to in discussing the exposition architecture. This remarkable unity, Schuyler pointed out, derived from the common classical style and the uniformity of height.[42] Now, this unity was, as any number of comments should have made clear, the singular virtue of the White City. It was a "triumph of *ensemble*." Schuyler also asserted that the landscape plan of Olmsted and Codman "was the key to the pictorial success of the Fair as a whole." Thus landscape design was fundamental to the White City's unity. The second condition which made the fair's architecture successful was its extraordinary magnitude of size and of scale, which Schuyler discussed at length and with reference to individual buildings, chiefly the Manufactures Building. The third condition was that the architecture was festal, temporary, illusory. It was this condition, Schuyler concluded, "which at once both completely justifies the architects of the Exposition in the course they have adopted, and goes furthest to render the results of that course ineligible for reproduction or for imitation in the solution of the more ordinary problems of the American architect."[43] To say as much is not to deprecate the classical style of the World's Fair buildings. "The White City," Schuyler concluded, "is the most integral, the most extensive, the most illusive piece of scenic architecture that has ever been seen." That should be praise enough, he said; it should not be argued that the fair had made any contribution to the development of architecture. "It is what you will, so long as you will not take it for an American city of the nineteenth century, nor its architecture for the actual or the possible or even the ideal architecture of such a city." His demurrer was fair enough. American cities of the nineteenth century could not be remade in the image of Rome. Most American architects, even those given to the classical style, would have conceded the point. But that point in no way diminished the achievement of the fair itself. Those who believed that architecture should be a correlation between structure and function had been reproached for admiring the fair buildings, said Schuyler. "But there is no inconsistency in entertaining at the same time a hearty admiration for the Fair and its builders and the hope of an architecture which in form and detail shall be so widely different from it as superficially to have nothing in common with it. Arcadian architecture is one thing and American architecture is another. The value of unity, the value of magnitude are common to the two, but for the value of illusion in the one there must be substituted in the other . . . the value of reality."[44]

Schuyler's assessment of the exposition architecture is balanced. It does not decry the classical style of the buildings, but advises that they should not be individually imitated. At the same time it applauds the virtue of both the unity and magnitude of that architecture. There lies the area of contention. The classical style had its limits, but there is no denying that American architects might have learned a valuable lesson from the other two conditions of the fair, and that lesson might have offset the negative effects of imitating classicism. Architectural unity and magnitude that is in scale, together with unified landscape design, would have enhanced the habitableness of American cities, made them more beautiful, more usable, more congenial, more refined, more coherent, by improving their physical aspect, their physiognomies, and thus transforming them into environments that augmented, rather than fragmented, the quality of life. This is not to argue that every Black City, so-called, should have been transformed into the White City. It is, however, to argue that the deaths of American cities might have been precluded, had their architecture been amalgamated rather than allowed to develop haphazardly. Such conclusions drawn from the exposition's site plan—which should be agreeable to the vast majority of architects and critics—have been repetitiously obscured by the preoccupation of architectural historians with the judgment of Louis Sullivan. It is a preoccupation that has sometimes resulted in critical myopia.

Louis Sullivan judged the exposition a disaster for our architecture because it popularized Renaissance and classical designs and thereby stymied the demand for new styles. "Thus," concluded Sullivan, "Architecture died in the land of the free and the home of the brave"—a statement at least as hyperbolic and banal as those made by the fair's sentimental devotees. "The damage wrought by the World's Fair will last for half a century from its date, if not longer. It has penetrated deep into the constitution of the American mind, effecting there lesions significant of dementia,"[45] declared Sullivan. In so saying he damned both the fair and Daniel H. Burnham's love of bigness. He also condemned the American public's taste in architecture, despite the fact that his own Transportation Building was probably the most popular building at the fair. Actually, Sullivan's conclusions, viewed in proper focus, reveal more about him than about the influence of the fair's architecture.

Certain criticisms need to be made about Sullivan's judgment. Too often regarded with unquestioning respect, that judgment has been allowed to stand as an ultimate commentary upon the architecture of the exposition; whereas even cursory study exposes that judgment as highly misleading and questionable, if not in fact exaggerative to the point of being nonsense. First of all, it was made thirty years after the fact, which is not to deny that Sullivan was opposed to classicism in 1893—though he raised no objection then to the classicism of the exposition—but which at least should suggest that his statement was influenced by his personal experiences of the years from 1893 to 1924. Those personal experiences were decidedly unpropitious. Sullivan was neglected. But he suffered neglect for a number of reasons, least of which was his unique designing—if indeed that was a factor at all. The very first of the reasons was the depression of 1893-1896. Its severity resulted in a drastic cutback in construction. The financial constrictions upon architectural firms finally led to Dankmar Adler's decision in 1895 to become consulting architect of the Crane Elevator Company in order to support his family.[46] Thus ended the partnership of Adler and Sullivan. Sullivan thereby lost the counsel and skills of a partner who was a masterful engineer as well as a genius in acoustical design and the details of construction technology, and whose contribution to their joint ventures has probably never received adequate recognition. Not only did Sullivan as architect suffer from the loss because he profoundly believed in the necessity of design that combined architecture and engineering, but also Sullivan as businessman suffered. He was a disagreeable person. "Emotionally erratic and given to strong drink in quantity, with an inflexible and arrogant personality, he made it difficult for even sympathetic clients to deal with him. He was a severe disciplinarian in his office, and he carried his extremely high standards into his business dealings. The result was that he was often admired and feared but rarely liked."[47] It is hardly surprising, then, that he lost commissions and became impoverished and neglected, however unfortunate these developments were for both him and American architecture.

Nevertheless, Sullivan's judgment upon the fair must be seen within this perspective of his own failure and its resultant disappointment. The fact is that his judgment was that of an embittered egocentric, an observation which is not intended in any way to depreciate his genius or his splendid achievement, but which should suggest that his pronouncements must be viewed skeptically. Sullivan's assessment of the exposition is in fact belied by developments in the Chicago school of architecture. Many buildings designed in the commercial style were erected after 1893. There was, for example, the Chicago Stock Exchange (1894) designed by Adler and Sullivan in a style that is strikingly similar to John Wellborn Root's Monadnock Building, except for Sullivan's incomparable decorative motifs on the ground floor. Later Sullivan himself had the opportunity to design the facade of the Gage Building (1898), the work of Holabird and Roche, and the entirety of the Carson, Pirie, Scott Store (1899, 1903-1904). Holabird and Roche, a leading firm in the designing of commercial style buildings which were in their simplicity perhaps advanced even beyond Sullivan's work, had such important commissions as the Marquette Building (1895), the Cable Building (1899), the Crown Building (1900), the Champlain Building (1903), the Chicago Building (1904), the Republic Building (1905), the Brooks

Building (1909-1910). Even the firm of D. H. Burnham, whom Sullivan rather maligned, continued to design commercial style structures, despite having taken on Charles B. Atwood as a replacement for Root. They designed the Reliance Building (1894-1895), the work of Atwood; the Fisher Building (1896), which contains Gothic, not classical, motifs; the Railway Exchange Building (1903); Chicago Business College (1910); Society Brand Building (1912-1913); and later additions to the Carson, Pirie, Scott store. Moreover, there were numerous Chicago style buildings designed by the younger legatees of the school, Richard E. Schmidt, George W. Maher, Dwight A. Perkins, Christian A. Eckstrom. Sullivan's most famous protégé, the young Frank Lloyd Wright, whom Sullivan had fired for taking outside commissions, was designing apartment buildings and houses: the Francis Apartments (1895), the Heller House (1897), the Robie House (1909). In short, Architecture did not die in the land of the free. And, as Carl Condit has concluded, "The view that the virus of the Columbian Exposition sapped the strength and spirit of the Chicago architects is wholly unsupported by the facts. One must look to later and more profound causes."[48] If there was a significant shift in the Chicago movement, Condit advises, then it occurred not in 1893 but in the period 1905-1910, when the concern of Chicago's architects shifted from commercial building to public buildings and residences.[49]

Certain other factors need to be considered. It may be said in fairness that the death of John Wellborn Root was a more significant factor in the fate that befell the Chicago school than was the World's Columbian Exposition. For if the Chicago school of architecture was the source of energy pushing toward a new style, then Root was clearly the nucleus of that energy. The respect with which he was regarded nationally made the simple eloquence of his advocacy of an organic style far more compelling than were the florid writings of Sullivan. Root's death deprived the Chicago movement of its most respected, most articulate, and most original architect. In this context it is worth noting that Root was more sincere in the pursuit of the premise that "form follows function" than was Sullivan himself. For example, George Davis, director general of the exposition, judged the Transportation Building, for which significantly Adler had no responsibility, as unsuitable for its exhibits—it was an impracticable design. As an additional example, Sullivan's original design for the Auditorium reportedly called for elaborate ornamentation. Commenting upon that design, Root is supposed to have said, "Louis couldn't build an honest wall without covering it with ornament"—a remark which made Sullivan so angry that he scrapped the original plan in favor of a simpler one that reveals the influence of Richardson's Marshall Field Wholesale Store.[50] The irony is that Sullivan's decorative motifs, however appealing they may be, were neither truly organic nor functional. As some of Sullivan's contemporaries remarked, what use are handsome decorative motifs eighteen stories high where they cannot even be seen? Root's death, though of profound significance, was not the only one that constituted a serious loss to the Chicago school. Adler died in 1900. Jenney, already aged and failing before the turn of the century, died in 1907. Wright removed himself to Japan and the Far West for twenty years. Burnham began to devote his energies to city planning and to projects in other cities. Then too, as Carl Condit has pointed out, the center of American culture concentrated increasingly in New York. Movements in literature and the arts that had begun in Chicago or elsewhere shifted to the eastern metropolis. Hamlin Garland's prophecies did not prove out. Architecture would lose its avant garde status among the American arts to literature and painting, not to be revived again until the importation of the International Modern style from the Bauhaus to Chicago. By World War I the impetus of the Chicago movement had spent itself. Louis Sullivan's judgment upon the exposition was quite simply irrelevant. But worse than that, it was damaging to whatever beneficial influence the exposition might have exercised. And the exposition was beneficial.

The most important architectural legacy of the World's Columbian Exposition derived from precisely that quality heretofore stressed: its unity, its triumph of *ensemble*. For that triumph led to the City Beautiful movement, an attempt to translate into the forms and environments of twentieth-century American cities the aestheticism and coherence that Frances Hodgson Burnett and others had deemed inherent in the White City as symbolic of the kingdom of God on earth. As observed in a recent commentary, "For all its critics, and despite Louis Sullivan's too-often quoted negative remarks, it [the exposition] was a splendidly coordinated classic triumph. Sullivan's own transportation building . . . fitted superbly within a setting of overall classic excellence, and it is really unfortunate that Sullivan's later writings painted a picture not entirely consistent with what modern scholars are just beginning to recognize as a triumph of early modern planning if not of architecture."[51] The statement suggests the genuinely beneficent legacy of the exposition. That legacy is city planning, which, in its modern guise, is attributable to Daniel Hudson Burnham, the spearhead of the City Beautiful movement. Burnham correctly discerned that America was on the threshold of constructing buildings of unprecedented magnitude. And it should be noted that, as Christopher Tunnard has commented, the classical style was better suited than most for such a development: "It was a flexible style, which could make a unity of a building by combining a boldness of plan with refinement of detail. It made possible the handling of entirely new building types, frequently of great scale, that a growing democracy required. These were the new state capitols, the railroad stations, and the public libraries, which are part of America's contributions to world architecture."[52] Burnham understood as much. Consequently he made it his first task to organize a large company, employing hundreds of architects and draftsmen, which would be able to take advantage of this new development. Burnham was not a great architect. But he was a great organizer, a consummate businessman—and in that respect, more distinctly in tune with his culture than any of his colleagues. Even Louis Sullivan conceded the genius of Burnham's discernment. It was, as he observed, the era of the formation of trusts, mergers, combinations; "The only architect in Chicago to catch the significance of this movement was Daniel Burnham, for in its tendency toward bigness, organization, delegation, and intense commercialism, he sensed the reciprocal workings of his own mind."[53] Nor does the gratuitous depreciation implied in Sullivan's comment negate Burnham's perception of future developments which escaped Sullivan's understanding and to which Burnham would try to bring a vision that was meant to benefit not only Burnham and his clients but the general public as well. The architect's difficult obligation is not only to the integrity of artistic expression and the desires of his client but also, and perhaps most importantly, to the welfare of the public, both present and future. For all his shortcomings as an artist, Burnham tried to honor that larger obligation.

Thus in 1902, having begun his association with Edward H. Bennett to whom he had lost the commission for West Point in the same year, Burnham completed a plan for the development of Washington, D.C., based upon the original plan of Charles L'Enfant which had long since been allowed to languish. His cohorts in devolving this plan were Charles Follen McKim, Augustus Saint-Gaudens, and Frederick Law Olmsted. "The Washington we see before us today is the result of their work."[54] Burnham thereafter elaborated city plans for Cleveland (1903), San Francisco (1904), and Manila and Baguio in the Philippines (1905). But his crowning achievement as an architect-planner was the plan of Chicago. It was something Burnham had wanted to undertake for over a decade and its final fruition in 1909 exemplified his civic-mindedness—he would accept no remuneration for his efforts. His comprehensive plan for his native city resulted from his belief that the urban environment should be designed "for men and women to live and for children to grow up in; his chief idea was to make conditions for working healthy and agreeable, and facilities for recreation both abundant and available."[55] In his remarks prefacing the detailed review of his plan, Burnham observed that urbanization was characteristic of the modern era, that along with it had come a widespread increase in wealth and enlarged participation of the public in politics. "As a natural result of these causes has come the desire to better the conditions of living. Men are becoming convinced that the formless growth of the city is neither economical nor satisfactory; and that over-crowding and congestion of traffic paralyze the vital functions of the city." Thus Burnham realized the trying vicissitudes of city life in terms that over sixty years later not only still pertain but also become insistent—partly because his vision remains unachieved. Chicago as well as other cities now recognized the fact, Burnham wrote, that the time had come to bring order out of the chaos that had resulted from rapid growth and the influx of variant nation-alities. "Among the various instrumentalities designed to accom-plish this result, a plan for a well-ordered and convenient city is seen to be indispensable." Such a plan, Burnham opined, must take into account the fact that the city was preeminently a center of industry and traffic; that commercial and transportation facil-ities must be bettered; that working people must have comfort-able, appealing, and restful homes, surroundings, and recreational facilities; that urban dignity and order, as essential to material progress, must be attained through impressive and interrelated groupings of buildings; and that expansion must be foreseen and provided for. All these general concerns Burnham's comprehensive plan of Chicago took into account.[56] Its purposes were to ration-alize the city's rail traffic primarily through a central union freight yard terminus; to integrate that traffic with harbors for water traffic; to develop the entire waterfront for recreation and leisure; to supplement the city's gridiron layout with diagonal arterials for ease of traffic flow; to revitalize Michigan Avenue and create a core inner-city area of civic monuments and parks with a grand Civic Center as climax; to eliminate slums by means of broad streets and enforced sanitation regulations—in short, to recreate Chicago as a city of social betterment, symmetrical ar-rangement, and grand vistas that befit its locale. Burnham's plan, as seems inevitable in America, would fail before the rapacity of profit-motivated developers—which is all the more reason to honor the monumentality and nobility of that plan.

The inspiration for the plan of Chicago was the World's Columbian Exposition, as Burnham said. The fair, for which he was so largely responsible, was, Burnham declared, "the beginning, in our own day and in this country, of the orderly arrangement of extensive public grounds and buildings." This beginning was a natural outgrowth of Chicago life. For Chicago was a commercial city whose scions of wealth had grown accustomed to planning for the common good and who believed the fair would surpass all previous expositions; they were also men who had learned that success depends upon securing the artisans best prepared to do a job. Hence the fair's unprecedented success. The fair's influence had initially effected a plan to improve the waterfront in order to attain the qualities of dignity, beauty, and convenience contained in the White City. That influence had expanded to encompass the whole city. The spirit that had led to the planning and creation of the exposition still prevailed in Chicago, Burnham argued. "Indeed, it seems to gather force with the years and the opportunities. . . . It conceals no private purpose, no hidden ends. This spirit—the spirit of Chicago—is our greatest asset. It is not merely civic pride: it is, rather, the constant, steady determination to bring about the very best conditions of city life for all the people."[57] In other words, that spirit was the sense of *communitas* which so many contemporary writers advocate and which they feel we may have lost entirely. In like vein Burnham argued that city planning, with its origins in Paris, and the experiences of innumerable cities throughout history, taught that the direction to greatness and prosperity "lies in making the city convenient and healthful for . . . its citizens; that civic beauty satisfies a craving of human nature . . .; that the orderly arrangement of fine buildings and monuments brings fame and wealth to the city; and that the cities which truly exercise dominion rule by reason of their appeal to the higher emotions of the human mind."[58]

Burnham was advocating a comprehensive planning that viewed the city as a total environment, whose physical aspects should reflect and promote beauty, coherence, enjoyment, unity. Thus the city should become a grand fulfillment of the triumph of *ensemble* contained in the Court of Honor. The city should contain visual climaxes, parks, lagoons, recreational facilities, streets like those at the exposition. As Burnham interpreted it, the influence of the White City was not toward imitating the classical style, but toward creating order and aesthetics in American cities. That point was made abundantly clear in Burnham's discussion of Chicago's civic center, whose effectiveness, he said, would depend upon "the character of the architecture displayed in the buildings themselves, in their harmonious relations one with another, and in the amount of the space in which they are placed. Surely the results attained at the World's Columbian Exposition in 1893 so amply proved the truth of these principles that it is not necessary to enlarge upon them. The attainment of harmony, good order, and beauty is not a question of money cost, for in the end good buildings are far cheaper than bad buildings."[59] Surely no one would quarrel with such principles. That the exposition inspired the plan of Chicago is hardly to its discredit. For as Wilbert Hasbrouck contends, in spite of its shortcomings that plan deserves positive appreciation as "the proto-typical city plan to which virtually every similar work undertaken ever since has been substantially indebted. What it did provide for was largely unprecedented, and important aspects of it have been realized."[60]

The fundamental insight and meaning of Burnham's plan can hardly be overstressed. What Burnham hoped for was the restoration of the coherence which he believed had characterized the major European cities of former eras. As Carl Condit has emphasized, "It is no longer so easy to condemn this passion for antiquity as it once was, especially in view of the new knowledge of urban history and the hopeless state of the contemporary urban milieu. Burnham's essential point was sound: whether architects had to confine themselves to the classical mode was arguable, but the chaos of the city made functional coherence and visual order, at least in the major civic areas, a matter of necessity."[61] Some critics and historians would dispute the point. Jane Jacobs, for example, very cogently and compellingly argues that "intricate minglings of different uses in the cities are not a form of chaos. On the contrary, they represent a complex and highly developed form of order." But she skews her argument in blaming the City Beautiful movement, which she regards as simply another form of Ebenezer Howard's Garden City concept, for subverting this complex and developed order through civic centers and other architectural or landscaping projects which alter the matrix of a city. Such undertakings as the City Beautiful, she says, "were primarily architectural design cults, rather than cults of social reform."[62] It is true that Burnham's emphasis was on architectural design. But it must be argued that, like the Social Gospelers and other reformers of his time, he saw urban planning as a means of creating an environment which preserved the city's social vitality and complexity while eliminating its visual disorder. Burnham's objective was not simply the aesthetic revitalization of the city but the ultimate realization of those social ideals that inhere in community identity. Burnham saw the city as an entity, and he set out to create the means whereby that entity could "be made an efficient instrument for providing all its people with the best possible conditions of living."[63] He wanted to facilitate circulation of people and traffic; to increase convenience and comfort for the citizenry; to enhance the dignity of the city. These were ultimately social goals. It may be true that a well-planned urban environment cannot predicate a responsible, civic-minded, well-behaved, and happy citizenry; but such an environment can at least alleviate some of the causes of urban decay and antisocial behavior. Thus, for example, Burnham's emphasis on public, rather than private, forms of transportation was quite sound. Wilbert Hasbrouck expresses some wonderment over Burnham's ignoring of the future of the automobile in his plan of Chicago. But Burnham knew better. As Jane Jacobs has remarked, "Cities have much more intricate economic and social concerns than automobile traffic. How can you know what to try with traffic until you know how the city itself works, and what else it needs to do with its streets?"[64] Burnham knew how the city works. Accommodating the city to the automobile, rather than the automobile to the city, would destroy the city's viability, as we have since learned through disastrous errors of judgment which effectively allowed highway engineers to usurp the duties of city planners. What Burnham learned from the White City about traffic was that a modern city must create mobility by means of public transportation. The White City provided varied means of transportation: boats, railroads, peddle cycles, a movable sidewalk, the Intramural Railway (an obvious prototype for the elevated "Loop" constructed in 1897). The "walking city" of the eighteenth century could not be reestablished. But public transportation could sustain urban vitality and preserve inner cities for the people. From the White City Burnham learned that and other valuable lessons.

In spite of these varied considerations, many critics and historians continue to cite Sullivan's comments and to belabor the presumed evil influence of the exposition. Thus, for example, Hugh Dalziel Duncan speaks of the plethora of public buildings in classical style erected after the exposition and asserts that the link between political symbol and classical form "soon became so deep that any civic building, to be really 'civic,' must be classical."[65] Even more recently Russell Lynes, again quoting Sullivan, says of that unhappy genius, "He was not far wrong in his estimate. Across the continent great railroad stations, libraries, state capitols, business buildings, museums, and memorials to heroes rose in the quasi-classic spirit and style of the impermanent palaces of the Court of Honor to squat as the permanent residue of the fair."[66] As examples he cites the railway station in Washington, the National Gallery, the New York Public Library, the Boston Public Library, the Jefferson Memorial, and the Lincoln Memorial. Such citations merely suggest the absurdity of the claim. Can one really believe that, for example, the National Gallery, erected nearly fifty years after the fair, was a direct result of the White City's influence? Did such structures owe nothing to the tradition and plethora of classical buildings in Washington and elsewhere dating back even to the eighteenth century?

After all, there was nothing novel about the use of classical or Renaissance styles in public buildings. Jefferson had fixed upon the classical style as most suitable for the government buildings of the early Republic and his decision had pertained ever since, especially after the completion of the Capitol Building during the Civil War. Furthermore, most American architects had been trained, either in Paris or in the United States, in using Renaissance or classical designs and they had been using them and advocating them long before the exposition came about. If the fair confirmed them in their bias, that is hardly surprising. Then too, the commercial style was largely just that—its employment had been confined mostly to commercial and industrial structures, with the exception of a few houses. That is not to argue that the commercial style would not or could not have become adopted for public buildings, but only to note its prevailing applicability, which continued well after the fair. The fair did not abort the Chicago style of architecture. Though its influence might possibly have furthered the Chicago style had the early plans of Root been fulfilled, its classical buildings probably effected one stylistic benefit: "At least the creators of the White City had accomplished a good deal toward smothering the grotesqueries of scroll-saw fretwork and Ruskinian dumpiness."[67] The classical style may not have been native, but neither was it alien. As an alternative to the Chicago style it was an anomaly, perhaps; but as an alternative to the often erratic eclecticism that had afflicted most of the nation's architecture, it was a blessing.

It must be argued, too, that advocates of an indigenous style of architecture were probably indulging a nationalistic fallacy. By this time in our history, given the rapidity of urban-industrial growth, America's architects should have been concerned, not with the attaining of a national style, but with the achievement of a desirable urban environment. Given the pluralism of our urban society, they should have been concerned to effect diverse but cohesive architecture, rather than a somewhat autocratic originality. In this context Henry Van Brunt drew the most logical of all conclusions from the architectural efforts of his times. The desire to achieve a characteristic style deserved respect, he argued, because we were dealing with difficult and unprecedented problems. "Our art has, to a certain extent, become polyglot, and architecture must now . . . evolve theories of design. Instead of floating with the tide of events, . . . and rendering service without effort to the evolution of a style, . . . we are constrained to exhaust our strength, to become morbid in our selfconsciousness, in making comparative analyses of many styles, and in endless experiments with formulas and dogmas." Such a struggle might be self-defeating, however necessary it was. But from that struggle we must conclude that there would never again develop such distinctive styles as the Greek, Roman, Mohammedan, Renaissance; that there could never again "come into existence a national style which shall keep strictly within any narrow bounds of architectural expression, excluding all others; but that all the historical demonstrations of art are necessary to constitute that larger and more copious language of form which is necessary to express in terms of art the rapid progress in the science of modern construction, and that many-sided and complicated civilization which it is the obvious destiny of our country to amalgamate, harmonize and justify out of all the civilizations of history."[68] Such a lesson might be learned from the White City. As watershed event, as hail and farewell, the World's Columbian Exposition indicated in its architectural and other features an ultimate future of cosmopolitanism and internationalism, and an inevitable end to nativism.

In addition, the exposition had provided a model for administrative management, delegation of authority, and cooperative endeavor. This large-scale mutual effort by architects, painters, and sculptors was unique in American experience. It may fairly be said that this was the first exposition in which art, not industry, was the main attraction. To have combined so well the industrial and the aesthetic was in itself a promising achievement. The comments of Candace Wheeler were fairly representative of views on how promising that achievement was. "The overwhelming value of the arts in sisterhood has probably never since the centuries of the antique world been so fully demonstrated," as it had been at the exposition, she wrote. Artists, sculptors, and art lovers owed to the fair the fact "that the field of artistic effort has been so greatly enlarged by examples of good painting and good sculpture as accessory to architecture. That it has also marked out a defined field for a class of effort, and that the lines of the painter and sculptor have been enlarged and made to embrace the highest and greatest work possible to mankind."[69] The accuracy of Wheeler's assessment was underscored by events. Inspired by his experiences with the White City, Charles Follen McKim enlisted the aid of fellow creators and devotees of the exposition—among them D. H. Burnham, Augustus Saint-Gaudens, Edward Simmons, Richard Morris Hunt, and Charles Eliot Norton—to fulfill his determination to found an American School of Architecture in Rome. The school, since broadened in scope and named the American Academy in Rome, was established in 1894. In addition, after the exposition opened, a group of sculptors and architects—prominent among them Augustus Saint-Gaudens, J. Q. A. Ward, Daniel Chester French, Olin Warner, Richard Morris Hunt, and Stanford White—established the National Sculpture Society. The society's purpose was to encourage the use of decorative sculpture in houses, public buildings, and parks; to educate the public taste in sculpture; and to hold exhibitions. From the time of the fair until the momentous Armory Show of 1913, the society would exercise a pervasive influence. Furthermore, the exposition itself had made familiar to the American public some sculptors who had previously been totally unknown. As a result of such developments, sculptors reaped the reward of enormous numbers of commissions after 1893, for works as adjuncts to railroad stations, public buildings, memorials. The commissions went not only to already prominent sculptors like Saint-Gaudens and French, but to a host of others as well. It would be a happy circumstance if the resultant works had significantly advanced the art of sculpture in America, but with few exceptions, primarily the works of Saint-Gaudens, they were undistinguished. Nevertheless, sculptors were kept busy and solvent.

The benefits of the exposition to painting were of similar nature and scope. Visitors to the fair had seen the art of decorative painting, of murals and frescoes, on a monumental scale, a novel experience for those who had not traveled in Europe. W. Lewis Fraser declared that the entire nation should be thankful to Chicago for having taken the initiative, through the exposition, of "showing to the people who are too busy to go abroad what a powerful adjunct to architectural effect painting may be; for proving what those who know our art best have for several years asserted, that our painters are particularly fitted for this branch of art activity; and for the hint, not to the builders of great public buildings only, but to those who seek beautiful and artistic homes."[70] Moreover, fairgoers had been given an opportunity to study the largest collection of paintings ever assembled. In the immediate aftermath of the interest in art thus aroused by the exposition municipal art societies were formed in many cities, chief among them perhaps the one founded in 1893 in New York which was headed by R. M. Hunt. Also in New York in 1895 was formed the Mural Painters Society, with John LaFarge as its president. The primary purpose of these societies was to sponsor exhibits and to promote decorative painting in public buildings and the hanging of artworks in commercial buildings. There was a greatly increased demand for mural decoration in public buildings, as for example, in the state capitols at Harrisburg, Saint Paul, and Des Moines, and in court buildings in New York and Baltimore. In addition to decorative painting in public buildings, there was increased use of such work in private residences, hotels, and clubs. Edwin Blashfield, for example, did mural works for the Lawyers'

Club in New York, the Bank of Pittsburgh, the Astoria Hotel, and the Huntington House in New York. Frederic Crowninshield's works decorated the Waldorf and Manhattan hotels in the same city. He also painted murals for the Marquand Chapel at Princeton and for several private residences. Will H. Low created murals for the Astoria and Plaza hotels and the mansion of Charles T. Yerkes, all in New York. The decorative paintings of George Maynard could be found in a large number of hotels, among them the grandiose Ponce de Leon in Saint Augustine, Florida. The Central Criminal Court House and the F. W. Vanderbilt house in New York contained works by Edward Simmons. All these murals were executed before 1900. It is clear even from such a partial listing that mural work was enjoying a new popularity and esteem.

Probably the most notable example of the new demand for decorative work was to be found in the Library of Congress, which was finished in 1897. At least here was the most lavish example. For the building was profusely ornamented with paintings, sculpture, colored marble, gilding, white granite, white enameled bricks. Among the sculptors who worked on it was Frederick Mac-Monnies, famed for his fountain at the exposition, and the muralists employed—Kenyon Cox, Edwin Blashfield, Walter MacEwen, Elihu Vedder, Edward Simmons, George Maynard, Walter Shirlaw, Gari Melchers, William Dodge—had all been involved with the exposition. Their work seemed nearly as colossal an undertaking as that at the fair. Whether it was of high quality is debatable; critics were more interested in the murals painted for the Boston Public Library (1895). The most impressive of these was a set of paintings depicting the Arthurian legend of the quest for the Holy Grail—the work of the well-known illustrator Edwin A. Abbey. Royal Cortissoz bestowed high praise on Abbey's murals, saying the impression they gave was one "of fine artistic pomp, of precisely that decorative bravura which means impressiveness without effort, splendor with serenity, brilliancy held in check by the decorative idea."[71] Had most of the mural work of the period deserved equivalent praise, then the legacy of the exposition would have been entirely beneficial. But American painters seemed unable to sustain the art. Few of the many murals done in the years following the exposition were of any great distinction. The majority were hackneyed imitations. Nevertheless, the World's Columbian Exposition had clearly served to create greater public admiration and desire for artwork. And the American artist, for a change, found both his status and his market improved, at least temporarily. The successes of John LaFarge, the genius of American mural work, and the impetus given to decorative painting by the influence of the White City gave hope for the future. Unimaginativeness of conception and thinness of style would eventually doom that hope. But in the 1890s it seemed that a renaissance impended in mural work. American artists were thought to be on the threshold of creating a great, new, and truly national art form through decorative painting.

Thus Russell Sturgis felt justified in concluding in 1896: "Mistakes have been made and will be made. Commissions have been given to the wrong men, or the right men have not yet found their way and have not yet learned to discriminate sufficiently between decorating a wall and merely putting a picture on it. Nevertheless, we are moving in the right direction, and if the movement continues, as I believe it will, the day is not far distant when our art shall worthily stand beside that of any other country."[72] The decorative works at the Boston Public Library later encouraged him to hold fast to his hope. And therein lies a most significant point. It was McKim, Mead & White, architects of the library, who were really responsible for those decorations. The lesson taught, from the early collaboration on Boston's Trinity Church of John LaFarge with Henry Hobson Richardson, at the invitation of the latter, to that massive collaboration at the Library of Congress, was that the painters were dependent upon the architects. As Herbert Croly, budding critic of American society, pointed out after the turn of the century, the virtue of American mural work was that "it is subordinated to architecture and keeps its place upon the wall. . . . But its popularity depends chiefly upon the buildings, with which these decorations have been associated and the way they have been advertised."[73] The success of American decorative painting must be intertwined with the success of American architecture—and forever overshadowed by it. That fact might have been both the blessing and the curse of our muralists.

In still other areas the influence of the exposition seemed at the time to be beneficent. It promised to further certain humanitarian ends. It is true, however, that the fair afforded little if any cause for America's ignored blacks or wretched poor to believe that a new day was at hand. Frederick Douglass had been justly disturbed by the implications of minuscule participation given blacks at the fair. Indeed, after 1896 blacks were effectively disenfranchised in the South, where Jim Crow principles were applied with increasing rigor throughout the early decades of the new century, while in the North public opinion was either indifferent or hostile to securing the rights of this oppressed minority. The infamous Chicago anti-black riots of 1919 lay ahead to confirm racism. Consequently, as one account has it, "In the face of the deteriorating conditions of the late nineteenth century, the dominant trends in Negro thinking shifted gradually from protest to accommodation."[74] Accommodation, it might be said, was clearly retreat. More and more blacks migrated to northern cities and there swelled the ranks of the poor who had not even the recourse of accommodation. For the oppressed the promised land seemed no nearer in the aftermath of the exposition. But for America's women at least the feminist achievements at the White City seemed both apex and prophecy. Bertha Palmer's ecstatic declaration at the dedication of the White City became translated into a straightforward shibboleth: "Columbus discovered a new world, but the Columbian Exposition has discovered woman."[75] No one might question which of the two discoveries was of greater import.

Women had had their own building at the Centennial Exposition in 1876, but their participation in that fair was insignificant by comparison with the role they played in Chicago. Here was evidenced not only American woman's managerial ability but also

her new financial and social independence. Both were manifested
in some curious ways, perhaps. One saw it, for example, in the
World's Columbian Laundry Company, owned, operated, and
managed by women, with shares of stock sold only to women.[76]
But more momentous and more conspicuous were the achievements of the Woman's Building and the Board of Lady Managers.
Feminists had no doubt about the significance of these achievements. Virginia C. Meredith wrote, "In the Columbian Exposition,
which celebrates a fifteenth century fact, the Board of Lady
Managers stands for a nineteenth century idea. . . . [Its creation]
may surely be considered a signal illustration of progress in the
New World." The Board was well funded by Congress, and such
financial recognition gave to its efforts a dignity that earned an
unusual and impressive degree of public interest. Its efforts illustrated the growing emphasis upon the worth of individual persons
and "the industrial freedom of women."[77] Alice Freeman Palmer
explained the larger and more lasting import of woman's triumph
at the fair when she wrote that throughout their labors the women
"showed organizing ability on a huge scale; they developed noteworthy leaders; what is more, they followed them . . .; their courage, their energy, their tact in the erection of a monument to
woman were astonishing; and the efforts of their central Board
were efficiently seconded by similar companies in every state."[78]
Such organization and endeavor created widespread respect for the
abilities and power of women. So convinced was Alice Freeman
Palmer of that fact that she foresaw no need for independent
buildings or organizations for women at future fairs. The era of
self-consciousness would end, special treatment of women would
be rendered needless as a result of the World's Columbian Exposition. There was truth in her prophecy, though it would be slow
to manifest itself.

Of immediate import to woman and perhaps of more lasting
influence upon American culture even than her presumed new
identity was the lesson of the fair that Alice Palmer discerned. She
called attention to the fact that at the fairgrounds women could

examine, many of them for the first time, numerous machines, such as sewing machines, designed to lighten their domestic chores. But much more importantly, at the exposition Americans had gained a new sense of beauty, not of ornament and decoration, "but that of proportion, balance, and ordered suitability of parts." Recalling that the Centennial Exposition had deeply influenced the domestic architecture and household decoration of the East—with frequently awful results, one might add—Palmer perceived that the proportion and order of the Columbian Exposition would have similar but better effects. "The Fair will do the same," she said, "but it will bring about a beauty of a higher, simpler sort. In people from every section, artistic taste has been developed, or even created; and not only in their houses, but in the architecture of their public buildings and streets shall we see the results." This new concept of beauty, largely the province of women, would become more usual for both sexes, she concluded.[79] She was quite right. Palmer did not mean that American cities and houses would be overrun by classicism. What she spoke of was a new sense of refinement—scale, order, decorousness—which was often lacking in the buildings that resulted from the collaboration between architects and businessmen. As William H. Jordy has suggested of the Chicago architecture of the three decades leading up to the exposition, it "impresses us with its rambunctiously masculine spirit, in the hardness, violence, and massiveness of forms." Women would help to bring about the replacement of what was crude with what was decorous. They would support academic norms in design, which "depended on softer esthetic criteria, less aggressive, more urbane."[80] The degree and precise nature of woman's influence in this realm is an open question, as Jordy suggests. But its nature is implied by a shift in domestic furnishings from the gaudy eclectic styles that antedate the exposition to the more simple, more tasteful furnishings and more subtle decorations of the subsequent decades, ushered in perhaps by the widely popular book *The Decoration of Houses* (1897), written by Edith Wharton and architect Ogden Codman.

Woman's role in the World's Columbian Exposition not only promised to influence the future of American taste but also provided impetus to the feminist movement in more tangible form. Despite the depression that began in 1893 and extended to 1896, the post-fair years saw a significant upswing in efforts to organize women laborers, who now constituted over 17 percent of the work force (over 4 million were employed in various jobs).[81] It is quite likely that the organizational network and mutual endeavor created by the Board of Lady Managers enhanced this movement, since some of the women involved in the state and national committees became active in the union movement. More certain, however, was the fact that the Woman's Congress and the Board evidenced the strengthening of the feminist movement through "the leadership of women with independent incomes or professional prestige."[82] The prominence of Bertha Palmer and other aristocratic women in the exposition's work earned tremendous journalistic publicity for the woman's movement and added to it the aura of upper class respectability. However, that development served quite ironically to underscore one of the unfortunate features of the woman's movement. Although among the most eloquent and effective advocates of woman's cause, black women were systematically excluded from membership in the major women's rights organizations. When Hallie Q. Brown of Wilberforce University urged Bertha Palmer to appoint a black member to the Board of Lady Managers, she was advised by the president that membership could be awarded only to a representative of a national organization. That advice, though excluding blacks from the Board, did have its beneficial effects. Brown immediately began urging black women's clubs to combine into an association. The clubs in Washington, D.C. had already formed the Colored Women's League. Now other leagues would follow. The National Association of Colored Women was founded in 1896, and by 1895 black women were provided with a national newspaper, *Woman's Era.*[83] Furthermore, though most of the credit must go to the General Federation of Women's Clubs set up in 1890, the various state committees organized through the efforts of the Board of Lady Managers must be given some credit for the inauguration in 1894 of the State Federations. The Parliament of Religions and the Woman's Congress also had their influences upon the woman's movement. "One was the permanent organization of the Jewish Women's Congress which had met in connection with the religious forum. This resulted in the National Council of Jewish Women."[84] That could only be considered a plus. "Another result was the stimulation of the peace movement among women. Miss Sarah Farmer, whose father's inventive genius had so largely contributed to the electrical success of the fair, was a leader in this. She also took a prominent part in the considerable growth, due to the influence of the Parliament . . . , of the Bahai doctrine."[85] In the wake of the exposition came several other woman-oriented organizations which it probably helped to engender: the National Congress of Mothers (1897), the National Consumers League (1899), the Junior League (1901). It is fair to conclude that what the World's Columbian Exposition provided for American women was a heightened awareness of their sexual identity and of the historic achievements of their sex, an introduction to the most up-to-date labor-saving devices for the home, an opportunity to influence the nation's taste in art and home furnishings, an official recognition of their civic standing and professional achievements, and an object lesson in effective methods of national and even international organization.

The latter point calls forth the subject of the World's Congress Auxiliary. The influence of the auxiliary extended well beyond the woman's movement. Its interests, after all, were almost totally catholic. They were an attempt to embrace the entirety of human knowledge and inquiry. That the auxiliary was regarded as momentous is attested by the sanguine view of the *Chicago Tribune:* "If there were no other supreme feature of the Fair the congresses would have constituted one in which the Columbian celebration has surpassed all which preceded it as the sunlight pales the rays of the full moon."[86] Their enthusiasm was shared by thousands of people who regarded the auxiliary as the most important feature of the exposition. The more judicious Charles Dudley Warner came away from the World's Congress Auxiliary feeling that the ambitious nature of the meetings was both their main virtue and their main failing. They were novel and they were large-scale; but he had finally to judge that they were not enormously valuable because the attendance of noted scholars, authors, and other leaders was too limited and because the purposes of the various meetings were too vague. Still, the auxiliary established the value of such meetings as a means for the exchange and diffusion of ideas and opinions. As such he deemed it certain to instigate subsequent congresses. He was right. Warner felt also that the auxiliary had stimulated the curiosity and interest of the general public and had revealed the eagerness of the American people to learn about artistic and intellectual matters. "The fair," he concluded, "is a great school, a university. It is hardly probable that in our day any other nation will attempt another exposition on so grand a scale. Future expositions are likely to be specialized. One in search of information could only attend this with profit on the eclectic system."[87] Thus the exposition itself and especially the World's Congress Auxiliary, overly ambitious though it may have been, were great educative affairs. They offered the American public the opportunity of learning on a broad and gigantic scale. The auxiliary's extraordinary catholicity made it cumbersome but also rewardingly instructive.

Interesting and inclusive as the auxiliary was, there is yet no doubt that by far its most important feature was the Parliament of Religions. The parliament was not merely the best-attended of the congresses; it was also the most promising, inclusive, and influential. Major significances of the parliament were its ecumenism and the openness of its deliberations. As one clergyman wrote, "The spirit of the gatherings was thoroughly in accord with its devotional expression. It was throughout religious, reverent, fraternal. It was also intense and profound. It reminded some who were present of the spirit of the great revival meetings led by a Finney or a Moody. It has been described as 'a holy intoxication.' Again and again it has been called Pentecostal."[88] That such a spirit could prevail among representatives of disparate faiths was extraordinary. It was that spirit which led the evangelically minded scientist Paul Carus to believe that the parliament had secured a new sense of breadth and charitableness in religion. He remarked upon the tolerant principles advocated by the oriental delegates and upon the remarkable circumstance that the Roman Catholic Bishop Keane had even supported the rebukes against Christian missionaries expressed by the Hindu monk Vivekenanda and the representatives of Jainism. True, there were a few narrow-minded advocates of Christianity as the only true faith. But Carus felt justified in concluding that the representatives of most religions spoke a new language dedicated to serving truth, which makes narrowness untenable. The parliament, he said, marked the beginning of "a new era in the evolution of man's religious life. . . . The whole movement indicates the extinction of the old narrowness and the beginning of a new era of a broader and higher religious life."[89] The parliament was merely a beginning for ecumenism, but it signaled the gradual decline of the sectarian spirit, and a coming rapprochement between science and religion in pursuit of the truth. The enthusiastic Carus organized a religious parliament extension society to serve these ends.

His enthusiasm was widespread. It was a source of gratitude to the man who was responsible for the parliament, John Henry Barrows. It was Barrows who probably best summarized the nature and the import of the parliament's work. It was remarkable, he wrote, as the first universal council ever held, and made even more remarkable as a meeting of religions which had formerly been the prime contributors to ethnic and national antipathies. People from all over the world, whose comments he referred to, recognized the enormous significance of such a meeting as the first truly ecumenical meeting in history. That meeting had been made possible by the spread of Christian missions, the study of comparative religions, the widespread use of the English language, international travel facilities, religious freedom in America, the opportunity offered by the exposition, and three years of hard work. The accomplished results surpassed expectations. Max Müller, probably the most famous scholar of comparative religions in Europe, regretted that he had not attended. In fact, his scholarly interest was well served by the parliament. The meetings were not expected to add new ideas or information to the study of comparative religions, but they had the beneficial effect of drawing popular attention to that study. It was for that reason, Barrows believed, that Daniel H. Burnham had said the parliament was about the only thing the world would remember of the fair after a thousand years and H. N. Higinbotham labeled it the "proudest work of our exposition." Greater than the White City, greater than the art and architecture, was the World's Parliament of Religions. It seems surprising that even the exposition's builders would feel so, but the reason was apparently that "while the fair was no novelty, the parliament was unique and unexampled, and purposed, in a great school of comparative theology, to bring the different faiths into contact and conference; to deepen the spirit of brotherhood; to emphasize the distinctive truths of each religion; to show why men believe in God and the future life; to bridge the chasm of separation between Christians of different names and religious men of all names; to induce good men to work together for common ends; and to promote the cause of international peace."[90] Not even Robert Ingersoll, the Great Infidel himself, could have denied the virtue of such an undertaking. Anything that might bring peace among the fractious faiths must be applauded even by sacrilegious persons. For religious peace would enhance societal peace. That is why Barrows asserted, "One of the best results of the parliament has been a better understanding, among enlightened minds, between Catholics and Protestants in America." In fact, Roman Catholic participation in the parliament—a generous, conciliatory, and far-sighted policy on the church's part—was perhaps chiefly responsible for its historic significance. The American Protective Association would pursue its acrimonious, invidious anti-Catholic crusade after the exposition; but that could not negate the inspiration and precedent of Catholic-Protestant fellowship established by the parliament.[91]

The ecumenical spirit that pervaded the parliament, the promise of fellowship among various faiths, the manifest desire to discern a religious truth that transcended sectarianism, the fraternalism among men of diverse ethnic and religious backgrounds—all these gave rise to a promise for the future of ecumenism that subsequent developments belied. But in 1893 who could have foreseen the extremely divisive and destructive xenophobia, imperialism, and warfare that torture the twentieth century? In our times the euphoria that infected the sponsors and participants of the World's Parliament of Religions may seem naive. But that is our loss, not their folly. As a contemporary historian has remarked of the thunderous approval audiences reportedly bestowed upon the spirit of toleration and liberality exuded in the parliament's meetings, "rather than smile at the naivete of that audience and of the anonymous reporter who covered the event, the reader two-thirds of a century later might do better to ask himself where the spirit of toleration and liberality has gone."[92] For that naivete was certainly superior to the divisiveness of such religious leaders as Billy Sunday, who, in the decade before World War I, denounced the concept of the fatherhood of God and brotherhood of man as nonsense, excoriated the Social Gospelers, and damned the World's Parliament of Religions as "one of the biggest curses that ever came to America."[93] It was the efforts of such men and the coming of fratricidal events that dissipated the influence of the parliament. But the fact that the promise of the World's Parliament of Religions has gone unfulfilled does not negate the inherent virtue of that promise; if anything it merely reveals how obtuse, how destructive the factionalism and the presumed sophistication of twentieth-century life have been. The chosen purposes and course of the parliament's delegates were eminently superior in their humanitarianism to the later policies and events that foredoomed them. Had the spirit of the parliament been fulfilled, some of the horror of the twentieth century might have been prevented.

That spirit did not, however, die aborning. Some of its effects were clear-cut, some were gradually revealed. Books issuing from the parliament and others inspired by it promoted the popular response. The speeches of the parliament were published. Participants in the parliament contributed to works on comparative religions in the aftermath of the fair. In 1895, for example, at least two such works appeared. One was *Great Religions of the World*, containing essays on such faiths as Confucianism, Buddhism, Islam, Zoroastrianism, and Christianity—the latter written by Washington Gladden. The second book, *Rays of Light from All Lands*, reproduced some of the speeches at the parliament and essays upon the holy works of various faiths. Its opening pages acclaimed the World's Parliament of Religions as having "made clearly manifest the welcome fact that the fundamental elements underlying the various faiths of mankind are far less conflicting than was formerly supposed." Its authors dedicated their work to the "Dawn of a New Era, wherein the Brotherhood of Man and Universal Sonship in God" would become the primary truths of every religion.[94] Such lofty principles proclaimed the hopefulness of those religious leaders who were dedicated to religious peace and cooperation.

One of the immediate effects of the parliament which created much interest at the time but which had no very pervasive results was the sojourn in the United States of representatives of various exotic faiths. The most prominent and popular of these representatives was Swami Vivekenanda. He remained first of all in Chicago, where he lectured and supposedly counseled John D. Rockefeller. Thereafter he made a three-year lecture tour of the nation, the purpose of which was to dispel falsehoods about Indian life that the Christian missionaries had propagated. But finally he became himself a Hindu missionary to the American people. "The eventual result was the founding in New York in 1894 of the Vedanta Society, which continues to this day as a mission-station for Eastern religion in America."[95] In the same year the Swami was invited to Cambridge by Mrs. Ole Bull to discuss Vedanta philosophy with her friends John Fiske, Thomas Wentworth Higginson, Irving Babbitt, Hugo Munsterberg, Alice Longfellow, Julia Ward Howe, and Gertrude Stein. He also spoke there with William James. In 1896 he was invited to lecture before the Graduate Philosophical Society at Harvard University.[96] Thus, although his lectures led to no widespread conversion of Americans to the Hindu faith, the tenets of his faith were disseminated among important members of America's intellectual and academic community. Another visitor was Ibrahim Kheirallah, whose lectures in conjunction with the parliament were responsible for the growth of the Baha'i faith in America. "By 1901 there were reported to be a thousand Babists (or Baha'is) in Chicago, four or five hundred in Kenosha, Wisconsin, another four hundred in New York City, and another thousand scattered across the country. . . . " A prominent convert to the faith was Phoebe Hearst, wife of Senator George Hearst and mother of the publisher William Randolph Hearst. One result of her efforts was the establishment in 1912 of the Baha'i house of worship in Wilmette, Illinois. The Buddhists also made some inroads. Probably as a result of the heady atmosphere of the parliament, one Japanese Buddhist came to San Francisco in 1899 to begin a proselyting mission among the Americans.[97] It is nearly impossible to gauge the results of such developments or the precise extent of their influence upon academic studies and fine arts because of similar developments, such as the importation of oriental ideas by Ernest Fenellosa, John LaFarge, Henry Adams, and Lofcadio Hearn. Then too, the oriental faiths as such have never enrolled many American adherents. But at the very least it may be assumed that they broadened the philosophic interests of a modest but influential number of American intellectuals, while they simultaneously converted a few citizens to some of these faiths which heretofore had been little known in America.

The parliament also had some influence upon the ecumenical

movement among the Christian faiths in America and internationally. John Henry Barrows pointed out that it required this parliament of all faiths to bring together the dissident Christian faiths. Washington Gladden argued later that it was highly significant that Christianity was responsible for the parliament: "no other form of faith would have suggested such a thing; this, in itself, indicates the likelihood that Christianity will be the solvent and unifier of faiths."[98] Christianity, however, had first to put its own house in order. Gladden had to concede that even in the year of the parliament, perhaps as a result of it, America was racked by ultra-Protestant bigotry aimed against Roman Catholics—he referred presumably to the American Protective Association as well as some fundamentalist denominations. The record of unification since has been a faltering one. But to its great credit, the parliament had set an example. It was an obvious forerunner of such organizations as the World Council of Churches. It foretold later organizations and conventions of representatives of the world's religions, such as the All-World Religious Federation begun in 1945 and the World Parliament of Religions held at Sivanandanagar Rishikish in 1953.

As a whole, the international impact of the exposition was outshone by that of the parliament. The White City had some meager influence upon the Paris Exposition of 1900, but it could hardly be expected that an American fair would exercise large influence abroad. Christopher Tunnard has asserted, however, "The architecture and city planning of the Fair actually influenced European cities, which were in some cases about to build new civic centers and open up new squares."[99] Many European visitors had been favorably impressed by the architecture and site planning of the exposition, but they saw the fair's major significance as an indication of American development. Their views confirmed the judgment of Frederick Jackson Turner that the center of American culture had shifted to the Old Northwest through that area's politicians, social ideals, immense commerce, developing culture. The exposition demonstrated the area's predominance. "The

White City which recently rose on the shores of Lake Michigan fitly typified its growing culture as well as its capacity for great achievement," Turner wrote. That area's complex and representative industries and commercial connections, its determination to preserve what was original and good in Western life, and its willingness to learn from the experiences of other sections "make it an openminded and safe arbiter of the American destiny."[100] Thus the World's Columbian Exposition symbolized the shift in political, social, and economic sway from the East to the West. In that shift lay the basis of America's emergent national unity. The values exemplified in the fair were not only Western but American.

Comments of foreign visitors said as much and more. The astute French novelist and critic Paul Bourget hailed the White City as a promise of progress in American art and the host city as a prophecy of the urban future. "Chicago, the enormous town we see expanding, the gigantic plant which grows before our eyes seems now in this wonderfully new country to be in advance of the age. But is not this more or less true of all America?"[101] This was the import of the exposition and of Chicago: that America was developing its own ideal. Bourget's comment indicates what in the long run was the most durable impression made upon European fairgoers. Remarking upon the unprecedented beauty and splendor of the exposition architecture, an English visitor concluded his observations with the opinion that it was really Chicago that was of predominant interest. "To the thoughtful observer from abroad," he wrote, "perhaps of more supreme interest than all the exhibits within Jackson Park was this young giant city of the West, with its striking architectural features that mark a distinct epoch in building engineering, with its teeming and polyglot population, with its phenomenally rapid commercial growth, with its web of concentrating railways, with all its feverish energy and enterprise."[102] It was a common response. The exposition was Chicago's creation, but Chicago itself was a greater exposition than its creation. Europeans recognized that fact; many Americans overlooked it. Perhaps the foremost value of the exposition was that it introduced Chicago to the world.

The laudatory responses of the public, both foreign and domestic, to the exposition also went a long way toward justifying the boastful pride of the Chicagoans, for it was they who deserved credit for the fair's success. They might take honest gratification from their achievement and its reception. Franklin H. Head declared that the fair had demonstrated that Chicago was no longer a rude, provincial town, "but a metropolitan city, one of the world's great capitals; one of its centres of intelligence, culture, intellectual and artistic power. . . . They [Chicagoans] have given to the world a vision of supreme beauty. . . . Their work is the inspiration of the century and its most priceless gift to the coming days. . . . In this vast work, its [Chicago's] public spirit, its loyalty to the highest ideals, its civic pride, and its enlightened liberality have won from all intelligent observers the gratitude" which must be forthcoming to those whose work lifts up the human race.[103] The praise, however extravagant, would doubtless have been taken in stride by Chicagoans. It seemed their rightful due. "But is the fair ended?" asked Charles Dudley Warner near the end of 1893. "Not in Chicago. Nothing is ended in Chicago. Every day is a day of new enterprise." Plans for new civic achievements were already under way even before the fair closed. "The people turning this over in their minds," said Warner, "are thinking about Chicago—always about the glory of Chicago."[104] And why not? Other cities had combated Chicago for the privilege of hosting the exposition, but the civic pride and largess of Chicago had secured that honor to her. Chicago's rivals scoffed from afar; they ridiculed the results of Chicago's undertaking in advance. But the realization of the White City had humbled their scorn, turned it to admiration and praise. Chicago had proved herself worthy of any endeavor, equal to any task. And so, as Richard Harding Davis aptly observed at the exposition's climax, "It is just as much the Chicago Fair to-day when it closes, amidst the congratulations and cheers of a whole people, as it was before the papers found they were on the wrong tack and veered about to praise it, and it will always be remembered as the Chicago Fair, and deserves to be so remembered."[105]

Thus the World's Columbian Exposition vindicated the pride of Chicagoans. If they had ever doubted their capacities, it restored their faith. It secured for future years their vision of Chicago's destiny. In their creation of the exposition Chicagoans not only fulfilled the spirit of their city but also provided to their fellow Americans a realized ideal of urban community, of metropolitan identity. Chicago, wrote Charles Dudley Warner, was a city with no yesterday. It had something more vital than a past. "More than any other community in this country it is a civic entity," he wrote, "not a mere aggregation of a million or two of men, but conscious of a personality in which is merged the personality of its citizens, as was the case in Rome and Florence. . . . In the minds of all its inhabitants is an image of something great, distinct, full of splendor, which is called Chicago. . . . With such a spirit nothing is impossible, nothing too exaggerated to be expected and worked for."[106] It was, no doubt, exposure to that spirit, the dynamic energy of Chicago, which was the most electrifying of experiences for many fairgoers. They might well have envied a city which evinced such a strong sense of community identity. The Chicago spirit, so thoroughly evidenced by the exposition, effected still other achievements even in the midst of the depression that prevailed from 1893 to 1896. In the same manner of individual civic-mindedness that resulted in the Crerar and Newberry libraries, Marshall Field unhesitatingly contributed $1 million for the conversion of the exposition's Fine Arts Palace into a museum. It would become known as the Field Columbian Museum. It would contain exhibits donated by foreign nations that had participated in the fair. It would also house impressive exhibits in geology, zoology, botany, ethnology, natural science; the Tiffany collections of gems and crystals; the Kunz collection of meteorites; models of the World's Fair statuary and the statue of Columbus; a science and technology library of 8,000 volumes. Quite appropriately it was also unique as a museum of industrial arts, including railways.[107] Besides this most immediate legacy of the exposition, there was its locale, Jackson Park, which the city planned to maintain and improve. Another illustrious Chicagoan, Potter Palmer, donated $200,000 for a Woman's Memorial Building which would contain meeting halls and exhibits of women's work from all nations. In such ways the entrepreneurs of that most materialistic of cities demonstrated that Chicago was ready to divert herself from the pursuit of Mammon to the furtherance of knowledge and art. Little wonder that the largess of Chicago's men of new and extraordinary wealth led Charles Dudley Warner to compare them to the merchant princes of Florence and Venice. They used their surplus wealth as patrons, not as pirates.

It must be recalled that the exposition itself was not entirely devoted to aesthetics, knowledge, and high-mindedness; part of its enchantment, and therefore part of its legacy, was the Midway Plaisance. Every county fair, state fair, and carnival since 1893 has had its midway, though few could have matched Chicago's. What the Midway Plaisance meant to Chicago was soon manifested in the White City amusement park on Sixty-third Street. It is possible that many people found the Midway to be their fondest recollection of the exposition, but that seems unlikely. Though the Midway gave rise to many replicas, though it assured the future of the Ferris Wheel, its dedication to ethnic celebrations and exotic pleasures was likely to remain in the memory as a curiosity rather than as either a revelation or an inspiration. This is not in any way to depreciate the Midway. The Ferris Wheel alone was remarkable, as actual and symbolic innovation—as a machine revolutionizing the world of amusement. As an arterial link between the exposition and south Chicago's Washington Park, the Midway was a suitably appealing site of international pleasures and cosmopolitanism. Nonetheless it was not the enticements of the Midway that moved people to mortgage their farms or borrow funds in order to travel to Chicago. The Midway was not in the mind of the old man who was reported to have left the Court of Honor and with tears in his eyes, to have told his gray-haired wife, "Well, Susan it paid even if it did take all the burial money."[108] Sentimental, yes, but the old man's opinion meant that there was value for your money in looking upon the White City; value not to be found before in his lifetime, nor that of many others. Thus, more important by far than the precedent of the Midway was that of the White City. It would attain partial reincarnation in subsequent American fairs—at New Orleans, Atlanta, Portland. The imitative Saint Louis Exposition of 1904, designed to celebrate the Louisiana Purchase and sprawled over twice the acreage of the Columbian Exposition, was a disaster financially and artistically. The truly great American fair that appropriated the image of Chicago's, and perhaps even improved upon it, was the Panama-Pacific International Exposition of 1915 which was held in San Francisco. Not surprisingly, its great structure, the Palace of Fine Arts, was the work of an American trained at the Beaux-Arts, Bernard Maybeck. But the scheme for this exposition as a whole, like that for the White City, provided a fine example for urban design. It is probably fair to conclude, however, that no American exposition has ever achieved the aesthetic or popular success that the White City evoked.

It is quite likely that a large part of the White City's success arose from very mundane considerations. The locus of American life had shifted from the farm to the city. But the city fell far short of providing an environment beneficial to its citizens. That is unfortunately still the case. The Black City was and remains a reality. By contrast, the White City suggested, not just on an artistic level but on a quite practical level, the possibility of evolving an urban environment that was satisfying, clean, and habitable. Some of the considerations involved in that possibility may seem pedestrian, even trifling, yet in sum they constitute a worthy alternative to the average maladministered city. Thus Charles Dudley Warner was quite right in calling attention to the amenities of the exposition: the abundance of drinking water (where were the public drinking fountains in American cities?);

the fine sanitation system with its routine of nightly removal of trash and debris (what city in America kept its streets cleaned of refuse?). "This is one of the most important lessons of the fair, namely, that any other city can by honest and intelligent management be kept clean. That no other city is kept clean . . . is considered a demonstration that the majority of voters do not want either an honest or an intelligent management."[109] The exposition demonstrated, to the contrary, that the desirability of cleanliness should be assumed and that a collection and disposal system was simple enough to achieve. As Richard Harding Davis observed of the exposition, "This is really a great city, with a street-cleaning department, a police and fire department, an electric light plant of its own, and what corresponds to a Mayor and a Board of Aldermen. In its way, the conception and the carrying out of the laws of this municipality is one of the most wonderful of the many wonderful features of the great fair."[110] Here was a model of how to run the modern city—efficiently, without corruption or scandal, and in the best interests of all its citizens. Chicago herself might have taken a lesson from the model she created.

In fact, if any American city was prepared to learn that lesson it was Chicago. Chicago had the leaders and the civic-mindedness to pursue the model. Julian Ralph reported two years after the close of the fair that the energy of Chicago's wealthy business leaders was endless. "Since the closing of the fair they have gone on, putting up scores of superb residences and office buildings, a majestic depot, pushing a stupendous drainage work, developing a superb palace of art, finishing three splendid libraries, bringing university life into prominence, and satisfying, in half a dozen directions, the demands of the cultivated element of the population."[111] Many of these projects had been started before the fruition of the fair, but their pursuit indicated continuing dedication to Chicago's advancement on the part of her prominent citizens. As for Chicago's citizenry as a whole, the exposition had confirmed them in a cosmopolitanism unexcelled in any of the world's capital cities, in the opinion of Julian Ralph. Given that cosmopolitanism and the fervor of her entrepreneurs, Chicago, as he saw it, seemed a totally different city from that arm-flexing municipality that had hosted the exposition. With her era of materialistic aggrandizement behind her, Chicago might, then, have been on the threshold of a magnificent civic blossoming. Its future seemed bright, since its present was promising; yet, as Julian Ralph noted, it was still industrial-commercial Chicago. "The rawness of the street scenes and street life of the city still offends the eye, and the makers of the finer Chicago . . . still hurry . . . to homes far distant from the belching steam and smoke filled crater of the volcanic town. . . . the filth in the streets, the bustle and clatter and worry and strain, are still so dreadful as to suggest the citadel of hades."[112] In short, the Black City persisted. The wondrous aura of the White City had left Chicago unregenerate. The getting and spending of money, the indulgence of appetites, the frenzied activity were not about to disappear suddenly.

Worse than that. Reformer William T. Stead remained appalled by Chicago's social evils. For the influence of the World's Columbian Exposition had neither diminished nor tempered those evils. Quite the contrary. Indeed, even some of the city's entrepreneurs behaved dubiously. Stead found that Chicago was happily spared from the rapaciousness of the vicious and frivolous rich—presumably because her millionaires were all self-made—but she had her share of the predatory rich, outstanding among them, as he saw it, being that member of the exposition board, Charles T. Yerkes. Predation here referred to the corrupting of politics. But there were also the predatory poor. And there were the criminals and whores—the miraculous White City had not converted them. The existence of the White City had, in fact, brought booming busines to the brothels. Nevertheless, Stead saw the exposition as an enormous boost to the forces of reform that had already been active in Chicago, whose superiority to other cities, he said, "was even more marked in social and municipal affairs than in the realm of commerce and the play of politics. For Chicago had become the ideal city of the world. . . . The great impulse, born of the World's Fair, led citizens to be transformed according to the best thought of the world's greatest thinkers."[113] Given the horrendous re-counting of evils that Stead's *If Christ Came to Chicago!* contains, it is difficult to determine the source of his optimism. There was the energy of Chicago's citizens; there was a new mayor following Carter Harrison's death; there was the civic-mindedness of many of the city's entrepreneurs. But respecting social evils, subsequent developments hardly bore out his hope. The age of Mickey Finn was just beginning, the age of Al Capone was yet to come. And Ada and Minna Everleigh would arrive in Chicago in 1899 to establish the Everleigh Club, the finest and most famous brothel in American history.

It was the rapaciousness of some of Chicago's citizens and the tacitly condoned indulgence of her social evils, along with the academicism of the exposition's architecture, that led some critics to draw the contrast between the White City and the Black City. A recent commentary has even suggested that the White City was a symbolic rejection of the real Chicago. But that view reveals blind spots. The White City, after all, arose in the midst of Chicago, not as an appendage to it but as a fulfillment of its spirit. Thus it suggested to the reform-minded, the Social Gospelers, that the Celestial City might arise out of the very bowels of Sodom, that one aspect of life need not forestall another—Babylon and Jerusa-lem might coexist. The kingdom of God might surmount Vanity Fair; the machine age need not debauch the Garden City. "Chica-go," Henry Adams recollected, "was the first expression of Amer-ican thought as a unity."[114] Wayne Andrews has succinctly dis-missed Adams's view with the assertion, "This was bunk."[115] In the limited sense in which Andrews takes Adams's comment as referring only to the architecture of the exposition he is right, but he also skews the point. Adams's statement occurs in his auto-biography in a chapter entitled "Chicago"—his sentence refers to Chicago, not merely to the exposition. He was discussing the exposition in the context of his desperate search for a formula or a symbol that would restore unity where he saw multiplicity, to reveal order where he saw chaos. His comment was preceded by the speculation that Chicago suggested the American people "might still be driving or drifting unconsciously to some point in thought . . .; and that, possibly, if relations enough could be observed, this point might be fixed."[116] It was at the exposition that Adams got his first intimation of that point in thought, the symbol of a new unity and energy to replace the old cosmic unity represented by the Virgin. That symbol was the dynamo, the mechanical and physical epitome of the Age of Energy. Thus within its larger context of philosophic predicament and quest, Adams's comment on Chicago refers to a concept that transcends the White City as such. Indeed, as a visitor he spoke of the fair as a "seductive vanity," and indulged the hucksterism of the Midway, the frivolity of the Ferris Wheel, and the enticements of water transport, electric fountains, and fireworks in the manner of the average fairgoer.[117] He was enthralled by the Court of Honor, especially Hunt's Administration Building, but that hardly faults his judgment. "Critics had no trouble in criticizing the classicism," he wrote, "but all trading cities had always shown traders' taste, and, to the stern purist of religious faith, no art was thinner than Venetian Gothic. All trader's [sic] taste smelt of bric-a-brac; Chicago tried at least to give her taste a look of unity."[118] The repetition of the latter word is telling. Henry Adams might be faulted for his limited appreciation of the commercial style, he might even in retrospect seem obsessed with a philosophic problem that we have come uneasily to live with; but his insight should not be taken lightly. The people of the old Northwest, he concluded, if they really knew what was good, might some day talk not of their politicians, but of Hunt, Richardson, LaFarge, Burnham, Saint-Gaudens, McKim, and White.[119] Even Louis Henry Sullivan would have had to admit that such men, especially Richardson, deserved continuing honor.

Adams's hopeful anticipation that Chicago suggested a concept of unity which might in the future draw together the disparate and seemingly fragmented elements of modern American life was probably the primary meaning of the World's Columbian Exposition and the city which hosted it. As a recent judgment observes, "Four images: the commercial buildings of the Loop; the academic Court of Honor . . .; the vast park and parkway system of [Chicago] . . .; the domestic felicity of the residential districts." No other city of the time possessed this contrast in urban image on such a scale or with such prominence as Chicago, nor surpassed the "contribution made in Chicago in all four of these aspects of design and planning. So much was this the case that had the city been fully conscious of the potential in its achievement, and had the disparate elements of its achievement been coordinated to maximum effect, then it is no exaggeration to say that a metropolitan ideal could have resulted from this integration of effort."[120] The Black City and the White City combined, alike evidencing the spirit of Chicago, revealed the potential for an urban environment which expressed and enhanced the primary unity within metropolitan diversity. For, on a mundane level, what Adams spoke of was equivalent to the value of harmony that so many commentators had read into the exposition. That value, however ephemeral, served at least to dispel fatalism over the future of an urban society. That is how Charles Eliot Norton viewed the matter. He was admittedly given to classicism, but his judgments suggested a larger concern. For example, in a letter to Henry Blake Fuller, who had drawn the contrast between the White City and the Black City, Norton expressed understanding for Fuller's dislike of the Black City, but admonished, "I think you should have sympathetic admiration, nay, even affection, for the ideal Chicago which exists not only in the brain, but in the heart of some of her citizens. I have never seen Americans from whom one could draw happier auguries for the future of America, than some of the men whom I saw at Chicago. The Fair, in spite of its amazing incongruities, and its immense 'border' of vulgarities, was on the whole a great promise, even a great pledge. It, at least, forbids despair."[121] Norton recognized that it was the energy of

Chicago itself that dispelled fatalism. For when his extreme enthusiasm about the fair elicited the question whether he might be considering moving to Chicago, he responded, "I like Chicago. I like the spirit, the civic power of the place." And in his public statements on the fair itself he called attention to the orderly arrangement of its grounds—an achievement universally applicable to the arrangement of urban grounds and buildings, regardless of the style of design of the latter. As he said, "The general design of the grounds and of the arrangement of the buildings was in every respect noble, original and satisfactory, a work of a fine art not generally included in the list of poetic arts, but one of the most important of them all to America—that of the landscape architect. Of all American artists, Frederick Law Olmsted, who gave the designs for the laying out of the grounds of the World's Fair, stands first in the production of great works which answer the needs and give expression to the life of our immense and miscellaneous democracy."[122] The World's Columbian Exposition was, in fact, the culminative achievement of America's greatest landscape architect, moving him from the romantic conception of landscape as substance to the fine arts view of landscape as form. "The Columbian Exposition incorporated many social and cultural values, and it reflected a new power of planners interested in comprehensive design." That new power was new wealth.[123] Olmsted's realization of that new power and his conceptualization of the urban community were certainly appropriate to the Garden City—or to any American city for that matter. It was surely just such values of harmony and design that Richard T. Ely had in mind when he advocated fulfillment of the truth that he presumed to be broadcast among the American public: "It is coming to be felt more and more that the city should be a work of art." Even more pointedly, as he argued, the city should become a "well-ordered household."[124] Daniel H. Burnham, referring to Pericles' Athens while arguing the need for the Chicago Plan, drew a similar conclusion: "In short, a commercial city is the one of all others that should be interested above all others in putting on a becoming dress and assuming a charming appearance."[125] After all, beauty attracts commerce. It is to our discredit, one might readily suspect, that the perceptions of Adams, Norton, Olmsted, Ely, Burnham, and a host of others went honored but unfulfilled in their own and our times.

What they were all saying, as a matter of fact, was best summarized by a distant relative of Henry Adams whose comments, since lost in the obscurity of time, are most worthy of recovery. There was one aspect of the exposition, John Coleman Adams wrote a few years after its close, which had not received sufficient attention. "Nothing in any of the exhibits within the walls of those great buildings . . . was half so interesting, so suggestive, so full of hopeful intimations, as the Fair in its aspect as a city by itself. In the midst of a very real and very earthly city, full of the faults which Chicago so preeminently displays, we saw a great many features of what an ideal city might be, a great many visions which perhaps will one day become solid facts, and so remove the blot and failure of modern civilization, the great city of the end of the century."[126] Here certainly was a point worth stressing. It was demonstrable in the 1890s that the future of America was urban. But it was not clear what the future of America's cities might be. Political corruption, commercial venality, rampant crime and vice, air pollution, traffic clutter, and lack of planning gave meager cause for hope that our cities would provide suitable and rewarding environments. Hence there were lessons to be learned from the World's Columbian Exposition as a city. The first lesson inhered in its system of arrangements which had been carefully planned: the layout and development of the grounds, the placement of buildings, the interlacing bridges, canals, and avenues. The prevision that had led architects, engineers, and landscape architects to relate all the fair's features to one another created a satisfying and intelligent result. One could study the fair as a whole or one could study its details. "They seemed to be the details of an organism, not the mere units of an aggregation." The same could be said of only a few of America's cities. "Life in our cities," Adams continued, "would be vastly easier if only they had been planned with some reasonable foresight as to results and some common sense prevision in behalf of the people who were coming to live in them. The great blemish upon our cities is the fact that their natural advantages have been squandered by uses which had no forethought of future needs. The blunders and stupidity of those who have developed them have laid heavy expense upon those who shall come after and try to remodel the territory they have spoiled." Adams was prophetic. He correctly foresaw that when the work of rehabilitation would be undertaken, "there will be anathemas profound and unsparing upon the shortsightedness which permitted narrow streets and omitted frequent parks and open squares; which reared monumental buildings, and failed to dig tunnels for local transportation; which carried sewage away in drain pipes, only to bring it back by the water tap."[127] It seems that there is little that is new in the problems of the cities.

Adams conceded that, given the rapidity of urban expansion and development in the nineteenth century, foresight was difficult. "But the trouble has been that the builders of our cities have been blind because they would not see. They have erred because they chose." It must be admitted that he was right. After all, there were precedents for city planning, such as Sir Christopher Wren's designs for London's reconstruction after the fire of 1666; and the rising rate of city populations could be forecast, just as the fair's planners were able to forecast the numbers of daily visitors. "Our mistakes are therefore gratuitous and wilful."[128] The White City itself was proof of Adams's point. System, arrangement, planning were possible and always had been. The White City further evidenced this possibility in the orderliness and cleanliness which Charles Dudley Warner had referred to. The millions of visitors to the fair had strewn its buildings and avenues with tons of debris, all cleaned away each night. Why not do the same in Chicago, New York, Boston? The White City had also demonstrated that huge crowds of Americans were capable of self-control. And, even had they not been, the White City, with its Columbian guards and its arrangements for traffic, provided a sense of total safety. There was no threat to life and limb in the White City—something of a contrast to Chicago's street traffic. Why could not this lesson be transferred to New York, for example? It never would be "as long as selfish and mercenary corporations are allowed to capture our thoroughfares and disregard the rights of the people in their use of them."[129] Adams here made a most telling point. The White City was created for the people, the entire public, its temporary citizens, and not for the profit or benefit of a few entrepreneurs. That fact was also exhibited in the fair's splendid facilities for eating, drinking, and cleanliness. The fairgoer, Adams commented, "was treated to the extraordinary experience of feeling that all this beauty, order, protection and display were for his sake, to minister to his enjoyment and to his ease."[130] Within the White City every person was sovereign. Therein all could experience the rights and privileges which belonged to citizens but which they were denied by the facts of urban life. The exposition provided the American citizen with a lesson in what he should expect his own city to be—that is, his own, not the politician's or the entrepreneur's. It taught that he need not submit to dirty streets, overbearing policemen, business control of thoroughfares. "Perhaps, as he understands all these things, he will long for a day to come when he can walk abroad with uplifted head, in the comfortable assurance that the city belongs to him and not to the corporations and the politicians." Adams was not advocating that the exposition's architecture be copied—in fact, he admonished against that, deplored the stupidities of academicism—but rather the possibility, revealed by the exposition, of effecting urban environmental beauty. "Such an era of real liberty in which the city is devoted to the good of the citizen is perfectly possible, but only under the same conditions as those which made the White City so conspicuous," Adams concluded. Those conditions included securing the best people to do their best work; realizing that personal comfort, safety, and enjoyment are worth having; recognizing that a desirable environment is a case of cause producing effect. When such conditions were met in New York, Boston, Chicago, then would the ideals of the White City be realized.[131] Alas, we are still waiting.

Though the lessons of the White City may not have been learned yet, that is no reason to doubt their continuing validity. It may be reason to doubt our society's wisdom. For the exposition, with its architecture, including state and foreign buildings, its site plan, its World's Congress Auxiliary, and even its Midway Plaisance, had arisen out of and served an earlier nineteenth-century ideal of unity through diversity—an ideal often ignored or disserved in the last century, but nonetheless worthy then and still worthy now. It would have been a mistake to reproduce the White City in urban centers throughout America. But that mistake could hardly have had more grievous results than the disorderliness of our cities and the hideousness of much of their architecture that continue to prevail as the norm. What has been done in the name of enterprise, on the one hand, and of organic architecture, on the other, is a travesty of both the ideals espoused by Louis Henry Sullivan and the ideals expressed in the World's Columbian Exposition. Modern architecture has had its triumphs and will continue to do so; but those triumphs have resulted from the conjoining of just those conditions Adams espoused—hiring the best people; recognizing the worth of comfort, beauty, safety; relating cause and effect—with enlightened investment and technological developments. Too frequently those triumphs exist in isolation. More often than not, it must be argued, we have what Ada Huxtable has called the architecture of destruction: the razing of buildings of the past to be replaced by sterile works reflecting the aesthetics of economics, a penitentiary style. Indeed, what has often been created in the name of functionalism is neither organic nor functional. It may pay, but it neither serves nor pleases. And, as Norman Mailer has pointed out, most of the time it is impossible to distinguish among the architecture of prisons, schools, hospitals, apartments, business offices. Instead of a harmony of diversity we have a chaos of conformity. Louis Sullivan would doubtless be appalled by much of our contemporary architecture. What would he have to say, for example, of "the architecture of brutality"? And what might he have to say, conversely, if the concept that not merely single buildings but entire cities should arise from organic precepts—a concept embodied in the White City and in Burnham's city plans—had come to its full fruition? That concept is the legacy of the White City.

Finally, the legacy of the White City inheres somewhere within the millions of words which re-created it or celebrated it in literature, magazines, newspapers, letters, diaries; and in architectural, art, and social histories. Its meaning may be elusive, difficult to assess. But fascination with its creation and its memory have been continuous. The exposition's hold upon the minds of its creators and its visitors was extraordinary and enduring. For the World's Columbian Exposition had afforded a novel and jubilant experience, an indulgence and an exultation, a satiety of both pleasure and beauty. It offered a peaceful interlude, a festive respite from the tawdriness, labors, and confusions of urban-industrial life. It was a consummation, a commingling of the contradictory forces and values of American life. And it was a wistful, langorous pause, a ritual celebration and consecration, before the onrush of time and events thrust American civilization irrevocably across the threshold of history into the cataclysmic twentieth century, with its mindless nationalisms, global wars, genocide, and fatalism. The White City embodied a moment of rapture, inspiration, and hope. As such it warrants rescue from the past, especially for a world in which celebration and aspiration too often have given way to confusion, destruction, and recrimination. The White City remains symbolic of a harmonious urban world still worthy of pursuit.

NOTES

Preface

1. Henry Steele Commager, *The American Mind* (New Haven, Conn.: Yale University Press, 1950), p. 41.

2. Here and elsewhere in this book the term culture is not used in a truly anthropological sense, but merely in its standard dictionary definition as a word designating characteristic social and intellectual attitudes, values, and beliefs.

3. Howard Mumford Jones, *The Age of Energy* (New York: Viking, 1971), p. 256.

Chapter 1

1. Howard Mumford Jones, *The Age of Energy* (New York: Viking, 1971), p. xii.

2. Ibid., p. 11.

3. Ibid., p. 18.

4. Arthur M. Schlesinger, *The Rise of the City, 1878-1898* (New York: Macmillan, 1933), p. 435.

5. Schlesinger, p. 53.

6. Ibid., p. 64.

7. Ray Ginger, *Age of Excess: The United States from 1877 to 1914* (New York: Macmillan, 1965), p. 36.

8. John Higham, *Strangers in the Land: Patterns of American Nativism 1860-1925* (New York: Atheneum, 1963), p. 50.

9. Ibid., pp. 51-54.

10. Harold U. Faulkner, *Politics, Reform, and Expansion* (New York: Harper & Row, 1959), p. 5.

11. Thomas C. Cochran and William Miller, *The Age of Enterprise* (New York: Harper & Row, 1961), p. 153.

12. Robert H. Walker, *Life in the Age of Enterprise* (New York: Capricorn Books, 1971), p. 58.

13. Cochran and Miller, p. 131.

14. Ibid., p. 146.

15. Ibid., p. 136.

16. Ibid., p. 153.

17. Samuel P. Hays, *The Response to Industrialism, 1885-1914* (Chicago: University of Chicago Press, 1957), p. 2.

18. Francis Wayland Ayer, "Advertising in America" in *One Hundred Years of American Commerce*, ed. Chauncey Depew (New York: D. O. Haynes & Co., 1895), 2:82.

19. See Andrew Carnegie, "Wealth," *North American Review* 148 (June 1889): 653-64.

20. Montgomery Schuyler, "The Works of the Late Richard M. Hunt," *Architectural Record* 5 (October-December 1895): 97, 98.

21. Max O'Rell [Paul Blouet], *Jonathan and His Continent* (New York: Cassell & Company, 1889), p. 20.

22. Ibid., pp. 55-56.

23. Dixon Wecter, *The Saga of American Society* (New York: Scribner's, 1937), p. 137.

24. Ibid., pp. 336-40.

25. Ibid., p. 344.

26. "The Limitations of Office Buildings," *Architecture and Building* 18 (May 6, 1893): 205.

27. John Wellborn Root, "A Great Architectural Problem," *Inland Architect* 15 (June 1890): 71.

28. George W. Sheldon, *Recent Ideals of American Art* (New York: D. Appleton, 1890), p. 2.

29. George Parsons Lathrop, "The Progress of Art in New York," *Harper's New Monthly Magazine* 86 (April 1893): 741.

30. Russell Sturgis, "The Field of Art," *Scribner's Magazine* 19 (March 1896): 390.

31. M. G. Van Rensselaer, "The New York Art Season," *Atlantic Monthly* 48 (August 1881): 198.

32. Frederic Crowninshield, "The Relation between Painter and Architect," *American Architect* 9 (February 26, 1881): 98.

33. Robert H. Walker, p. 170.

34. Paul de Rousiers, *American Life*, trans. A. J. Herbertson (Paris and New York: Firmin-Didot, 1892), p. 414.

35. H. Wiley Hitchcock, *Music in the United States: A Historical Introduction* (Englewood Cliffs, N.J.: Prentice-Hall, 1969), p. 143.

36. Irving Sablosky, *American Music* (Chicago: University of Chicago Press, 1969), pp. 96-97.

37. Ronald L. Davis, *Opera in Chicago* (New York: Appleton-Century, 1966), p. 46.

38. John Tasker Howard, *Our American Music*, 4th ed. (New York: Thomas Y. Crowell, 1965), pp. 280-81.

39. Sablosky, pp. 88-93.

40. Hitchcock, p. 82.

41. Ibid., p. 128.

42. Ibid., pp. 130-38.

43. Howard, pp. 326-27.

44. Sablosky, p. 103.

45. Howard, pp. 244-46.

46. Hitchcock, p. 115.

47. Sigmund Spaeth, *A History of Popular Music in America* (London: Phoenix House, 1948), p. 197.

48. Ibid., p. 265; also pp. 231-78 passim.

49. Ibid., pp. 235-36, 193, 240.

50. Hitchcock, pp. 119 ff.

51. Spaeth, p. 252.

52. Jay Martin, *Harvests of Change: American Literature, 1865-1914* (Englewood Cliffs, N.J.: Prentice-Hall, 1967), pp. 18-19.

53. Schlesinger, p. 250.

54. Martin, p. 21.

55. Frank Luther Mott, *Golden Multitudes* (New York: R. R. Bowker, 1947), p. 183.

56. Ibid., pp. 310-11.

57. Ibid.

58. "The Contributors Club," *Atlantic Monthly* 54 (November 1884): 718.

59. William Dean Howells, "Editors Study," *Harper's New Monthly Magazine* 75 (September 1887): 639-41.

60. Charles Dudley Warner, "Modern Fiction," *Atlantic Monthly* 51 (April 1883): 472.

61. Myron Matlaw, ed., *The Black Crook and Other Nineteenth-Century American Plays* (New York: E. P. Dutton, 1967), p. 320.

62. Brander Matthews, "The Dramatic Outlook in America," *Harper's New Monthly Magazine* 78 (May 1889): 94.

63. Dion Boucicault, "The Future American Drama," *Arena* 2 (November 1890): 649.

64. Marvin Felheim, *The Theater of Augustin Daly* (Cambridge: Harvard University Press, 1956), p. 235.

65. Quoted in Percy MacKaye, *Epoch* (New York: Boni and Liveright, 1927), 2: 132.

66. Montrose Jonas Moses, *The American Dramatist* (Boston: Little, Brown, 1911), pp. 111-12.

67. Joseph Harker, *Studio and Stage* (London: Nisbet, 1924), p. 105.

68. Ibid., p. 103.

69. Walker, p. 141.

70. Ibid., pp. 142-43.

71. Ibid., p. 149.

72. Schlesinger, p. 157.

73. Josiah Strong, *Our Country*, ed. Jurgen Herbst (Cambridge, Mass.: Belknap, 1963), p. 172.

74. Winthrop S. Hudson, *American Protestantism* (Chicago: University of Chicago Press, 1961), p. 111.

75. Russell H. Conwell, *Acres of Diamonds* (New York: Harper & Brothers, 1915), pp. 92, 136.

76. Hudson, p. 125.

77. James Bryce, *The American Commonwealth*, 3d ed. (New York: Macmillan, 1895), 2: 707.

78. Ibid., p. 704.

79. John Tracy Ellis, *American Catholicism* (Chicago: University of Chicago Press, 1956), p. 101.

80. Ibid., p. 104.

81. Nathan Glazer, *American Judaism* (Chicago: University of Chicago Press, 1957), pp. 45-46.

82. Charles Howard Hopkins, *The Rise of the Social Gospel in American Protestantism, 1865-1915* (New Haven, Conn.: Yale University Press, 1940), pp. 3, 26, 54.

83. Charles F. Thwing, *The Working Church* (New York: Baker and Taylor, 1889), p. 65.

84. Richard T. Ely, *Social Aspects of Christianity, and Other Essays* (New York: Thomas Y. Crowell, 1889), p. 19.

85. Ibid., pp. 76-77.

86. Strong, p. 166.

87. Ibid., pp. 160-67.

88. Lyman Abbott, "The Place of the Individual in American Society," in *The United States of America*, ed. Nathaniel Southgate Shaler (New York: D. Appleton, 1894), 3: 1258.

89. Francesco Cordasco, ed., *Jacob Riis Revisited* (Garden City, N.Y.: Doubleday, 1968), p. 4.

90. Ibid., p. 125.

91. Walker, p. 187.

92. Bryce, 2: 275-76.

93. George W. Cable, *The Negro Question*, ed. Arlin Turner (Garden City, N.Y.: Doubleday, 1958), p. 164.

94. W. T. Harris, "Education in the United States," in *The United States of America*, 3: 969.

95. Ibid., pp. 1010-11.

96. Edwin Grant Dexter, *A History of Education in the United States* (New York: Macmillan, 1906), pp. 494-98.

97. Ibid., p. 294.

98. D. C. Gilman, "Science in America," in *The United States of America*, 3: 1045.

99. Walker, p. 54.

100. Faulkner, p. 21.

101. J. C. Furnas, *The Americans: A Social History of the United States* (New York: Capricorn Books, 1969), 2: 642-45.

102. Matthew Arnold, *Civilization in the United States* (Boston: Cupples and Hurd, 1888), p. 168.

103. Jones, pp. 197-200.

104. Bryce, 1: 642.

105. John A. Garraty, *The New Commonwealth, 1877-1890* (New York: Harper & Row, 1968), p. 231.

106. Ibid., p. 226.

107. Ginger, p. 116.

108. de Rousiers, p. 363.

109. Andrew Carnegie, *Triumphant Democracy* (New York: Scribner's, 1886), p. 1.

110. Henry Steele Commager, *The American Mind* (New Haven, Conn.: Yale University Press, 1950), pp. 45-46.

111. H. N. Higinbotham, *Report of the President to the Board of Directors of the World's Columbian Exposition* (Chicago: Rand, McNally, 1898), p. 9.

112. Telford Burnham and James F. Gookins, *Chicago the Site of the World's Fair of 1892* (Chicago: Rand, McNally, 1889), p. 7.

113. Higinbotham, pp. 7-14.

114. Rossiter Johnson, ed., *A History of the World's Columbian Exposition* (New York: D. Appleton, 1897), 1: 4.

Chapter 2

1. Clarence Clough Buel, "Preliminary Glimpses of the Fair," *Century Magazine*, n.s. 23 (February 1893): 615.

2. Theodore Dreiser, *Dawn* (New York: Horace Liveright, 1931), p. 296.

3. Henry B. Fuller, *The Cliff-Dwellers* (New York: Harper & Brothers, 1893), p. 243.

4. Bessie Louise Pierce, *A History of Chicago, 1871-1893* (New York: Alfred A. Knopf, 1957), 3: 5-6.

5. James W. Sheahan and George P. Upton, *The Great Conflagration* (Chicago: Union Publishing Co., 1871), p. 329.

6. "Cheer Up," *Chicago Tribune*, 11 October 1871.

7. Pierce, p. 17.

8. Louis H. Sullivan, *The Autobiography of an Idea* (New York: Dover Publications, 1956), pp. 200-201.

9. Quoted in James P. Holland, "Chicago and the World's Fair," *Chautauquan* 17 (May 1893): 137.

10. Quoted in Pierce, p. 19.

11. Paul de Rousiers, *American Life*, trans. A. J. Herbertson (Paris and New York: Firmin-Didot, 1892), p. 73.

12. Sir Lepel Henry Griffin, *The Great Republic* (New York: Scribner and Welford, 1884), pp. 40-41.

13. Rudyard Kipling, *American Notes* (New York: Manhattan Press, 1889), pp. 215, 218.

14. Buel, p. 615.

15. Pierce, p. 67.

16. Ibid., pp. 97-98.

17. Ibid., p. 94.

18. Ibid., p. 109.

19. Ibid., p. 149.

20. Paul Bourget, from *Outre-Mer Impressions of America* in *As Others See Chicago*, ed. Bessie Louise Pierce (Chicago: University of Chicago Press, 1933), p. 387.

21. Quoted in Pierce, *A History of Chicago*, p. 141.

22. Ibid., pp. 156-57.

23. Ibid., p. 163.

24. Ibid., p. 178.

25. Dixon Wecter, *The Saga of American Society* (New York: Scribner's, 1937), p. 143.

26. C. H. Blackall, "Notes of Travel. Chicago. II," *American Architect* 22 (December 31, 1887): 313-14.

27. Ibid., p. 314.

28. C. H. Blackall, "Notes of Travel. Chicago. III," *American Architect* 23 (February 25, 1888): 89.

29. "Editorial," *Building* 5 (September 11, 1886): 122.

30. John W. Root, "Architectural Ornamentation," *Inland Architect* 5, Extra No. (April 1885): 54.

31. Barr Ferree, "Chicago—The Buildings. II," *Architecture and Building* 16 (January 9, 1892): 17.

32. Clarence A. Hough, "The Art Institute of Chicago," *Art and Archaeology* 12 (September-October 1921): 145, 149.

33. Lena M. McCauley, "Some Collectors of Paintings," *Art and Archaeology* 12 (September-October 1921): 163-67.

34. Leon Stein, ed., "Introduction," *Theodore Thomas: A Musical Autobiography* (New York: Da Capo Press, 1964), pp. A22-A23.

35. Charles Edward Russell, *The American Orchestra and Theodore Thomas* (1927; rpt. Westport, Conn.: Greenwood Press, 1971), p. 104.

36. H. Wiley Hitchcock, *Music in the United States* (Englewood Cliffs, N.J.: Prentice-Hall, 1969), p. 82.

37. Ronald L. Davis, *Opera in Chicago* (New York: Appleton-Century, 1966), p. 45.

38. Ibid., pp. 45-48 passim.

39. Hamlin Garland, *Crumbling Idols* (Cambridge: Belknap, 1960), p. 119.

40. Jay Martin, *Harvests of Change: American Literature, 1865-1914* (Englewood Cliffs, N.J.: Prentice-Hall, 1967), p. 249.

41. Emmett Dedmon, *Fabulous Chicago* (New York: Random House, 1953), p. 203.

42. Harriet Monroe, *A Poet's Life* (New York: Macmillan, 1938), p. 116.

43. Hugh Dalziel Duncan, *The Rise of Chicago as a Literary Center from 1885 to 1920* (Totowa, N.J.: Bedminster Press, 1964), pp. 36, 43.

44. "What Chicago People Read," *Critic*, n.s. 20 (September 23, 1893): 200-201.

45. [Will Payne], "Chicago's Higher Evolution," *Dial* 13 (October 1, 1892): 206.

46. Edward G. Mason, "Chicago," *Atlantic Monthly* 70 (July 1892): 37.

47. Ibid.

48. Max O'Rell, *A Frenchman in America* (New York: Cassell Publishing Company, 1891), p. 209.

49. Pierce, *A History of Chicago*, 3: 22.

50. Ibid., p. 516.

51. Lloyd Lewis and Henry Justin Smith, *Chicago: The History of Its Reputation* (New York: Harcourt, Brace, 1929), p. 172.

52. G. W. Steevens, *The Land of the Dollar* (Edinburgh: William Blackwood and Sons, 1897), pp. 144-45.

53. *The Ten Best States of America* (Cedar Rapids, Iowa: Republican Printing Company, 1893), p. 86.

54. Washington Gladden, "Sunday in Chicago," *Century Magazine*, n.s. 23 (November 1892): 151.

55. Pierce, *A History of Chicago*, 3: 324.

56. Ibid., p. 423.

57. Ibid., p. 425.

58. Ibid., p. 545.

59. Charles Dudley Warner, *Studies in the South and West* (New York: Harper & Brothers, 1889), p. 195.

60. William T. Stead, *If Christ Came to Chicago!* (Chicago: Laird & Lee, 1894), p. 25.

61. Ibid., p. 133.

62. Ibid., pp. 142, 41.

63. Dedmon, pp. 143-47.

64. Herbert Asbury, *Gem of the Prairie* (Garden City, N.Y.: Garden City Publishing Company, 1942), p. 137.

65. Pierce, *A History of Chicago*, 3: 149.

66. Carter H. Harrison, *Growing Up with Chicago* (Chicago: Ralph Fletcher Seymour, 1944), p. 110.

67. Stead, pp. 73-74.

68. Asbury, p. 146.

69. Pierce, *A History of Chicago*, 3: 355.

70. Duncan, p. 71.

71. Ibid., p. 3.

72. Stead, p. 127.

73. Theodore Dreiser, *The Titan* (Cleveland: World Publishing Company, 1946), p. 6.

Chapter 3

1. H. N. Higinbotham, *Report of the President to the Board of Directors of the World's Columbian Exposition* (Chicago: Rand, McNally, 1898), p. 15.
2. Ibid., pp. 21-22.
3. Charles Moore, *Daniel H. Burnham: Architect, Planner of Cities* (Boston: Houghton Mifflin, 1921), 1: 32.
4. Frederick Law Olmsted, "The Landscape Architecture of the World's Columbian Exposition," *Inland Architect* 22 (September 1893): 19.
5. Rossiter Johnson, ed., *A History of the World's Columbian Exposition* (New York: D. Appleton, 1897), 1: 135.
6. Moore, p. 35.
7. Ibid., p. 40.
8. Ibid., p. 42.
9. Ibid., p. 43.
10. Daniel Hudson Burnham and Francis Davis Millet, *The Book of the Builders* (Chicago: Columbian Memorial Publication Society, 1894), p. 25.
11. Harriet Monroe, *John Wellborn Root* (Boston: Houghton Mifflin, 1896), pp. 242-43.
12. Burnham and Millet, p. 22.
13. Ibid.
14. Ibid., pp. 23, 28.
15. Quoted in Moore, p. 47.
16. Burnham and Millet, p. 37.
17. "Chicago," *American Architect* 28 (April 19, 1890): 38.
18. "Editorial," *Architecture and Building* 12 (March 15, 1890): 122.
19. "Chicago," *American Architect* 28 (June 21, 1890): 180.
20. "Columbian Exposition Notes," *Architecture and Building* 15 (October 7, 1891): 190.
21. Burnham and Millet, pp. 38-39.
22. "Editorial," *American Architect* 32 (June 6, 1891): 142.
23. Johnson, pp. 161-62.
24. *A Week at the Fair* (Chicago: Rand, McNally, 1893), p. 35.
25. Quoted in Johnson, p. 35.
26. Higinbotham, p. 34.
27. Burnham and Millet, pp. 35-36.
28. Johnson, p. 156.
29. Ibid., pp. 156, 145.
30. Ibid., p. 156.
31. Higinbotham, pp. 199-200.
32. Johnson, pp. 158-59.
33. Hubert Howe Bancroft, *The Book of the Fair* (Chicago: Bancroft Company, 1893), p. 67.
34. Higinbotham, p. 36.
35. Johnson, p. 153.
36. Higinbotham, pp. 109-10.
37. Johnson, pp. 57-62.
38. Ibid., pp. 62-63.
39. Ibid., pp. 63-64.

40. Higinbotham, pp. 230-31, 250.

41. Ibid., p. 132.

42. Ibid., pp. 138-40.

43. Ibid., pp. 219-20.

44. Johnson, p. 193; Higinbotham, p. 45.

45. James B. Campbell, *Campbell's Illustrated History of the World's Columbian Exposition* (Chicago: N. Juul & Co., 1894), 2:386.

46. Johnson, 2:2.

47. Ibid., 1:110.

48. John J. Flinn, ed., *Official Guide to the World's Columbian Exposition* (Chicago: Columbian Guide Co., 1893), p. 30.

49. Higinbotham, p. 193.

50. *Rand, McNally & Co.'s Handbook of the World's Columbian Exposition* (Chicago: Rand, McNally, 1893), p. 22.

51. Flinn, p. 31.

52. Campbell, 1:166.

53. *Rand, McNally & Co.'s Handbook*, pp. 22-23.

54. Higinbotham, pp. 117-18.

55. John W. Chadwick, "Why the Fair Must Be Open on Sunday," *Forum* 14 (September 1892-February 1893): 548-49.

56. Bishop J. L. Spalding, D.D., "Why the World's Fair Should Be Opened on Sunday," *Arena* 7 (December 1892-May 1893): 46-47.

57. Elizabeth Cady Stanton, "Sunday at the World's Fair," *North American Review* 154 (1892): 254-56.

58. Higinbotham, pp. 237-46.

59. Johnson, 1:159.

60. Barr Ferree, "Chicago—The World's Fair. IV," *Architecture and Building* 16 (February 20, 1892): 87.

61. Julian Ralph, *Harper's Chicago and the World's Fair* (New York: Harper & Brothers, 1893), p. 1.

62. Marquis de Chasseloup-Laubat, "A Frenchman on the World's Fair and America," *American Architect* 39 (January 28, 1893): 59.

63. "Editorial," *Inland Architect* 17 (April 1891): 30.

64. Olmsted, p. 21.

65. Flinn, p. 77.

66. Carl Condit, *American Building Art: The Nineteenth Century* (New York: Oxford University Press, 1960), p. 219.

67. "Chicago," *American Architect* 36 (May 28, 1892): 133. For a detailed discussion of the engineering at the fair see E. C. Shankland, chief engineer, "The Construction of the Buildings, Bridges, etc., at the World's Columbian Exposition," *Inland Architect* 22 (August 1893): 8-9.

68. Ralph, p. 241.

69. "The Area of the Liberal Arts Building at Chicago," *American Architect* 42 (December 23, 1893): 151.

70. Johnson, 1:190.

71. Ibid., p. 189.

72. Ibid., p. 187.

73. Ibid., pp. 146-47.

74. Burnham and Millet, p. 47.

75. Johnson, 1:177-80.

76. Higinbotham, pp. 156-57.

77. Ibid., pp. 156-59.

78. Johnson, 1:261.

79. Ibid., p. 266.

80. 'Chicago," *American Architect* 38 (November 26, 1892): 133.

81. Johnson, 1:264.

82. Higinbotham, pp. 161-63.

83. Johnson, 1:267.

84. Campbell, p. 190.

85. Ibid.

86. Johnson, 1:270-71.

87. Harriet Monroe, *Commemoration Ode* (Chicago: Printed for the Author, 1892), p. 12.

88. Harriet Monroe, *A Poet's Life* (New York: Macmillan, 1938), pp. 130-31.

89. Johnson, 1:276-77.

90. Ibid., pp. 277-80.

91. Campbell, p. 191.

92. Johnson, 1:284-88.

93. Quoted in ibid., pp. 288-95.

94. Quoted in ibid., pp. 295-306.

95. Monroe, *A Poet's Life*, p. 130.

96. Higinbotham, p. 165.

97. Johnson, 1:306.

98. Campbell, p. 250.

99. Johnson, 1:340-45.

100. Quoted in ibid., pp. 345-51.

101. Higinbotham, p. 211.

102. "Ready for a World," *Chicago Tribune*, 2 May 1893.

103. Higinbotham, pp. 211-12.

104. James W. Shepp and Daniel B. Shepp, *Shepp's World's Fair Photographed* (Chicago: Globe Bible Publishing Co., 1893), p. 8.

105. *A Week at the Fair*, p. 35.

106. Clarence Clough Buel, "Preliminary Glimpses of the Fair," *Century Magazine* 45 (February 1893): 615.

107. Walter Besant, "A First Impression," *Cosmopolitan* 15 (September 1893): 531.

108. Benjamin Harrison, "Points of Interest," *Cosmopolitan* 15 (September 1893): 611.

109. "Achieved Is the Glorious Work," *Chicago Tribune*, 1 May 1893.

110. Andrew Carnegie, "Value of the World's Fair to the American People," *Engineering Magazine* 6 (January 1894): 418.

111. Shepp and Shepp, p. 9.

112. Frank D. Millet et al., *Some Artists at the Fair* (New York: Charles Scribner's Sons, 1893), p. 82.

Chapter 4

1. Peter B. Wight, "The Great Exhibition Reviewed," *American Architect* 42 (October 7, 1893): 8.

2. Henry Van Brunt, "The Architectural Event of Our Times," *Engineering Magazine* (January 1894): 432-33.

3. Mrs. Schuyler Van Rensselaer, "The Fair Grounds," in *A Week at the Fair* (Chicago: Rand, McNally, 1893), p. 74.

4. James W. Shepp and Daniel B. Shepp, *Shepp's World's Fair Photographed* (Chicago: Globe Bible Publishing Co., 1893), p. 8.

5. Montgomery Schuyler, "Last Words about the World's Fair," *Architectural Record* 3 (January-March 1894): 297.

6. Talbot Hamlin, *Forms and Functions of Twentieth-Century Architecture* (New York: Columbia University Press, 1952), 2:578-79.

7. Quoted in Charles Moore, *Daniel H. Burnham: Architect Planner of Cities* (Boston: Houghton Mifflin, 1921), 1:79.

8. Halsey C. Ives, "Introduction," *The Dream City* (St. Louis, Mo.: N. D. Thompson Publishing Co., 1893), n.p.

9. John J. Flinn, ed., *Official Guide to the World's Columbian Exposition* (Chicago: Columbian Guide Company, 1893), pp. 41-42. All subsequent data on dimensions and features are taken from this *Guide* unless otherwise noted.

10. *The Dream City*, n.p.

11. Lorado Taft, *The History of American Sculpture* (New York: Macmillan, 1924), p. 322.

12. Van Rensselaer, p. 129.

13. *Conkey's Complete Guide to the World's Columbian Exposition* (Chicago: W. B. Conkey Company, 1893), pp. 46-47.

14. Taft, p. 342.

15. Van Rensselaer, pp. 75-76.

16. Henry Van Brunt, "Architecture at the World's Columbian Exposition," *Century Magazine*, n.s. 22 (May 1892): 92.

17. Ibid., p. 93.

18. Ibid., p. 96.

19. "What Mrs. Van Rensselaer Says," in *Rand, McNally & Co.'s Handbook of the World's Columbian Exposition* (Chicago: Rand, McNally, 1893), p. 62.

20. Rossiter Johnson, ed., *The History of the World's Columbian Exposition* (New York: D. Appleton, 1897), 2:178.

21. "What Mrs. Van Rensselaer Says," p. 62.

22. Henry Van Brunt, "Architecture at the World's Columbian Exposition, II," *Century Magazine*, n.s. 22 (July 1892): 394.

23. Hubert Howe Bancroft, *The Book of the Fair* (Chicago: Bancroft Company, 1893), pp. 342-43.

24. *The Dream City*, n.p.

25. Bancroft, p. 343.

26. "Chicago," *American Architect* 37 (August 20, 1892): 116.

27. *The Magic City* (St. Louis, Mo.: Historical Publishing Company, 1894), n.p.

28. "What Mrs. Van Rensselaer Says," p. 62.

29. Barr Ferree, "Architecture at the World's Fair," *Engineering Magazine* 5 (August 1893): 657.

30. *A Week at the Fair*, p. 132.

31. Ferree, p. 656.

32. Van Brunt, "The Architectural Event of Our Times," p. 438.

33. "What Mrs. Van Rensselaer Says," p. 62.

34. Schuyler, p. 298.

35. Ibid., p. 298.

36. *Memorial Volume: Dedicatory and Opening Ceremonies of the World's Columbian Exposition* (Chicago: Stone, Kastler & Painter, 1893), p. 59.

37. *The Dream City*, n.p.

38. Ferree, p. 654.

39. Ibid., p. 658.

40. Quoted in *The Dream City*, n.p.

41. Quoted in Larzer Ziff, *The American 1890's* (New York: Viking, 1966), p. 21.

42. S. K., "The Columbian Exposition—IV. The Ensemble," *Nation* 57 (August 24, 1893): 133.

43. Carl Condit, *The Chicago School of Architecture* (Chicago: University of Chicago Press, 1964), p. 136.

44. "The World's Fair Buildings," *American Architect* 38 (November 5, 1892): 86.

45. *The Dream City*, n.p.

46. "The World's Fair Buildings," p. 86.

47. "What Mrs. Van Rensselaer Says," p. 63.

48. Candace Wheeler, "A Dream City," *Harper's New Monthly Magazine* 86 (May 1893): 836.

49. Flinn, ed., p. 73.

50. Henry Van Brunt, "Architecture at the World's Columbian Exposition. V," *Century Magazine*, n.s. 22 (October 1892): 897, 901.

51. Van Rensselaer, p. 77.

52. Ferree, pp. 657-58.

53. Julian Hawthorne, *Humors of the Fair* (Chicago: E. A. Weeks & Co., 1893), p. 59.

54. Johnson, 2:383.

55. "Architectural Aberrations. No. 6—The Government and the World's Fair," *Architectural Record* 3 (January-March 1893): 336.

56. "What Mrs. Van Rensselaer Says," p. 63.

57. *The Illinois Building and Exhibits Therein at the World's Columbian Exposition* (Chicago: John Morris Company, 1893), p. 9.

58. "What Mrs. Van Rensselaer Says," p. 63.

59. Montgomery Schuyler, "State Buildings at the World's Fair," *Architectural Record* 3 (July-September 1893): 61.

60. F. D. Millet, "The Designers of the Fair," *Harper's New Monthly Magazine* 85 (November 1892): 878.

61. Frank D. Millet et al., *Some Artists at the Fair* (New York: Charles Scribner's Sons, 1893), pp. 10-13.

62. Julian Ralph, *Harper's Chicago and the World's Fair* (New York: Harper & Brothers, 1893), p. 143.

63. Millet et al., pp. 66-67.

64. *Rand, McNally & Co.'s Handbook*, p. 52.

65. Royal Cortissoz, "Color in the Court of Honor at the Fair," *Century Magazine*, n.s. 24 (July 1893): 332-33.

66. Cortissoz's use of the word construction to describe the manner of execution of this mural is interesting. An artwork so vast seems not to have been limned, but rather built section by section like a house. For an idea of how the various painters approached this work see C. C. Buel, "Preliminary Glimpses of the Fair," *Century Magazine*, n.s. 45 (February 1893): 620.

67. Millet et al., p. 14.

68. *Rand, McNally & Co.'s Handbook*, pp. 56-57.

69. Taft, pp. 456-57.

70. Bancroft, pp. 132-33.

71. Cortissoz, p. 327.

72. Millet et al., p. 18.

73. Ibid., p. 21.

74. W. Lewis Fraser, "Decorative Painting at the World's Fair," *Century Magazine*, n.s. 24 (May 1893): 15.

75. Ibid., p. 21.

76. Millet et al., *Some Artists at the Fair*, p. 28.

77. Ibid.

78. Ibid., p. 35.

79. Cortissoz, p. 332.

80. Millet et al., pp. 77-78.

81. Bancroft, p. 101.

82. Ellen M. Henrotin, "An Outsider's View of the Woman's Exhibit," *Cosmopolitan* 15 (September 1893): 561.

83. Millet et al., p. 78.

84. Maud Howe Elliott, ed., *Art and Handicraft in the Woman's Building of the World's Columbian Exposition* (Chicago: Rand, McNally, 1894), p. 45.

85. Ibid., p. 53.

86. Fraser, p. 21.

87. Candace Wheeler, "Decorative Art," *Architectural Record* 4 (April-June 1895): 411.

88. H. N. Higinbotham, *Report of the President to the Board of Directors of the World's Columbian Exposition* (Chicago: Rand, McNally, 1895), p. 183.

89. Johnson, 1:465-68.

90. *Rand, McNally & Co.'s Handbook*, p. 113.

91. Charles Edward Russell, *The American Orchestra and Theodore Thomas* (1927; rpt. Westport, Conn.: Greenwood Press, 1971), p. 209.

92. Johnson, 1:465, 468-69.

93. "Music at the World's Fair," *Dial* 14 (June 1, 1893): 329.

94. Higinbotham, p. 252.

95. Russell, pp. 212-36.

96. Higinbotham, p. 252.

97. Johnson, 1:469.

98. Higinbotham, p. 221.

99. Ibid., p. 213.

100. Johnson, 1:469.

101. Ibid., pp. 470-71.

102. Irving Sablosky, *American Music* (Chicago: University of Chicago Press, 1969), p. 105.

103. Johnson, 1:469.

104. Ibid., p. 472.

105. Sigmund Spaeth, *A History of Popular Music in America* (London: Phoenix House, 1948), p. 260.

106. Johnson, 1:473.

107. Bancroft, pp. 253-54. See also Johnson, 3:347-52.

108. *Dictionary Catalog, Being Part III of Catalog of "A.L.A." Library: 5000 Volumes for a Popular Library.* Selected by the American Library Association and shown at the World's Columbian Exposition. (Issued by U.S. Bureau of Education.)

109. Elliott, ed., pp. 126, 133-37. See also Johnson, 3:467-70.

110. Johnson, 1:432-33.

111. "Nature's Own Stage," *Daily Inter Ocean*, 31 August 1893.

112. Otis Skinner, *Footlights and Spotlights* (Indianapolis, Ind.: Bobbs-Merrill, 1924), p. 210.

113. W. L. B. Jenney, "A Talk on Architecture at the World's Columbian Exposition," *Inland Architect* 21 (April 1893): 35.

114. Van Brunt, "The Architectural Event of Our Times," p. 431.

115. Schuyler, "Last Words about the World's Fair," p. 299.

116. Ibid., p. 300.

117. Arthur Sherburne Hardy, "Last Impressions," *Cosmopolitan* 16 (December 1893): 196.

118. William Anderson Coffin, "The Fair as a Work of Art," in *History of the World's Columbian Exposition*, ed. Rossiter Johnson, 2:515.

119. Benjamin Harrison, "Points of Interest," *Cosmopolitan* 15 (September 1893): 611.

120. Thomas A. Janvier, "A Retrospective Forecast," *Cosmopolitan* 15 (September 1893): 617.

121. P. B. Wight, "After Ten Years," *Inland Architect* 21 (February 1893): 5.

122. "Current Magazines," *Architectural Review* 2 (April 3, 1893): 29.

123. "A Frenchman on the World's Fair and America," *American Architect* 39 (January 28, 1893): 58-59.

124. Paul Bourget, "A Farewell to the White City," *Cosmopolitan* 16 (December 1893): 136-37.

125. Edmund Mitchell, "International Effects of the Fair," *Engineering Magazine* 6 (January 1894): 468.

126. Ibid., p. 472.

127. Walter Besant, "A First Impression," *Cosmopolitan* 15 (September 1893): 533.

128. James P. Holland, "Chicago and the World's Fair," *Chautauquan* 17 (May 1893): 136.

Chapter 5

1. Ben C. Truman, *History of the World's Fair* (Philadelphia: Mammoth Publishing Co., 1893), p. 451.

2. *The Dream City* (St. Louis, Mo.: N. D. Thompson Publishing Co., 1893), n.p.

3. Candace Wheeler, "A Dream City," *Harper's New Monthly Magazine* 86 (May 1893): 840.

4. Homer Saint-Gaudens, ed., *The Reminiscences of Augustus Saint-Gaudens* (New York: Century Company, 1913), 2:73.

5. *The Magic City* (St. Louis, Mo.: Historical Publishing Company, 1894), n.p.

6. *The Columbian Gallery* (Chicago: Werner Company, 1894), n.p.

7. Trumbull White and William Iglehart, *The World's Columbian Exposition, Chicago, 1893* (Philadelphia: International Publishing Co., 1893), p. 337.

8. Charles M. Kurtz, *Official Illustrations from the Art Gallery of the World's Columbian Exposition* (Philadelphia: George Barrie, 1893), p. 10.

9. John J. Flinn, ed., *Official Guide to the World's Columbian Exposition* (Chicago: Columbian Guide Company, 1893), p. 62.

10. Ibid., p. 64.

11. *Rand, McNally & Co.'s Handbook of the World's Columbian Exposition* (Chicago: Rand, McNally, 1893), p. 153.

12. *Revised Catalogue, Department of Fine Arts* (Chicago: W. B. Conkey Company, 1893).

13. Quoted in Hubert Howe Bancroft, *The Book of the Fair* (Chicago: Bancroft Company, 1893), pp. 671-72.

14. Ibid., p. 672.

15. William A. Coffin, "The Columbian Exposition.—II. Fine Arts: The United States Section," *Nation* 57 (August 10, 1893): 97.

16. Bancroft, p. 678.

17. Ibid., p. 679.

18. William Walton, *World's Columbian Exposition: Art and Architecture* (Philadelphia: George Barrie, 1893), 1: 20 and opposite p. 4.

19. H. H. Ragan, *Art Photographs of the World and the Columbian Exposition* (n.p.: Photograph Publishing Company, 1893), p. 33.

20. Rossiter Johnson, ed., *The History of the World's Columbian Exposition* (New York: D. Appleton, 1897), 3:397.

21. Bancroft, p. 685.

22. William A. Coffin, "The Columbian Exposition.—III. Fine Arts: Pictures by American Artists—Sculptural and Pictorial Decoration," *Nation* 57 (August 17, 1893): 115.

23. Bancroft, p. 686.

24. Ibid.

25. Walton, 1:13.

26. General Lew Wallace, "Introduction," *Famous Paintings of the World* (New York: Fine Arts Publishing Company, 1894), n.p.

27. Walton, p. 14.

28. *Buildings and Art at the World's Fair* (Chicago: Rand, McNally, 1894), p. 97.

29. Wallace, n.p.

30. *The Columbian Gallery*, n.p.

31. Johnson, 3:406.

32. *Buildings and Art at the World's Fair*, p. 183.

33. William A. Coffin, "The Columbian Exposition.—I. Fine Arts: French and American Sculpture," *Nation* 57 (August 3, 1893): 80.

34. Johnson, 3:402.

35. John C. Van Dyke, "Painting at the Fair," *Century Magazine*, n.s. 26 (July 1894): 446.

36. Walton, 1:51.

37. Ibid., p. 52.

38. White and Iglehart, pp. 362-63.

39. *World's Columbian Exposition, 1893, Chicago: Catalogue of the Russian Section* (St. Petersburg: Imperial Russian Commission, 1893), pp. iii-iv.

40. Walton, 1:53.

41. Johnson, 3:409.

42. Walton, 1:58.

43. Ibid., pp. 61-62.

44. H. C. Payne, "Painting and Sculpture at the World's Fair," *Inland Architect* 22 (August 1893): 4.

45. *Classification of the World's Columbian Exposition* (Chicago: Donohue & Henneberry, 1891), pp. 1, 3-13, 33-41, 59-74.

46. Frank Millet et al., *Some Artists at the Fair* (New York: Scribner's, 1893), pp. 46-47.

47. "Big Things at the World's Fair," *Architecture and Building* 18 (June 24, 1893): 293.

48. Johnson, 3:328.

49. W. E. Hamilton, *The "Time-Saver." A Book Which Names and Locates 5,000 Things at the World's Fair* (Chicago: Cushing Printing Company, 1893), passim.

50. Truman, p. 210.

51. White and Iglehart, p. 106.

52. Ibid., p. 109.

53. Johnson, 3:286.

54. *The Columbian Gallery*, n.p.

55. Truman, p. 221.

56. Johnson, 3:281.

57. Bancroft, p. 140. Bancroft devotes 220 pages to the Manufactures and Liberal Arts Building and its exhibits, suggesting the utter impossibility of considering here the entirety of those exhibits.

58. Truman, p. 355.

59. "The Electricity Building at the Fair," *Scientific American* 69 (October 7, 1893): 229.

60. Truman, pp. 356-57.

61. Bancroft, p. 400.

62. "The Largest Search-Light in the World," *Architecture and Building* 19 (August 26, 1893): 105.

63. Murat Halstead, "Electricity at the Fair," *Cosmopolitan* 15 (September 1893): 578.

64. J. P. Barrett, *Electricity at the Columbian Exposition* (Chicago: R. R. Donnelly & Sons Company, 1894), p. 4.

65. Flinn, p. 87.

66. Bancroft, p. 308.

67. Robert H. Thurston, "An Era of Mechanical Triumphs," *Engineering Magazine* 6 (January 1894): 456.

68. White and Iglehart, p. 268.

69. Ibid., p. 299.

70. Truman, p. 341.

71. James B. Campbell, *Campbell's Illustrated History of the World's Columbian Exposition* (Chicago: N. Juul & Co., 1894), 2:489.

72. Ibid., 1:299.

73. White and Iglehart, p. 437.

74. "Well Done, Mrs. Palmer," *Chicago Tribune*, 6 May 1893.

75. Truman, pp. 175, 182.

76. Ibid., p. 177.

77. Bancroft, p. 267.

78. Ibid., p. 291.

79. Johnson, 1:430.

80. Ibid., p. 453.

81. Flinn, p. 56.

82. *Rand, McNally & Co.'s Handbook*, p. 101.

83. See *The Illinois Building and Exhibits Therein at the World's Columbian Exposition, 1893* (Chicago: John Morris Company, n.d.).

84. Truman, p. 458.

85. Ibid., p. 509.

86. *Buildings and Art at the World's Fair*, n.p.

87. Truman, p. 509.

88. *The Magic City*, n.p.

89. Ibid., n.p.

90. White and Iglehart, p. 551.

91. Ibid., pp. 542-43.

92. Johnson, 2:413-14.

93. Ibid., p. 430.

94. Ibid., pp. 422-23.

95. White and Iglehart, p. 561.

96. "Within the Midway Plaisance," *Columbian Gallery*, p. 1.

97. M. P. Handy, ed., *Official Catalogue of the Exhibits on the Midway Plaisance, Group 176* (Chicago: W. B. Conkey, 1893), passim.

98. Johnson, 3:433-34.

99. *The Dream City*, n.p.

100. "Within the Midway Plaisance," p. 1.

101. White and Iglehart, pp. 569-70.

102. Johnson, 3:437.

103. Truman, pp. 575-76.

104. Johnson, 3:437.

105. White and Iglehart, p. 583.

106. Truman, p. 551.

107. W. J. H., *Street in Cairo* (n.p.: Egypt-Chicago Exposition Co., 1893), p. 3.

108. Handy, ed., p. 22.

109. *A Complete "Guide" to the Egyptological Exhibit in the Cairo Street Concession at the World's Columbian Exposition, Chicago* (Chicago: Thayer & Jackson Stationery Co., 1893), p. 10.

110. W. J. H., p. 7.

111. James W. Shepp and Daniel B. Shepp, *Shepp's World's Fair Photographed* (Chicago: Globe Publishing Co., 1893), p. 512.

112. *The Dream City*, n.p.

113. Ibid.

114. "Within the Midway Plaisance," pp. 3-4.

115. Ibid., pp. 4-5.

116. *The Magic City*, n.p.

117. W. J. H., p. 15.

118. Sigmund Spaeth, *A History of Popular Music in America* (London: Phoenix House, 1948), p. 197.

119. *A Brief History of the Invention and Construction of the Ferris Wheel* (Chicago: Ferris Wheel Co., 1893), n.p.

120. Shepp and Shepp, p. 502.

121. *A Brief History of the Invention and Construction of the Ferris Wheel*, n.p.

122. *The Columbian Gallery*, n.p.

123. "World's Fair Notes," *Architecture and Building* 18 (May 6, 1893): 213-14.

124. *The Columbian Gallery*, n.p.

125. "Display of Fireworks at the Columbian Exposition," *Scientific American* 69 (December 2, 1893): 359.

126. N.H.D., "Columbian Expectoration," Correspondence, *Nation* 57 (November 2, 1893): 328.

127. Percy MacKaye, *Epoch* (New York: Boni & Liveright, 1927), 2:314.

128. Ibid., p. 346.

129. Quoted in ibid., p. 328.

130. *Handy Guide to Chicago* (Chicago: Rand, McNally, 1893), p. 57.

131. Ibid., p. 60.

132. Quoted in Herbert Asbury, *Gem of the Prairie* (New York: Garden City Publishing Co., 1942), pp. 61, 89, 155, 142-43, 146, 151, 172-76.

133. Ibid., pp. 181-86.

134. Ibid., pp. 117-41.

135. Hamlin Garland, *A Son of the Middle Border* (n.p.: Grosset & Dunlap, 1917), pp. 258-61.

136. William Dean Howells, "Letters of the Altrurian Traveler. II," *Cosmopolitan* 16 (December 1893): 218.

137. Ibid., p. 219.

138. Ibid., pp. 220-23.

139. Ibid., p. 232.

Chapter 6

1. Charles Carroll Bonney, *World's Congress Addresses* (Chicago: Open Court Publishing Company, 1900), p. iii.

2. H. N. Higinbotham, *Report of the President to the Board of Directors of the World's Columbian Exposition* (Chicago: Rand, McNally, 1898), pp. 326-27.

3. Thomas B. Bryan, "World's Congress Auxiliary," in Trumbull White and William Iglehart, *The World's Columbian Exposition, Chicago, 1893* (Philadelphia: International Publishing Co., 1893), p. 620.

4. Higinbotham, pp. 327-28.

5. Rossiter Johnson, ed., *A History of the World's Columbian Exposition* (New York: D. Appleton, 1898), 4:4.

6. Ibid., pp. 8-9.

7. Ibid., pp. 10-12.

8. Ibid., p. 6.

9. Ibid., pp. 6-8.

10. "Address Delivered by Mrs. Potter Palmer," in *The Congress of Women*, ed. Mary Kavanaugh Oldham Eagle (Chicago: Beezley Publishing Co., 1894), p. 28.

11. Ibid., p. 25.

12. Laura DeForce Gordon, "Woman's Sphere from a Woman's Standpoint," in ibid., pp. 74-76.

13. Hanna K. Korany, "The Glory of Womanhood," in ibid., p. 360.

14. Juliet Corson, "The Evolution of Home," in ibid., pp. 717-18.

15. Charlotte C. Holt, "The Woman Who Has Come," in ibid., pp. 190-93.

16. Mrs. Carrie K. Sherman, "Characteristics of the Modern Woman," in ibid., p. 766.

17. Isabel Wing Lake, "The Tempted Woman," in ibid., pp. 574-75.

18. Helen L. Bullock, "Power and Purposes of Women," in ibid., pp. 143, 147.

19. Ellen M. Henrotin, "The Financial Independence of Women," in ibid., pp. 348-53.

20. Mary A. Greene, "Legal Condition of Woman in 1492-1892," in ibid., pp. 41-52.

21. Cara Reese, "We, the Women," in ibid., p. 329.

22. Lucy Stone, "The Progress of Fifty Years," in ibid., pp. 58-61.

23. Quoted in Johnson, 4:77-79.

24. Bertha Honoré Palmer, "Closing Address," *World's Congress of Women*, pp. 820-24.

25. Ibid., p. 824.

26. Quoted in Johnson, 4:94.

27. Quoted in ibid., pp. 103-4.

28. Quoted in ibid., p. 105.

29. Ibid., p. 117.

30. Quoted in ibid., p. 119.

31. Ibid., pp. 140, 158.

32. Ibid., pp. 160-61.

33. Quoted in ibid., p. 161.

34. Ibid., pp. 162-63.

35. Quoted in "The Congress of Authors," *Dial* 15 (July 16, 1893): 30.

36. Ibid., p. 30.

37. Ibid., p. 30.

38. Quoted in Johnson, 4: 166-67.

39. Ibid., p. 169.

40. Walter Besant, "Literary Conferences," *Contemporary Review* 65 (January 1894): 124.

41. Johnson, 4:174.

42. Ibid., pp. 175-76.

43. Stewart Culin, "Retrospect of the Folk-lore of the Columbian Exposition," *Journal of American Folk-lore* 7 (January-March 1894): 51, 54.

44. Johnson, 4:169-70.

45. Quoted in ibid., pp. 170-71.

46. William Leuchtenburg, ed., *Frontier and Section: Selected Essays of Frederick Jackson Turner* (Englewood Cliffs, N.J.: Prentice-Hall, 1961), p. 37.

47. Ibid., pp. 52, 56, 61.

48. Johnson, 4:180.

49. Quoted in ibid., p. 218.

50. Henry Van Brunt, "The Growth of Characteristic Architectural Style in the United States," in *Proceedings of the Twenty-Seventh Annual Convention of the American Institute of Architects*, ed. Alfred Stone (Chicago: Inland Architect Press, 1893), pp. 242-53 passim.

51. Barr Ferree, "Economic Conditions of Architecture in America," in ibid., pp. 228-41 passim.

52. Quoted in Johnson, 4:403.

53. Quoted in ibid., p. 415.

54. Quoted in ibid., p. 440.

55. Ibid., p. 221.

56. Ibid., p. 223.

57. Ibid., p. 225.

58. Ibid., pp. 226-27.

59. Bonney, pp. 1, 9.

60. John Henry Barrows, ed., *The World's Parliament of Religions* (Chicago: Parliament Publishing Company, 1893), 1:82.

61. Johnson, 4:227-28.

62. Ibid., pp. 228-29.

63. H. K. Carroll, "The Present Religious Condition of America," in *The World's Parliament of Religions*, ed. John Henry Barrows (Chicago: Parliament Publishing Company, 1893), 2:1162.

64. Ibid.

65. Ibid., p. 1165.

66. Lyman Abbott, "Religion Essentially Characteristic of Humanity," in ibid., 1:499.

67. Ibid., pp. 499-500.

68. F. G. Peabody, "Christianity and the Social Question," in ibid., 2:1024.

69. Ibid., pp. 1026-28.

70. Richard T. Ely, "Christianity as a Social Force," in ibid., p. 1059.

71. Ibid., pp. 1060-61.

72. Washington Gladden, "Religion and Wealth," in ibid., pp. 1068-70.

73. A. W. Small, "The Churches and the City Problems," in ibid., p. 1080.

74. Ibid., pp. 1080-81.

75. Ibid., pp. 1082-83.

76. W. T. Stead, "The Civic Church," in ibid., p. 1209.

77. Ibid., p. 1209.

78. Ibid., pp. 1212-15.

79. Paul Carus, "Science a Religious Revelation," in ibid., pp. 980-81.

80. James M. Cleary, "Religion and Labor," in ibid., pp. 1066-67.

81. "Addresses of B. W. Arnett and the Hon. J. M. Ashley," in ibid., pp. 1101-4.

82. Fannie Barrier Williams, "What Can Religion Further Do to Advance the Condition of the American Negro?" in ibid., pp. 1114-15.

83. J. R. Slattery, "The Catholic Church and the Negro Race," in ibid., pp. 1104-6.

84. Frances E. Willard, "A White Life for Two," in ibid., p. 1232.

85. Elizabeth Cady Stanton, "The Worship of God in Man," in ibid., pp. 1234-36.

86. Julia Ward Howe, "What Is Religion?" in ibid., p. 1251.

87. Antoinette Brown Blackwell, "Woman and the Pulpit," in ibid., pp. 1148-50.

88. Henrietta Szold, "What Has Judaism Done for Woman?" in ibid., p. 1056.

89. Lydia Fuller Dickinson, "The Divine Basis of the Cooperation of Men and Women," in ibid., pp. 502-7.

90. Bonney, p. 12.

91. Barrows, ed., 1:157-60.

92. Ibid., p. 169.

93. Ibid., p. 183.

94. Ibid., p. 184.

95. Bonney, p. 77.

96. Ibid., p. 85.

97. Ibid., p. 88.

98. Thomas B. Bryan, "World's Congress Auxiliary," in *The World's Columbian*

Exposition, Chicago, 1893, ed. Trumbull White and William Iglehart (Philadelphia: International Publishing Co., 1893), pp. 627-28.

99. John Henry Barrows, "Results of the Parliament of Religions," *Forum* 18 (September 1894): 57.

100. Max Müller, "The Real Significance of the Parliament of Religions," *Arena* 11 (December 1894): 1, 6.

Chapter 7

1. Rossiter Johnson, *A History of the World's Columbian Exposition* (New York: D. Appleton, 1897), 1:487.

2. Ibid., p. 490.

3. Trumbull White and William Iglehart, eds., *The World's Columbian Exposition, Chicago, 1893* (Philadelphia: International Publishing Co., 1893), p. 640.

4. Ben C. Truman, *History of the World's Fair* (Philadelphia: Mammoth Publishing Co., 1893), p. 605.

5. Ibid., p. 607.

6. "Fate of Chicago World's Fair Buildings," *Scientific American* 75 (October 3, 1896): 267.

7. Ibid.

8. Truman, p. 610.

9. Johnson, 4:161.

10. F. Hopkinson Smith, "A White Umbrella at the Fair," *Cosmopolitan* 16 (December 1893): 152.

11. Julian Hawthorne, *Humors of the Fair* (Chicago: E. A. Weeks & Company, 1893), n.p., p. 46.

12. Richard Watson Gilder, "The Vanishing City," *Century Magazine*, n.s. 24 (October 1893): 868.

13. Hugh Dalziel Duncan, *The Rise of Chicago as a Literary Center from 1885 to 1920* (Totowa, N.J.: Bedminster Press, 1964), p. 73.

14. "Mrs. Burnett's 'Two Little Pilgrims' Progress,' " *Critic*, n.s. 24 (November 23, 1895): 342.

15. Frances Hodgson Burnett, *Two Little Pilgrims' Progress* (New York: Scribner's, 1895), p. 8.

16. Ibid., p. 135.

17. Ibid., p. 183.

18. Ibid., p. 186.

19. See Chapter 3.

20. Tudor Jenks, *The Century World's Fair Book for Boys and Girls* (New York: Century Company, 1893), p. 230.

21. Marietta Holley, *Samantha at the World's Fair* (New York: Funk & Wagnalls, 1893), p. 235.

22. Ibid., p. 473.

23. Clara Louise Burnham, *Sweet Clover: A Romance of the White City* (Boston: Houghton, Mifflin, 1896), p. 137.

24. Ibid., pp. 201-2.

25. Ibid., p. 410.

26. Henry B. Fuller, *With the Procession* (New York: Harper & Brothers, 1895), p. 87. The contrast between the White City and Black City has been dourly pursued in

Ray Ginger's *Altgeld's America: The Lincoln Ideal versus Changing Realities* (1958).

27. Robert Herrick, *Memoirs of an American Citizen* (New York: Grosset & Dunlap, 1905), p. 192.

28. Robert Herrick, *The Common Lot* (New York: Macmillan, 1904), p. 21.

29. William Dean Howells, "Letters of an Altrurian Traveler. II," *Cosmopolitan* 16 (December 1893): 221.

30. Ibid., p. 232.

31. William H. Jordy, *American Buildings and Their Architects* (Garden City, N.Y.: Doubleday, 1972), p. 79.

32. "Howells on the Fair," *Chicago Tribune*, 30 October 1893.

33. "Editorial," *Architectural Review* 3 (September 1894): 33.

34. Ibid.

35. Christopher Tunnard, *The Modern American City* (Princeton, N.J.: D. Van Nostrand Company, 1968), p. 47.

36. Henry Van Brunt, "The Architectural Event of Our Times," *Engineering Magazine* 6 (January 1894): 431.

37. Ibid., pp. 432-33.

38. Barr Ferree, "Architecture," *Engineering Magazine* 5 (June 1893): 396.

39. W. L. B. Jenney, "A Talk on Architecture at the World's Columbian Exposition," *Inland Architect* 21 (April 1893): 35.

40. S. K., "The Columbian Exposition—IV.," *Nation* 57 (August 24, 1893): 132-33.

41. P. B. Wight, "The Great Exhibition Reviewed. VII. As an Educator," *American Architect* 42 (December 30, 1893): 159.

42. Montgomery Schuyler, "Last Words about the World's Fair," *Architectural Record* 3 (January-March 1894): 292.

43. Ibid., p. 299.

44. Ibid., p. 300.

45. Louis Sullivan, *The Autobiography of an Idea* (New York: Dover Publications, 1956), pp. 324-25.

46. Hugh Dalziel Duncan, *Culture and Democracy* (Totowa, N.J.: Bedminster Press, 1965), p. 419.

47. Carl W. Condit, *The Chicago School of Architecture* (Chicago: University of Chicago Press, 1964), p. 161. For more detailed discussion of Sullivan and the exposition see David H. Crook, "Louis Sullivan and the Golden Doorway," *Journal of the Society of Architectural Historians* 26 (December 1967): 250-58; and Dimitri Tselos, "The Chicago Fair and the Myth of the 'Lost Cause,' " ibid. 26 (December 1967): 259-68.

48. Ibid., p. 200.

49. Ibid., p. 161.

50. Quoted in Thomas E. Tallmadge, *Architecture in Old Chicago* (Chicago: University of Chicago Press, 1941), pp. 159-66.

51. Wilbert H. Hasbrouck, ed., "Introduction," in Daniel H. Burnham and Edward H. Bennett, *Plan of Chicago* (1909; rpt., New York: Da Capo Press, 1970), pp. v-vi.

52. Tunnard, pp. 47-48.

53. Sullivan, p. 314.

54. Christopher Tunnard and Henry Hope Reed, *American Skyline* (New York: New American Library, 1956), p. 146.

55. Ibid., p. 151.

56. Burnham and Bennett, *Plan of Chicago*, pp. 1, 4.

57. Ibid., pp. 6-8.

58. Ibid., pp. 14, 30.

59. Ibid., p. 117.

60. "Introduction," in ibid., p. vii.

61. Carl Condit, *Chicago, 1910-29: Building, Planning, and Urban Technology* (Chicago: University of Chicago Press, 1973), p. 61.

62. Jane Jacobs, *The Death and Life of Great American Cities* (New York: Modern Library, 1969), pp. 222, 375.

63. Burnham and Bennett, p. 1.

64. Jacobs, p. 7.

65. Duncan, *Culture and Democracy*, p. 416.

66. Russell Lynes, *The Art-Makers of Nineteenth Century America* (New York: Atheneum, 1970), pp. 480-81.

67. J. C. Furnas, *The Americans: A Social History of the United States* (New York: Capricorn Books, 1969), 2:766.

68. Henry Van Brunt, "The Growth of Characteristic Architectural Style in the United States," in *Proceedings of the Twenty-Seventh Annual Convention of the American Institute of Architects*, ed. Alfred Stone (Chicago: Inland Architect Press, 1893), pp. 243, 252.

69. Candace Wheeler, "Decorative Art," *Architectural Record* 4 (April-June 1895): 410, 411.

70. W. Lewis Fraser, "Decorative Painting at the World's Fair," *Century Magazine*, n.s. 24 (May 1893): 15.

71. Royal Cortissoz, "Mural Decoration in America I," *Century Magazine*, n.s. 29 (November 1895): 116.

72. [Russell Sturgis], "The Field of Art," *Scribner's Magazine* 19 (February 1896): 260.

73. Herbert Croly, "American Artists and Their Public," *Architectural Record* 10 (January 1901): 260.

74. August Meier and Elliott M. Rudwick, *From Plantation to Ghetto* (New York: Hill and Wang, 1966), p. 171.

75. Ellen M. Henrotin, "Woman's Part at the World's Fair," *Review of Reviews* 7 (May 1893): 422.

76. See Alice C. Woolger, *The Exposition Study Class Review* 1 (November 1892): back cover.

77. Virginia C. Meredith, "Woman's Part at the World's Fair," *Review of Reviews* 7 (May 1893): 417.

78. Alice Freeman Palmer, "Some Lasting Results of the World's Fair," *Forum* 16 (December 1893): 517.

79. Ibid., pp. 520-21.

80. William H. Jordy, pp. 78, 79.

81. Eleanor Flexner, *Century of Struggle* (Cambridge, Mass.: Belknap Press, 1966), p. 193.

82. Ibid., p. 218.

83. Ibid., pp. 186-89.

84. Ernest R. Groves, *The American Woman* (New York: Greenberg, 1937), p. 326.

85. Ibid., p. 326.

86. "The World's Fair Congresses," *Chicago Tribune*, 29 October 1893.

87. [Charles Dudley Warner], "Editor's Study," *Harper's New Monthly Magazine* 87 (October 1893): 801.

88. F. Herbert Stead, "The Story of the World's Parliament of Religions," *Review of Reviews* 9 (March 1894): 300.

89. Paul Carus, "The Dawn of a New Religious Era," *Forum* 16 (November 1893): 391-92.

90. John Henry Barrows, "Results of the Parliament of Religions," *Forum* 18 (September 1894): 55-58.

91. Ibid., p. 63.

92. Paul A. Carter, *The Spiritual Crisis of the Gilded Age* (DeKalb: Northern Illinois University Press, 1971), p. 210.

93. Quoted in Jacob Henry Dorn, *Washington Gladden* (Columbus: Ohio State University Press, 1967), pp. 387-88.

94. E. C. Towne, A. J. Canfield, and George J. Hagar, eds., *Rays of Light from All Lands* (New York: Gay Brothers & Company, 1895), pp. xiii, iii.

95. Carter, pp. 217-18.

96. Ibid., p. 218.

97. Ibid., pp. 217-19.

98. Washington Gladden, *Recollections* (Boston: Houghton Mifflin, 1909), p. 359.

99. Tunnard, p. 47.

100. Frederick Jackson Turner, "The Problem of the West," *Atlantic Monthly* 78 (September 1896): 297.

101. Paul Bourget, "A Farewell to the White City," *Cosmopolitan* 16 (December 1893): 135.

102. Edmund Mitchell, "International Effects of the Fair," *Engineering Magazine* 6 (January 1894): 472.

103. Franklin H. Head, "The Fair's Results to the City of Chicago," *Forum* 16 (December 1893): 524-25.

104. Charles Dudley Warner, "The Last Day of the Fair," *Harper's Weekly* 37 (November 11, 1893): 1075.

105. Richard Harding Davis, "The Last Days of the Fair," *Harper's Weekly* 37 (October 21, 1893): 1002.

106. Warner, "The Last Day of the Fair," p. 1074.

107. John T. Bramhall, "The Field Columbian Museum," *Harper's Weekly* 38 (August 4, 1894): 738. In later years the museum fell into disuse, but it was restored and now serves as the Museum of Science and Industry.

108. Quoted in Palmer, p. 519.

109. Warner, "The Last Day of the Fair," p. 1074.

110. Davis, p. 1002.

111. Julian Ralph, "A Recent Journey through the West. IX—Chicago since the Fair," *Harper's Weekly* 39 (November 16, 1895): 1088.

112. Ibid., p. 1088.

113. William T. Stead, *If Christ Came to Chicago!* (Chicago: Laird & Lee, 1894), p. 420.

114. Henry Adams, *The Education of Henry Adams* (Boston: Houghton Mifflin, 1927), p. 343.

115. Wayne Andrews, *Architecture in Chicago and Mid-America* (New York: Atheneum, 1968), p. xiii. I do not intend any discredit of Wayne Andrews in this remark. In the same book he advocates the view that Sullivan's opinion of the exposition was too limited, that the fair and its aftermath served the fortunate diversity of American life and inspired the erection of some buildings, classical in design, which were masterpieces;

some of them, like McKim, Mead & White's Pennsylvania Station, have tragically fallen to the wrecker's ball.

116. Ibid., p. 343.

117. Worthington Chauncey Ford, ed., *Letters of Henry Adams* (Boston: Houghton Mifflin, 1938), p. 33.

118. Adams, p. 340.

119. Ibid., p. 341.

120. Jordy, p. 82.

121. Sarah Norton and M. A. DeWolfe Howe, eds., *Letters of Charles Eliot Norton* (Boston: Houghton Mifflin, 1913), 2:218.

122. Quoted in Charles Moore, *Daniel H. Burnham: Architect, Planner of Cities* (Boston: Houghton Mifflin, 1921), 1:78-79.

123. Albert Fein, *Frederick Law Olmsted and the American Environmental Tradition* (New York: George Braziller, 1972), p. 14.

124. Richard T. Ely, *The Coming City* (New York: Thomas Y. Crowell, 1902), pp. 60-61.

125. Moore, 2:102.

126. John Coleman Adams, "What a Great City Might Be—A Lesson from the White City," *New England Magazine*, n.s. 14 (March 1896): 3.

127. Ibid., p. 4.

128. Ibid., p. 5.

129. Ibid., p. 8.

130. Ibid., p. 10.

131. Ibid., p. 12.

INDEX

373

INDEX

INDEX

Pennell, Joseph, 191
Perkins, Dwight A., 306
Perry, Bliss, 38
Philadelphia, 28, 87, 177, 249
Phillips, Wendell, 37
Phillipson, Emil, 163
Pierce, R. H., 260
Pingree, Hazen S., 39
politics: corruption of, 38-40; election of 1888, 40; election of 1892, 86, 107, 109; national, 39-40; state, 39; urban, 38-39, 71
Poole, William F., 251
Post, George B., 77, 78, 132, 134, 137, 157
Potter, Edward C., 100, 119, 120, 181, 192
Potter, Mrs. O. W., 236
Powderly, Terence V., 29
Pratt, Bela L., 100
Pretyman, William, 98-99, 154
Price, Bruce, 79
Proctor, A. P., 148, 180-81
prostitution, 27-28, 38; in Chicago, 69-70, 230, 231-32, 243, 339-40
Pulitzer, Joseph, 33
Pullman, George M., 50, 100, 227
Pung, Kwang Yu, 265
Pyle, Howard, 191

railroads, 41, 205-6; and Chicago, 48, 50; and exposition, 86-87, 205-6, 335; growth of, 5, 205-6
Ralph, Julian, 47, 92, 154, 338-39
Rappe, Thornburg (baroness), 208
recession of 1893, 4, 86, 170, 304, 324, 335
Redpath, James, 38
Reed, Thomas, 39
Reese, Cara, 244
Rehan, Ada, 24, 207
Reid, Robert, 160, 189
Reinhart, Charles S., 99, 162, 191
religion, 28-32, 67-68, 89-91, 240, 243, 263-82, 324, 326-32; ecumenism, 326-32; Judaism, 30, 68, 268, 276; Kingdom of God on Earth, 31, 113, 270-71, 273, 275, 291-92, 293, 296, 308, 340; leading denominations, 29, 268-69; Protestantism, 28, 30-32, 68, 269-74, 328, 332; Roman Catholicism, 29, 68, 268, 269, 276-77, 278, 328-29, 332; secularism, 30-33, 275-76; Social Gospel, 28-31, 267-76, 279, 291, 313, 329, 340

Remington, Frederic, 191
Reuchi, Shibata, 265
Revell, Alexander H., 100
Richardson, Henry Hobson, 11, 12, 51, 57, 301, 307, 341; and Marshall Field Wholesale Store, 11, 51, 52, 307
Richter, Max, 251
Rideout, Alice B., 100, 144, 166
Riis, Jacob, 32-33, 38
Riley, James Whitcomb, 21
Rimmer, William, 15
Robinson, Theodore, 191
Rockefeller, John D., 5, 330
Rodin, Auguste, 195
Roebuck, Alvah, 50
Rogers, John, 15, 192
Rohl-Smith, Carl, 183
Root, George Frederick, 61
Root, John Wellborn, 11-12, 51, 54, 77-78, 99, 119, 305, 306-7, 315; Monadnock Building, 56; Rookery Building, 55
Rosenfeld, Monroe H., 19
Rowland, Henry A., 36
Royce, Josiah, 258, 262
Russell, Lillian, 229
Ryerson, Martin, 49

Saint-Gaudens, Augustus, 15, 59, 79, 100, 122, 128, 181, 192, 309, 317, 318, 341; statue of *Diana*, 15, 128
Saint-Gaudens, Louis, 181
Saint Louis Exposition (1904), 337
Saint Peter's Church, Rome, 81, 92, 97, 124, 136
Saint-Saëns, Camille, 170
Sandburg, Carl, 44
Sankey, Ira S., 28
Sargent, D. A., 193
Sargent, John Singer, 186-87, 193
Sayers, Henry J., 20
Schaff, Philip, 267
Schakovsky, Mary A. (princess), 208
Schiff, Jacob, 15
Schladermundt, H. T., 157
Schlesinger, Arthur, 3
Schmidt, Richard E., 306
Schouler, James, 257
Schuyler, Montgomery, 9, 117, 136, 151, 176, 190, 301-3
Schwab, Charles H., 43, 100
Scott, Sir Walter, 21, 64
sculpture, 15, 59, 317-18. *See also* World's Columbian Exposition, sculpture
Sears, Richard, 50

INDEX

Van Rensselaer, Mrs. Schuyler, 14, 115, 117, 120, 124, 128, 131, 132, 136, 144, 147, 150, 151

Vaux, Calvert, 83

Vedder, Elihu, 14, 105, 319

Verestchagin, Vasily, 196

Vinton, Frederick, 189

Vivekenanda, Swami, 327, 330-31

von Brousart, Frau Ingeborg, 208

von Kasetowsky, Frau Professor, 208

Von Moltke, Helmuth, 213

Waagen, M. A., 126

Wacker, Charles H., 100

Wallace, Lew, 21, 64, 191, 192-93, 286

Waller, Thomas, 110

Walton, William, 187, 190, 194, 195, 196-97

Ward, Aaron Montgomery, 50

Ward, Mrs. Humphrey, 22

Ward, J. Q. A., 100, 192, 317

Ward, Lester, 36, 263

Warner, Charles Dudley, 23, 44, 68, 191, 251-52, 253, 289, 326, 333, 335, 336, 337-38, 345

Warner, Olin L., 148, 192, 212, 317

Washburne, Hempstead, 104

Washington, Booker T., 34

Washington Park, 76, 83, 100, 216, 336

Watson, Carrie, 69-70, 231

Watterson, Henry, 107, 108

Wecter, Dixon, 51

Weir, J. Alden, 99, 100

Wells, David, 251

Westinghouse Company, 98, 198, 202, 204

Wharton, Edith, 10, 323

Wheeler, Candace, 145, 167-68, 181, 259, 317

Whistler, James A. M., 186, 191

White, Stanford, 15, 128, 191, 298, 317, 341. *See also* World's Columbian Exposition, Agricultural Building

Whitehouse, F. M., 168

Whiting, Arthur, 18

Whitman, Walt, 14

Whittier, John Greenleaf, 237

Wight, Peter B., 114, 177, 300

Wilkins, Mary E., 64

Willard, Frances E., 27, 236, 243, 249, 267, 279

Williams, Fannie Barrier, 277-79

Wilson, Woodrow, 258

Wise, Isaac Mayer, 30, 267, 268

Wolkonsky, Serge (prince), 265

Woman's Christian Temperance Union (WCTU), 27, 243, 249, 287

women, 9-10, 37-38, 105-6, 131, 163-67, 207-9, 210, 239-49, 262-63, 265, 279-80, 283, 321-25, 335; and arts and letters, 10, 18, 21-22, 24; and feminism, 37-38, 208-9, 239-49, 280, 323-24; and reform, 33; and suffrage, 37, 243, 244, 246, 279; and temperance, 27

Woodberry, George Edward, 36, 255

Woodbury, Charles H., 189

Woodhull, Victoria, 38

World's Columbian Exposition, 1, 6, 19, 25, 26, 35, 40, 42, 43, 45, 48, 53, 61, 62, 65, 68, 69, 70, 72, 73-74, passim

— Administration Building, 78, 99, 110, 122, 124-26, 131, 137, 140, 150, 155-57, 169, 181, 212, 288, 341

— Agricultural Building, 78, 99-100, 128-31, 134, 137, 157-58, 198, 206, 207, 210, 288, 291, 293

— architecture, 78-79, 95, 97, 114-53, 175-78, 180, 259-60

— art, 84, 98-100, 152, 154-68, 175, 183-97; murals, 152, 154-56, 157-58, 159-63, 165-68, 169, 212

— Art Building, 79, 83, 84, 99, 128, 147, 148, 149, 150, 151, 183-97, 199, 288, 289, 335

— attendance, 91, 284

— Bird's-Eye View of, 93

— campaign to locate in Chicago, 42-43

— Casino, 119, 287

— Casino Pier, 119, 211

— Chicago Day, 210

— closing, 286-87

— Columbian Guards, 87, 111

— committee on grounds and buildings, 76, 77, 175

— Corporation and organization, 75, 85-86, 89, 90-91, 100, 110, 172, 224, 227, 236

— costs and financing, 85-86

— Court of Honor, 78, 81, 110, 116, 118, 119-37, 157-58, 181, 210, 216, 226, 292, 293, 300, 301-2, 312, 314, 336, 341, 342

— dedication, 100-109

— electricity at, 97-98, 198, 204, 226-27

— Electricity Building, 78, 98, 131, 132, 135, 157, 183, 202, 204, 288, 289

— Festival Hall, 119, 168-71, 287

— fires, 87-88, 226, 287-88

Dear Parents:

Congratulations! Your child is taking the first steps on an exciting journey. The destination? Independent reading!

STEP INTO READING® will help your child get there. The program offers five steps to reading success. Each step includes fun stories and colorful art or photographs. In addition to original fiction and books with favorite characters, there are Step into Reading Non-Fiction Readers, Phonics Readers and Boxed Sets, Sticker Readers, and Comic Readers—a complete literacy program with something to interest every child.

Learning to Read, Step by Step!

Ready to Read   Preschool–Kindergarten
• big type and easy words • rhyme and rhythm • picture clues
For children who know the alphabet and are eager to begin reading.

Reading with Help   Preschool–Grade 1
• basic vocabulary • short sentences • simple stories
For children who recognize familiar words and sound out new words with help.

Reading on Your Own   Grades 1–3
• engaging characters • easy-to-follow plots • popular topics
For children who are ready to read on their own.

Reading Paragraphs   Grades 2–3
• challenging vocabulary • short paragraphs • exciting stories
For newly independent readers who read simple sentences with confidence.

Ready for Chapters   Grades 2–4
• chapters • longer paragraphs • full-color art
For children who want to take the plunge into chapter books but still like colorful pictures.

STEP INTO READING® is designed to give every child a successful reading experience. The grade levels are only guides; children will progress through the steps at their own speed, developing confidence in their reading.

Remember, a lifetime love of reading starts with a single step!

Visit us on the Web!
StepIntoReading.com
randomhousekids.com

Educators and librarians, for a variety of teaching tools, visit us at RHTeachersLibrarians.com

ISBN 978-0-7364-3594-9 (trade) — ISBN 978-0-7364-8181-6 (lib. bdg.)
ISBN 978-0-7364-3595-6 (ebook)

Printed in the United States of America   10 9 8 7 6 5 4 3 2 1

DISNEY PRINCESS

Beauty and the Beast

by Melissa Lagonegro

illustrated by
the Disney Storybook Art Team

Random House 🏠 New York

Belle is kind
and smart.
She loves
to read.

Gaston wants
to marry Belle.
She does not
like him.

Belle's father, Maurice,
is an inventor.
He goes on a trip.

Maurice gets lost

in the forest.

Wolves surround him!

He finds a castle.

He goes inside.

Maurice meets
magical objects.
Lumiere is a candlestick.
Cogsworth is a clock.

The castle belongs
to the Beast.
He locks Maurice
in a cell.

Belle finds Maurice.
She asks the Beast
to free her father.

She tells the Beast
to keep her instead.
The Beast agrees.

Belle meets

the magical objects

in the castle.

Lumiere sings.

Belle explores
the castle.
She finds a magic rose.

The Beast finds Belle.

He grabs the rose.

Belle is scared!

Belle leaves the castle.

Wolves surround her.

She is in danger!

The Beast arrives.

He fights the wolves.

He saves Belle!

Belle returns
to the castle.
She and the Beast
become good friends.
They spend time outdoors.

Belle teaches the Beast
to dance.

They are happy.

Belle sees her father
in a magic mirror.

He looks sick.

Belle leaves
to help him.
The Beast is sad
when Belle leaves.

Gaston wants
to find the Beast.

He goes to the castle.

He attacks the Beast!

The Beast is hurt.

Belle is very sad.

"I love you,"

says Belle.

The Beast
is really a prince!
Belle's love changes him
into a human.
They live happily
ever after.

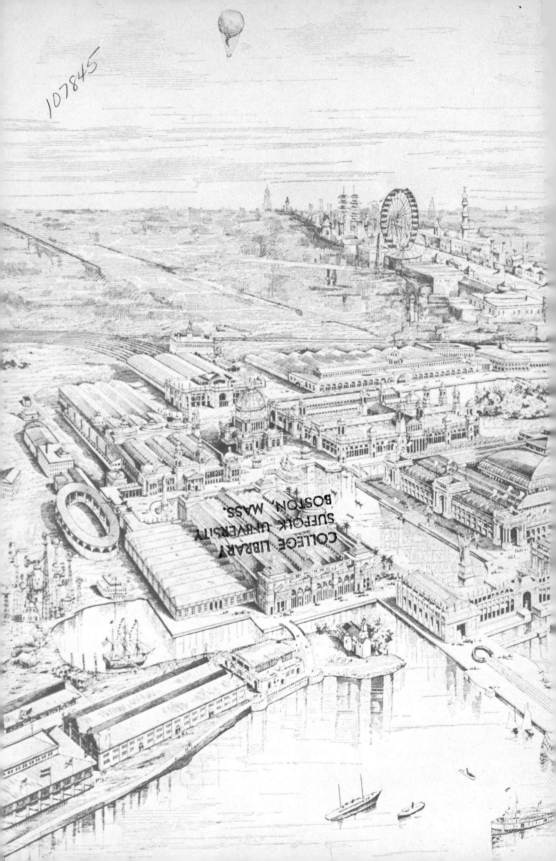

107845